New Perspectives:

Portfolio Projects for Business Communications

Carol M. Cram

Capilano University, North Vancouver, BC

COURSE TECHNOLOGY
CENGAGE Learning™

Australia • Brazil • Japan • Korea • Mexico • Singapore • Spain • United Kingdom • United States

COURSE TECHNOLOGY
CENGAGE Learning™

New Perspectives: Portfolio Projects for Business Communications

Vice President, Publisher: Nicole Jones Pinard

Executive Editor: Marie L. Lee

Associate Acquisitions Editor: Brandi Shailer

Senior Product Manager: Kathy Finnegan

Associate Product Manager: Leigh Robbins

Editorial Assistant: Julia Leroux-Lindsey

Director of Marketing: Cheryl Costantini

Marketing Manager: Ryan DeGrote

Marketing Coordinator: Kristen Panciocco

Developmental Editor: Pam Conrad

Senior Content Project Manager: Jennifer Goguen McGrail

Composition: GEX Publishing Services

Text Designer: Steve Deschene

Art Director: Marissa Falco

Cover Designer: Marissa Falco

Proofreader: Suzanne Huizenga

Indexer: Rich Carlson

For product information and technology assistance, contact us at
Cengage Learning Customer & Sales Support, 1-800-354-9706
For permission to use material from this text or product, submit all requests online at **cengage.com/permissions**
Further permissions questions can be emailed to
permissionrequest@cengage.com

Some of the product names and company names used in this book have been used for identification purposes only and may be trademarks or registered trademarks of their respective manufacturers and sellers.

Microsoft and the Office logo are either registered trademarks or trademarks of Microsoft Corporation in the United States and/or other countries. Course Technology, Cengage Learning is an independent entity from the Microsoft Corporation, and not affiliated with Microsoft in any manner.

Disclaimer: Any fictional data related to persons or companies or URLs used throughout this book is intended for instructional purposes only. At the time this book was printed, any such data was fictional and not belonging to any real persons or companies.

ISBN-13: 978-1-4390-3746-1

ISBN-10: 1-4390-3746-9

Course Technology
20 Channel Center Street
Boston, Massachusetts 02210
USA

Cengage Learning is a leading provider of customized learning solutions with office locations around the globe, including Singapore, the United Kingdom, Australia, Mexico, Brazil, and Japan. Locate your local office at:
international.cengage.com/region

Cengage Learning products are represented in Canada by Nelson Education, Ltd.

To learn more about Course Technology, visit **www.cengage.com/coursetechnology**
To learn more about Cengage Learning, visit **www.cengage.com**

Purchase any of our products at your local college store or at our preferred online store **www.ichapters.com**

Printed in the United States of America
1 2 3 4 5 6 7 8 9 13 12 11 10 09

Preface

The New Perspectives Series' critical-thinking, problem-solving approach is the ideal way to prepare students to transcend point-and-click skills and take advantage of all that business communication tools have to offer.

The goal of this new Portfolio Projects text is to provide review of critical business communications concepts, hands-on instruction using selected applications to teach skills related to the concepts, and multiple exercises to give students many opportunities to put the concepts and skills they've learned into action.

With the New Perspectives Series, students understand *why* they are learning *what* they are learning, and are fully prepared to apply their skills to real-life situations.

About This Book

This book provides a thorough, hands-on overview of business communications concepts and applications, and includes the following:

- Fifteen business communications portfolio projects designed to teach students how to write common business documents including e-mails, reports, proposals, and presentations
- Multiple exercises in each project that give students hands-on practice in creating and revising business documents
- Three exercises in each project that cover the document development process: Practice, Revise, and Create
- Coverage of how to use Word to facilitate the document creation process, including working with styles, mail merge, outlining, and sections
- Coverage of how to use PowerPoint to create compelling presentations
- Coverage of how to use Outlook to organize e-mail messages, add signature lines, and create folders
- Numerous examples of business documents that students can use as templates to help them create meaningful documents of their own

This book is the perfect supplement to any Business Communications textbook, providing opportunities for students to apply the concepts they have learned to solve real-world business problems and to produce work that is up to professional standards.

System Requirements

This book assumes a typical installation of Microsoft Office 2007 and a typical installation of Microsoft Windows Vista Ultimate (with the Aero feature turned off), Windows Vista Home Premium, or Windows Vista Business. (Note: You can also complete the projects in this book using Windows XP.) The browser used for any steps that require a browser is Internet Explorer 7.

The New Perspectives Portfolio Projects Approach

Context
Each project focuses on a specific document type, such as a proposal, brochure, or sales letter, and provides students with seven distinct exercises.

Document Essentials
Each project includes extensive conceptual information that provides students with practical tips and techniques for creating the project document. Numerous screen shots provide examples for students to adapt. Tables present document creation guidelines in an easy-to-read format that students can immediately apply.

Key Points
Key Points, which appear in the margin in labeled boxes, offer expert advice and best practices to help students better understand how to create useful business documents.

Technology Skills
Each project includes a Technology Skills section, which provides hands-on coverage of a set of software skills related to the project document. Examples of technology skills include how to use outlining in the project on proposals, how to animate charts in the project on sales presentations, and how to create and modify styles in the project on brochures.

Tips
Tips, which appear in the margin in labeled boxes, provide helpful hints and shortcuts for more efficient use of the software. The Tips appear in the margin at key points throughout the Technology Skills sections to provide students with extra information when and where they need it.

Assessment
Each project includes seven exercises: a Technology Skills exercise, a Practice exercise, a Revise exercise, a Create exercise, and three case studies.

My Portfolio
The text concludes with a summary exercise, My Portfolio, in which students select documents they have completed in the projects or create new documents to include in a personal portfolio. Students can then use their portfolios to demonstrate to current or prospective employers their business communications skills and related software skills, showcasing their capabilities and talents.

Reference
A combination Glossary/Index promotes easy reference of conceptual and technology-related material.

COURSECASTS

Our Complete System of Instruction

CourseCasts – Learning on the Go. Always available…always relevant.
Want to keep up with the latest technology trends relevant to you? Visit our site to find a library of podcasts, CourseCasts, featuring a "CourseCast of the Week," and download them to your mp3 player at http://coursecasts.course.com.

Ken Baldauf, host of CourseCasts, is a faculty member of the Florida State University Computer Science Department where he is responsible for teaching technology classes to thousands of FSU students each year. Ken is an expert in the latest technology trends; he gathers and sorts through the most pertinent news and information for CourseCasts so your students can spend their time enjoying technology, rather than trying to figure it out. Open or close your lecture with a discussion based on the latest CourseCast. Visit us at http://coursecasts.course.com to learn on the go!

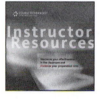

Instructor Resources
We offer more than just a book. We have all the tools you need to enhance your lectures, check students' work, and generate exams in a new, easier-to-use and completely revised package. This book's Instructor's Manual, PowerPoint presentations, data files, solution files, figure files, and a sample syllabus are all available on a single CD-ROM or for downloading at http://www.cengage.com/coursetechnology.

Skills Assessment and Training
SAM 2007 helps bridge the gap between the classroom and the real world by allowing students to train and test on important computer skills in an active, hands-on environment. SAM 2007's easy-to-use system includes powerful interactive exams, training or projects on critical applications such as Word, Excel, Access, PowerPoint, Outlook, Windows, the Internet, and much more. SAM simulates the application environment, allowing students to demonstrate their knowledge and think through the skills by performing real-world tasks. Powerful administrative options allow instructors to schedule exams and assignments, secure tests, and run reports with almost limitless flexibility.

Acknowledgments

My students are first in line for thanks. Their enthusiasm and willingness to learn and grow continue to inspire me. I also wish to thank my friend, mentor, and colleague, Dr. Thomas McKeown. I also want to thank the New Perspectives team: Marie Lee, Executive Editor; Kathy Finnegan, Senior Product Manager; Brandi Shailer, Associate Acquisitions Editor; Leigh Robbins, Associate Product Manager; Julia Leroux-Lindsey, Editorial Assistant; Jennifer Goguen McGrail, Senior Content Project Manager; Christian Kunciw, MQA Supervisor; and Serge Palladino, MQA tester. My thanks to the following Advisory Board members for their helpful feedback: Brenda Carey, Campbell University; Duane Franceschi, Canyon College; James Katzenstein, California State University; Kevin Pratt, Columbia College; David Swarts, Clinton Community College, and Lisa Turner, Missouri State University. Thanks as well to the following textbook reviewers for their thoughtful insights: Domenic Bruni, University of Wisconsin; Anthony Corte, University of Illinois; Linda Glassburn, Cuyahoga Community College; Michael Evans, Columbia College; Kristie Loescher, University of Texas; Nan Nelson, Phillips Community College of the University of Arkansas; and Vesta Whisler, Valdosta State University. As always, special thanks to my wonderful mom and dad and ever-tolerant husband Gregg and daughter Julia. Finally, I wish to thank Pam Conrad, my Developmental Editor, for her incredible patience, good humor, support, and encouragement. She is truly a jewel.

– Carol M. Cram

Table of Contents

Objectives

- Define business writing
- Identify reader action
- Develop clarity
- Identify formatting requirements
- Understand reader needs
- Use a positive tone
- Use writing tools in Word

Business Communications Overview

Introduction

In business, you write to accomplish specific goals in a timely manner. Every document you write should communicate a clear message that readers can understand quickly and easily.

In this project, you define business writing, identify techniques for developing a clear, reader-centered business writing style, and explore how the appearance of a business document influences the way in which the reader understands the content. You also examine the crucial role that the reader plays in the communication process and learn how to develop a positive tone that encourages rather than commands the reader to act. Finally, you explore how to use some of the writing tools included with Microsoft Word to help you improve your writing style.

Starting Data Files

Project.01

Tech_01.docx
Practice_01.docx
Revise_01.docx
Case1_01.docx
Case2_01.docx
Research_01.docx

Business Communication Essentials

Four activities take place in the business communication process. First, a reader receives a document—either in paper or electronic form; and second, the reader reads the document. However, communication has not yet taken place because the reader also needs to understand the message—the third activity in the business communication process. At this point, you might decide that communication has occurred so long as the reader understands the message. However, in business writing, the reader needs to go further. The fourth activity in the business communication process is that the message must require the reader to take some kind of action.

Defining Business Writing

Business writing is writing that communicates the information a reader needs to take a specific action. In business writing, the reader plays the central role in the business communication process.

You probably already have experience writing essays, term papers, and short stories. When you write an essay or a short story, you write to communicate with your reader, just as you write to communicate with your reader in a business situation. However, the desired *results* of the communication differ. You write an essay or term paper to convince your reader of your point of view on a specific topic, and you write a short story to entertain or inspire your reader. Every document you write in business is designed to lead the reader to take a specific action.

Identifying Reader Action

In business, you must always keep in mind the action you want the reader to perform as the result of reading your business communication. Suppose you are asked to write a proposal requesting funding for a new playground at a local school. What action do you want your reader to take as the result of reading the proposal? Obviously, you want the reader to give you the funding you requested. Alternatively, suppose you write a short e-mail asking the reader to attend a meeting. What action do you want the reader to take? You want the reader to attend the meeting. Now, imagine you receive the following e-mail:

> *Discussions took place regarding the need to organize an event for this holiday season. Many staff members were in favor of such an event.*

After reading the e-mail, you will probably ask, *What am I supposed to do? Am I being asked to help organize the event? Attend the event? Save the date for the event?* Either you need to wait for *another* e-mail that contains more information or you need to send an e-mail to request more information so you know exactly what action you should take. Both of these actions waste time, and more importantly, do not lead to the desired reader action.

Before you write a business document, you should identify exactly what action you require of your reader. Figure 1-1 lists some typical business documents, along with the general action expected of the reader.

| Figure 1-1 | Sample reader actions |

Document	Expected Reader Action
Sales letter describing an exciting new tour of Antarctica	Purchase the tour
Letter requesting a recommendation	Provide you with a recommendation
Proposal to purchase a new computer system	Approve your proposal
Letter offering a job to an applicant	Accept the job
E-mail asking to attend a meeting	Attend the meeting

The actions listed in Figure 1-1 might seem obvious. However, sometimes writers focus on what *they* feel they need to say instead of what the *reader* actually needs to read. Compare the two e-mails in Figure 1-2.

| Figure 1-2 | Vague and action-oriented messages |

VERSION 1 – Expected Action Unclear

As a student in your business communication course a few years ago, I learned a great deal about how to communicate effectively with my reader. Since taking your course, I have worked for two companies. Both jobs have really helped me improve my communication skills. Now I need a new challenge and so I'm applying for a new job as a marketing assistant with Preston Consultants in Seattle. I just know that my qualifications are perfectly suited for this new job and, even better, the job is close to my home and provides great benefits. I hope you'll let me know if you're able to help me. Thank you!

VERSION 2 – Expected Action Clarified

I was a student in your business communication course two years ago. At the end of the course, you very kindly gave me permission to use your name as a reference to help me with my job search efforts. You also said that you would write a letter of recommendation.

I have applied for a position as a marketing assistant with Preston Consultants in Seattle. Janet Cox, the personnel director, has asked me for a reference from one of my college instructors. Could you send a letter of recommendation to Sally Lee at 208 Bayview Drive, Seattle, WA, 98241?

Please call me at 206-555-2233 if you would like to discuss my request or require further information. I appreciate your help in this matter.

Key Point

In business, you write to get results.

Eventually, the reader of the Version 1 message would guess that the writer is requesting a recommendation. The Version 1 message does not provide enough information, and so the reader action in response to this message might be one of the following: reply to this message with a request for details, thereby wasting both the reader's time and the writer's time, or ignore the message altogether. Neither action is what the writer wants.

The Version 2 message tells the reader exactly what to do and, even better, exactly how to do it. The writer makes a clear request for a recommendation and provides the reader with the specific details the reader needs in order to fulfill the request. When you clarify what action your reader should take as the result of reading your business message, you show respect for the reader, and most importantly, you increase your chances of getting exactly what you want.

Developing Clarity

Because the goal of business writing is to provide your readers with the information they need to take a desired action, you need to make sure that the message you communicate is as clear and easy to understand as possible. You can use the following techniques to make your business writing clear and concise:

• Select precise words
• Use active voice
• Use everyday vocabulary
• Eliminate wordiness

Selecting Precise Words

You need to choose words that communicate your message clearly and precisely so that your readers are left with no doubt about your meaning. What message is the writer communicating to readers in the following sentence?

It is important to point out that the company is in serious financial trouble.

Readers will not be pleased by this message, particularly if they are employees or shareholders in the company. They will be particularly frustrated by the phrase *serious financial trouble*. Part of their frustration will be because they don't have enough information to know exactly what the phrase *serious financial trouble* means. This phrase as used in the sample sentence means almost nothing simply because readers can interpret it in many different ways, depending on their point of view. For some readers, *serious financial trouble* could mean that the company is on the point of bankruptcy, whereas for other readers, the phrase could mean that the company has lost a portion of its profits. The problem is that readers cannot determine exactly what the phrase means.

Here is a much more reader-friendly and clear alternative:

The 2011 financial statements for Go Green Packing show a 20% decrease in profits.

The revised sentence uses precise words. The phrase *serious financial trouble* is replaced with the more meaningful phrase *20% decrease in profits* and a time frame (2011) for the loss is defined. Readers will still not be pleased by the message, but at least they will have specific information that they can use to make a decision about investment or employment opportunities at Go Green Packing.

Figure 1-3 lists three vague sentences with underlined words and phrases that need clarification. The Problems and Comments column describes the ways in which the underlined words are unclear, and the Precise Meaning column shows the sentences rewritten with precise words and phrases.

Figure 1-3	Rewriting vague sentences

Vague Sentence	Problems and Comments	Precise Meaning
Your <u>order</u> will be filled <u>soon</u>.	What order? When will it be filled?	Your order for 300 electric cars will be filled by May 3.
The <u>report</u> is full of <u>errors</u>.	What report? What errors?	The *Water Sources on Bowen Island* report contains several grammatical errors and incorrectly states that all residents receive water from wells.
<u>We</u> are meeting later <u>today</u>.	Who is meeting? When? Why?	The Sales Department will meet at 4 p.m. today (June 3) to analyze the 2011 sales figures.

Each of the rewritten sentences in Figure 1-3 uses precise words and phrases to provide the reader with specific information. For example, instead of *soon*, you provide a date and instead of *report*, you specify which report.

Using Active Voice

You use the least number of words and convey your message with maximum clarity when you use the active voice. In an **active voice** sentence, the noun that performs the action in the sentence comes before the verb and is the subject of the sentence. Here is an example of an active voice sentence:

The shipping clerk purchased the packing materials.

The active voice sentence puts the doer of the action first. The active voice is *active* because the subject of the sentence, the shipping clerk, *performs* the action.

The opposite of an active voice sentence is a passive voice sentence. In a **passive voice** sentence, the noun that performs the action in the sentence follows the verb and is the direct object of the sentence. The noun that receives the action rather than performs the action is the subject of the sentence. Here is the preceding sentence written in the passive voice:

The packing materials were purchased by the shipping clerk.

The sentence is called *passive* because the subject of the sentence is *packing materials*, and is the noun in the sentence that *receives* the action (*were purchased*), rather than *performs* the action.

When you rewrite a passive voice sentence in the active voice (*The shipping clerk purchased the packing materials*), you eliminate the words *by* and *were*. Neither of these words enhances the meaning of the sentence. They only serve to make the sentence longer. Figure 1-4 compares several passive and active voice sentences. In every case, the sentence written in the active voice communicates the message with fewer words, greater clarity, and more energy.

Key Point

Sentences in the active voice are usually shorter than sentences in the passive voice.

Figure 1-4 ▶ **Passive vs. active voice**

Passive Voice	Active Voice
The sales representatives were questioned by the marketing director.	The marketing director questioned the sales representatives.
The rent was raised.	The landlord raised the rent. *Note:* In this passive sentence, no noun performs the action (raised). To put the sentence into the active voice, you must supply a subject, such as *The landlord*, in this example.
The store was overwhelmed with hundreds of customers rushing in to buy the latest bestseller.	Hundreds of customers rushed into the store to purchase the latest bestseller.
The refund check for $400 was issued by Acacia Financing.	Acacia Financing company issued a refund check for $400.

Using Everyday Vocabulary

Effective business writers choose everyday words to communicate their messages. However, not so long ago, a sentence such as the following would have been perfectly acceptable:

As per our recent conversation, I am sending you the information about what packing supplies Go Green Packing has to offer.

In the twenty-first century, this rather stilted phrasing sounds pretentious. Rarely in normal conversation do we use the Latin phrase *as per* (meaning *with regard to*), so why would we want to use it in writing? Here is a clear alternative:

As we discussed on April 2, I am sending you information about the packing supplies you can purchase from Go Green Packing.

In business, you will often read documents filled with stock phrases that add extra words with little or no meaning. Figure 1-5 lists common stock phrases and their less wordy alternatives.

Figure 1-5	Common stock phrases

Wordy Stock Phrase	Conversational Alternative
In the event that	If
Due to the fact that	Because
Please do not hesitate to call me.	Please call me.
I'd like to take this opportunity to thank you.	Thank you.
I'd be more than happy to accede to your request.	I am happy to assist you. (How can you be more than happy?)
It has come to my attention	No alternative; omit use of this phrase

You get the idea! Instead of using old-fashioned stock phrases that contribute little to the message you want to communicate, find phrases that you can use such as *Thank you for contacting me regarding ...*, *Please call me if you need assistance*, *Thank you for your attention to my application*, and *Enclosed are...* and then use them where appropriate.

As you develop your business writing skills, you need to develop techniques that help you speed up the writing process. You do not want to stare for hours at a blank computer screen every time you need to dash off an e-mail or a letter. You can use stock phrases—but only those that clarify your meaning, rather than obscure it.

Eliminating Wordiness

How would you react if you received an e-mail containing the following message?

In keeping with the current trend toward downsizing operations to afford a more equitable distribution of resources, it would be indicated, in 2011, that certain steps be taken, perforce, that expenses related to operations be reduced and trimmed down in accordance with recent policies approved in principle by shareholders.

Do you have any idea what the writer means? You could probably figure out some kind of meaning—but only after you have read the sentence several times. Here is what the sentence really means:

We need to reduce our operating costs in 2011.

Why didn't the writer say so? Make sure that everything you write can be understood the *first time someone reads it*. If your reader needs to read a sentence two or even three times to understand it, the sentence is just not clear. The reader will move on to the next task and your opportunity to communicate your message is lost. Often all you need to do is to remove excess words and say exactly what you mean. Figure 1-6 shows suggested edits to sentences that contain unnecessary words.

Figure 1-6	Editing wordy sentences

Wordy Sentence	Reader Response	Straight to the Point
Your application, which we received with pleasure last week, will be reviewed by us at a later date yet to be decided.	*Just tell me when you will review my application.*	We will review your application by July 30.
I wish to take this opportunity to extend my thanks to you for the work that you did to help me on the account we worked on from the Carter company.	*I'm in danger of falling asleep before I get to the end of this sentence.*	Thank you for helping me with the Carter account.
The meeting that will be held on May 3 will need to address a variety of issues that are all in some way related to our participation in the upcoming sales conference.	*What are we meeting about?*	On May 3, we will meet to discuss our participation in the June sales conference.

You will go a long way toward developing an effective business writing style when you select words that express your meaning precisely, when you write most of your sentences in the active voice, when you use everyday vocabulary, and finally, when you eliminate excess words that contribute little to the message you want to communicate.

Identifying Formatting Requirements

An effectively formatted document presents information in a clear and easy-to-understand way. Readers should be able to see at a glance the purpose of the document and its main points. In fact, many busy businesspeople frequently just scan a document to determine if they need to read it. If the main points are not immediately apparent, the reader might set the document aside and go on to another task.

You will learn how to format specific types of documents, such as letters, reports, and brochures, as you progress through this text. In this section, you will focus on general formatting principles related to document layout and content organization.

Adapting Document Layout

The **layout** of a document refers to the positioning of the text on the page. Figure 1-7 shows how the layout of a simple message can drastically affect its readability.

Figure 1-7 — Layout comparison

Version 1: Poor Layout

Thank you for your order to ship 300 ceramic garden pots from Toronto to Paris. Your shipment will leave our warehouse on May 1.
Here is the information related to your shipment:
Items: 300 ceramic garden pots
Packing methodFoam chips/foam-lined crates
Receiving distributor (Paris):   Marie Fontaine at France Air
100 rue de Charenton 75011 Paris
Packing cost: $1200
Shipping cost: $800
The total cost of your order is $2000 plus 7% tax for a total of $2140. Our invoice, which includes package tracking information, is attached. If I can be of further assistance, please call me at (416) 555-1299. Thank you again for placing your order with Go Green Packing.

Version 2: Professional Layout

Thank you for your order to ship 300 ceramic garden pots from Toronto to Paris. Your shipment will leave our warehouse on May 1.

Here is the information related to your shipment:

Items:	300 ceramic garden pots
Packing method	Foam chips/foam-lined crates
Receiving distributor (Paris):	Marie Fontaine at France Air
	100 rue de Charenton 75011 Paris
Packing cost:	$1200
Shipping cost:	$800
Subtotal	$2000
Tax	$140
Total	$2140

Our invoice, which includes package tracking information, is attached. If I can be of further assistance, please call me at (416) 555-1299. Thank you again for placing your order with Go Green Packing.

In Version 1, cramped and inconsistent spacing makes the information about the shipment very difficult to read. In Version 2, much more white space appears around the text. From the reader's point of view, the most important part of the message is the information about the shipment. Just by changing the positioning of this information, you make the information stand out for the reader.

Where possible, you can also choose to present items in a list format, which means using bullets or numbers to format each item. Figure 1-8 compares the readability of items presented in a sentence and the same items presented in a list.

Sentence Version

The reader needs to mentally separate out the items and may miss something.

I will be pleased to process your order as soon as we receive a sample vase, the packing option you require (foam chips or bubble wrap), the distributor's contact information, and customs forms.

List Version

The reader can check off each item to be sure nothing is missed.

I will be pleased to process your order as soon as we receive the following items:

- Sample vase
- Packing option required (foam chips or bubble wrap)
- Distributor's contact information
- Customs forms

Organizing Content

The appearance and layout of a document can be perfect and still fail to communicate if the writer has not organized the content in a way that promotes understanding. Figure 1-9 compares the content presented in the form of a paragraph of plain text with the same content organized by headings into meaningful chunks of information.

Figure 1-9 **Comparison of plain text content and organized content**

Version 1: Plain Text

The Marketing Department at Go Green Packing has developed three kinds of printed materials to advertise our new shipping options: brochures, bookmarks, and posters. Each type of printed material includes descriptions and pricing options for the packing options. We suggest you send the brochure to customers on your mailing list and include the bookmark with every purchase of packing materials. You can send the poster to post offices, company mailrooms, and retail warehouses in your target area.

Version 2: Content Organized with Headings

New Marketing Materials

The Marketing Department at Go Green Packing has developed three kinds of marketing materials to advertise our new shipping options. Each type of printed material includes descriptions and pricing options for the packing options. Please distribute these materials as follows:

Brochures

Send to all customers on your mailing list.

Bookmarks

Include a bookmark with every purchase of packing materials.

Posters

Send to post offices, company mail rooms, and retail warehouses in your target area.

You can use a variety of techniques to organize content to maximize readability. First, you can use headings and subheadings to separate content into manageable bites. Headings help your readers understand your document at a glance. For example, in Version 1, readers need to read and absorb the entire paragraph before identifying what they need to do. In Version 2, the use of a main heading (New Marketing Materials) and three subheadings (Brochures, Bookmarks, Posters) helps readers to quickly identify the new marketing materials and how they are to distribute them.

You can also use tables to organize content into an easy-to-read format. Figure 1-10 shows how a paragraph of text is broken into components suitable for presentation in table form. Readers appreciate tables because they present information clearly and succinctly.

Figure 1-10 **Organizing content in a table form**

Version 1: Content presented in a paragraph
The reader needs to study the paragraph closely to determine when to perform each action.

Arrive at 7:15 a.m. and open the premises. The alarm needs to be disarmed. Prepare the coffee. At 7:30 a.m. ensure that the doors to the public are unlocked. Greet customers and direct them to the appropriate department. Take a 15-minute break at 10:30 and 2:30. Take lunch at noon for 30 minutes. No customers should be admitted after 4:30 p.m. At 4:45 p.m., contact the janitorial staff and provide directions regarding specific areas to clean. At 5:00 p.m., the premises need to be locked and the alarm needs to be set before you leave the premises.

Version 2: Content presented in table form
The reader can see at a glance exactly what to do throughout the day.

Daily Schedule

Time	Activity
7:15	Open the premises and disarm the alarm
7:20	Prepare coffee
7:30	Unlock the doors to admit customers
7:30 to 4:30	Greet customers and direct them to the appropriate department
10:30 to 10:45	Morning break
Noon to 12:30	Lunch
2:30 to 2:45	Afternoon break
4:30	Close the doors to customers
4:45	Advise the janitorial staff about specific areas to clean
5:00	Lock the premises and set the alarm

Effective business writers do not stop with the text of a message. After making sure their message is written clearly, they spend time formatting the text with headings, subheadings, lists, and tables as appropriate to ensure that readers can understand the message quickly and easily.

Understanding Reader Needs

You can write a business document very clearly and still not communicate effectively with your reader. For example, an e-mail that consists of only the sentence *Attend the meeting at 2 p.m.* has communicated a message. However, the recipient of the message is still left with many questions, such as *Where is the meeting?*, *What date is the meeting?*, *Who will be at the meeting?*, and *Do I need to bring anything to the meeting?*. When you write in business, you need to centralize the role of the reader. You do so by writing both clearly *and* effectively.

Identifying Reader Needs

The reader must understand what you write and then be able to act accordingly. When the writer of a business document does not focus on the central position of the reader in the communication process, communication does not take place, and the time of both the writer and the reader is wasted. In today's fast-paced business world, wasting time costs money.

You use the **5W technique** to identify the information your reader needs to take a required action and then develop a reader-centered vocabulary. The 5W technique consists of five *W* words and one *H* word as follows: Who, What, Where, When, Why, and How.

Using the 5W Technique

You are probably familiar with the Who, What, Where, When, Why, and How sequence of questions that newspaper writers use to identify the information they need to write a news article. In business, you can use these questions to help you focus your attention on the information that your reader needs. You use the *5W* technique before you start to write a document so you can gather all the information you need to include in the document.

Suppose you need to write an e-mail asking your supervisor to hire an administrative assistant who can help you with administrative duties. Before you start to write the e-mail, think about the information your supervisor needs to make the decision. Jot down a series of *W* questions (in no particular order) that will help you identify the information you need to provide in the e-mail. Figure 1-11 lists some of the questions and sample answers for an e-mail that requests an administrative assistant.

Key Point

In business writing, you ask questions to identify reader needs and gather information to include in the document.

| Figure 1-11 | Sample questions and answers to identify reader needs |

Question Word	Sample Question	Sample Answers
Who	Whom should we hire?	Specify the person's name and qualifications if you have someone specific in mind. Suggest a method for recruiting if you need to hire someone. For example, suggest advertising in the local paper or contacting an employment agency.
What	What duties would the new assistant perform?	Refer to a job description supplied by the Human Resources Department, if available, to identify the duties required and then list them in the memo. Use a bulleted list to present the duties in an easy-to-read format.
Where	Where would the new assistant work? For example, is a new workstation or computer needed?	Identify an area in the office that would be suitable for a new workstation. The supervisor will also want to know if new equipment and office furniture are required. If so, identify the costs involved.
When	When should we hire the assistant?	Specify when the new assistant should start, as well as a possible work schedule. Will the assistant work part-time? Full-time?
Why	Why should we hire an assistant?	Provide a rationale for hiring the assistant. How can the assistant help the business? The supervisor will want to know if spending money on a new assistant will contribute to making the office more productive and, most importantly, more profitable.
How	How much should we pay the assistant?	Research the pay scale for assistants in similar positions and then provide the supervisor with a range.

The answers you identify help you determine the information you need to include in your e-mail. Your goal is to anticipate questions your reader might have and then answer them. If you do your job well as the writer, your reader should be able to read the e-mail and reply with an approval. When you leave out important information, you waste your reader's time. For example, if you forget to mention what duties the new assistant will perform, your reader will need to e-mail or phone you to get clarification.

After you have gathered the information generated from the 5W questions, you can start to organize the content so that it makes sense to your reader. When you use the 5W technique to anticipate the questions your reader might have, you can usually reduce the number of communications required to come to an agreement. Figure 1-12 shows a completed version of the e-mail.

Key Point

Any steps you can take to reduce the number of times two people need to contact each other to make a decision will pay off in saved time and greater productivity.

Figure 1-12	Completed e-mail requesting an assistant

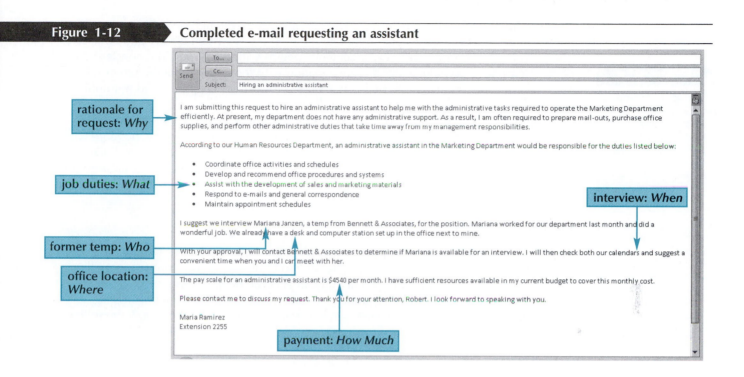

rationale for request: *Why*

job duties: *What*

former temp: *Who*

office location: *Where*

interview: *When*

payment: *How Much*

Using a Reader-Centered Vocabulary

Good business writers select words that focus on the reader, not on the writer. To understand the importance of using a reader-centered vocabulary, compare the two versions of the message shown in Figure 1-13.

Figure 1-13	Writer-centered message and reader-centered message

Version 1: Writer-centered message

We note with pleasure that our Web site was visited and a request for a copy of our Spring 2011 catalog was made. We are pleased to enclose our catalog along with a free sample of our new Premium Best Bubble Wrap.

Our online questionnaire was completed which resulted in a request for our shipping products. Pages 3 to 12 in the catalog provide a full list of our shipping products. We've also included in our catalog our reference guide to all the packing supplies for retail operations that we carry.

Again, we thank you for requesting one of our Go Green Packing 2011 catalogs. Please call us at (206) 555-1299 or e-mail us at orders@gogreenpacking.com to place an order. Remember that our new secure online ordering system can also be used to order our products directly from our Web site at www.gogreenpackingcorp.com.

Version 2: Reader-centered message

Thank you for visiting the Go Green Packing Web site and requesting a copy of the Spring 2011 catalog. Enclosed are a catalog and a free sample of Premium Best Bubble Wrap. You can use Premium Best to protect delicate objects such as china and glassware.

When you completed the online questionnaire, you mentioned your interest in shipping products. You will find a full list of these products on pages 3 to 12 in the catalog, as well as a reference guide at the back of the catalog that lists all packing supplies for retail operations.

Again, thank you for requesting a Go Green Packing 2011 catalog. If you would like to place an order or if you have further questions, please call me at (206) 555-1299 or e-mail me at orders@gogreenpacking.com. You can also log on to www.gogreenpackingcorp.com and place your order.

In Version 1, every reference to the writer (we, our, us) is underlined. As you can see, the writer dominates the message. Although the message is written clearly and concisely, it lacks warmth because almost every sentence begins with *we* or *our*. The constant use of these pronouns communicates a preoccupation with the concerns of the writer rather than the concerns of the reader. Only once does the word *you* appear—and not until the very end of the message, in the phrase *we thank you*.

To help you focus on the reader in a business document, such as an e-mail, a letter, or a memo that you write directly to an individual, start as many sentences as possible with *you* or *your*. In Version 2 of the message, every reference to the reader is underlined. Now the reader takes center stage in a message that replies to a specific request from the reader and helps to encourage new sales.

Using a Positive Tone

As you have learned, the reader plays a crucial central role in business writing. When you need to write a negative message, you need to think about how your reader will react if you don't word the message carefully. In general, people respond very strongly to negative stimuli and give it more significance than it deserves. If negative words are so powerful, why do we use them so often in business writing? Think about how the following sentence makes you feel:

> We **regret** to inform you that we **cannot** process your order **until** you send us two copies of the product specifications.

As a customer receiving this message, you might feel as if you were somehow at fault for the delay of your order. The message feels negative because it includes the words shown in bold. The words *regret* and *cannot* are obviously negative and the word *until* feels slightly threatening. Now consider the positive alternative:

> We **will be glad** to process your order **as soon as** you send us two copies of the product specifications.

This small change from negative to positive makes the sentence much more pleasing to read and acknowledges the importance of the reader. Remember that the central purpose of business writing is to get the reader to take a required action. If your negative tone offends the reader, the reader might not feel inclined to act. Instead, the reader might either ignore the message, or worse, take the opposite action to the one you intended. In either case, *effective* communication does not occur.

Figure 1-14 lists sentences containing negative words and offers alternative versions that use a positive tone. The use of negative words to communicate a message can alienate the reader. The reframed versions do not *water down* the message or leave out information. You can use a positive tone while still conveying your message accurately.

Figure 1-14 ▶ Using a positive tone

Negative Version	Positive Version	Comments
This report contains too many errors to submit to the Board as written.	Please correct punctuation and grammar in the report on Relocation Options before submitting it to the Board.	Tell the reader what actions can be taken to correct the problem rather than focusing only on the problem.
Your application for the position of marketing manager has been rejected.	The successful candidate had over 15 years of experience in a similar position.	Saying *no* in a way that retains the reader's goodwill requires some finesse—and a specific structure, which you will study in more detail in a later project.

Figure 1-14	Using a positive tone (*continued*)

Negative Version	Positive Version	Comments
We are sorry to hear of the problem you've had with our product.	Thank you for letting us know about the loose bolts on the chair you purchased from us on July 3. We will certainly exchange the chair for a new one.	The customer never has a problem! Acknowledge the reader and the specific situation, and then provide assistance.
There is nothing to be done about the team's total lack of ideas.	The team needs to work together to develop new ideas. I suggest we ask a facilitator to help us get back on track.	Find a positive action.

Figure 1-15 shows an example of a message that uses a positive tone to request additional information from a customer regarding a cost estimate. Frequent references to the reader (*you*) and positive words and phrases such as *pleased, provide,* and *I look forward* contribute to the upbeat and optimistic tone of this message.

Figure 1-15	Example of a positively-worded message

Thank you for requesting packing services from Go Green Packing. I understand that your company manufactures glass vases and that you need to know the cost of packing 3000 vases for shipment to Asia.

I will be pleased to send you a cost estimate as soon as we receive the following items:

- Sample vase
- Packing option (foam chips or bubble wrap)
- Distributor's contact information
- Customs forms

Please send us the above information by June 30 so that I can provide a cost estimate for your order. If you have any questions or require further assistance, please call me at (206) 555-1299. Thank you for your interest in Go Green Packing. I look forward to hearing from you.

Technology Skills – Using Writing Tools in Word

Microsoft Word includes a variety of tools that you can use to help you write clearly and effectively. You can enliven your writing by using the **Thesaurus** feature to help you find synonyms and antonyms that clarify your meaning. You do not use the thesaurus to find *big words* that make your writing sound important. Readers have no time to think about the meaning of *missive* when you mean *letter*, or *eschew* when you mean *avoid*. You use the **Spelling & Grammar** feature to identify spelling and grammar errors and suggest corrections. The Technology Skills steps cover these skills:

- Use the Thesaurus to find synonyms
- Change settings for the Spelling & Grammar feature
- Use the Spelling & Grammar feature to check for errors

To use the Thesaurus feature:

▶ 1. Open the file **Tech_01.docx** located in the Project.01 folder included with your Data Files and then, to avoid altering the original file, save the document as **Writing Tools** in the same folder.

▶ 2. Read the description of Go Green Packing. As you can see, the word *provide* appears three times (once as *provides*), and other adjectives such as *massive* and *brilliant* do not sound quite right for a business document.

▶ 3. Press [**Ctrl**]+[**F**] to open the Find and Replace dialog box, type **provide**, click the **Find Next** button, and then click the **Cancel** button to close the Find and Replace dialog box. The word *provides* is not very precise and is certainly overused in this document.

▶ 4. Click the **Review** tab, and then click the **Thesaurus** button in the Proofing group. The Research task pane opens showing a list of synonyms for *provide*.

▶ 5. Click **supply** in the list of synonyms. Another list of synonyms for *supply* appears. After studying the list, you decide you prefer *supply*.

▶ 6. Click the **Back** button near the top of the Research task pane, move the mouse pointer over **supply**, then click the **list arrow** that appears, as shown in Figure 1-16.

| **Figure 1-16** | **Using the Thesaurus** |

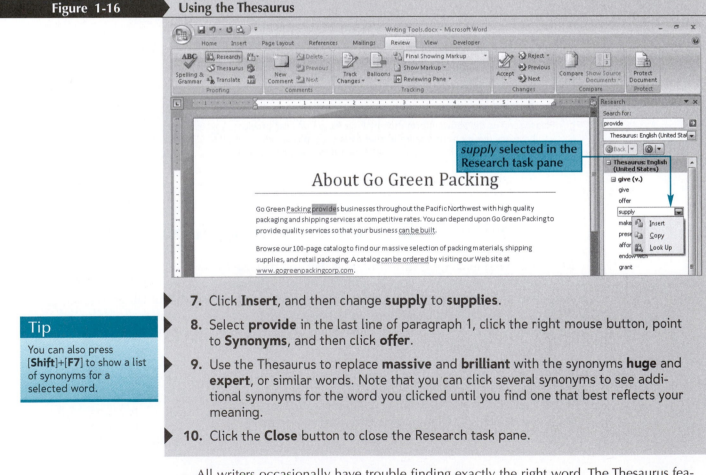

▶ 7. Click **Insert**, and then change **supply** to **supplies**.

▶ 8. Select **provide** in the last line of paragraph 1, click the right mouse button, point to **Synonyms**, and then click **offer**.

▶ 9. Use the Thesaurus to replace **massive** and **brilliant** with the synonyms **huge** and **expert**, or similar words. Note that you can click several synonyms to see additional synonyms for the word you clicked until you find one that best reflects your meaning.

▶ 10. Click the **Close** button to close the Research task pane.

Tip

You can also press [**Shift**]+[**F7**] to show a list of synonyms for a selected word.

All writers occasionally have trouble finding exactly the right word. The Thesaurus feature alone won't make you a great writer, but it will help you out when you get stuck staring at a blank screen. When writer's block hits, you can type a word that is close to the meaning you want and then use the Thesaurus to provide you with options. Within minutes, you can usually get yourself back on track.

You can use the Spelling & Grammar feature to check for errors. The Grammar feature even finds passive voice sentences that you can rewrite in the active voice.

To find passive voice sentences:

1. Click the **Office** button (🏢), click **Word Options**, and then click **Proofing**.

2. Click the **Mark grammar errors as you type** check box (the Check grammar with spelling check box will also be selected) if it is not already selected, click the **Writing Style** list arrow, click **Grammar & Style**, click the **Settings** button, scroll down and be sure the **Passive Sentences** check box in the Style area is checked, click **OK**, click **Recheck Document**, click **Yes**, and then click **OK**.

3. Click the **Spelling & Grammar** button in the Proofing group, and then, if the sentence with *Pacific time* is highlighted, click **Ignore Once**. The Grammar check thinks *time* is a capitalization error; however, it is correct as lowercase, so you ignore the error.

4. Click **Ignore Once** to skip Your Name, and then, if *Packing* in the first sentence is highlighted, click **Ignore Once**. The Grammar check thinks *Packing* is a capitalization error; however, since it is part of the company name, you ignore the error. The construction *can be built* is highlighted because it is in the passive voice.

5. Click **Explain**, read the description of the passive voice, then close the Word Help dialog box.

6. Select the text **your business can be built** in the Spelling and Grammar dialog box, and then type **you can build your business** as shown in Figure 1-17.

Figure 1-17 Correcting a passive voice sentence

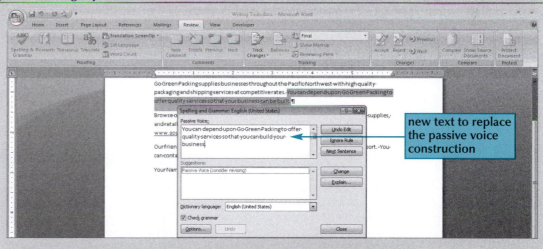

7. Click **Change**, note that the passive construction **can be ordered** is highlighted, select **A catalog can be ordered** in the Spelling and Grammar dialog box, type **You can order a catalog**, click **Change**, and then click **OK**.

8. Type your name where indicated, save the document, print a copy, and then close the document.

Tip

Respond to questions and highlighted terms as appropriate if your order does not match steps.

Practice	Identify Reader Needs

You work for Dawn Bennett, the vice president of marketing at Go Green Packing in Seattle, a packing and distribution company dedicated to using environmentally friendly packaging products. Dawn is concerned that the action required by the reader is not clear in many of the business documents her employees send to customers and colleagues. Dawn asks you to analyze three messages and then rewrite them so that the reader knows exactly what to do.

Follow the steps below to identify and specify reader actions.

1. Open the file **Practice_01.docx** located in the Project.01 folder included with your Data Files, and then to avoid altering the original file, save the document as **Reader Needs** in the same folder.

2. Read the directions at the beginning of the document. You need to ask clarifying questions that will help readers know what action is required of them for each of the three messages. You then need to rewrite each message so the required action is stated clearly for the reader. You can provide additional details if you want and use more than one sentence.

3. Refer to Figure 1-18 to view a sample response using a different message.

Figure 1-18	**Sample response for reader actions**

Reader Needs

Message	Reader Action	Clarifying Questions
It is important to note that the Accounting Department is requiring that travel expense forms must be completed by all personnel and submitted to the accounting assistant in a timely manner. Jason McDonald will process the forms when he gets them.	Send completed travel expense forms to the accounting assistant in a timely manner.	Who must fill out the travel expense forms? Who are the completed forms sent to? Why are the forms needed? How long do I have to submit a form?

Message 1

It is important to note the Accounting Department is requiring that travel expense forms must be completed by all personnel and submitted to the accounting assistant in a timely manner. Jason McDonald will process the forms when he gets them.

Rewrite: Please send your completed travel expense form to Jason McDonald, the accounting assistant, within ten days of the completion of your business trip. Accounting needs the form and all proper documentation in order to process the request for reimbursement.

4. Write your own entries in the appropriate areas of the Reader Needs document.

5. Use the Thesaurus to help you find appropriate synonyms and then use the Grammar feature to find and correct any passive voice constructions.

6. Type your name in the location indicated in the footer, save the document, print a copy, and then close the document.

Revise | Clarity and Tone

Some of the employees in the Administration office at Go Green Packing use a long-winded style to write their memos, letters, and even e-mails, while others use negative words and a brusque tone. Your supervisor wants to hold a one-day business writing seminar to teach these employees how to write clearly and with a reader-friendly tone. She has prepared ten poorly written sentences that she will use in the seminar as part of one writing exercise. Some of the sentences lack clarity, use passive voice constructions, and include outdated vocabulary, and some sentences use a curt, unprofessional tone. She asks you to create an answer key for the exercise by rewriting each sentence using the techniques you have learned in this project.

Follow the steps below to rewrite sentences to enhance clarity and improve tone.

1. Open the file **Revise_01.docx** located in the Project.01 folder included with your Data Files, and then to avoid altering the original file, save the document as **Clarity and Tone Exercises** in the same folder.
2. Read the directions at the beginning of the document. You need to use the techniques you have learned in this project to rewrite ten sentences.
3. Rewrite the sentences in the document as directed. Use the Thesaurus and Grammar features to help you write clear, reader-friendly sentences.
4. Type your name in the location indicated in the footer, save the document, print a copy, and then close the document.

Create | Reader-Oriented Message

You are working in the Human Resources department of a large retail store, which has recently been receiving a worrisome number of customer complaints. Your supervisor asks you to help her draft a message to Jolene Ng, the director of the department, to propose a seminar to train front line staff in handling customer complaints. Ms. Ng is a real stickler for detail, so your supervisor asks you to use the 5W technique to help you identify all the information that Ms. Ng will need to help her make a decision about whether to approve the seminar.

Follow the steps below and use the 5W technique to gather information needed to write a business communication.

1. Complete the table below with information about the seminar request. Note that you will need to make up information. Use fictitious but realistic details.

Information for a Seminar Request
When will we hold the seminar?
Who will attend the seminar and who will conduct the seminar? *Hint*: Specify how many employees will attend the seminar. Also describe the speaker, who could be someone from the company or a local expert.

Information for a Seminar Request (*continued*)

What topics will be covered at the seminar? *Hint*: Check the Internet to find descriptions of similar seminars and then list some of the topics.

Where will the seminar be held? *Hint:* Specify whether the seminar will be held on the company premises or at a local hotel or conference center.

Why do we need to hold a seminar? *Hint:* List at least two reasons why you think employees need to learn how to handle customer complaints better.

How much will it cost the company to hold the seminar? *Hint:* Ms. Ng will be particularly interested in the answer to this question. Identify a cost for the speaker (if any), a cost for the rental of a seminar room if required, and a cost for lunch for the number of participants. Include the total cost.

2. In Word, compile all the information into a three- to four-paragraph message to Ms. Ng.
3. Include some of the information in a table or a list so that the information is as easy to read as possible.
4. Write clear sentences in the active voice and use a pleasant, reader-friendly tone.
5. Save the message as **Customer Service Seminar Request**, print a copy, and then close the document.

Apply | Case Study 1

Capstone College   Students in the Digital Arts Department at Capstone College in San Francisco are just completing their 10-month program. As part of their graduation requirements, the students exhibit samples of their work in a class exhibition. You work as a program assistant for the Digital Arts Department and need to invite all faculty members to the exhibition. You open the message that your predecessor wrote the year before and discover that some rewriting and formatting are required before you can send the message to faculty members to advertise the current exhibition. To complete this case study, you rewrite the invitation asking the staff to attend the graduating class exhibition.

1. Open the file **Case1_01.docx** located in the Project.01 folder included with your Data Files, and then save the document as **Graduating Class Exhibition** in the same folder.
2. Read the message and consider ways to improve the writing style and organization.
3. Rewrite paragraph 1 so that it invites faculty to the exhibition. You can remove most of the existing text and extend the invitation in the first sentence.

4. Modify paragraph 2 so that it clearly communicates the following information about the exhibition:

    a. Date is two weeks after the current date

    b. Time is 6 p.m.

    c. Location is the Digital Arts Department on the fifth floor of the Maple Building

5. Rewrite paragraph 3 to improve its tone. You might find that you can eliminate almost all of paragraph 3 and replace it with a friendly request to attend the exhibition and show support for the students.

6. Use the Spelling & Grammar feature to find and correct grammar errors in the message, and then read the message carefully to find and correct any errors that the Spelling & Grammar checker did not identify.

7. Read the revised message carefully. Consider how the reader will react to the content. Will the reader feel pleased to attend the exhibition? Can the reader quickly identify the information about the exhibition? Remember, you can use bullets or indents to present the details about the exhibition if you want.

8. Include your name in the footer as indicated, print a copy of the document, save the document, and then close it.

Apply | Case Study 2

Otter Bay Kayaking Adventures Tourists from all over the world journey to Juneau, Alaska, to enjoy the stunning scenery and a wide variety of outdoor activities. As an assistant in the Marketing Department, you are responsible for editing and proofreading all the documents used to market the company. The owner of the company, Kay Johnson, has just written a new company description that she wants to post on the About Us page on the company's Web site. Kay wrote the description in a hurry and knows that she probably included several passive voice sentences and unclear constructions. To complete this case study, you will rewrite the company description so the message is clear and reader-centered.

1. Open the file **Case2_01.docx** located in the Project.01 folder included with your Data Files, and then save the document as **Company Description** in the same folder.

2. Use the Spelling & Grammar feature to find and correct grammar errors in the document. If the Grammar feature does not find any passive sentences, check the settings using the Office button and be sure, for example, that Grammar & Style is selected. Also, click the Recheck document button to reset the document.

3. Read the document carefully and correct any additional errors.

4. Evaluate the sentence structure and word choices, and then rewrite sentences as needed to make the company description clear and easy to read. Make sure that every sentence is written in the active voice.

5. Use headings to organize the information. For example, you might divide the document into four sections: Company Overview, Company Background, Expansion Plans, and Contact Information.

6. Type your name in the footer as indicated, and then print a copy of the document.

7. Evaluate the printed copy carefully, and then make further changes, if necessary. Sometimes, you can find additional errors when you read the printed version of a document.

8. Enter any new edits, save the document, print a copy, and then close the document.

Research | Case Study 3

The Internet has become a good source of information about grammar rules and usage. Several Web sites provide a user-friendly interface to help you find answers to grammar questions. To complete this case study, you explore a grammar Web site and record information about three grammar issues of your choice.

1. Open the file **Research_01.docx** located in the Project.01 folder in your Data Files, and then save the document as **Researching Grammar Issues** in the same folder.

2. Open your Web browser, and then search for Web sites that provide information about grammar rules and guidelines. *Hint:* Use search terms such as *grammar*, *grammar rules*, and *grammar guidelines*.

3. Select a Web site and then explore it to find information about three grammar issues that interest you. For example, you may want to know how to use *that* correctly in a sentence, or the difference between *it's* and *its* or when to use *lay* and *lie*. *Hint:* Some Web sites include an index that you can use to see all the topics available.

4. In the table provided in the Researching Grammar Issues document, identify each of the grammar issues you have selected and then summarize the information provided on the Web site about each issue. Provide examples where possible. Note that some of the topics will include a great deal of information. Look for topics that describe specific grammar problems clearly and succinctly. For example, choose a topic such as *split infinitives* rather than a broad topic such as *verbs*.

5. Type your name as indicated in the footer, save the document, print a copy, and then close the document.

E-Mail

Introduction

E-mail provides you with a quick and efficient way to communicate with people in all areas of your life, including work, school, family, and friends. To survive and thrive in the electronic universe, you need to develop strategies for writing clear e-mails that communicate exactly the message you intend.

In this project, you will explore the uses of e-mail and learn how to write effective e-mails that use an appropriate tone and format. You also learn how to use Outlook to create a signature block and how to create folders in Outlook. Another important skill you learn is how to take a screen shot of your program window.

Starting Data Files

Project.02

Tech_02.docx
Practice1_02.docx
Practice2_02.docx
Revise_02.docx
Case1_02.docx
Research_02.docx

E-Mail Essentials

In the twenty-first century, messages flash across the digital airways at lightning speed. You can engage in e-mail conversations with the coworker sitting yards away in the same office or with a client on the other side of the globe. E-mail provides you with a quick and efficient way to communicate with people in all areas of your life, including work, school, family, and friends. To survive and thrive in the electronic universe, you need to communicate exactly the message you intend.

Understanding E-Mail Uses

Every day, millions of e-mails transmit messages, documents, and files. In fact, e-mail has almost replaced regular mail as the distribution system of choice for letters and many forms of advertising. Even bills and greeting cards can be distributed by e-mail. Figure 2-1 describes some of the most common ways in which e-mail is used in business situations.

Figure 2-1 ▶ **Common uses for e-mail in business**

Business Use for E-Mail	Description

Sending routine business messages	• Examples include:
	   • Confirm attendance at a meeting.
	   • Ask a question.
	   • Provide requested information.
	• Keep routine business messages short—usually no longer than one screen.
	• Get to the point of the message in the first sentence and use an efficient but friendly tone.
	• Include all the information that the reader needs to respond. Every time your reader must reply to you to obtain clarification, you waste both your time and your reader's time.

Replying to messages	• Provide requested information, including attachments. • Answer a question, such as the time and place of a meeting. • Confirm attendance at a meeting, speaking engagement, and so on.

Forwarding messages	• Consider carefully whether the person to whom you are forwarding the message wants or needs to receive it. Ask permission, if necessary.
	• Include a message with the forwarded e-mail. Examples include:
	   • *Here is the e-mail from Sara Warren concerning your vacation request.*
	   • *As you requested, I'm forwarding you the agenda for the meeting on July 4.*

Investigating business opportunities	• Include a personal introduction to differentiate the e-mail from a scam:
	   • *Your name from was forwarded to me from a colleague of mine, Allison Watson, who recommended that I contact you. I am the Personnel Director at Maple Enterprises in Toronto.*
	• State clearly the business opportunity:
	   • *I would like to set up a series of ergonomic consultations with you. In addition, Maple Enterprises would like you to advise us regarding the redesign of all our workstations. We employ 50 people.*
	• Specify a time and date for further contact:
	   • *Are you available at 2 p.m. on May 3? I would like to set up a meeting in our office at 1799 Bay Street in Toronto. I anticipate the meeting lasting approximately two hours, which would allow time for you to conduct a preliminary assessment of our workstations.*

Figure 2-1	Common uses for e-mail in business (*continued*)

Business Use for E-Mail	Description
Sending attachments	• Limit the size of attachments. • Check with recipients if they are able to receive large files. • Convert files to Rich Text Format (.rtf) or Portable Document Format (.pdf) when possible so that all recipients can read the files regardless of software. • Use a file compression program, such as WinZip, to compress large files before sending them. • Use an online file transfer service to send very large files containing graphics, presentations, or movies.
Sharing information messages	• Use the acronym FYI (For Your Information) in the subject line so readers know that the e-mail does not require any action. • Describe the FYI attachment in the text of the e-mail and summarize its relevance to the recipient.
Distributing solicited advertising or information	• Use to send information or advertising to individuals who have given their permission to receive it, usually by opting in. This type of advertising can be extremely effective because it costs little, provides information that interests the recipient, and saves paper.
Sending personal messages	• Check your employer's Terms of Service or Acceptable Use Policy (AUP) to determine whether you can send personal e-mails from your workplace. An AUP is a set of rules that specifies how people in an organization may use the Internet. For example, an AUP can limit the amount and type of data a user can download from the Internet.

Writing Subject Lines

One of the greatest favors you can do for the recipients of your e-mails is to write a good subject line. A **subject line** provides information about the e-mail that the reader sees before opening the e-mail. Figure 2-2 shows four possible subject lines for the same e-mail.

Figure 2-2	Four versions of one subject line

Version	Example
Version 1:	Meeting
Version 2:	Agenda for tomorrow's meeting
Version 3:	Marketing Meeting at 2 p.m. on June 3 to discuss several issues that have recently arisen as a result of the development of our new line of keyboards
Version 4:	Agenda for Marketing Meeting: 2 p.m. June 3

You know right away that the brief Version 1 subject line, *Meeting,* is too short and too vague. The recipient will immediately want to know what meeting you are talking about, and where and when it will take place. The Version 2 subject line, *Agenda for Tomorrow's Meeting,* is not accurate for anyone who receives the e-mail on a different day than when it was sent. The Version 3 subject line provides far too much information. Some writers believe that long subject lines help their readers, but the opposite is generally the case. Readers do not want to read 50 words just to determine the content of an e-mail. Also, because long subject lines do not fit in the subject text box in most e-mail programs, recipients might not even see the whole line.

The Version 4 subject line in Figure 2-2 wins hands down for clarity and effectiveness. You know right away that the e-mail contains an agenda for a specific meeting (the Marketing Meeting) at a specific time (2 p.m.) and on a specific day (June 3). You cannot confuse the e-mail with an e-mail concerning the Sales Meeting on April 3 or the Production Meeting on November 19. Figure 2-3 presents guidelines for writing effective subject lines.

Key Point

A relevant subject line not only helps the recipient know immediately the content of the e-mail but also helps the recipient file the e-mail appropriately.

Figure 2-3	Guidelines for writing effective subject lines

Guideline	Description
Always include a subject line	• Avoid leaving the subject line blank. Many people delete, without even opening, e-mails that do not include text in the subject line.

Keep the subject short and informative	• Use no more than eight to 10 words and omit articles, pronouns, and other short words, such as *a*, *the*, and *you*.
	   • **Unacceptable Subject**: *The latest update of the Coordinators' Manual for you to review*
	   • **Acceptable Subject**: *Updated Coordinator's Manual for review.*

Indicate an action	• Ensure the reader can determine what action, if any, is being requested in the e-mail.
	   • **Vague Action**: *New Brochure*
	   • **Specific Action**: *New brochure to proofread* or *New brochure to distribute to clients*

Use punctuation judiciously	• Avoid exclamation marks because they often indicate that a message is spam or is not intended for business purposes.
	   • **Unprofessional**: *Great News for Sales Reps!!!!*
	   • **Professional**: *New Incentive Package for Sales Reps*

Reduce the repetition of *RE:*	• Where possible, break subject lines after several replies to reduce the repeated *RE:*. The new e-mail should use a new subject line that reflects the progress made in the exchange. For example, after four e-mail responses to *Submit Fall Catalog Items*, you could start a new e-mail with the subject line: *16 new items for Fall Catalog.*

Avoid spam triggers	• Avoid subject lines that may trigger a spam filter.
	   • The subject line *Free Stuff Coming Your Way!!!* will likely activate a filter that prevents the e-mail from reaching your reader's Inbox.
	 • De-spam your subject lines as follows:
	   • Avoid starting subject lines with verbs that demand action such as *Save*, *Buy*, and *Get*.
	   • Avoid *you* and *your*.
	   • Do not include words such as *free*, *at no cost*, and *free of charge*.

Using an Appropriate Tone

How would you feel if you received the following e-mail message?

> *George*
> *As I TOLD you in our phone conversation yesterday, you MUST contact me immediately. If I don't hear from you by the end of the day, I will presume that you are no longer interested in our services. Good day.*

Would you want to continue doing business with someone who could send such an e-mail? Two things make the tone of this e-mail unacceptable. First, the writer uses all capital letters to emphasize two of the words (TOLD and MUST). One of the conventions in the digital world is that words written in all capital letters signify shouting, which is not something you want to do to a business associate. Second, the writer includes words that the reader could easily interpret as a threat: *If I don't hear from you....* You need to use care when writing a phrase that begins with *If* in an e-mail. The reader can so easily misinterpret your meaning.

To help you maintain an appropriate tone in your e-mail, imagine that your e-mail message has been magnified 300 times and displayed on a huge banner spanning your local freeway. When you send e-mail, always consider that your readers can so easily forward your message to hundreds of people and then print and distribute it to hundreds more. Make sure that every e-mail you send is professional in both content and tone. Figure 2-4 presents guidelines for using an acceptable tone in your e-mails.

Figure 2-4 — **Guidelines for creating an acceptable e-mail tone**

Guideline	Description
Understand legal implications	• Be aware that e-mail messages can be used as evidence in a court of law. Employees who write damaging e-mails about a company leave the company open to legal proceedings and even prosecution. • Never send any message in an e-mail that you would not want the world to read. Your e-mail can stay in your reader's Inbox for years, just waiting to be retrieved as evidence.
Use polite words	• Use polite words such as *please* and *thank you*. Most people do not respond positively to direct orders made in an e-mail. • **Unacceptable**: *Pick up the financial report and deliver it to the accountant.* • **Acceptable**: *Please pick up the financial report and deliver it to the accountant.*
Avoid extreme brevity	• Avoid sending extremely short e-mails. • **Too short**: *Sure.* • **Reader-friendly**: *Thank you for asking me to attend the March 28 presentation. I will definitely be there!* • When writing short e-mails from a personal digital assistant (for example, a BlackBerry) or a phone, avoid sounding too abrupt. • **Too abrupt**: *Not now. Later.* • **Reader-friendly**: *Can we meet at 2 p.m. instead?*
Write correctly	• Use correct grammar and avoid slang. • **Unprofessional**: *R u going to the mtg on Thurs? I hope to atend, but if I dont, pls get me handouts.* • **Professional**: *Are you attending the Marketing Meeting on Thursday, May 23? I hope to attend, but if I am not there, could you obtain extra copies of any handouts? Thanks!*
Limit emoticons	• Use emoticons very rarely to inject humor only where appropriate. An **emoticon** is a symbol that usually represents an expression on a face: the emoticon :-) represents a smiling face and the emoticon ;-) represents a wink.
Limit abbreviations	• Avoid e-speak such as *LOL* for *laughing out loud*, *BRB* for *be right back*, *IMHO* for *in my humble opinion*, *BTW* for *by the way*, and *AYPI?* for *and your point is?*. Abbreviations can confuse and even irritate readers who may feel the writer lacks professionalism. • Avoid any abbreviation that your reader might not know. Using abbreviations without an explanation is writer-centered, not reader-centered, writing.

You can think of e-mail as a very intimate form of communication. The screen containing the e-mail is just inches from your reader's eyes. The reader is usually alone at the computer and, in some work situations, quite isolated from other workers. For many hours, e-mail might be the only contact a person has with coworkers. As a result, every negative word and every offhand remark can get analyzed far beyond the intention of the writer. Take special care to make sure that every e-mail you write uses a pleasant and friendly tone to communicate your message clearly and precisely.

Formatting E-Mails

You should develop and use a set format for every e-mail. You do not want to waste time thinking about how to start and end an e-mail. Find a format you like and stick with it. To understand the importance of formatting, compare the two e-mails shown in Figure 2-5.

Figure 2-5 ▶ **Comparison of e-mail formats**

VERSION 1: Poorly Formatted E-Mail Message
Please let me know if you are able to attend the marketing meeting at 10 am on Monday, May 2. We will be discussing the results of the marketing research survey that Paul administered to customers in Oregon, Washington, Idaho, and Montana. You should already have received hard copy of the research results in internal mail. Please bring these along to the meeting. After the meeting we'll go to Harborview Bistro for a light lunch. Call me if you have any questions. Thanks!

VERSION 2: Well Formatted E-Mail Message
Hi Joan,

Please let me know if you are able to attend the marketing meeting at 10 a.m. on Monday, May 2. We will be discussing the results of the marketing research survey that Paul administered to customers in Oregon, Washington, Idaho, and Montana.

You should already have received hard copy of the research results in internal mail. Please bring these along to the meeting.

After the meeting, we'll go to Harborview Bistro for a light lunch. Call me if you have any questions. Thanks!

Ron Lee
Greenock Communications
1788 West Georgia Street
Vancouver, BC V6B 1A4
(604) 555-5566

Both e-mails contain exactly the same information. Which e-mail do you find easier to read? Version 1 is missing a salutation, closing, and writer identification. In addition, the lack of paragraphs makes the message difficult to read. In Version 2, a friendly salutation appropriate for a coworker (*Hi Joan,*) is included along with the identification of the writer in a full signature block that includes the writer's contact information. In addition, the e-mail divides the message into easy-to-read paragraphs and includes a friendly closing (*Thanks!*).

When you take a few extra moments to format your e-mails, you increase your chances of actually having your e-mails read and acted upon. Figure 2-6 presents tips for formatting e-mails effectively.

Figure 2-6 ▶ **E-mail formatting tips**

Guideline	Description
Include a salutation	• For e-mails to colleagues and clients you know, begin e-mails with *Hi* or *Hello* followed by the person's name. • For e-mails to new contacts, use *Hello,* on its own when you do not know the person's name or *Dear* followed by the person's name. • Avoid starting an e-mail with just the name of the reader. There is a subtle difference in tone between *Hi Janice,* and *Janice.* Just using the person's name sounds too abrupt.
Use paragraph spacing	• Insert a blank line between the salutation and the first paragraph of an e-mail and then between each paragraph.

| Figure 2-6 | E-mail formatting tips (*continued*) |

Guideline	Description
Use standard formatting	• Avoid modifying the appearance of the text in an e-mail and use the standard white background. Fancy fonts and backgrounds are distracting and unprofessional. Also, many people set e-mail programs to ignore enhancements.
Limit paragraph length	• Keep paragraphs relatively short—no more than three to five lines at the most. • Include only one main idea in each paragraph. Readers find long paragraphs tiring to read, particularly when the paragraph fills a screen.
Close an e-mail	• Include a friendly closing. Options include *Thanks!*, *Cheers!*, and *Regards.*

Identifying E-Mail Program Features

You will generally use an e-mail program such as Microsoft Outlook, Gmail, or Yahoo! Mail to send and receive e-mail. All e-mail programs share common features. In this project, all the examples and exercises use Microsoft Outlook; however, you can complete the exercises using another e-mail program. If you use a different e-mail program, just remember that the placement of a feature might be slightly different from the figures. If you are not able to find a feature, refer to your e-mail program's Help.

Figure 2-7 provides a description of common features of an e-mail message window. Some of these features are discussed in more detail later in the project.

| Figure 2-7 | Common features in an e-mail message window |

Feature	Description
Message header	Area of the e-mail window that includes information such as To:, Cc:, Bcc:, and Subject line.
To:	Type the e-mail address of the person or people who should receive the information; use your address book feature to quickly fill in each address.
Cc:	Type the e-mail address of any person who should receive a copy of the e-mail; people who receive a copy generally are not expected to reply to the e-mail message.
Bcc:	Type the e-mail address of any person who should receive the e-mail message but who you do not want others to know is receiving the e-mail.
Subject line	Type a short, meaningful subject line.
Message window	Type the body of your e-mail message; keep the message concise and the information clear.
Send	Click the Send button to send the e-mail.
Reply	Click the Reply button to respond only to the person who sent the e-mail.
Reply All	Click the Reply All button to respond to all people listed in the e-mail header area (the To:, Cc:, and Bcc: text boxes). Use the Reply All button sparingly to avoid cluttering up people's Inboxes with unnecessary e-mails.
Forward	Click the Forward button to send the message on to one or more people; type the e-mail addresses in the message header.
Attach file	Click the Attach file button to attach a document, such as a meeting agenda; the name of the attached file appears in the Attached text box.

Technology Skills — Handling E-Mail in Outlook

You can send e-mail directly from Word, from Outlook, or from another e-mail application such as Gmail or Yahoo! Mail. If you use Outlook as your e-mail client, you can also take advantage of its many features for handling e-mail including creating signature blocks, attaching a file, and creating folders.

A **signature block** contains text or pictures or both that is added automatically to the end of every e-mail you send. A typical signature block includes the sender's name, job title, company, business address (including a Web address, if applicable), and phone numbers. You should limit the number of lines in your signature block to no more than five and omit inspirational quotations, marketing information, and pictures that waste space and can increase the time required to download the e-mail.

The Technology Skills steps cover these skills:

- Add a signature block
- Attach a file
- Create folders
- Take a screen shot

To add a signature block to an e-mail:

Tip
Read Help for your e-mail program if the features covered in this Technology Skills section are not readily apparent.

1. Launch Outlook.

2. Click **Tools** on the menu bar, and then click **Options**.

3. Click the **Mail Format** tab, click **Signatures**, and then click **New**.

4. Type **Cara O'Neil** as the name of the signature, click **OK**, and then type the name and contact information for Cara O'Neil in the Edit signature area, as shown in Figure 2-8.

Figure 2-8 ▶ **Signature block information**

a different e-mail address will appear here

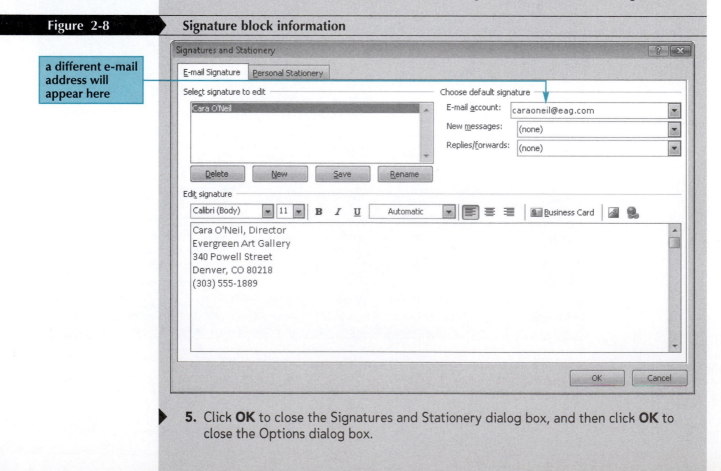

5. Click **OK** to close the Signatures and Stationery dialog box, and then click **OK** to close the Options dialog box.

6. Click the **New** button to open a new, blank e-mail message.

7. Verify that the signature block for Cara O'Neil is added to the blank e-mail.

An **attachment** is a file, such as a document file, presentation file, spreadsheet file, or image file. An attachment travels with an e-mail message. Some e-mail clients limit the size of an attachment that can be sent or received. Be sure to check if there are any size limitations with the recipient of an e-mail attachment before sending it. Also, be sure to scan any attachments you receive for viruses before opening the attachment. Next, you attach a file to an e-mail message.

To attach a file:

1. Be sure a message window is open.

2. Click the **Attach File** button in the Include group.

3. Navigate to the file **Tech_02.docx** located in the Project.02 folder included with your Data Files.

4. Click **Tech_02.docx**, and then click **Insert**. The file is attached to the e-mail message as indicated by the information in the Attached text box. See Figure 2-9.

Figure 2-9   **E-mail message window with signature and attached file**

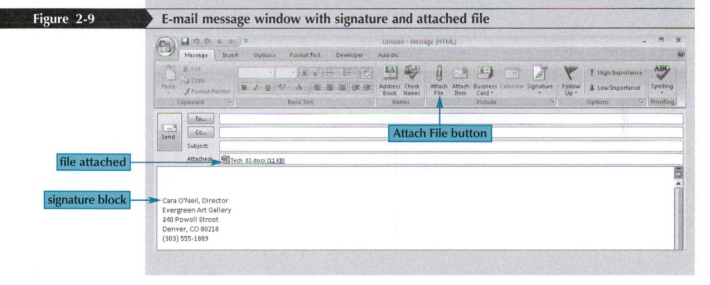

Sometimes, you might find it helpful to be able to take a screen shot of the information on your screen. Pressing the PrntScrn button captures an image of your screen and copies it to your computer memory. You can then paste the image into a Word document. Once the screen shot is copied into a Word document, you can work with it like you would any image—that is, you can crop it, resize it, and so on. Next, you take a screen shot of your Outlook screen.

To take a screen shot of the program window:

1. Press the **PrntScrn** button on your computer's keyboard.

2. Launch Word, and then press [**Ctrl**]+[**V**]. An image of the Outlook screen appears in Word.

3. Save the document as **Signature Block and Folders**, keep the document open, return to Outlook, and then close the e-mail without saving it.

Many businesspeople routinely receive hundreds of e-mails every day. A good way to sort, categorize, and keep track of e-mails is to create folders. A folder is often represented in your e-mail program by a folder icon. You can open a folder to display its contents, and you can close a folder when you do not need to see its contents. You can create folders, called *subfolders*, within a folder. For example, you could create a folder called *Client Questions* and then drag every e-mail containing a question from a client into the Client Questions folder. In this way, you keep all the e-mails containing client questions together in one area. Next, you create folders.

To create folders in Outlook:

▶ **1.** Click the **New** button list arrow on the Standard toolbar, and then click **Folder**.

▶ **2.** Type **Client Support** as the folder name, expand **Personal Folders** if it is not expanded, and then click **Inbox** in the Select where to place the folder list box, as shown in Figure 2-10. The Client Support folder will become a subfolder of the Inbox.

Figure 2-10 ▶ **Creating a new folder**

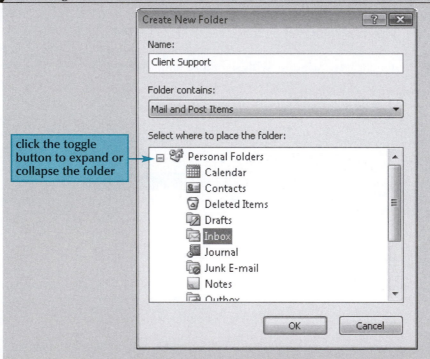

▶ **3.** Click **OK**. The new Client Support folder appears as a subfolder in the Inbox folder.

▶ **4.** Repeat Steps 2 and 3 to create two additional subfolders in the Inbox folder: name one **Reference** and name the other one **Sales**.

The three new folders appear in the Mail task pane, as shown in Figure 2-11. To help you organize your files, you can drag an e-mail to its folder after you have attended to it.

Figure 2-11   New folders created in the Inbox

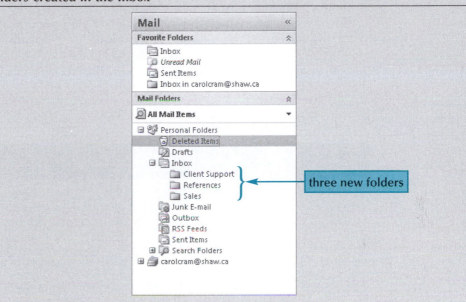

> **5.** Press the **PrntScrn** button on your computer's keyboard.

> **6.** Switch to the document you created in Word, press [**Enter**] twice, and then press [**Ctrl**]+[**V**].

> **7.** Type your name at the bottom of the document, save the document, print a copy, and then exit Word.

If you are working on a shared computer, you might need to delete information specific to you. For example, you might need to delete your signature block or any folders you created so that the program does not contain any information related to you. Next, you delete your signature block and the folders you created.

To remove the signature block and folders:

> **1.** Click **Tools** on the menu bar, click **Options**, and then click **Mail Format**.

> **2.** Click **Signatures**, click **Delete**, click **Yes**, click **OK**, and then click **OK**.

> **3.** Right-click the **Client Support** folder, click **Delete "Client Support"**, and then click **Yes**.

> **4.** Delete the **Reference** and **Sales** folders.

> **5.** Exit Outlook.

Practice | **Routine E-Mails**

As the president of Office Ease Solutions, Jerry Wong develops customized ergonomic solutions for clients throughout North America and distributes a wide range of ergonomic products, including keyboards, mice, office chairs, and desks. Business is booming, and Jerry frequently gets bogged down by a constantly overflowing e-mail Inbox. He asks you to help him out by replying to two e-mails he has received—one from a supplier and one from a client. Figure 2-12 includes the text of the two e-mails Jerry has received along with notes from Jerry regarding the information you need to include in the replies.

Figure 2-12 | **Information for two e-mails**

E-Mail 1	
Sender 1	Rick Watson at Bay Street Printing
Message from Rick Watson	*Please send me the product descriptions you want to include in the 2011 product catalog. We need the descriptions by May 1 so that we can have the catalog printed by June 1. Also, how many copies did you want of the catalog and would you like us to deliver the catalogs?*
Notes from Jerry for Reply	Please tell him you're attaching descriptions of the 300 products to be included in the 2011 catalog and apologize for sending the descriptions two days late. We want 10,000 copies and will pick them up on June 1. Also ask to see a copy of the catalog cover so our marketing manager can approve it.

E-Mail 2	
Sender 2	Donna Wells, director of human resources at Lakeside College
Message from Donna Wells	*Jana Ramal, my colleague at Dundas College in Toronto, recommended I contact you regarding the need to upgrade our offices. We are interested in purchasing ergonomically designed mice, keyboards, and office furniture for the 300 staff at Lakeside College. Could we schedule a time in the next week (any time Wednesday or Thursday is good for me) for a representative from Office Ease Solutions to visit me at the college?*
Notes for Reply	Thank her for contacting us and include a statement about how products distributed by Office Ease Solutions help reduce strain and injuries in the workplace. Confirm that I will meet her in her office at the college at 10 a.m. on Wednesday, April 3. Also tell her that you're attaching our product catalog and draw her attention to the new vertical mouse described on page 45. Mention that her colleague at Dundas College (Jana Ramal) purchased the vertical mouse for her staff and was very pleased with the resulting reduction in back and neck pain reported by staff.

Follow the steps below to write the two e-mails for Jerry.

1. Launch Outlook and create a new signature block called **Office Ease Solutions** with the following information:
   Your Name, Marketing Assistant
   Office Ease Solutions
   1500 Bay Street
   Toronto, ON M5W 2E6
   (416) 555-4422
2. Start a new message in Outlook, type **Rick Watson** in the To: line, and then enter an appropriate subject line for the e-mail to Rick Watson.
3. Attach the file **Practice1_02.docx**.

4. In the body of the e-mail, type an appropriate salutation, press [**Enter**] twice, and then write the first paragraph of the e-mail. Use a polite tone and include the apology and the information about the product descriptions.

5. Press [**Enter**] twice following the first paragraph, and then write a second paragraph. Include the information about the number of copies and the pick-up date.

6. In a third paragraph, ask the question about the catalog cover.

7. Press [**Enter**] twice following the third paragraph, and then type an appropriate closing such as *Thanks!* or *Regards.* You choose the closing you prefer.

8. Use the PrntScrn key to record a picture of the Outlook screen, paste the screen image in Word, and then save the Word document as **Office Ease Solutions E-mails**.

9. In Outlook, save the e-mail (click the **Save** button). A draft of the e-mail will be saved using the text you entered in the subject line. If you wish to revise the draft, you can open the e-mail from the Drafts folder.

10. Close the e-mail, and then start a new e-mail message.

11. Repeat the above steps to write the reply to the e-mail from Donna Wells. You determine how to divide the text for the e-mail into three or four paragraphs. Include an appropriate salutation and closing. Be sure to attach the file **Practice2_02.docx**.

12. Use the PrntScrn key to record a picture of the Outlook screen, paste the screen image in the Word document you created in step 8, save a draft of the e-mail message so you can open it again if you need to make changes, and then close the e-mail.

13. In Outlook, create two new folders in the Inbox folder called **Suppliers** and **Clients**.

14. Use the PrntScrn key to record a picture of the Outlook screen, paste the screen image on page 2 of the Word document, double-click in the area at the bottom of page 1 of the document (the footer area), type your name, exit the footer area, save the document, print a copy, close the document, and then exit Word.

15. In Outlook, delete the two folders and the signature block, and then exit Outlook.

Revise | E-Mail Tone

Jerry Wong, your boss at Office Ease Solutions, has discovered that some of his colleagues find his e-mails too harsh, while others sometimes feel his e-mails are unprofessional. Jerry thought he was being efficient by writing short e-mails, but in reality he often offended associates and some of his customers with his brusque tone. Jerry asks you to rewrite three of his more curt e-mails. Follow the steps below to revise some of Jerry's e-mails.

1. Start Word, open the **Revise_02.docx** file located in the Project.02 folder included with your Data Files, and then to avoid altering the original file, save the document as **E-Mail Tone Revisions** in the same folder.

2. Read the directions at the beginning of the document. You need to apply the concepts you have learned to write positive versions of each of Jerry's replies.

3. Write your own replies in the appropriate areas of the document. Note that you can include additional information where appropriate so that the e-mails are clear, polite, and complete.

4. Type your name where indicated in the footer of the document, save the document, print a copy, close the document, and then exit Word.

Create | **Vacation Request E-Mail**

You are planning an eight-day vacation to a location of your choice and have decided to enlist the help of an associate who has just launched a business as a freelance travel agent. You provide your associate with information about your vacation plans in an e-mail. Follow the steps below to write an e-mail requesting information.

1. Complete the table below with information about your vacation plans.

Information for an E-Mail
What is the name of the associate who will be making your vacation arrangements?
Where do you wish to go for your vacation? Select just one location.
What are the dates of your vacation?
What are your requirements? For example, you can specify that you would like your associate to book your flights, rent you a car, find you accommodations, and arrange activities. Note that you can list your requirements on separate lines, select the text, and then apply bullets (click the Bullets button in the Basic Text group). Your goal is to make sure that your vacation requirements are clear and easy to read.
How many people are going on the vacation and what are their names?

2. In Outlook, create a signature block using your personal contact information.
3. Start a new e-mail message and include an appropriate subject line.
4. Enter a salutation that includes your associate's name.
5. Using the format you learned in this project, write the text of the e-mail in three to four paragraphs. Include all the information your associate will need to book your trip. Make sure you leave a blank line between each paragraph. Include a bulleted list if appropriate.
6. Include an appropriate closing.
7. Use the PrntScrn key to record a picture of the Outlook screen and then paste it in a Word document, type your name below the screen in Word, save the document as **Vacation Plans E-mail**, print a copy, close the document, and then exit Word.
8. Save a draft of the e-mail in Outlook so you can open it again if you need to make changes, and then close the e-mail.
9. Delete the signature block, and then exit Outlook.

Apply | Case Study 1

Capstone College   Students in the Digital Arts Department at Capstone College in San Francisco, California, are just completing their 10-month program. Joanne Vance, the coordinator of the program, encourages students to correspond with her via e-mail to resolve concerns, make requests, and ask questions related to the program. To complete this case study, you write the text for two e-mails to Joanne Vance on the topics provided.

1. In Outlook, create a signature block containing your name and contact information.
2. In Outlook, write an e-mail that requests a letter of reference from Joanne Vance. Determine what details Ms. Vance needs to fulfill your request and provide that information in three or four paragraphs. For example, Ms. Vance might need the name and address of the person to whom she should send the reference. In addition, you might want to ask Ms. Vance to describe a skill or subject in which you have excelled.
3. Type **Letter of Reference** as the subject line.
4. Include a salutation and a closing.
5. Save a draft of the message.
6. Use the PrntScrn key to record a picture of the Outlook screen, paste the screen image in a Word document, and then save the document as **Capstone College E-Mails**.
7. In a new e-mail message, write to Ms. Vance informing her that you are attaching your term essay titled *Employment Opportunities in the Digital Arts* to the e-mail. Make the subject **Essay Attached** and ask Ms. Vance to let you know when you can pick up the essay following the end of term. Also thank Ms. Vance for her patience during the year. Remember to attach the file Case1_02.docx.
8. Include a salutation and a closing, and then save a draft of the e-mail in Outlook.
9. Use the PrntScrn key to record a picture of the Outlook screen, paste the screen image in the Word document, type your name at the bottom of the document, print a copy, save and close the document, and then exit Word.
10. In Outlook, delete the signature block, and then exit Outlook.

Apply | Case Study 2

Otter Bay Kayaking Adventures   Every day during the summer season in Juneau, Alaska, tourists from many cruise ships book tours with Otter Bay Kayaking Adventures. As an assistant in the Marketing Department, you spend most mornings catching up on e-mails with other tour operators in Juneau, with tour organizers on the cruise ships, and with local businesses. To complete this case study, you write an e-mail on behalf of Otter Bay Kayaking Adventures.

1. In Outlook, create a signature block containing your name and the following contact information:
   [Your Name], Marketing Assistant
   Otter Bay Kayaking Adventures
   149 Seward Street
   Juneau, AK 99804
   (907) 555-3311
2. Start a new e-mail in Outlook to Martin Green, the owner of Silver Star Catering in Juneau. You are considering using his company for the boxed lunches and snacks that are provided to tour participants. You need to request a price quote from Martin.
3. Enter **Request for Catering Proposal** as the subject and then include an appropriate salutation. This e-mail is your first contact with Martin.

4. Following the salutation, write three short paragraphs containing the following information:

   a. Introduce yourself as the marketing assistant at Otter Bay Kayaking Adventures and state that you would like a price quote for snacks and boxed lunches.

   b. Inform Martin that you would like the following items included:

      i. Snacks: a bottle of fruit juice, a granola bar, and a package of trail mix

      ii. Boxed lunch: a sandwich (you determine two types; for example, chicken salad sandwich), cookies, raw vegetables, fruit, and a bottle of water

   c. Ask Martin to e-mail you with a price quote for 50 boxed lunches and 75 snacks. Tell him that he can call you at (907) 555-3311 if he needs more information.

5. Include the closing you prefer (for example, *Thanks.* or *Regards.*)

6. Save a draft of the e-mail.

7. Use the PrntScrn key to record a picture of the Outlook screen, paste the screen image in a new Word document, save the document as **Catering E-Mail**, type your name below the picture of the screen, print a copy, save and close the document, and then exit Word.

8. In Outlook, delete the signature block, and then exit Outlook.

Research | Case Study 3

The pervasive presence of electronic junk mail, also known as spam, will probably not diminish any time soon. Junk mail usually advertises products and services without the permission of the people reading it. Aside from being annoying, junk mail can be dangerous. Often senders of junk mail embed viruses into the messages they send. Viruses are programs or pieces of code that are loaded on your computer without your knowledge and then run without your permission. When you open a message that contains a virus, the virus is activated, sometimes with devastating results. To complete this case study, you gather information on how you can protect yourself from receiving junk mail and spam.

1. Open the file **Research_02.docx** located in the Project.02 folder included with your Data Files, and then to avoid altering the original file, save the document as **Reducing Junk Mail** in the same folder.

2. Open your Web browser and conduct a search for Web sites that provide advice about preventing junk e-mail and spam. Search terms you can use include *anti-spam guidelines*, *reducing spam*, and *reducing junk mail.*

3. Find a Web site that provides guidelines that you can use to protect yourself from receiving unwanted junk e-mail and spam.

4. Enter the required information about the Web site in the space provided in the Reducing Junk Mail document.

5. Type your name in the footer where indicated, save the document, print a copy, close the document, and then exit Word.

Objectives

- Identify memo uses
- Organize memo content
- Format a memo
- Create custom border lines in Word
- Convert text to tables in Word
- Use bullets and numbering in Word

Memos

Introduction

The definition of the word **memorandum** is *to be remembered*. You write a memo when you want to communicate information that is important enough *to be remembered*. For many years, most memos were relatively short. In fact, most memos were very similar to the average e-mail sent in business today. As you learned in Project 2, you send an e-mail to remind someone of an event, provide the recipient with information he or she needs to file or remember, make a simple request, and so on. For short messages, the e-mail method of distribution has all but replaced the memo. However, memos still have a place in business writing today.

In this project, you identify ways in which memos are used in business, how to organize content for a memo, and how to format a memo. You also review how to work in Word to create custom borders, convert text into a table form, and use lists to clarify content presentation.

Starting Data Files

Project.03

Tech_03.docx
Practice_03.docx
Revise_03.docx
Case1_03.docx

Memo Essentials

When you are deciding whether to send a message as an e-mail or as a memo, think about the length of your message and what you want your reader to do with the information. If the information can fit in a one-screen e-mail and if your reader can read the message quickly and then act upon it, file it, or delete it, you should send the message as an e-mail. However, if the information requires one to three pages and if you want your reader to retain the information, preferably in printed form, you should write a memo. The key word is *printing*. If your message is substantive enough to require printing and retaining on paper, you serve your reader best by formatting the message in a memo, even if you will be sending the memo as an attachment to an e-mail.

Identifying Memo Uses

You use the memo form to communicate substantive information that the reader is likely to reference, print, and act upon. You can classify information suitable for a memo into one of three categories: **defining procedures**, **making requests**, and **summarizing progress**. Figure 3-1 describes each of these categories.

Figure 3-1 | Memo categories

Memo Category	Description
Defining procedures	• Use to inform coworkers or clients about specific policies and procedures. • Describe the procedure in the first paragraph. • Use numbered steps to present any actions associated with the procedure.
Making requests	• Use to make a request for something that the reader will need to consider carefully and possibly spend significant funds on. • For example, you could write a memo to accompany a purchase order for a piece of expensive equipment or to accompany a work order that requests a substantial renovation to your office. The memo provides the rationale for the request. • State the request in the first paragraph. • Use formatting options, such as tables and bulleted or numbered lists, to present the rationale for the request and any details the reader requires in order to grant the request.
Summarizing progress	• Use to summarize activities, provide a progress report, or explain strategies. • State the context for the summary in the first paragraph. • Present the summary information in the form of tables and/or bulleted lists so readers can identify important information at a glance.

Organizing Memo Content

All three of the memo categories discussed previously share the same basic organizational structure. Each memo includes a purpose statement at the beginning, an action statement or statements at the end, and sufficient details in the body of the memo to ensure that the reader can take the required action. To remember these memo requirements, think *PDA* for *Purpose Statement, Details,* and *Action Request*. Figure 3-2 shows a summarizing progress memo with the PDA elements highlighted.

Figure 3-2   A summarizing progress memo with *PDA* elements highlighted

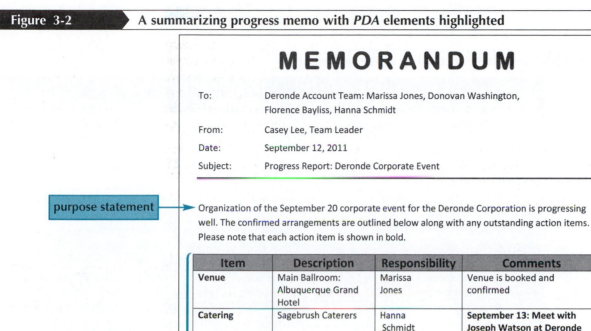

MEMORANDUM

To:	Deronde Account Team: Marissa Jones, Donovan Washington, Florence Bayliss, Hanna Schmidt
From:	Casey Lee, Team Leader
Date:	September 12, 2011
Subject:	Progress Report: Deronde Corporate Event

purpose statement → Organization of the September 20 corporate event for the Deronde Corporation is progressing well. The confirmed arrangements are outlined below along with any outstanding action items. Please note that each action item is shown in bold.

details in the form of an easy-to-read table with action items bolded →

Item	Description	Responsibility	Comments
Venue	Main Ballroom: Albuquerque Grand Hotel	Marissa Jones	Venue is booked and confirmed
Catering	Sagebrush Caterers	Hanna Schmidt	**September 13: Meet with Joseph Watson at Deronde Corporation to finalize dinner menu items**
Entertainment	Desert Rats Trio to play oldies for dancing from 9 p.m. to midnight	Marissa Jones	Band is booked and confirmed
Transportation	Albuquerque Coaches to transport employees to the hotel at 6 p.m. September 20 and back to the company at midnight	Donovan Washington	**Need to finalize schedule for 5 coaches to transport 500 employees to and from the event**
Merchandise	500 Deronde Corporation sweatshirts for all employees	Florence Bayliss	**September 19: Need to transport boxes to the venue**

action statements → Please send all updates to me by September 17 for inclusion in the September 18 progress report that will confirm final arrangements. Also, please attend the final progress meeting on September 19 at 10 a.m. Thanks to all your hard work, this event is shaping up to be one of Prism's best events!

Purpose Statement

The **purpose statement** provides the reader with a reason to read the memo. Here is a clear purpose statement for a request memo that lets the reader know right away the main topic of the memo:

I am requesting permission to purchase new furniture for our office reception area in order to improve its appearance and ensure the comfort of visiting clients.

The reader understands right away that the memo relates to the purchase of furniture and anticipates that the memo will provide the details needed to approve the purchase.

A purpose statement should be reasonably short and simple. You do not need to provide every detail about your memo in the purpose statement. Instead, you use the purpose statement to provide your reader with a context for reading the remaining paragraphs and for understanding what action is expected. The purpose statement is an expansion of the subject line. A **subject line** consists of a short phrase, and a purpose statement turns this short phrase into a complete sentence. Figure 3-3 shows sample subject lines and purpose statements for three situations in which memos would be written.

Figure 3-3 **Sample subjects and purpose statements**

Situation	Subject Line	Purpose Statement	Expected Action
You need to ask your supervisor if you can attend a workshop on how to improve your leadership skills.	Request to Attend Leadership Workshop	I am requesting permission to attend the *Improve Your Leadership Skills* workshop sponsored by the Albuquerque Chamber of Commerce.	You want the reader to approve your request.
You need to inform coworkers of the procedures required to book large venues for special events.	Procedure for Booking Large Venues	The city of Albuquerque requires all consultants to use its new procedure for booking large venues, such as the convention center and stadium. The required procedure is outlined below.	You want your readers to use the correct procedure to book large venues.
You need to summarize progress for members of a committee that is organizing a retirement party for an employee.	Progress Update: Marissa's Retirement Party	With two weeks to go before Marissa's retirement party on March 3, the committee has completed the arrangements outlined below. Action items are highlighted in bold.	You want your readers to know which action items are still outstanding and who is responsible for each item.

The purpose statement can sometimes consist of two sentences. The first sentence defines the purpose of the memo, and the second sentence directs the reader's attention forward to the details contained in the body of the memo.

Details

The *D* in PDA stands for *Details*. Most readers do not have time to read several long paragraphs of text to extract the important details. Readers want—and need—to identify the details as quickly as possible. Consider again the purpose statement discussed previously:

I am requesting permission to purchase new furniture for our office reception area in order to improve its appearance and ensure the comfort of visiting clients.

A memo that begins with this purpose statement needs to include details about the request so that the reader can decide whether to approve the purchase of new furniture.

You can use the 5W technique discussed in Project 1 to determine appropriate details to include. Remember that the **5W technique** consists of five *W* words and one *H* word as follows: Who, What, When, Where, Why, and How. Figure 3-4 shows sample questions and answers that can be used to write the office furniture request memo.

Figure 3-4 **Using the 5W technique to determine memo content**

Question	Answer
Why do we need new furniture?	To improve the appearance of our reception area and ensure a pleasant waiting experience for our clients.
What furniture do we need?	Two couches, two lamps, and two end tables.
Where will we purchase the furniture?	The Office Barn currently has great deals on office furniture.
When do we want the furniture?	If we purchase the furniture on November 3, we can take delivery on November 5.
Who will order the furniture?	I can order the furniture from The Office Barn.
How much will the furniture cost?	Total price will be $5000 to $6500.

You use the 5W technique to help you identify all of the details required for a memo. When you ask questions that you think the reader might have, you are thinking from the reader's point of view. You are therefore less likely to leave out important information. Figure 3-5 shows a properly formatted request memo with sufficient details based on the answers to the 5W questions.

Figure 3-5 **A properly formatted request memo with sufficient details**

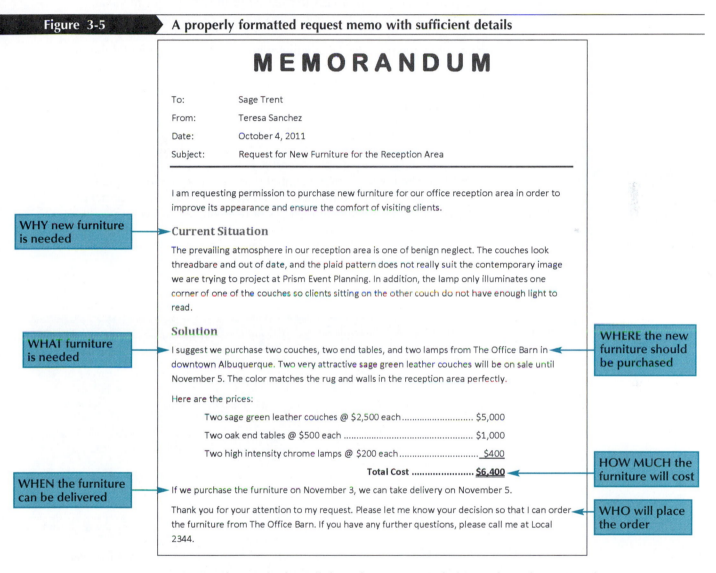

Now, the reader has all the information needed to make a decision. When you include sufficient details in a memo, you make your reader's job much easier.

Action Request

The *A* in PDA stands for *Action Request*. You need to end a memo with a sentence or two that requests a specific action from the reader. This action can be as simple as asking the reader to call you with any questions or to attend a meeting to discuss an issue further. Two examples of appropriate action statements that you can adapt for most memos follow:

If you have any questions or require further information, please call me at Extension 2285.

Let's meet at 2 p.m. on April 3 to discuss this matter further. You can call me at Extension 2285 to let me know if that time works for you or to suggest a different time.

The last sentence of a memo states clearly the required action and provides the means for the reader to perform that action, whether by calling, meeting, or sending something.

Formatting a Memo

Busy readers appreciate memos that use a standard memo format. Readers want the various components of a memo to appear in a consistent position and with consistent formatting. Fancy fonts, unnecessary graphics, and garish colors can do more harm than good when they distract the reader from the central purpose of the memo. Readers should be able to scan an effectively formatted memo quickly to find the information they need. In fact, you can maximize your chances of receiving a positive response by presenting the information in an attractively formatted memo that the reader can print and perhaps distribute to others, such as other decision makers at a meeting. Figure 3-6 describes issues related to formatting a memo.

Figure 3-6 ▶ **Memo formatting issues**

Formatting Issue	Description
Heading	• Include the word *Memorandum* at the top of the page, usually centered and in a large font size. • Include four heading components: To:, From:, Date:, and Subject: • At the end of the memo, include a line indicating attachment(s), how many, and the name of each if appropriate. • Include a line regarding the number of pages if the memo is longer than one page, or include that information in the header/footer by using a phrase such as Page 2 of 3. • Omit a salutation such as Dear and a closing that includes the sender's name. • Save time by using the same format for the heading for all the memos you write.
Body	• Use the full-block format, which means that each paragraph begins at the left margin and the first line of each paragraph is *not* indented. • Use headings, tables, and bulleted/numbered lists to present information. • Avoid long sections of text.

Many readers will lose interest in the memo if no clues are provided regarding the relative importance of the information being presented. You can help the reader access the information in the memo quickly and efficiently by using formatting to draw attention to specific blocks of information. Figure 3-7 compares an unformatted procedures memo with a formatted version.

Figure 3-7 Comparison of unformatted and formatted procedures memos

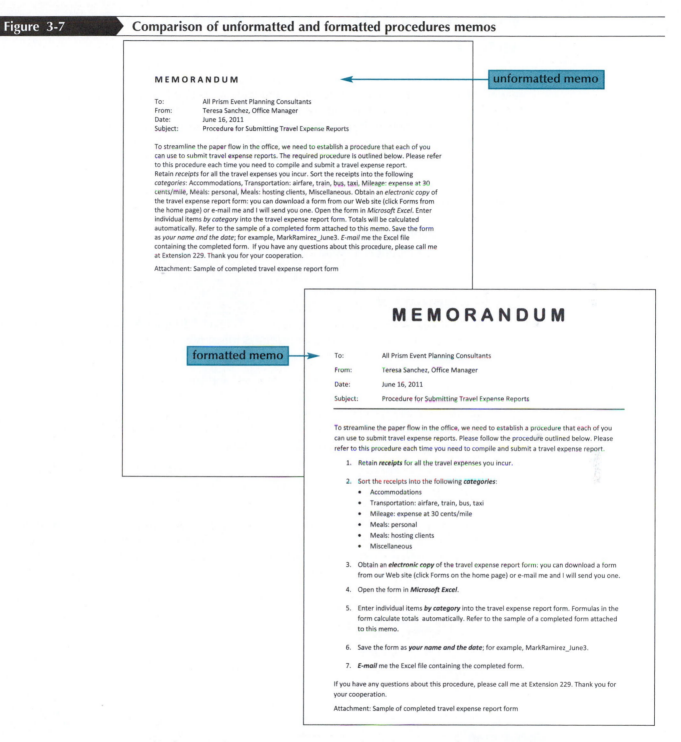

The formatted memo communicates the information much more effectively than the unformatted memo in the following ways:

- The Memorandum heading is centered at the top of the page and is in a different font size.
- Information is presented in numbered steps and bulleted lists.
- Key words are presented in bold and italics.
- Plenty of white space is used to increase readability.

Technology Skills – Using Borders, Tables, and Lists

You can use a variety of Word features to organize content in a memo to maximize reader understanding. For example, you can create a custom border to separate the heading information from the body of the memo, present information in a table, or format a list with numbers or bullets. You create a **table** to display information in a grid-like structure with columns and rows. You **number** items in a list when the items correspond to steps in a procedure. You use **bullets** when you want to present a list in which the order of items is not important. The Technology Skills steps cover these skills:

- Add a custom border
- Convert text to a table
- Create a numbered list and adjust line spacing
- Format a list with a custom bullet

To add a custom border:

1. Open the file **Tech_03.docx** located in the Project.03 folder included with your Data Files, and then to avoid altering the original file, save the document as **Formatted Memo** in the same folder.

2. Enter your name in the heading information, and then click the **Show/Hide ¶** button ¶ in the Paragraph group to turn on the display of formatting marks if they do not already appear. Whenever you format text, particularly text formatted with borders, you should work with the Show/Hide ¶ button selected so that you can easily see spacing, tabs, and paragraph breaks.

3. Click at the **paragraph mark** below Subject, click the **Border** list arrow in the Paragraph group, and then click **Borders and Shading**. You work in the Borders and Shading dialog box when you want to create a customized line.

4. As shown in Figure 3-8, select the required style, color, and width, click **None** in the Setting area, and then click the top of the diagram in the Preview area to indicate where you want the border added. You can add a border above, below, to the right, or to the left of a paragraph, or to any combination of these locations.

Tip

If clicking the Show/Hide ¶ button ¶ hides the formatting marks, click the button again to show them.

Figure 3-8 **Selecting options in the Borders and Shading dialog box**

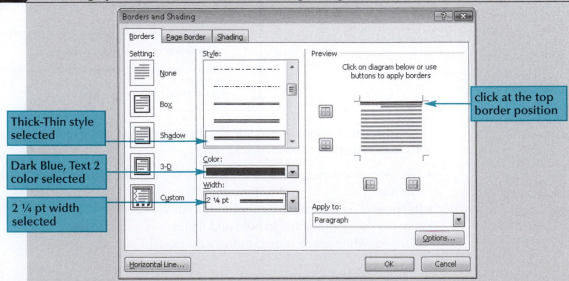

5. Click **OK** and then save the document. A border with the settings you selected appears between the heading information and the body of the memo.

Sometimes you may receive a document containing text formatted in columns separated by tabs. This text is often better displayed in a table. The following steps cover how to convert text formatted in columns separated by tabs into a table.

To convert text to a table:

1. Scroll down the document to the tabbed list that follows the first paragraph and note the number of columns required to present the information. You can see that four columns are necessary for Client, Event, Location, and Consultant.

2. Select the eight lines of tabbed text from **Client** through **Clarice King**.

3. Click the **Insert** tab, click the **Table** list arrow, and then click **Convert Text to Table**. The number 9 appears in the Number of columns text box in the Convert Text to Table dialog box. Word determines the number to enter in this text box by adding one to the greatest number of tabs in one line in the selected list.

4. Click **OK**, and then click below the new table. As you can see, the table is not correctly formatted. Word suggested nine columns for the table because the first row of text included eight tabs. Each tab is considered the division between two table columns. As a result, when the text was converted, nine separate columns were created. You need to undo the operation and remove the extra tabs.

5. Click the **Undo** button 🔄 on the Quick Access toolbar, and then note the number of tabs between each of the four column headings in the first line of the tabbed list. You can see that several tabs appear between each entry. See Figure 3-9. Apparently, the person who formatted this list was trying to line up the column headings with the information below them.

Figure 3-9 ▶ **Tabs in the tabbed list**

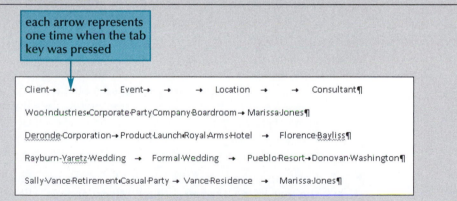

each arrow represents one time when the tab key was pressed

6. Click to the right of *Client* in the first line, press the **Delete** key to remove the first tab, press the **Delete** key again to remove the second tab so only one tab appears between *Client* and *Event*, and then remove the extra tabs in the rest of the first line so that just one tab appears between *Event*, *Location*, and *Consultant*, as shown in Figure 3-10.

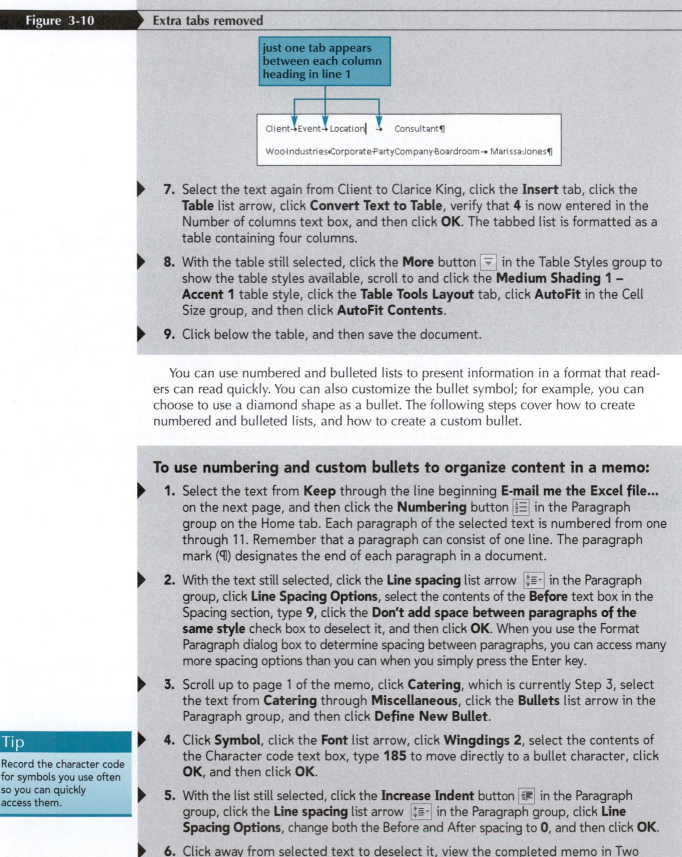

Figure 3-10 ▶ **Extra tabs removed**

just one tab appears between each column heading in line 1

Client→Event→Location| → Consultant¶

Woo·Industries◦Corporate·Party◦Company·Boardroom→ Marissa·Jones¶

▶ 7. Select the text again from Client to Clarice King, click the **Insert** tab, click the **Table** list arrow, click **Convert Text to Table**, verify that **4** is now entered in the Number of columns text box, and then click **OK**. The tabbed list is formatted as a table containing four columns.

▶ 8. With the table still selected, click the **More** button ▼ in the Table Styles group to show the table styles available, scroll to and click the **Medium Shading 1 – Accent 1** table style, click the **Table Tools Layout** tab, click **AutoFit** in the Cell Size group, and then click **AutoFit Contents**.

▶ 9. Click below the table, and then save the document.

You can use numbered and bulleted lists to present information in a format that readers can read quickly. You can also customize the bullet symbol; for example, you can choose to use a diamond shape as a bullet. The following steps cover how to create numbered and bulleted lists, and how to create a custom bullet.

To use numbering and custom bullets to organize content in a memo:

▶ 1. Select the text from **Keep** through the line beginning **E-mail me the Excel file...** on the next page, and then click the **Numbering** button ▤ in the Paragraph group on the Home tab. Each paragraph of the selected text is numbered from one through 11. Remember that a paragraph can consist of one line. The paragraph mark (¶) designates the end of each paragraph in a document.

▶ 2. With the text still selected, click the **Line spacing** list arrow ▤▼ in the Paragraph group, click **Line Spacing Options**, select the contents of the **Before** text box in the Spacing section, type **9**, click the **Don't add space between paragraphs of the same style** check box to deselect it, and then click **OK**. When you use the Format Paragraph dialog box to determine spacing between paragraphs, you can access many more spacing options than you can when you simply press the Enter key.

▶ 3. Scroll up to page 1 of the memo, click **Catering**, which is currently Step 3, select the text from **Catering** through **Miscellaneous**, click the **Bullets** list arrow in the Paragraph group, and then click **Define New Bullet**.

Tip

Record the character code for symbols you use often so you can quickly access them.

▶ 4. Click **Symbol**, click the **Font** list arrow, click **Wingdings 2**, select the contents of the Character code text box, type **185** to move directly to a bullet character, click **OK**, and then click **OK**.

▶ 5. With the list still selected, click the **Increase Indent** button ▤ in the Paragraph group, click the **Line spacing** list arrow ▤▼ in the Paragraph group, click **Line Spacing Options**, change both the Before and After spacing to **0**, and then click **OK**.

▶ 6. Click away from selected text to deselect it, view the completed memo in Two Pages view, turn off the display of formatting marks, save the document, print a copy, and then close the document.

In your role as assistant to Teresa Sanchez, the office manager at Prism Event Planning in Albuquerque, you are responsible for writing memos to keep the company's event planning consultants informed about current and ongoing contracts, office procedures, and other issues as they arise. Teresa has noticed that many of the memos written by the consultants at Prism Event Planning contain useful information but they are poorly organized. She decides to write a memo that provides employees with tips on how to organize a memo. She has started the memo and asks you to provide appropriately organized content.

Follow the steps below to complete a memo.

1. Open the file **Practice_03.docx** located in the Project.03 folder included with your Data Files, and then to avoid altering the original file, save the document as **Memo Organization** in the same folder.
2. Type your name and the current date where indicated in the document.
3. Click to the right of Subject:, press the Tab key, and then type **How to Organize a Memo**.
4. Insert a custom border under the Subject line. Make sure you select a style, color, and width for the line.
5. Click to the left of *This memo describes each of these components in turn*, and then write a sentence to describe the PDA components of a memo.
6. Click at the end of paragraph 2 after a *sample purpose statement follows:*, press the Enter key, and then type a purpose statement you could use to begin a memo that requests permission to attend a workshop titled *How to Handle Customer Complaints*. Make the purpose statement clear and straightforward so that the reader knows a decision is required.
7. Indent the purpose statement on the left and right, and apply italics to it so that it stands out. To indent text from the right, click the Line spacing button in the Paragraph group, click Line Spacing Options, and then change the Right Indent to .5 in the Indentation section.
8. In the Content Organization area, create a bulleted list of the six words used in the 5W technique. Format the list with a custom bullet style. You select an appropriate bullet symbol.
9. Indent the bulleted list so it left-aligns with the purpose statement and change the spacing after each item to 3 pt. Remember to deselect the Don't add space between paragraphs of the same style check box in the Spacing area on the Indents and Spacing tab of the Paragraph dialog box.
10. Click after *situations follows:* in the last paragraph of the memo (under Action Statement), and then press the Enter key.
11. Type an action statement that asks the reader to call to discuss the proposal further or to ask questions. Include a phone number where you can be contacted. Format the action statement in the same way you formatted the purpose statement.
12. Save the document, print a copy, and then close the document.

| Revise | **Summarizing Progress Memo** |

You are working as part of a team responsible for organizing a career fair at a local college. The coworker responsible for writing a memo after each team meeting to summarize the team's progress is ill and asks you to record the team's progress after the next meeting. You open the memo your coworker wrote about the previous meeting and revise it with information about the team's current progress. You also modify the memo's format to present the information more clearly.

Follow the steps below to revise and format a memo.

1. Open the file **Revise_03.docx** from the Project.03 folder included with your Data Files and then to avoid altering the original file, save the document as **Team Meeting Progress Memo** in the same folder.
2. Read the text of the memo and note how the information is difficult to read. Think about how you could reformat the information so that team members can easily determine their duties.
3. Format the memo heading information attractively: center, bold, and increase the font size of *MEMORANDUM,* increase the After spacing between each of the four lines of heading information, and add a custom border so it appears between the Subject line and the body of the memo.
4. Change the memo date to **April 2**, and then change the dates in the last paragraph in the body of the memo to **April 10** and **April 12**.
5. In the first line of the tabbed text, remove extra tabbed characters and then after Responsibility, press the Tab key once and type **Comments/Action**.
6. Select the tabbed text and convert it to a table. The table should consist of four columns, with the fourth column (Comments/Action) currently blank. To be useful, the table in a progress memo should specify exactly what tasks remain to be done. The Comments/Action column provides a space for entering this information.
7. Refer to the information in Figure 3-11 and then edit the information in the memo to reflect the team's current progress.

| Figure 3-11 | **Information for progress memo** |

Progress Memo Details

Dave O'Malley is responsible for the venue, which is in the large gym. Comment that the venue is booked and confirmed.

Kirsten Wong is responsible for catering, which will be provided by the college cafeteria. Note that Kirsten needs to meet with Joyce Ng, the catering manager, to confirm availability of beverages and snacks.

Joe Czerny is responsible for entertainment; he has confirmed booking of the Glendale Jazz Trio. They will be paid $300 after their performance.

Lara Singh and Joe Czerny are responsible for booking exhibitors at the career fair. They have now booked 20 exhibitors. They need to contact each exhibitor to confirm arrival time at the fair and ask if additional assistance is required.

Kirsten Wong is responsible for organizing raffle tickets for 20 prize draws. She has confirmed all the prizes.

8. Format the table with the table design of your choice. Note that you can remove check marks from the boxes in the Table Style Options group so the table displays the information in exactly the way you want.

9. Apply numbers to the list of items in column 1 of the table, and then click the Decrease Indent button in the Paragraph group so the numbers appear closer to the left edge of the table. Adjust the column widths; use AutoFit if you wish.

10. Adjust spacing where necessary so the memo fits on one page, save the document, print a copy, and then close the document.

| Create | **Request Memo** |

You work at a company that has a policy of funding employees to take courses to develop their skills. In order to qualify for funding, you are required to write a request memo to your supervisor. You decide that you would like to take a course at a local college—you determine the course subject and its applicability to your job. To ensure that you address all the questions your supervisor may ask, you start by answering a series of questions and then you write and format the memo.

Follow the steps below to answer questions and then write a memo requesting funding for a course.

1. Answer the questions listed in the table below. Use fictional, but realistic information.

Request Memo Questions
What course do you want to take?
What are some topics covered in the course related to your job?
Where is the course offered?
Why (and how) will taking this course help you in your job?
When will you take this course?
Who recommended this course? (or Who will take over your duties if you need to leave early one day a week to attend the course?)
How much does the course cost?
When do you need to register?

2. In a new document in Word, set up a heading for the memo. Make the heading **MEMORANDUM** in a large font size. You can also add a space between each letter and apply bold and a color of your choice.

3. Include the name of your instructor or supervisor in the *To:* line and your name in the *From:* line. Include the current date and an appropriate subject line.

4. Create a custom border to separate the heading from the body of the memo.

5. Start the memo with a purpose statement that also implies the action you expect from your supervisor (e.g., to approve your request for funding to take a work-related course).

6. Organize the details regarding your request in an attractive, easy-to-read format. Use a table and bullets to present some of the information. Format the table attractively.

7. Conclude the memo with an action statement that includes your contact information.

8. Adjust spacing if necessary to fit the memo on one page, save the document as **Course Request Memo**, print a copy, and then close the document.

Apply		**Case Study 1**

Capstone College   Students in the Digital Arts Department at Capstone College in San Francisco are looking forward to a week of Spring Break in the middle of their 10-month program. You have volunteered to work on the social committee to organize a Spring Break trip for interested students. The president of the committee, Sara Wells, has written a memo that she wants to distribute to the students to determine their interest in a skiing trip. Writing is not Sara's strong suit; she asks you to look at the memo and rewrite it. To complete this case study, you edit Sara's memo.

1. Open the file **Case1_03.docx** located in the Project.03 folder included with your Data Files, and then save the document as **Spring Break Skiing Trip** in the same folder.

2. Read the memo and consider ways in which you could improve the writing style and organization. At present, the memo does not really say much. Most students would glance at it and then discard it. They would not know what they were supposed to do.

3. Consider how you could rewrite the memo to include information about an upcoming skiing trip and request that students contact you if they are interested.

4. Write a good purpose statement to start the memo. You want to inform students that the purpose of the memo is to determine their interest in the Spring Break skiing trip. The first paragraph should also include some kind of motivational statement such as *We'd like to organize a fantastic Spring Break skiing trip!*

5. Determine the details required for the memo. Use the 5W technique to help you determine appropriate details. For example, you could ask questions such as *Where will the trip go?*, *How much will it cost?*, *Where will the students stay?*, and *What activities are available in addition to skiing?*. You will probably be able to think of many more questions. Jot down the answers to the questions on a separate sheet of paper and then refer to them as you rewrite the memo. Conduct some research on the Internet to find information about ski resorts in California so that you can describe possible destinations. Remember that the purpose of the memo is to encourage students to participate in the trip. As a result, you want to make sure you provide them with enough information to make a positive decision.

6. Include an action statement in the final paragraph. You need to provide students with a way to answer you. You might consider including a tear-off form at the bottom of the memo that includes check boxes. Students can fill in the form, tear it off, and drop it off at a specified location such as a classroom. You want to make replying to the memo with an expression of interest as easy as possible. Figure 3-12 shows a sample tear-off form that you may want to adapt for your memo. You can create the dashed line using the Borders and Shading dialog box. You can create the check boxes by inserting a symbol. A check box symbol can be created using the Wingdings 2 Character code 163.

Figure 3-12   **Sample tear-off form**

☐ **YES!** I am interested in a Spring Break skiing trip.

☐ **NO!** I've made other plans.

If you are interested, please give us your name, e-mail address, and phone number:

Name	
Phone Number	
E-Mail Address	

7. Modify the formatting of the memo. For example, you might change the color of the Memorandum heading and add a custom border below the heading lines. You may need to adjust the top and bottom margins so the memo fits on one page.
8. Type your name and the current date where indicated, save the document, and then print a copy.

Apply | Case Study 2

Otter Bay Kayaking Adventures   Every day during the summer season, tourists from the many cruise ships that sail into Juneau book tours with Otter Bay Kayaking Adventures. As the marketing assistant for the company, you are in charge of developing new marketing campaigns and producing marketing materials. A two-day training course on how to market adventure tour companies online is being held in Anchorage and you feel the company would benefit if you attended. Kay Johnson, the owner of the company and your boss, prefers to receive all requests from her staff in writing. As a result, you need to put together a memo that provides Kay with all the information she needs to make a decision about whether or not to fund the training course and your travel expenses. To complete this case study, you write a memo to Kay Johnson requesting permission and funding to attend the class.

1. Start a new blank document and save it as **Funding Request Memo**.
2. Use the 5W technique to help you determine what information to include in the memo. Jot down answers on a separate sheet of paper. Make up fictional, but realistic details about the seminar location, topics, cost, and so on.
3. Begin the memo with a purpose statement and then provide Ms. Johnson with compelling reasons why her company should fund your attendance at the training course. *Hint:* Ms. Johnson is most likely to respond positively if she sees a benefit to her company, so think about how the online marketing skills presented in the course will help Otter Bay Kayaking Adventures attract more customers.

4. Present all the information about the training course. Use a table to display the information in an easy-to-read format. Include a bulleted list as needed.

5. Include an action statement at the end of the memo. Remember that the goal of the memo is to convince Ms. Johnson to fund your attendance at the training course in Anchorage.

6. Format the memo attractively with a heading and a custom border, save the memo, print a copy, and then close the document.

| Apply | **Case Study** 3 |

Power Up Communications You have just started working as the office manager for Power Up Communications, a new company that provides communication training seminars to clients in the Phoenix area. As the company's office manager, you assist with the preparation of materials for use in the training seminars. Your supervisor asks you to draft a procedures memo to use as an example for seminar participants. To complete this case study, you write a memo outlining the steps involved in completing a common task.

1. Start a new blank document and save it as **Procedures Memo**.

2. Write and format a memo that informs readers of the procedures required to perform a task with which you are familiar. Examples of tasks include how to apply for a student loan, how to set up an Instant Messaging account on MSN, how to take public transit from your home to your school, how to request funds for a specific project at work, how to open and close a store, and so on.

3. Include an appropriate subject line and an introductory paragraph that provides a purpose statement defining the task and providing a rationale for it. Provide six to eight numbered steps after the introductory paragraph that the reader would follow to accomplish the task. You can also include bulleted items within some of the steps, if appropriate.

4. Complete the memo with a sentence that offers to provide more information if required. Include a phone number or e-mail address.

5. Format the memo attractively with a heading and a custom border, save the memo, print a copy, and then close the document.

Objectives

- Identify letter types
- Structure everyday letters
- Format letters
- Determine when to use a form letter
- Identify the components of a form letter
- Use mail merge in Word

Everyday Letters

Introduction

You can define an **everyday letter** as a letter that communicates relatively neutral information for common business situations. This information can be distributed in the form of an e-mail or in a letter printed on the company letterhead and mailed in an envelope. You create a **form letter** when you need to send the same or similar information to a large number of recipients. You can personalize the letter by adding the name and address of each recipient and other information specific to the recipient.

In this project, you explore the various types of everyday letters, learn how to structure and format an everyday letter, identify the purpose and components of a form letter, and use Word's Mail Merge function to create a form letter and merge it with a data source.

Starting Data Files

Project.04

Tech_04.docx
Practice_04.docx
Revise_04.docx
Case1_04.docx

Everyday Letters Essentials

Most businesses spend the bulk of the time they devote to correspondence writing every-day letters, whether in the form of letters printed on paper or in e-mails. Everyday letters are also written by individuals to companies. For example, an individual may write a request letter to a company to ask for information about a product or service. The key feature of all everyday letters is that they should be short and to the point. The reader should understand the purpose of the everyday letter quickly and then respond accordingly.

Identifying Letter Types

Most everyday letters fall into one of the following five categories: request, confirmation, transmittal, acceptance, and personal. Figure 4-1 summarizes the purpose of each of these types of everyday letters.

| Figure 4-1 | Everyday letter types |

Letter Type	Purpose	Example
Request	To request items or services	A travel agency requests information about tours to Ireland from an Irish tour operator.
Confirmation	To confirm an agreement, a meeting, or an event	A speaker confirms with an event planner that he will deliver a presentation at an upcoming conference.
Transmittal	To accompany an attachment such as a report, a resume, promotional materials, or a shipped order	A consultant submits to the school board a report she was hired to write on playground safety.
Acceptance	To say yes to a reader's request	A human resources director informs a job applicant that he has been hired.
Personal	To say thank you or to offer congratulations or condolences; these letters are generally handwritten and personalized	A business associate congratulates a colleague on a promotion.

> **Key Point**
>
> In business terms, goodwill can very quickly lead to increased sales and improved levels of customer satisfaction.

Regardless of content, all everyday letters share a similar purpose, which is to generate goodwill. You can define **goodwill** as the positive feeling or impression that a company's reputation creates in the mind of a customer. Whenever you need to write an everyday letter, think of the letter as your opportunity to promote goodwill for your business.

Structuring an Everyday Letter

All types of everyday letters share a similar format as follows:

- The first paragraph includes the reason for the letter and usually includes a reference to the reader.
- The second paragraph provides additional details. Some everyday letters may present details in two paragraphs, but one paragraph is sufficient for most everyday letters.
- The last paragraph thanks the reader and invites action and/or further contact.

With this three-paragraph structure, you should be able to write almost any everyday letter quickly and easily.

Developing Request Letters

You write a **request letter** when you need to ask for something specific from your reader. Because e-mail is now the preferred way to distribute messages, many requests are sent as e-mails. The structure of a request letter is the same as the structure of a request e-mail message. Figure 4-2 shows how to develop a typical request for travel information in three paragraphs.

Figure 4-2   **Request letter structure**

Paragraph	Purpose	Example
Paragraph 1	State the request	Option 1: No previous contact I am writing to request information about your tours of Ireland. I am working with a corporate client who wishes to provide a trip to Ireland for 10 employees and their guests. The trip is scheduled for the last three weeks in June of this year. Option 2: Previous contact Thank you for speaking with me on March 2 about your tours of Ireland. As I indicated in that conversation, I require information to plan a trip to Ireland on behalf of my corporate client. The trip is scheduled for the last three weeks in June of this year.
Paragraph 2	Provide additional details (use a bulleted list if appropriate)	Please provide me with the following information: • Suggested itinerary for a three-week tour that includes Dublin, Belfast, Cork, and a one-week stay in a cottage in the west of Ireland • Suggested hotels; the budget is €150 per night • Suggested cottage rentals in the west of Ireland • Suggested activities suitable for active couples • Transportation options • Estimated cost of the trip
Paragraph 3	Close positively and invite further contact	Please call me at (505) 555-1770 if you have any questions about my request. Thank you for your quick attention to this request. I look forward to hearing from you soon.

Developing Confirmation Letters

You write a **confirmation letter** when you need to confirm a formal agreement with a client. For example, you could write a confirmation letter to thank an associate for agreeing to speak at a conference and to provide details about the conference. Figure 4-3 shows a sample confirmation letter. Notice that the letter in Figure 4-3 communicates the conference details successfully because of the use of tabs with dot leaders. The reader can identify the most important information at a glance.

Figure 4-3	Sample confirmation letter

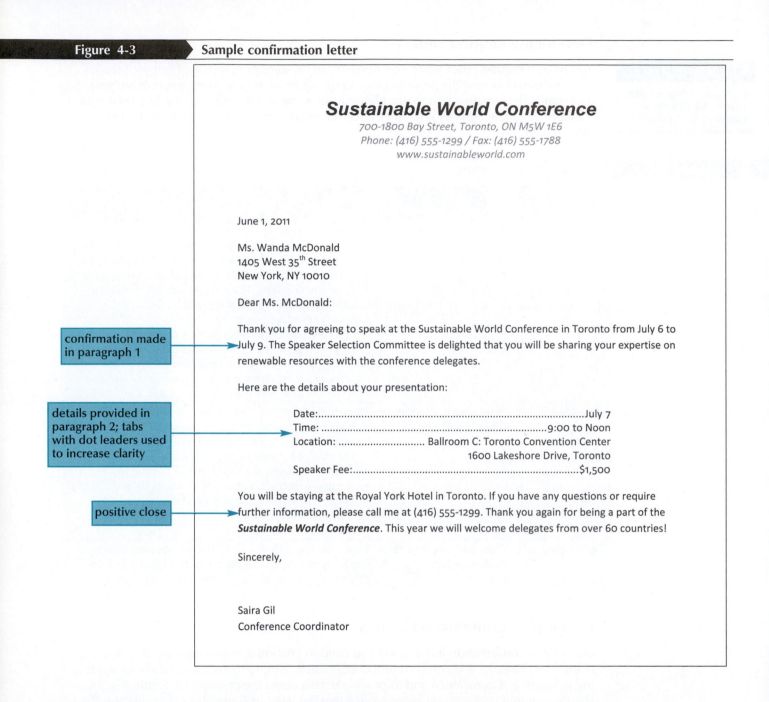

confirmation made in paragraph 1

details provided in paragraph 2; tabs with dot leaders used to increase clarity

positive close

Sustainable World Conference

700-1800 Bay Street, Toronto, ON M5W 1E6
Phone: (416) 555-1299 / Fax: (416) 555-1788
www.sustainableworld.com

June 1, 2011

Ms. Wanda McDonald
1405 West 35th Street
New York, NY 10010

Dear Ms. McDonald:

Thank you for agreeing to speak at the Sustainable World Conference in Toronto from July 6 to July 9. The Speaker Selection Committee is delighted that you will be sharing your expertise on renewable resources with the conference delegates.

Here are the details about your presentation:

Date:..July 7
Time: ....9:00 to Noon
Location: .... Ballroom C: Toronto Convention Center
                                            1600 Lakeshore Drive, Toronto
Speaker Fee:...$1,500

You will be staying at the Royal York Hotel in Toronto. If you have any questions or require further information, please call me at (416) 555-1299. Thank you again for being a part of the *Sustainable World Conference*. This year we will welcome delegates from over 60 countries!

Sincerely,

Saira Gil
Conference Coordinator

Developing Transmittal Letters

You write a **transmittal letter** to accompany an attachment such as a formal report or proposal, a contract or other legal document, or samples and information requested by a client. The purpose of the transmittal letter is to provide the reader with information about the enclosure. For example, you could write a transmittal letter to accompany a proposal you wrote to the local government to improve traffic safety in your neighborhood. Your transmittal letter could include a brief summary of the enclosed proposal and a description of the action you hope local government will take as a result of reading the proposal. Sometimes, transmittal letters are referred to as **cover letters**. Figure 4-4 shows how to develop a typical transmittal letter in three paragraphs.

| Figure 4-4 | Transmittal letter structure |

Paragraph	Purpose	Example
Paragraph 1	State why you are writing, thank the reader if appropriate, and specify the attachment	Thank you for providing me with the opportunity to submit the enclosed proposal titled *Maple Road Traffic Safety Solutions*. The purpose of the proposal is to request that the municipality install a stop sign at the intersection of Maple Road and 1st Street in Baltimore.
Paragraph 2	Provide additional information about the attachment	As discussed in the proposal, 40 traffic accidents have occurred at the intersection of Maple Road and 1st Street since 1990. Data concerning these accidents, along with traffic patterns at different times of the day over a six-month period, is included in the proposal. A stop sign would help prevent more accidents by reducing traffic speed and volume because those motorists who do not want to stop will find an alternate route. Installation of a stop sign will also contribute significantly to the safety of pedestrians in the neighborhood.
Paragraph 3	Close positively and invite further contact	Please call me at (410) 555-1770 if you have any questions about the attached proposal or if you need any additional information. Thank you for your immediate attention to this matter. I look forward to hearing from you.

When you include a well-formatted transmittal letter with a report, proposal, or other attachment, you signal to your reader that you consider the enclosure to be important and deserving of consideration. From the point of view of the reader, a transmittal letter provides a context for the enclosure and includes additional information that the reader might need to help make a decision.

Developing Acceptance Letters

In an **acceptance letter**, you respond positively to a request made by a reader. For example, you write an acceptance letter to offer someone a job or a refund. In an acceptance letter, you give the good news right away, provide details if required, and close positively. As shown in Figure 4-5, the purpose of the first sentence in the acceptance letter is to tell the reader right away that he got the position. The tone of an acceptance letter should be positive and friendly.

Figure 4-5 ▶ **Correctly structured acceptance letter**

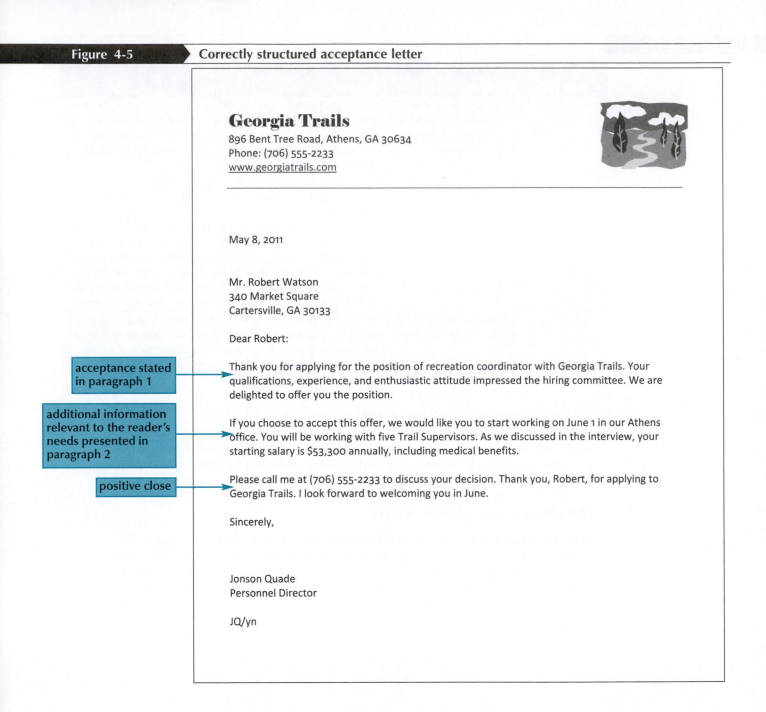

acceptance stated in paragraph 1

additional information relevant to the reader's needs presented in paragraph 2

positive close

Georgia Trails
896 Bent Tree Road, Athens, GA 30634
Phone: (706) 555-2233
www.georgiatrails.com

May 8, 2011

Mr. Robert Watson
340 Market Square
Cartersville, GA 30133

Dear Robert:

Thank you for applying for the position of recreation coordinator with Georgia Trails. Your qualifications, experience, and enthusiastic attitude impressed the hiring committee. We are delighted to offer you the position.

If you choose to accept this offer, we would like you to start working on June 1 in our Athens office. You will be working with five Trail Supervisors. As we discussed in the interview, your starting salary is $53,300 annually, including medical benefits.

Please call me at (706) 555-2233 to discuss your decision. Thank you, Robert, for applying to Georgia Trails. I look forward to welcoming you in June.

Sincerely,

Jonson Quade
Personnel Director

JQ/yn

Developing Personal Letters

Personal letters include thank you letters, letters of congratulations, and letters offering condolences. You write a thank you letter to show appreciation for a client, thank a person who interviews you for a job, and for any other situation in which the personal contact of a thank you letter can generate goodwill. In business, you often write a letter of congratulations to a client who has been promoted or who has secured a substantial contract. Everyone appreciates being congratulated and in business the offering of congratulations can certainly promote goodwill. The letter of condolence is, of course, one of the most difficult letters to write. However, these letters are also among the most important.

You usually handwrite personal letters, although sometimes you may create a form letter to send thank you letters to multiple recipients. A handwritten letter shows that the writer has taken some time to consider the contents of the letter and the individual who will receive it. Figure 4-6 shows a handwritten letter of congratulations.

Figure 4-6 **Sample letter of congratulations**

March 14, 2011

Dear Amy:

Congratulations! I just heard about your promotion to marketing director. You certainly deserve it.

I'm sure you're excited to put all your great ideas to work. I am looking forward to seeing what wonderful new marketing campaigns you will develop.

I wish you every success in your new position.

Sincerely,

Kevin

The personal letter follows the same basic structure as any other everyday letter. You specify the specific situation in the first paragraph, provide some additional personal observations in the second paragraph, and then close positively in the last paragraph.

Formatting Letters

You need to pay attention to three principal areas when formatting a business letter as discussed next and in Figure 4-7:

• Include an attractive letterhead
• Select a business letter format such as block or modified block
• Apply the punctuation style for the salutation and complimentary closing

Figure 4-7 **Letter formatting requirements**

Letter Element	Description
Letterhead	• Include the following components: • Company name • Logo or company slogan, if available • Company street address • Company phone and fax numbers • Company e-mail address or Web site address • Limit the total height of the letterhead to no more than 1 to 2 inches.
Letter format	• When using the **block** letter format, start all lines at the left margin. • When using the **modified block** letter format, indent the date and closing lines to the center of the page and indent the first line of each paragraph five spaces.
Punctuation style	• Follow the salutation with a colon and the complimentary closing with a comma.

Of the two letter formats, the block format is easiest to use because you do not need to worry about setting tabs or indenting paragraphs. Which letter format you use depends on your own preferences and those of the organization where you work. When you are hired by a company, you will be expected to use the letter format that the company uses. Figure 4-8 compares the two letter formats. Note that the letterhead is simple and easy to read.

Figure 4-8	Letter formats

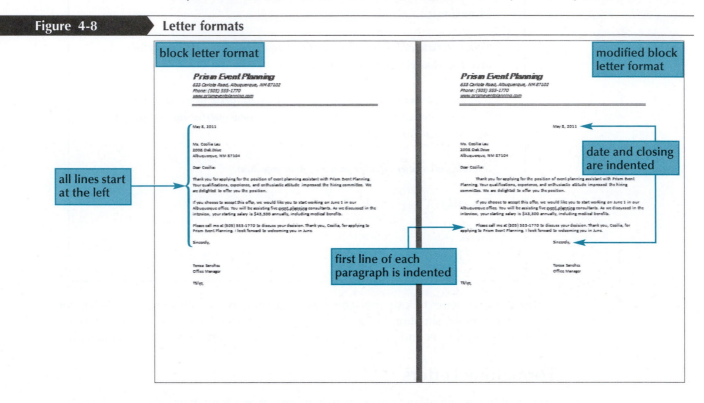

Determining When to Use a Form Letter

As you have learned, businesses use e-mail most frequently to communicate with individual clients about issues specific to the client's needs. However, when the company needs to communicate information that is common to a great number of clients, the company usually sends a **form letter**. A form letter contains both a basic message that you want many people to receive and customized information that is personalized for each recipient. For example, a Human Resources Department would create a form letter to send to employees about an upcoming healthcare plan enrollment deadline. The name, address, and specific healthcare plan would change from letter to letter, but the basic information about which healthcare plans are available, the representatives to meet with, and the time and place of the sign-up would stay the same in each letter.

Identifying the Components of a Form Letter

Key Point

If a form letter is well constructed, the recipient will not think of it as a form letter but rather as a personalized communication.

A form letter consists of two components: a main document and a data source. The **main document** contains all the common information required for every letter and contains merge fields for the variable information that differs in each letter. The merge fields correspond to fields in the data source. You can create the main document as a new document or you can create it from an existing document. The **data source** contains all of the variable information for each recipient of the letter, such as the person's name and address and the product or service purchased. The data source contains **fields**, such as FIRST NAME and LAST NAME. The variable information for each person is entered in the fields in the data source. A **record** in a data source is a collection of variable information for one person. You can create the data source from scratch or you can create it from an existing data source. Every time you open a main document, a message appears asking you to navigate to and select the data source.

After you create the main document and the data source, you insert merge fields in the main document. The merge fields replace the placeholders you originally entered in the main document. Once you have inserted the merge fields, you merge the main document with the data source to create the personalized form letters. When a merge takes place, the merge fields in the main document are replaced with the corresponding information in the data source.

You need to spend time writing the text for the form letter and thinking carefully about the type of variable information you require *before* you create the data source and before you begin the merge process. You also need to spend time creating a well-constructed data source—one that allows the most flexibility when placing merge fields in the main document.

Creating the Main Document

When you write a form letter, your first task is to determine what information will remain the same from letter to letter and what information will be variable information. **Variable information** is the information that will be different in each printed form letter. You usually write a draft of a form letter that includes **placeholders** to indicate where variable information should go.

Determining where to place variable information in a form letter requires some thought. You need to consider carefully how you may want to personalize the content for each recipient of a form letter. For example, you can personalize whole sentences, or you can just personalize the occasional word or phrase. In either case, you include a placeholder for the variable information.

Creating the Data Source

After you have established what type of variable information you require for a form letter, you need to create a data source that contains the variable information for each person who will receive the form letter. You usually use a database, such as one created in Access, as your data source. You can also use your contacts lists in Outlook if that list contains the variable information you need.

You want to create a data source that is as flexible as possible. Instead of creating a data source that includes the field NAME, you might create a data source that includes the fields TITLE, FIRST NAME, LAST NAME, and SALUTATION. Setting up four different fields for the name allows you to personalize how the person's name appears in the form letter. For example, in the Address block the person's name might be written as Dr. William Conrad, in the salutation it might be written as Dr. Conrad or William, and in the body of the letter, it might be written as William.

Inserting the Merge Fields and Running the Merge

After you have created the data source, you need to replace the placeholders in the main document with merge fields from the data source. In Word, you highlight the placeholder you want to replace, and then you use the Insert Merge Field command in the Write and Insert Fields group on the Mailings tab. In the dialog box that opens, you select the merge field you want to insert. Chevrons appear around each field name inserted in the main document; for example, <<SALUTATION>>.

The final step in the merge process is to run the merge and then view the merged letters. You should always view each individual letter before printing to verify that all the variable information appears correctly.

Key Point

Create two or three records in your data source, and then run the merge to verify that all the variable information appears in the main letter as expected. If not, you can easily add or remove fields from the data source before adding additional records.

Technology Skills—Merging Letters in Word

You use the **Mail Merge** function in Word to produce personalized form letters in which each letter contains the basic message you want all recipients to receive, along with variable information such as the recipient's address and other custom information. In Word, you use the commands on the Mailings tab to set up and run a mail merge. The Technology Skills steps cover these skills:

- Initiate a mail merge
- Customize a data source
- Enter information in a data source
- Add mail merge names to a main document
- Preview a merged letter and correct errors

To initiate a mail merge:

▶ 1. Open the file **Tech_04.docx** located in the Project.04 folder included with your Data Files and then, to avoid altering the original file, save the document as **Transmittal Form Letter** in the same folder.

▶ 2. Read the letter and note where placeholders, such as [INSIDE ADDRESS], have been inserted in the form letter. The placeholders will be replaced with the merge fields that contain the variable information.

▶ 3. Click the **Mailings** tab, click the **Start Mail Merge** button in the Start Mail Merge group, and then click **Step by Step Mail Merge Wizard**. The Mail Merge task pane opens at Step 1 of 6.

▶ 4. Verify that Letters is selected as the document type, and then click **Next: Starting document**.

▶ 5. Verify that Use the current document is selected as the starting document, and then click **Next: Select recipients**. In the Mail Merge Wizard, the main document is referred to as the starting document.

You can create a data source from scratch or you can use an existing data source and adjust it as needed. When you create a data source from scratch, you work in the New Address List dialog box, which contains the fields that are most commonly included in a form letter. Usually, you need to add some new fields and delete fields you don't want. Next, you customize a data source.

To customize a data source:

▶ 1. Click the **Type a new list** option button in the Select recipients area, and then click **Create** in the Type a new list area. The New Address List dialog box opens.

▶ 2. Click **Customize Columns** to open the Customize Address List dialog box, click **Home Phone** in the list of fields, click **Delete**, click **Yes**, and then delete the **Work Phone** and **E-Mail Address** fields.

▶ 3. Click **Add**, type **Event**, and then click **OK**. You can add as many new mail merge fields as you want.

▶ 4. Click **Add**, type **EventDate**, click **OK**, and then add **Invoice**, **Message**, and **Salutation**. You create a field for Salutation so that you can customize how you want to enter the greeting line. For some recipients, you may wish to write *Dear Mr. Adams*, while for other recipients, you may wish to write *Dear Lisa*.

Tip

You save time when you arrange field names in the order in which you will insert them in the main document.

5. With **Salutation** still selected, click **Move Up** until Salutation follows the Last Name field, and then click **OK**. You return to the New Address List dialog box. In this dialog box, you enter information about each recipient of your form letter.

Once you have created fields for your data source and you have arranged them in a logical order, you are ready to enter the data for each person who will receive the form letter. When you enter the data, you can leave a field blank. For example, if a person's address consists of just one line, you can leave the Address2 field blank. Next, you enter data in the data source file.

To enter information into a data source:

1. Type **Mr.**, and then press the **Tab** key to move to the First Name field.

2. Enter the remaining information for George Adams, as shown in Figure 4-9.

Figure 4-9 **Information for record 1**

Title	Mr.
First Name	George
Last Name	Adams
Salutation	Mr. Adams
Company	Gold Mark Enterprises
Address 1	1700 Palace Road
Address 2	Suite 300
City	Santa Fe
State	NM
ZIP Code	87112
Country	[Leave Blank]
Event	the launch of Paints on Parade, your new line of household paints
EventDate	May 3
Invoice	$9400
Message	During the event, you mentioned your interest in working with us again to sponsor a charitable event. I think your idea of featuring the new Paints on Parade would work very well. I will contact you in a few weeks to discuss plans.

3. Click **New Entry**, and then enter the information for record 2, as shown in Figure 4-10.

Figure 4-10 **Information for record 2**

Title	Ms.
First Name	Lisa
Last Name	DeMarco
Salutation	Lisa
Company	[Leave Blank]
Address 1	1200 Alameda Road
Address 2	[Leave Blank]
City	Albuquerque
State	NM
ZIP Code	87102
Country	[Leave Blank]
Event	the wedding of your daughter Roquela
EventDate	May 15
Invoice	$15,800
Message	Your daughter looked stunning on her special day! I am so glad Roquela and Harrison enjoyed the wedding of their dreams. I am sure you must be very proud.

Tip

Use filenames beginning with the same word or phrase for files used in the same merge in order to keep files together in your file management program.

4. Click **OK**, navigate to the location where you are storing files for this book, type **Transmittal Form Letter Data Source**, click **Save**, and then click **OK**.

When you create a new form letter, you should enter just a few records and then test the merge. Often, after conducting a test merge, you will find that you need to add or remove field names, change some of the common information in the form letter, or adjust punctuation and spacing in the form letter. Once your form letter and your data source are set up, you replace the placeholders in your main document with merge fields from your data source. When the merge is run, the merge fields in the main document are replaced with the personalized information in the corresponding fields in the data source. Next, you replace placeholders in the main document with merge fields.

To add mail merge fields to a main document:

1. Click **Next: Write your letter**, select the **[INSIDE ADDRESS]** placeholder, press the **Delete** key, click **Address block** in the Mail Merge task pane, click **OK** to accept the default settings, and then press the **Enter** key once, if necessary, to add one blank line between the inside address and salutation.

2. Select the **[SALUTATION]** placeholder, press the **Delete** key, and then click the **Insert Merge Field** list arrow in the Write & Insert Fields group to display the list of fields.

Tip

If the Insert Merge Field dialog box opens, click Cancel and then click the Insert Merge Field list arrow to display the list of available fields.

3. Click **Salutation**, and then type a **colon** (:).

4. Follow the process described in steps 2 and 3 to insert the corresponding merge fields for the placeholders **[Event]**, **[EventDate]**, **[Invoice]**, and **[Message]** in the appropriate places in the letter, as shown in Figure 4-11.

Figure 4-11 ▶ **Mail merge fields inserted in the main document**

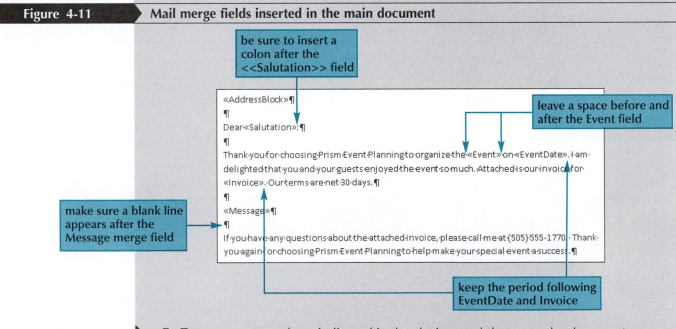

5. Type your name where indicated in the closing, and then save the document.

After you enter the merge fields into the transmittal letter, you preview each letter to make sure that the variable information appears correctly. Often you will need to make changes to the common information or to punctuation and spacing in the main document or to the information entered in the data source. Next, you preview a merged letter and make corrections to the main document.

To preview a merged letter and correct errors:

▶ 1. Click **Next: Preview your letters**, and then read the first paragraph of the letter for George Adams. The first sentence does not sound right now that the variable information is entered. The sentence *Thank you for choosing Prism Event Planning to organize the the launch of Paints on Parade, your new line of household paints on May 3.* contains two errors. The word *the* appears twice and a comma is needed after *paints* because that is the end of the clause *your new line of household paints.*

▶ 2. Read the second paragraph. A noun is needed at the end of the phrase *the new Paints on Parade.* For example, the phrase should be *the new Paints on Parade product line.*

▶ 3. Click the **Next Record** button |>>| in the Mail Merge task pane to see the letter for Lisa DeMarco, and then read the letter for Lisa to find errors. Again the word *the* is repeated in the first sentence. Fortunately, the rest of the letter is fine.

▶ 4. Click **Previous: Write your letter** at the bottom of the Mail Merge task pane to move to Step 4, select **the** before <<Event>> in the first line of the first paragraph, and then press the **Delete** key.

▶ 5. Click **Previous: Select recipients** to move to Step 3, click **Edit recipient list**, click **Transmittal Form Letter Data Source** in the Data Source area of the Mail Merge Recipients dialog box, and then click **Edit**. The Edit Data Source dialog box opens.

▶ 6. Press the **Tab** key to scroll to the entry under **Event** for George Adams, and then type a comma (,).

▶ 7. Tab to **Message**, use the arrow keys to move to the sentence that begins *I think your idea,* and then delete the sentence **I think your idea of featuring the new Paints on Parade will work very well.**

▶ 8. Click **OK**, click **Yes**, click **OK**, click **Next: Write your letter**, click **Next: Preview your letters**, and then click **Next: Complete the merge**.

▶ 9. Click **Edit individual letters**, click **OK** to merge all records into a new document, print a copy of both letters, save the document as **Transmittal Form Letter Merged**, and then close the document.

▶ 10. Click the **Preview Results** button in the Preview Results group on the Mailings tab to deselect it, and then save and close the main document. If you want to print individual letters, you can run the merge again.

Tip

The Preview Results button is a toggle button that lets you switch between seeing the merge fields and the variable information in the form letter.

As a special events coordinator at Prism Event Planning, you have written a form letter to send to suppliers to confirm arrangements for a special event. Now you need to add merge fields for variable information and then merge the main document with a data source containing information about two suppliers. Follow the steps below to set up the main document and then merge it with a data source.

1. Open the file **Practice_04.docx** located in the Project.04 folder included with your Data Files and then, to avoid altering the original file, save the document as **Event Suppliers Form Letter** in the same folder.
2. Read the letter and notice the placeholders.
3. Open the Mail Merge task pane, and then use the letter as the main document.
4. Use the placeholders in the main letter to help you create a customized data source that contains only the field names you need for the letter. Note that you will need to delete field names you will not use and present the field names in a logical order. You will need to add some field names. Be sure to keep all the field names you will need for the Address block.
5. Refer to Figure 4-12 to enter information for the first of two suppliers in your data source.

Figure 4-12 **Information for record 1**

Placeholder	Variable Information
Title	Ms.
First Name	Sheila
Last Name	Laval
Salutation	Ms. Laval
Company	Twilight Entertainment
Address	2309 West 9th Street
City	Albuquerque
State	NM
ZIP Code	87102
Contact Date	March 2, 2011
Event	Rhonda Watson and Juan Redondo wedding
Supply	a three-piece trio to provide dance music at the wedding reception
Cost	$3500
Event Date	March 19, 2011
Start Time	7:00 p.m.
End Time	11:00 p.m.
Location	the Grand Ballroom at the Marriott, 432 Central Avenue in Albuquerque
Message	Rhonda and Juan would like a mix of music, including rock, pop, and Latin. For their special dance, Rhonda and Juan have asked for "Close to You."

6. Add a second supplier and enter appropriate information. Make up fictitious but realistic details. For example, you could enter information about a supplier of a gourmet birthday cake for a 21st birthday party.
7. Save the data source as **Event Suppliers Form Letter Data**, replace the placeholders in the main document with the field names, review the letters, and then make adjustments to the main document and data source if necessary.
8. Save the merged document as **Event Suppliers Form Letter Merged**, print a copy of the two letters, and then in the main document, deselect Preview Letters and save and close the document.

Revise | Request Letter

You have been asked to review the request letter sent by the event planners at Prism Event Planning to determine the special events needs of their clients. The request letter is efficient, but lacking in goodwill. Follow the steps below to reorganize the request form letter so that it includes a friendly opening and a goodwill closing, and then create a main document and data source containing records for two clients.

1. Open the file **Revise_04.docx** located in the Project.04 folder included with your Data Files and then, to avoid altering the original file, save the document as **Client Request Letter** in the same folder.

2. Read the letter to identify areas of concern. As you can see, the letter presents the request clearly; however, the tone is too abrupt.

3. Click at the beginning of paragraph 1, and then write a sentence that thanks the reader for contacting Prism Event Planning to organize his or her [EVENT] scheduled for [EVENT DATE]. Remember that the purpose of this first sentence is to acknowledge the reader and to refer to the reader's own situation.

4. For the second sentence in paragraph 1, type **In order to provide you with an accurate price quote, additional information that only you can provide is needed**. This sentence communicates the request. In this case, the request is for the reader to provide additional information. The next paragraph provides the details so the reader knows what to send.

5. Press the **Enter** key once to move the next sentence to paragraph 2, and then type **Please** as the first word.

6. Click after the last sentence in the letter, and then write a sentence that asks the reader to call you at (505) 555-1770 if he or she has further questions. Include a placeholder for the client's first name.

7. Write a sentence that informs the reader that you look forward to receiving the requested information at his or her earliest convenience.

8. Open the Mail Merge task pane, and then use the letter as the main document.

9. Create a customized data source that contains only the field names you need for your letter. Note that you will need to delete field names you will not use and present the field names in a logical order. You will need to add some field names. Be sure to keep all the field names you will need for the Address block.

10. Enter information for two clients. Make the date of each event 10 to 14 days after November 11, 2011 and the deadline four or five days before the event date.

11. Save the data source as **Client Request Letter Data**, replace the placeholders in the main document with the merge field names, review the letters, and then make adjustments to the main document and data source if necessary.

12. Save the merged document as **Client Request Letter Merged**, print a copy of the two letters, and then in the main document, deselect Preview Letters and save and close the document.

Create | Acceptance Form Letter

You work for a private foundation that awards grants to organizations and individuals involved in community service projects. One of your jobs is to inform grant applicants that they have received a grant for a specific project. The acceptance letter you write should include a short description of the grant (for example, running a homeless shelter or setting up a day care center), the amount of the grant, and any other relevant information. Follow the steps below to write a draft of the acceptance letter you could write to inform successful grant applicants.

1. Complete the table below with the information you need for each of the three paragraphs in the form letter. Define what field names you will need for variable information. Note that you will need to make up information. Use fictitious but realistic details.

Information for paragraphs in the acceptance form letter
Paragraph 1 Text
Paragraph 1 Field Names
Paragraph 2 Text
Paragraph 2 Field Names
Paragraph 3 Text
Paragraph 3 Field Names

2. In Word, set up the main document for the acceptance letter, and then save the document as **Acceptance Letter**.

3. Format the letter using the Full Block format, include the current date, and create an attractive letterhead for the foundation. You determine the name and address. Make sure you include a phone number and a Web site address.

4. Note that you can use the Line spacing button in the Paragraph group on the Home tab to change the line spacing of the letterhead to 1.0 and remove After paragraph spacing.

5. Include your name in the closing of the main document.

6. Open the Mail Merge task pane, and then create a customized data source that contains only the field names you need for your letter. Note that you will need to delete field names you will not use and present the field names in a logical order. You will need to add some field names. Be sure to keep all the field names you will need for the Address block.

7. Enter information for two grant recipients, save the data source as **Acceptance Letter Data**, replace the placeholders in the main document with the field names, review the letters, and then make adjustments to the main document and data source if necessary.

8. Save the merged document as **Acceptance Letter Merged**, print a copy of the two letters, and then in the main document, deselect Preview Letters and save and close the document.

Apply | Case Study 1

Capstone College In your position as the program assistant for the Digital Arts Department at Capstone College in San Francisco, you assist the department coordinator with a variety of letter writing tasks. The department recently received a donation of $20,000 from Carl Beauville, a former student who now owns his own company called Beauville Animation at 300 Bayview Drive, San Francisco, CA 94332. As a result of a recent fund-raising campaign, more such donations are expected. To complete this case study, you write a thank you letter to Carl, and then adapt it as a form letter and send it to one other donor.

1. On paper, write a draft of the letter to Carl to thank him for the donation. Include a short description of how the money will be used to purchase new computers for the animation program. Mention how these new computers will assist students to develop cutting edge skills.
2. Determine the location of variable information in Carl's letter and assign placeholders for the merge field names.
3. Open the file **Case1_04.docx** located in the Project.04 folder included with your Data Files, and then save the document as **Thank You Form Letter** in the same folder.
4. Based on your draft letter to Carl, edit the thank you letter and include placeholders for variable information.
5. Open the Mail Merge task pane, and then create a data source that contains only the field names you need for your letter.
6. Enter information for Carl Beauville and one other donor.
7. Save the data source as **Thank You Form Letter Data**, add field names to the document, review the letters, and then make adjustments to the main document and data source if necessary.
8. Save the merged document as **Thank You Form Letter Merged**, print a copy of the two letters, and then in the main document, deselect Preview Letters and save and close the document.

Tip

Note that you will need to delete field names you will not use and present the fields names in a logical order. You will need to add some field names. Be sure to keep all the field names you will need for the Address block.

Apply | Case Study 2

Otter Bay Kayaking Adventures Every day during the summer season, tourists from the many cruise ships that sail into Juneau book tours with Otter Bay Kayaking Adventures. As an assistant in the Marketing Department, you are responsible for corresponding with cruise ship companies to make requests, confirm tour arrangements, and transmit sales literature. To complete this case study, you write a form letter to confirm tour arrangements, create a data source containing information for two recipients of the form letter, and run a mail merge to produce two confirmation letters.

1. Start a new blank document and save it as **Kayaking Tours Confirmation Letter**.
2. Format the letter using the Full Block format, include the current date, and create an attractive letterhead. The information is: Otter Bay Kayaking Adventures, 149 Seward Street, Juneau, AK 99804, Phone: (907) 555-3311, Web site: *www.otterbaykayaking.com*.
3. Note that you can use the Line spacing button in the Paragraph group on the Home tab to change the line spacing of the letterhead to 1.0 and remove after paragraph spacing.

4. Write a draft of the form letter that you would send to the cruise ship tour coordinators to confirm arrangements for an adventure tour. Include the following information in your letter:
   a. Your company offers two adventure tour options: Half Day Sea Kayaking and Full Day Whitewater Rafting.
   b. The letter should include placeholders for the name of the cruise ship, the number of guests, the tour name, the tour date, and the tour cost.
   c. The first paragraph of the letter should thank the cruise ship for registering passengers for one of the two tours.
   d. The second paragraph should provide additional details, such as the number of guests, the tour date, and the tour cost. You can display this information in the form of a list if you wish.
   e. The last paragraph should provide contact information and should close positively.
5. Include your name in the closing of the main document and save the document.
6. Open the Mail Merge task pane, and then create a data source that contains only the field names you need for your letter. Note that you will need to delete field names you will not use and present the field names in a logical order. You will need to add some field names. Be sure to keep all the field names you will need for the Address block.
7. Enter information for two cruise ships in your data source.
8. Save the data source as **Kayaking Tours Data**, add field names to the document, review the letters, and then make adjustments to the main document and data source if necessary.
9. Save the merged document as **Kayaking Tours Confirmation Letter Merged**, print a copy of the two letters, and then in the main document, deselect Preview Letters and save and close the document.

Research | Case Study 3

You can download templates for a variety of business documents from the Microsoft Office Templates Web site. The templates available include a good selection of business letters and memos for various occasions. If you are unsure about the content and formatting of a letter you want to write, you can check out the content included in the templates from the Microsoft Office Templates Web site. You can often get some very good ideas about appropriate content and formatting. To complete this case study, you decide to download and adapt two business letters for a company of your choice.

1. Start Word, click the Office button, and then click New.
2. Scroll to and click Letters in the list under Microsoft Office Online.
3. Click Business in the list of letter types, and then click Thank you letters.
4. Scroll through the thank you letters listed. You need to select one that you can adapt for a business of your choice.
5. Select the letter you want to adapt, click Download, and then click Continue. In a few moments, the document should appear in Word.
6. Modify the content of the letter in Word so it contains information relevant to a company of your choice. Include an inside address and modify the letterhead so that it includes your name and address. You may need to remove or adapt placeholders.
7. Save the letter as **Office Sample Letter.docx**. Note that you may need to specify the .docx file type if the downloaded document has a .doc file extension.
8. Be sure your name appears in the closing as indicated, print a copy, and then close the document.

Objectives

- Analyze sales letter characteristics
- Identify reader benefits
- Use the persuasive message structure
- Modify color in a piece of clip art
- Rotate, resize, and position a clip art picture
- Create a WordArt object
- Modify, rotate, and position a WordArt object

Sales Letters

Introduction

As any successful entrepreneur will tell you, a successful business thrives on repeat business. A business, therefore, needs to ensure that every document sent to a customer satisfies the needs of the customer and encourages the customer to buy again from the company. A sales letter differs from other letters and messages sent from a company only in terms of its primary focus. The primary purpose of a **sales letter** is to encourage the customer to purchase a specific product or service. For all other business documents, the generation of sales is a secondary purpose.

In this project, you examine the characteristics of a sales letter, identify how to structure a sales letter to generate reader interest in a product or service, and learn how you can customize clip art and WordArt in Microsoft Word.

Starting Data Files

Project.05

Tech_05.docx
Practice_05.docx
Revise_05.docx
Case1_05.docx

Sales Letters Essentials

Sales letters play a vital role in helping a business get and keep customers. Like all business documents, sales letters are reader-centered. Every sales letter you write should accomplish the following goals:

- Stress the *benefit* of the purchase to the reader
- Use the *persuasive message structure* to maximize the chance of getting a positive response from the reader
- Define the reader *action* as a purchase

Analyzing Sales Letter Characteristics

To determine the importance of the BPA characteristics, study the ineffective sales letter shown in Figure 5-1.

Figure 5-1	**Text of an ineffective sales letter**

Dear Guest

Dolphin Cove Resort is a great seaside resort that features wonderful ocean view suites. We also provide you with many different spa treatments that are designed to make our guests feel better.

Dolphin Cove Resort is located on a private sandy beach just minutes from famed Waikiki Beach on the wonderful island of Oahu. Diamond Head, scenic drives along the wild north coast, and exciting Honolulu are all easily accessible. In addition to spa treatments, we provide our guests with the opportunity to engage in many other activities including golfing, kayaking, sailing, snorkeling, big game fishing, and fine dining. Our chef is famous for his tasty cuisine.

If Dolphin Cove Resort sounds like the kind of place you'd like to return to, our enclosed brochure will provide additional information. We will process a reservation.

Dolphin Cove Resort currently sends this sales letter to its former guests to encourage them to return. As you can see, the letter focuses almost exclusively on the writer. In fact, virtually every sentence starts with a reference to the writer. In paragraph 1, the subject of the first sentence is *Dolphin Cove Resort*, and the subject of the second sentence is *we*. As you learned in Project 1, you should avoid starting too many sentences with *we* or the name of the company. This heavy focus on the writer excludes the reader, who will then be unlikely to respond positively.

You can summarize the weaknesses in the letter shown in Figure 5-1 as follows:

- Frequent references to the writer: *we, Dolphin Cove Resort, our*
- Few references to the reader: *you* occurs only twice
- Description of features (*list of activities, proximity to attractions, luxurious accommodations*) instead of benefits (*relaxation, excitement, privacy*)
- Ineffective organizational structure: starts with a description of the product instead of thanking readers for their previous stays and then confuses the reader by jumping from one topic (location) to another topic (activities) and then back to the first topic (location)
- Abrupt request for action: *We will process a reservation.*

If you received this letter, would you be inclined to pick up the phone and book a room?

When you write a sales letter, you want to do the opposite of each of these points. You want to minimize references to the writer and maximize references to the reader. You also want to describe features in terms of benefits that appeal strongly to your reader, and you want to use the persuasive message structure to encourage the reader to recognize these benefits. Finally, you want to include a gentle, encouraging request for action.

Identifying Reader Benefits

A sales letter needs to show the reader the benefits of purchasing a product or service. A **benefit** is something that the reader values and that the reader can assume will be received as a result of purchasing the product.

Before you write a sales letter, you need to identify and then describe some of the benefits your readers might obtain as a result of purchasing your product or service. Figure 5-2 lists some common benefits that customers expect and provides an example of each.

Figure 5-2	Customer benefits

Benefit	Example
Saving money	A sales letter from a manufacturer of electric cars specifies the incredible mileage and describes to readers how they will have money left over from their transportation budget to spend on dining out or going on vacation.
Reducing stress	A sales letter from a resort hotel describes to readers how the stresses of everyday life melt away as soon as they dip a toe into the swirling waters of the ocean view Jacuzzi.
Having more leisure time	A sales letter from an investment service explains to readers how, if they invest wisely, they can retire young with plenty of money to travel the world.
Being admired	A sales letter from a personal training service describes to readers how beautiful and admired they will be after they have completed a personalized training program.

Matching Benefits to Features

After you have identified the benefits your customers expect, you need to determine how your product or service can provide these benefits. To do this, you need to focus on specific features of your product or service. A **feature** is a characteristic of a product or service. For example, a *no tipping policy* is a feature offered to passengers on a cruise ship. The benefit of this *no tipping policy* feature to customers is that they do not need to search for spare change every time they buy a drink, nor do they have to set aside money to distribute at the end of the cruise to various service staff. The benefit could be defined as *convenience* or it could be defined as *saving money*. How you describe the *no tipping policy* feature depends on which benefit you want to emphasize with your potential customers.

For example, if the benefit you want to stress is *convenience*, you could write:

On Pacific Waves Cruise ships, you forget about cash from the moment you step on board until the moment you depart the ship. All expenses, including gratuities, are included in your cruise package. Leave your wallet in your room and dance the night away!

If the benefit is *saving money*, you could write:

You pay one low price for your cruise. You don't need to bring another dime because gratuities are included in the cruise price. In fact, members of the service staff are not permitted to accept tips.

Although the feature being described is exactly the same in both examples, the benefit differs. Figure 5-3 lists a series of features along with examples of benefits.

Figure 5-3 **Features and benefits**

Feature	Benefit
Computer with an extraordinary amount of storage space	Convenience: easily store large files, such as movies and graphics
Hotel within walking distance of a theme park	Saving money: no need to rent a car or pay extra for transportation
Airplane with increased leg room	Comfort: an easy and enjoyable flight
Nonstick cookware	Saving time: cleanup is quick and easy

Matching Benefits to a Target Audience

Key Point

Readers respond to a product if they think it will help them in some way.

You identify benefit categories such as *relaxation* or *meeting people* and then develop a sales letter for each category. You usually need to develop several versions of a sales letter, with each version targeted to different groups of customers. Figure 5-4 compares two versions of the first paragraph of a sales letter targeted at corporate customers. Version 1 focuses on the benefit of employee satisfaction and Version 2 focuses on the benefit of cost effectiveness. Both versions can also include references to other benefits; for example, Version 1 could also mention the benefit of cost effectiveness. However, the principal focus of each version should be on one specific benefit.

Figure 5-4 **Target audience comparison**

Version 1: Employee Satisfaction Benefit

Your employees work hard for you all year and have made your company a success. When the time rolls around for your annual sales meeting, you can show your employees how much you appreciate them by holding your meeting at Dolphin Cove Resort. Here, you have access to all the seminar rooms and business services you need, and your employees can enjoy all the recreational activities they have earned.

Version 2: Cost-Effectiveness Benefit

Your annual sales meeting should celebrate your company's successes without breaking your company's budget. You need a venue that includes spacious seminar rooms, efficient business services, reasonably priced catering, and guest rooms large enough for two or three employees to share. At Dolphin Cove Resort, you can take advantage of several corporate packages customized to the budget you set.

Readers rarely respond positively to a list of product features unless those features happen to relate strongly to perceived benefits.

Using the Persuasive Message Structure

The *P* in BPA stands for **persuasive message structure**. You use the persuasive message structure to lead readers slowly to a request for action. This structure is based on the psychology of persuasion. Suppose you wanted to ask your supervisor for a raise and you anticipate some resistance. Would you blurt out the request *Please give me a raise* without any preamble? This approach might be clear and direct, but it will probably not produce a positive response. Your supervisor is taken by surprise and not given any reason to consider your request.

The persuasive message structure is opposite to the structure you learned in previous projects. For e-mails, memos, and everyday letters, you need to state the purpose as quickly as possible and then present any details the reader requires to make a decision. The purpose of a sales letter is to persuade someone to buy something; however, readers need more persuasion than a simple *buy me* statement. The persuasive message structure consists of four parts as follows:

1. Engage the reader
2. Stimulate interest
3. Provide details
4. Inspire action

Figure 5-5 describes each of the four components of the persuasive message structure.

Figure 5-5   **Components of the persuasive message structure**

Component	Description
Engage the reader	• Focus on the benefits relevant to the reader. • Use the second person *you* to speak directly to the reader. • Use descriptive words to paint a vivid picture for the reader. • Use action verbs and the active voice. • Sample first paragraph for a sales letter promoting a resort: *Your busy life brings you a great deal of fulfillment, but it can also drain your energy. You need a vacation that can relieve your stress and restore your energy. You work hard and you deserve to relax in luxury.*
Stimulate interest	• Visualize your reader engaged in some kind of activity and then use words that put the reader at the center of the action. • Use action verbs to *show* how readers can be involved with the product or service. • Sample statement to stimulate interest in a kayaking tour that stresses the benefit of excitement: *Feel the adrenaline rush as you plunge your paddle into the swirling waters and launch your kayak down a rushing mountain stream.*
Provide details	• Position details and cost information after you have motivated the reader to make a purchase. A sales letter that starts with cost information such as *Buy now and receive a 20% discount* is unlikely to hold a reader's attention. • State cost information clearly and without embellishment. • Avoid *hype* phrases such as *the incredibly low price of* or *this one time only offer.*
Inspire action	• Provide readers with the information they need to make a purchase. • Keep the paragraph short and to the point. • Include the phone number and/or e-mail address even when they are included in the company letterhead. A phrase such as *Call me at the above number* is not very reader friendly because the reader will need to physically look up to the letterhead to find the number. • Make the last sentence motivational and positive. Negative: *If you would like to make a reservation, you need to contact me by March 20 at the very latest.* Positive: *Please contact me by March 20 to reserve your place in paradise.*

Each of the four parts of the persuasive message structure requires at least a paragraph and sometimes two. As a result, the average sales letter requires four or five paragraphs and usually fills most of the page.

Figure 5-6 shows a sales letter designed to attract membership in a fitness club. The benefits stressed are that the reader will feel healthy, comfortable, and beautiful by working out in the club's friendly, fun, and attractive environment. As you read the letter, notice how the persuasive message structure is used to engage the reader and lead slowly to a request for action. The letter in Figure 5-6 is completely reader-centered.

Figure 5-6 Sales letter showing the four-part structure

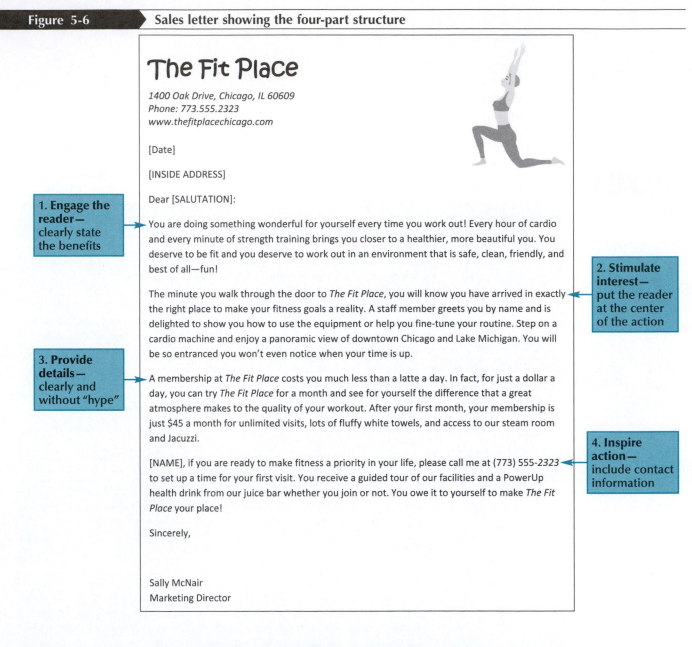

The Fit Place

1400 Oak Drive, Chicago, IL 60609
Phone: 773.555.2323
www.thefitplacechicago.com

[Date]

[INSIDE ADDRESS]

Dear [SALUTATION]:

1. Engage the reader— clearly state the benefits

You are doing something wonderful for yourself every time you work out! Every hour of cardio and every minute of strength training brings you closer to a healthier, more beautiful you. You deserve to be fit and you deserve to work out in an environment that is safe, clean, friendly, and best of all—fun!

2. Stimulate interest— put the reader at the center of the action

The minute you walk through the door to *The Fit Place*, you will know you have arrived in exactly the right place to make your fitness goals a reality. A staff member greets you by name and is delighted to show you how to use the equipment or help you fine-tune your routine. Step on a cardio machine and enjoy a panoramic view of downtown Chicago and Lake Michigan. You will be so entranced you won't even notice when your time is up.

3. Provide details— clearly and without "hype"

A membership at *The Fit Place* costs you much less than a latte a day. In fact, for just a dollar a day, you can try *The Fit Place* for a month and see for yourself the difference that a great atmosphere makes to the quality of your workout. After your first month, your membership is just $45 a month for unlimited visits, lots of fluffy white towels, and access to our steam room and Jacuzzi.

4. Inspire action— include contact information

[NAME], if you are ready to make fitness a priority in your life, please call me at (773) 555-*2323* to set up a time for your first visit. You receive a guided tour of our facilities and a PowerUp health drink from our juice bar whether you join or not. You owe it to yourself to make *The Fit Place* your place!

Sincerely,

Sally McNair
Marketing Director

Technology Skills—Editing Clip Art and WordArt

Key Point

If you use clip art in a business document, you should customize it in some way that makes it unique because all businesses that use Microsoft Office have access to the same library of clips.

Clip art refers to premade graphic files such as drawings, pictures, sounds, and animations that are available to copy and paste into your documents. The generic term for all these files is **clips**. Microsoft Word provides a library of clips that you access through Word's Clip Art task pane. If used sparingly, clip art drawings and pictures can enhance the appearance of a document. A **WordArt** object is a drawing object that contains text you can format with a variety of shapes, patterns, and orientations. The Technology Skills steps cover these skills:

- Modify color in a piece of clip art
- Rotate, resize, and position a clip art picture
- Create a WordArt object
- Modify, rotate, and position a WordArt object

To modify color in a piece of clip art:

► 1. Open the file **Tech_05.docx** located in the Project.05 folder included with your Data Files, and then to avoid altering the original file, save the document as **Sales Letter with Formatted Letterhead** in the same folder. The document contains the text of the sales letter sent to corporate clients. A picture of a dolphin appears at the top of the document.

► 2. Click the **Show/Hide ¶** button ¶ in the Paragraph group to turn on the formatting marks. Whenever you work with graphics, you should work with the formatting marks showing so that you can easily see positioning changes.

► 3. Right-click the **clip art picture** of the dolphin, and then click **Edit Picture**. The clip art picture is enclosed in the drawing canvas and the Drawing Tools Format tab appears. You can use the tools on the Drawing Tools Format tab to edit components of the clip art picture.

> **Tip**
>
> Use the Undo command on the Quick Access tool-bar any time you do not get the results you expect.

► 4. Click the **purple shaded area**, and then press the **Delete** key.

► 5. Click the middle of the dolphin (currently white), click the **Format** tab on the Drawing Tools tab, click the **Shape Fill** list arrow in the Shape Styles group, point to **Gradient**, click **More Gradients**, and then click the **Two colors** option button in the Colors section.

► 6. Click the **Color 1** list arrow, select **Blue**, **Accent 1**, **Darker 50%**, click the **Color 2** list arrow, select **Blue**, **Accent 1**, **Lighter 80%**, and then click the top right Variant style in the Variants area.

► 7. Click **OK**, click the **black line** at the head area, press and hold the [**Ctrl**] key, and then click the other four lines that make up the outline of the dolphin as shown in Figure 5-7.

Figure 5-7 **Selecting the outline lines**

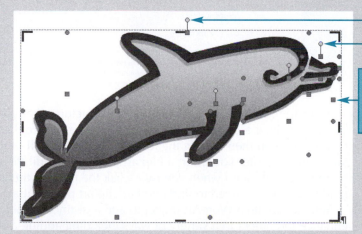

green rotation handles appear for each selected line; you should see five

selection handles appear around each of the five selected outline lines

► 8. Click the **Shape Fill** list arrow in the Shape Styles group, and then click **Purple**, **Accent 4**, **Lighter 80%**.

► 9. Right-click a blank area of the drawing canvas, click **Expand**, point the mouse at the top left of the drawing canvas, click and drag to select all components that make up the dolphin picture, click the **Group** button 回▾ in the Arrange group, and then click **Group**.

The picture of the dolphin is attractively colored and all the components that make up the picture are combined into one object that you can easily rotate, resize, and position. Next, you resize and position the clip art picture.

To resize and position a clip art picture:

1. With the dolphin picture still selected, click the **Rotate** button in the Arrange group, and then click **Flip Horizontal**.

2. Click the **launcher** in the Size group, select **100%** in the Height box in the Scale area, type **40**, press [**Tab**], type **40**, and then click **OK**.

3. Drag the dolphin picture below the drawing canvas (anywhere on the document is fine at this point), click the white space where the drawing canvas had appeared (crop marks will appear), and then press the **Delete** key.

4. Drag the dolphin to the top right corner of the document as shown in Figure 5-8, and then click away from the picture to deselect it.

> **Tip**
>
> You delete the drawing canvas because it is no longer needed and so you can more accurately place the clip art picture.

Figure 5-8 | **Dolphin picture sized and positioned**

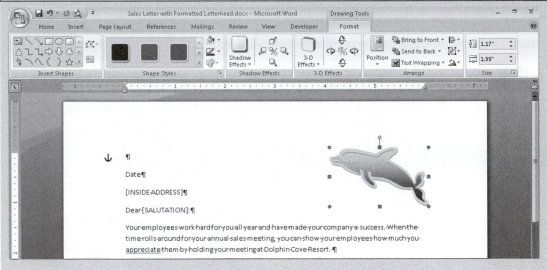

You can modify most (but not all) clip art pictures that you insert in a Word document by right-clicking a clip and clicking Edit Picture to place the picture in the drawing canvas. You can then modify the formatting of any or all of the components that make up the picture. If, after you insert a clip art picture, the Edit Picture option does not appear on the shortcut menu when you right-click the picture, then you will not be able to modify it. You will need to find another clip art picture that you can modify.

You can create a WordArt object to add a distinctive look to your letter, and then enhance the object in a variety of ways including adding a shadow effect, a gradient effect, and rotating the text. Next, you create a WordArt object from the words *Dolphin Cove Resort* and then display the object vertically along the left side of the page.

To create and modify a WordArt object:

1. Click the **Page Layout** tab, click **Margins**, click **Custom Margins**, change the Left margin to **2**, click **OK**, and then adjust the position of the dolphin so that its tail extends about one-half inch beyond the right edge of the text (to 5.5).

2. Click to the left of **Date** at the top of the document, click the **Insert** tab, click **WordArt** in the Text group, and then click the top left WordArt style.

3. Type **Dolphin Cove Resort** as the WordArt text, and then click **OK**.

> **Tip**
>
> Use the ruler to help position the dolphin. If the ruler is not showing, click the View Ruler button at the top of the right scroll bar.

4. Click the **launcher** in the Size group, click the **Colors and Lines** tab, click the **Color** list arrow in the Fill area, click **Blue**, **Accent 1**, **Lighter 60%**, select the contents of the **Transparency** text box in the Fill area, type **50**, and then press the **Tab** key.

5. Click the **Size** tab in the Format WordArt dialog box, select the contents of the **Absolute** text box in the Height area, type **.5**, press [**Tab**] two times, and then type **8.5** for the Absolute width.

6. Click the **Layout** tab in the Format WordArt dialog box, click the **Square** layout, click the **Left** option button, and then click **OK**.

Tip

You change the layout to Square so that you can use your mouse to position the WordArt object anywhere on the page.

You continue to modify the WordArt object. Next, you add a shadow and then rotate and position the WordArt object so it creates an attractive element in the left margin.

To modify, rotate, and position a WordArt object:

1. Click the **Shadow Effects** button in the Shadow Effects group, click the **Shadow Style 1** in the Drop Shadow area, click the **Shape Outline** arrow in the WordArt Styles group, click **No Outline**, click the **Nudge Shadow Down** button three times in the Shadow Effects group, and then click the **Nudge Shadow Right** button three times.

2. With the WordArt object still selected, click the **Rotate** button in the Arrange group, and then click **Rotate Left 90°**.

3. Click the **View** tab, click **One Page** in the Zoom group, and then use your mouse to position the WordArt object, as shown in Figure 5-9.

Figure 5-9   **WordArt object positioned on the page**

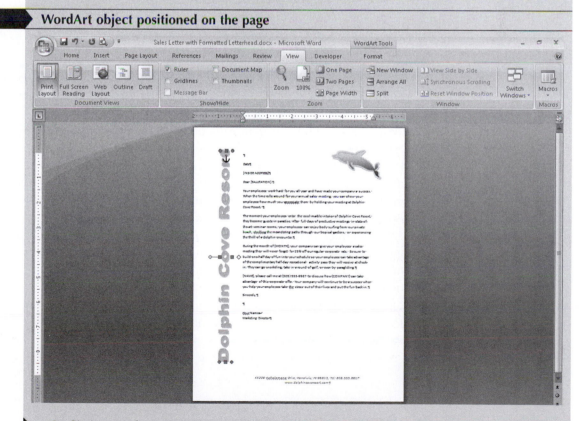

4. Click away from the WordArt object, click **Page Width** in the Zoom group, scroll as needed to see the closing, type your name where indicated in the closing, save the document, print a copy, and then close the document.

Practice	**Targeted Sales Letters**

Gary Novak, the marketing director at The Palms Resort in Maui, and your supervisor, wants to edit an existing sales letter so he can send it to two target audiences—active travellers interested in water sports and travellers interested in spa treatments and relaxation. The members of both of these target audiences have stayed at The Palms Resort before.

Figure 5-10 describes the features of The Palms Resort that are most likely to interest the two target audiences and inspire them to return. You will use this information to help you determine appropriate benefits to include in the sales letters.

Figure 5-10 ▸ **Resort features for target audiences**

Audience 1: Active travellers interested in surfing, kayaking, and snorkeling	
Features	The Palms Resort is located on a pristine white sand beach with direct access to a marina well stocked with kayaks, fishing boats, and jet skis. In addition, a sheltered cove teeming with tropical fish and ideal for snorkeling is located a five- minute walk from the resort. Surfing lessons are provided along with guided kayaking tours. The sunset kayaking tour is particularly popular.
Audience 2: Travellers interested in spa treatments and relaxation	
Features	The Palms Resort includes one of Maui's premier spas. Guests at the spa enjoy access to a private outdoor spa deck that overlooks the tropical gardens. Herbal teas, tropical juices, and soothing music relax guests before they enter the 15,000 square foot, full-service spa that includes a comprehensive range of skin and body treatments, scrubs, clay wraps, facials, and traditional Hawaiian healing massages.

Follow the steps below to identify benefits for the two target audiences and then to edit an existing sales letter.

1. Refer to Figure 5-10 to identify one benefit for each of the two target audiences. Remember that a benefit is something that the reader values and expects to receive as the result of purchasing the product.
2. Write a draft of the first paragraph of the sales letter for each of the two target audiences. Remember to engage the reader by focusing on the benefit you identified. Use the second person *you*, choose descriptive words that paint a vivid picture, and select action verbs. For example, instead of writing *You will be able to relax on our private terrace,* you can use action verbs and the active voice to write *Feel the stress melt away as you sink into a luxuriously padded deck chair on our private terrace and sip a restorative juice concoction while gazing at lush tropical gardens. You have all the time in the world.* Note that coming up with an effective first paragraph takes time; experiment with a variety of approaches. Make up realistic but fictional details.
3. Open the file **Practice_05.docx** located in the Project.05 folder included with your Data Files and then, to avoid altering the original file, save the document as **The Palms Resort Sales Letters** in the same folder.

4. Read the letter and note where information specific to each target audience is needed. You need to replace the text in paragraphs 1 and 2 with text that will be relevant to the target audiences. You also need to replace text in square brackets.

5. Use the paragraph you wrote for step 2 to modify the letter for audience 1—the active travellers interested in water sports. Include a second paragraph that stimulates interest. In this paragraph, you can put your reader at the center of the action.

6. Create an attractive letterhead for the sales letter that creates the company name as a WordArt object that you modify and a piece of edited clip art. Note that you cannot edit all clip art pictures. After you have inserted a clip art picture, right-click it to view the shortcut menu. If the Edit Picture option appears on the shortcut menu, you can modify the various components that make up the clip art picture. If the Edit Picture option is not available, delete the clip art picture and select another one.

7. Type your name where indicated in the closing.

8. Press [Ctrl]+[A] to select the entire letter, press [Ctrl]+[C] to copy the entire letter, insert a new page 2, and then press [Ctrl]+[V] to paste the letter on page 2.

9. Revise the copied letter so that it can be sent to target audience 2—the travellers interested in a relaxing spa vacation.

10. Save the document, and then print a copy of both letters.

| Revise | **Writer-Oriented Sales Letter** |

You have just started working as a marketing assistant at GreenArt Landscaping. The sales letter that the company had been sending to inform local homeowners about landscaping services is poorly organized and too aggressive. In addition, the letterhead is out of date. You have been asked to rewrite the sales letter using the techniques you have learned in this project and then to create an attractive letterhead that includes a WordArt object and a modified clip art picture.

Follow the steps below to rewrite the sales letter and create a new letterhead.

1. Open the file **Revise_05.docx** located in the Project.05 folder included with your Data Files and then, to avoid altering the original file, save the document as **GreenArt Landscaping Sales Letter** in the same folder.

2. Read the letter and note its poor tone. Benefits are not stressed, and the constant use of the company name and the third person plural (we, our) puts the focus firmly on the company and not the reader.

3. Use the techniques you have learned in this project to rewrite the letter. Note that the revised letter should be approximately five paragraphs long. Make any assumptions you wish about the company.

4. Replace the company name with a WordArt object that you modify.

5. Format the contact information attractively. Note that you can choose to place the company information in a footer at the bottom of the page or as part of the letterhead.

6. Insert a clip art picture appropriate for a landscaping service (for example, a clip art picture of a tree), and then modify the clip art picture. You can choose to delete objects from the clip art picture, change the fill color of selected objects, add a shadow or 3D effect, and so on. Note that you cannot edit all clip art pictures. After you have inserted a clip art picture, right-click it to view the shortcut menu. If the Edit Picture option appears on the shortcut menu, you can modify the various components that make up the clip art picture. If the Edit Picture option is not available, delete the clip art picture and select another one that you can modify.

7. Size and position the clip art picture so it complements the letterhead. Make sure that it doesn't overwhelm the document. You can choose to position the clip art picture at the bottom of the document if you wish.

8. Type your name where indicated in the closing, save the document, and then print a copy.

Create | **Sales Letter for Study Tour**

You work as the departmental coordinator of the Humanities Department at Western View College in Colorado. Each year during the summer, your department conducts a study tour to a different part of the world for groups of up to 20 students. You need to draft a sales letter that advertises the current year's study tour to current students. All of these students have taken courses in the Humanities department; however, none of them has participated in a study tour.

Follow the steps below to write the sales letter and create a new letterhead for Western View College.

1. Complete the table below with the information you need to help you write the sales letter. Note that you will need to make up information. Use fictitious but realistic details.

Information for a Sales Letter
Study Tour Theme and Location (for example, Renaissance Art in Italy or Archeology in Egypt)
Characteristics of Target Audience (for example, students pursuing a humanities degree who could participate in the study tour as part of their summer term)
Features of the Tour
Benefits for Students

2. Create a new document in Word, and then save it as **Study Tour Sales Letter**.

3. Create an attractive letterhead using the following address information. Make *Western View College* a WordArt object.

   Western View College
   3400 Aspen Way, Pueblo, Colorado 81002
   (719) 555-7956
   www.westernviewpueblo.com

4. Include a clip art picture that you have modified in some way. You determine where best to place the picture to balance the letterhead. Note that you cannot edit all clip art pictures. After you have inserted a clip art picture, right-click it to view the shortcut menu. If the Edit Picture option appears on the shortcut menu, you can modify the various components that make up the clip art picture. If the Edit Picture option is not available, delete the clip art picture and select another one that you can modify.

5. Write a sales letter that will encourage students to sign up for a study tour to the location you have chosen. You can decide all the details about the tour including the theme, dates, cost, and registration deadlines. Remember to engage the reader, stress the benefits to students of participating in the study tour, and stimulate interest through the use of strong descriptive words and action verbs. Make any assumptions you wish about Western View College and the study tour.

6. Type your name in the closing, print a copy of the letter, and then save and close the document.

Apply | Case Study 1

Capstone College In your position as the program assistant for the Digital Arts Department at Capstone College in San Francisco, you assist the department coordinator with a variety of letter writing tasks. Your supervisor has asked you to draft a letter that the department can use to recruit new students into the program. You open the sales letter that was written last year by your predecessor and discover that some rewriting and formatting are required. To complete this case study, you rewrite the sales letter.

1. Open the file **Case1_05.docx** located in the Project.05 folder included with your Data Files, and then save the document as **Digital Arts Sales Letter** in the same folder.

2. Read the letter and then rewrite it using the techniques you learned in this project. You need to engage the reader, stress the benefits to students of taking the Digital Arts program, and stimulate interest through the use of strong descriptive words and action verbs. You can add additional information if you want.

3. Create an attractive letterhead using the address information provided. Make *Capstone College* a WordArt object. Do not include a clip art picture.

4. Type your name where indicated in the closing.

Apply | Case Study 2

Otter Bay Kayaking Adventures Tourists from all over the world enjoy kayaking trips led by the friendly guides at Otter Bay Kayaking Adventures in Juneau, Alaska. One of the company's principal target markets is the group of tour coordinators who work on the cruise ships that dock in Juneau every day throughout the summer season. These tour coordinators are responsible for informing cruise ship passengers of the various recreational activities available in Juneau. One of your jobs as an assistant in the Marketing Department is to help develop sales materials, including sales letters. To complete this case study, you write a sales letter to promote the half day sea kayaking tour and the full day whitewater rafting adventure to cruise ship tour coordinators.

1. Start a new blank document and save it as **Kayaking Sales Letter**.

2. Write a draft of a sales letter that you would send to the cruise ship tour coordinators to promote two tours: *Half Day Sea Kayaking* and *Full Day Whitewater Rafting*. You will need to create interesting reader-centered descriptions of these tours to appeal to the tour coordinators who organize trips for passengers on the cruise ships. You can refer to the following information to help you plan and write the letter:

   • A benefit to tour coordinators of selling a tour from Otter Bay Kayaking Adventures is that the company's long-standing reputation as one of the area's foremost tour providers ensures passengers will have a great experience.

Tip

This sales letter could be constructed as a form letter, which you learned about in Project 4.

- A benefit to cruise ship passengers is the chance to view wildlife up close and have an Alaskan adventure.
- A gourmet boxed lunch is included with every tour, along with all the required equipment and clothing.
- The Half Day Sea Kayaking tour costs $75 and the Full Day Whitewater Rafting adventure costs $135. Search the Web to find information about sea kayaking and whitewater rafting in Alaska that you can adapt for the sales letter.
- Offer tour coordinators a package rate if more than 10 passengers sign up for a tour on any one day.

3. Create an attractive letterhead using the following information: Otter Bay Kayaking Adventures, 149 Seward Street, Juneau, AK 99804, Phone: (907) 555-3311, Web site: *www.otterbaykayaking.com*. Instead of creating a WordArt object, use bold, italics, and different font sizes to highlight information in the letterhead.

4. Insert a clip art picture of a kayak, edit the picture, and then position it in the letterhead. Note that you cannot edit all clip art pictures. After you have inserted a clip art picture, right-click it to view the shortcut menu. If the Edit Picture option appears on the shortcut menu, you can modify the various components that make up the clip art picture. If the Edit Picture option is not available, delete the clip art picture and select another one that you can modify.

5. Add placeholders for variable information such as Inside Address and Recipient, type your name in the closing, save the document, and then print a copy.

Research | **Case Study 3**

You can download templates for a variety of business documents from the Microsoft Office Templates Web site. The templates available include a good selection of sales letters that you can adapt. To complete this case study, you download and adapt a business letter for a company of your choice.

1. Start Word, click the Office button, click New, and then scroll to and click Letters in the list under Microsoft Office Online.
2. Click Business in the list of letter types, and then click Sales letters.
3. Scroll through the sales letters listed. You need to select one that you can adapt for a business of your choice.
4. Select the letter you want to adapt, click Download, and then click Continue. In a few moments, the document should open in Word.
5. Modify the letterhead so that it includes the name of a fictitious business. You may need to remove or adapt placeholders. Make any formatting changes you wish so that the letterhead is clear and attractive.
6. Modify the content of the letter in Word so it contains information relevant to a business of your choice. Include placeholders for the data, inside address, and any other variable information you wish to include.
7. Include an appropriate clip art picture that you have modified.
8. Save the letter as **Office Sales Letter.docx**. Note that you may need to specify the .docx file type if the downloaded document has a .doc file extension.
9. Be sure your name appears in the closing, print a copy, and then close the document.

Objectives

- Use persuasive techniques in a refusal letter
- Structure a refusal letter
- Write complaint letters
- Reply to complaint letters
- Create envelopes in Word
- Create labels in Word

Messages with Negative News

Introduction

A letter or e-mail message that communicates **negative news** communicates information that the reader considers unwelcome. For example, a letter that refuses an application for a job is a negative news letter because the reader will likely be disappointed that the job application was not successful. You classify a message that communicates negative news as a form of **persuasive correspondence**. When the message you are writing contains negative news, you need to write it in a way that retains the goodwill of the reader and persuades the reader to accept the negative news as fair and reasonable. If you are writing in response to a complaint, you need to acknowledge the concern and persuade the reader to accept the resolution to the complaint.

In this project, you learn how to structure a reader-friendly refusal letter, write a complaint letter that gets results, write an appropriate reply to a complaint letter sent by a customer, add an envelope to a letter, and create a sheet of labels.

Starting Data Files

Project.06

Tech_06.docx
Practice_06.docx
Revise_06.docx
Case1_06.docx
Case2_06.docx

Messages with Negative News Essentials

Imagine you have spent many weeks putting together a proposal for something that means a great deal to you. Perhaps you have proposed a significant change in your work situation or you have requested funding for a project that is dear to your heart. You send off your proposal and feel satisfied that you have done everything possible to plead your case.

Several weeks later, an official-looking letter arrives. You open it anxiously, sure it contains a positive response to your proposal. Figure 6-1 shows the letter you receive.

Figure 6-1	Poorly structured refusal letter

Birch County Planning Committee
3409 West Mall, Kansas City, KS 66104
Phone: (913) 555-1066
www.birchcountykansas.com

September 12, 2011

Applicant
100 Maple Drive
Kansas City, KS 66112

Dear Applicant:

We regret to inform you that your proposal to build a new playground at Birch Drive Elementary School has been rejected.

We receive many proposals such as yours. While your proposal had merit, the funding committee cannot approve it. Consider applying again next year. Good luck.

Sincerely,

Planning Committee

How do you feel after reading the letter? Deflated? Angry? Upset? A message that communicates negative news should not evoke any of these emotions. After reading a negative news message, you will inevitably feel a certain amount of disappointment; however, if the message is written well, you should not feel angry or upset.

You can learn a great deal about how *not* to structure a message that communicates negative news by analyzing a poorly written message. Look again at the refusal letter shown in Figure 6-1. The refusal letter begins with the impersonal salutation *Dear Applicant,* instead of the recipient's name, abruptly states the rejection *We regret to inform you*, and then goes on to try to explain the rejection but without providing any helpful information. At the end, the terse wording falls far short of friendly. The writer probably did not intend any ill will toward the reader, but the trite *Good luck* comes off sounding hurtful instead of helpful. In addition, the letter is signed by the Planning Committee so the reader does not even have the name of an individual to call or write to for more information.

Using Persuasive Techniques in a Refusal Letter

You employ many of the same techniques you use for a sales letter to write a refusal letter—or any message that informs the reader that something he or she values has been rejected. In fact, both types of letters are persuasive letters. When you write a sales letter, you persuade your reader to buy your product or service. When you write a **refusal letter**, you persuade your reader to accept that the refusal is fair and reasonable.

Key Point

An effective negative news letter does not alienate or anger the reader.

The primary goal of a refusal letter is not to say *no*. You need to think of a refusal letter as an opportunity to help the reader accept the negative news, and if appropriate, determine how he or she could receive a letter of acceptance at another time.

To understand how a refusal letter could be a helping letter, try to identify with your reader's feelings and goals. The reader is hoping for good news but worries about receiving bad news. You need to write a refusal letter that lets the reader down slowly, clarifies the reason for the refusal, and then provides some kind of alternative.

Structuring a Refusal Letter

You structure a refusal letter according to the level of emotional investment the reader has in receiving a positive response. If the *no* situation is relatively neutral and the reader has little emotional investment, you can use the **direct approach** to structure the refusal. For example, if you are refusing an invitation to attend a meeting, you can write a short e-mail as follows:

> *Thank you for inviting me to the planning committee meeting on September 13. I have a previous engagement and so I will not be able to attend. However, I am excited to hear about the progress made by the committee members and look forward to receiving the minutes of the meeting.*

In this situation, the reader does not need to be led slowly to a *no* because the reader has little emotional investment in the situation. You can state the refusal in the first sentence or two and then close positively.

When the refusal might have an emotional impact on the reader, you need to use the **persuasive refusal structure**. This structure consists of five paragraphs as described in Figure 6-2.

Figure 6-2	Five-paragraph structure for a refusal letter

Paragraph	Analysis
Paragraph 1: Thank you	• In the first sentence, thank the reader for the contact. • In the second sentence, build goodwill with the reader: be polite but not effusive.
Paragraph 2: Context	• Provide the reader with the rationale behind the decision. • Present information neutrally as you build toward the refusal. • Provide the reader with the opportunity to anticipate the *no* before you actually state it. • Present the context for the refusal in a fair and reasonable way.
Paragraph 3: No	• Say no clearly, but diplomatically and without using any negative words. Note that you can use *not* when you pair it with a positive word such as *not accepted* instead of *rejected*.
Paragraph 4: Positive alternative	• Provide some hope in the form of a positive alternative.
Paragraph 5: Positive close	• Thank the reader again and then provide your contact information, if appropriate.

Figure 6-3 shows how the refusal letter shown in Figure 6-1 is rewritten using the five-paragraph refusal structure.

Figure 6-3 **Effective refusal letter**

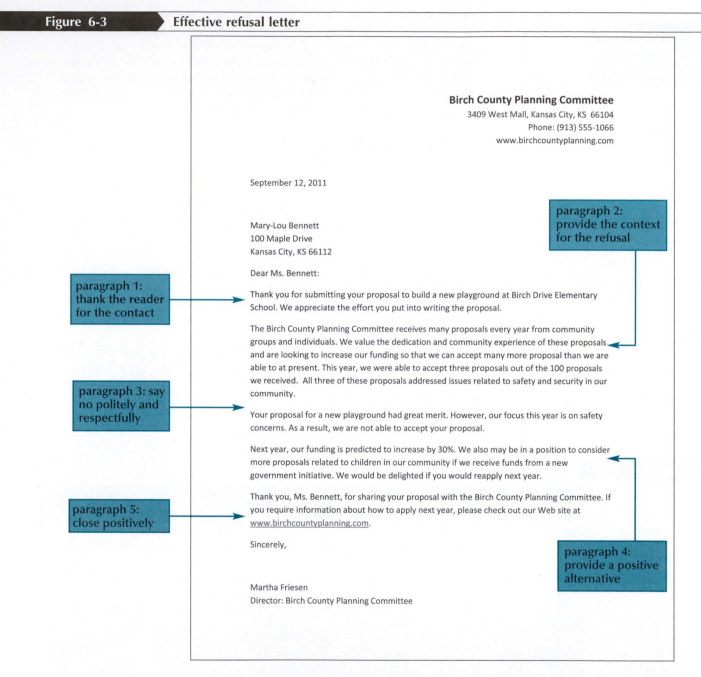

Birch County Planning Committee
3409 West Mall, Kansas City, KS 66104
Phone: (913) 555-1066
www.birchcountyplanning.com

September 12, 2011

Mary-Lou Bennett
100 Maple Drive
Kansas City, KS 66112

Dear Ms. Bennett:

paragraph 1: thank the reader for the contact

Thank you for submitting your proposal to build a new playground at Birch Drive Elementary School. We appreciate the effort you put into writing the proposal.

paragraph 2: provide the context for the refusal

The Birch County Planning Committee receives many proposals every year from community groups and individuals. We value the dedication and community experience of these proposals and are looking to increase our funding so that we can accept many more proposal than we are able to at present. This year, we were able to accept three proposals out of the 100 proposals we received. All three of these proposals addressed issues related to safety and security in our community.

paragraph 3: say no politely and respectfully

Your proposal for a new playground had great merit. However, our focus this year is on safety concerns. As a result, we are not able to accept your proposal.

paragraph 4: provide a positive alternative

Next year, our funding is predicted to increase by 30%. We also may be in a position to consider more proposals related to children in our community if we receive funds from a new government initiative. We would be delighted if you would reapply next year.

paragraph 5: close positively

Thank you, Ms. Bennett, for sharing your proposal with the Birch County Planning Committee. If you require information about how to apply next year, please check out our Web site at www.birchcountyplanning.com.

Sincerely,

Martha Friesen
Director: Birch County Planning Committee

You need to take more time to write a refusal letter that readers can accept as fair and reasonable than you need to write an abrupt refusal letter that leaves the reader with negative feelings toward you and your company or organization. The time taken to write a well-constructed refusal letter is time well spent. Companies and organizations benefit in the long run when they make sure that every letter—even a refusal letter—engenders goodwill.

Writing a Complaint Letter

People generally write complaint letters because they are angry and upset about poor service or a defective product. However, the purpose of a complaint letter should not be to vent anger. Instead, the purpose of a complaint letter is to state exactly what the company can do to address the situation. The complaint letter needs to use a positive, respectful tone, include details about the problem, and state clearly but politely what compensation the writer expects. When you take the emotion out of a complaint letter and substitute a clear and rational request for a specific action, you are more likely to see positive results.

Consider the complaint letter shown in Figure 6-4. Although some of the writer's complaints are valid, he is not likely to receive a positive response from the resort.

| Figure 6-4 | Ineffective complaint letter |

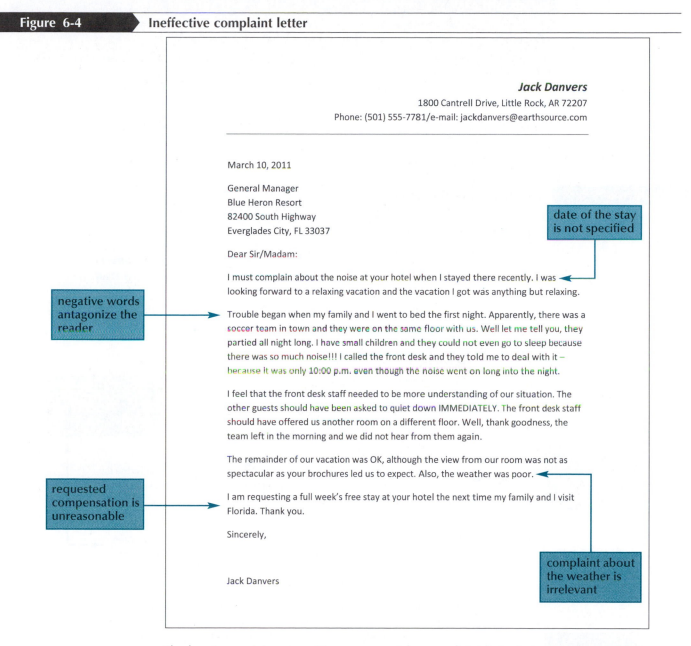

Jack Danvers
1800 Cantrell Drive, Little Rock, AR 72207
Phone: (501) 555-7781/e-mail: jackdanvers@earthsource.com

March 10, 2011

General Manager
Blue Heron Resort
82400 South Highway
Everglades City, FL 33037

Dear Sir/Madam:

I must complain about the noise at your hotel when I stayed there recently. I was looking forward to a relaxing vacation and the vacation I got was anything but relaxing.

Trouble began when my family and I went to bed the first night. Apparently, there was a soccer team in town and they were on the same floor with us. Well let me tell you, they partied all night long. I have small children and they could not even go to sleep because there was so much noise!!! I called the front desk and they told me to deal with it – because it was only 10:00 p.m. even though the noise went on long into the night.

I feel that the front desk staff needed to be more understanding of our situation. The other guests should have been asked to quiet down IMMEDIATELY. The front desk staff should have offered us another room on a different floor. Well, thank goodness, the team left in the morning and we did not hear from them again.

The remainder of our vacation was OK, although the view from our room was not as spectacular as your brochures led us to expect. Also, the weather was poor.

I am requesting a full week's free stay at your hotel the next time my family and I visit Florida. Thank you.

Sincerely,

Jack Danvers

date of the stay is not specified

negative words antagonize the reader

requested compensation is unreasonable

complaint about the weather is irrelevant

The key to receiving a positive response to a complaint letter is to state the problem clearly and to specify reasonable compensation. You might not receive the exact compensation you request but you will probably get at least a portion.

You use the four-paragraph structure described in Figure 6-5 to write a complaint letter.

| Figure 6-5 | Four-paragraph structure for a complaint letter |

Paragraph	Analysis
Paragraph 1: Context for the complaint	• State that you have a concern with the service or product and specify when and where you made the purchase.
Paragraph 2: Details about the complaint	• Use neutral language to describe the problem as precisely as possible.
Paragraph 3: Compensation expected	• Provide additional details, if necessary, and then state exactly what compensation you require.
Paragraph 4: Positive close	• Provide contact information and close positively.

Figure 6-6 shows an example of an effectively written complaint letter.

| Figure 6-6 | Effective complaint letter |

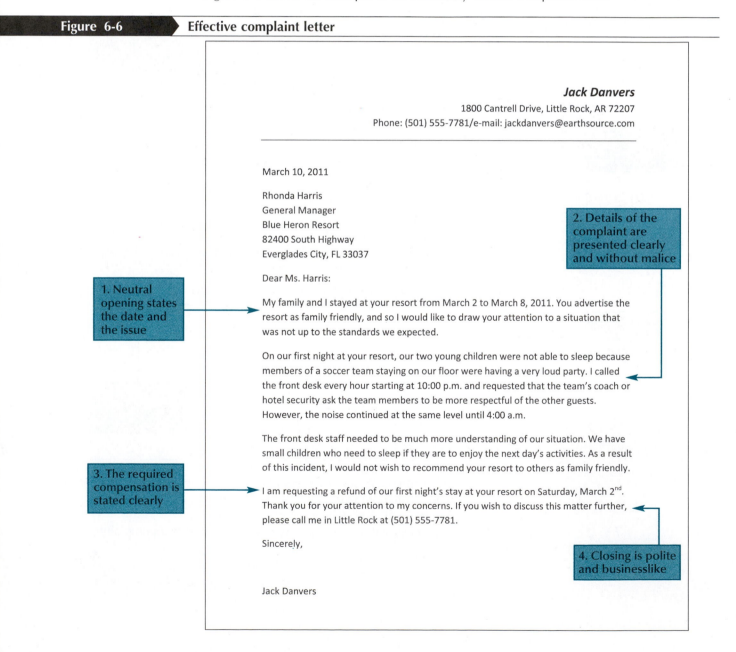

Jack Danvers
1800 Cantrell Drive, Little Rock, AR 72207
Phone: (501) 555-7781/e-mail: jackdanvers@earthsource.com

March 10, 2011

Rhonda Harris
General Manager
Blue Heron Resort
82400 South Highway
Everglades City, FL 33037

Dear Ms. Harris:

My family and I stayed at your resort from March 2 to March 8, 2011. You advertise the resort as family friendly, and so I would like to draw your attention to a situation that was not up to the standards we expected.

On our first night at your resort, our two young children were not able to sleep because members of a soccer team staying on our floor were having a very loud party. I called the front desk every hour starting at 10:00 p.m. and requested that the team's coach or hotel security ask the team members to be more respectful of the other guests. However, the noise continued at the same level until 4:00 a.m.

The front desk staff needed to be much more understanding of our situation. We have small children who need to sleep if they are to enjoy the next day's activities. As a result of this incident, I would not wish to recommend your resort to others as family friendly.

I am requesting a refund of our first night's stay at your resort on Saturday, March 2nd. Thank you for your attention to my concerns. If you wish to discuss this matter further, please call me in Little Rock at (501) 555-7781.

Sincerely,

Jack Danvers

1. Neutral opening states the date and the issue

2. Details of the complaint are presented clearly and without malice

3. The required compensation is stated clearly

4. Closing is polite and businesslike

When you write a complaint letter, you need to focus on the effect it will have on your reader. No one wants to read an angry tirade. Instead, use a neutral tone to state your complaint and then request reasonable compensation. Avoid all negative words except *not* when used with a positive word. For example, write *We were not pleased with the service* rather than *We were very angry about the service*. The difference between *not pleased* and *angry* is subtle but important. The phrase *not pleased* implies that a positive outcome could be negotiated, while *angry* is antagonistic and leaves little room for a mutually acceptable solution. Writing a letter that antagonizes your reader is not a productive use of your time because it will not lead to a positive result.

Replying to a Complaint Letter

If you receive a complaint letter in the course of your work, the first question you need to ask is *What does the reader want?*. Regardless of the details of the complaint, the first thing the reader wants is acknowledgement that the company has listened to the complaint and is making an attempt to address it. For some complaint letters, your simple acknowledgement of the issue and an apology are sufficient. If the complaint letter also requests compensation, your reply can either grant the compensation or provide an alternative.

The reply to a complaint letter is particularly challenging if you are not able to give the reader the compensation he or she requested. In this situation, you use the refusal letter structure to lead the reader to acknowledge that alternative compensation is fair and reasonable. Figure 6-7 describes how to adapt the refusal letter structure to reply to a complaint letter.

> **Key Point**
>
> Use the refusal letter structure to reply to a complaint letter when you are not able to provide the compensation requested by the reader.

Figure 6-7 | **Structure for a reply to a complaint letter**

Paragraph	Analysis
Paragraph 1: Context for the complaint	• Thank the reader for informing you about the issue. Clearly describe the writer's concern as you understand it and avoid negative words such as *problem*; include an apology if appropriate.
Paragraph 2: Details about the complaint	• Describe the situation with the aim of leading the reader to recognize that the requested compensation cannot be granted.
Paragraph 3: Compensation offered	• Describe the compensation that can be granted; instead of describing what you cannot do, describe what you can do.
Paragraph 4: Positive close	• Close positively with a request to the reader to contact you if further clarification is required.

Figure 6-8 shows how the refusal letter structure is used to reply to the complaint letter shown in Figure 6-4 that demanded unreasonable compensation.

Figure 6-8 Reply to an unreasonable complaint letter

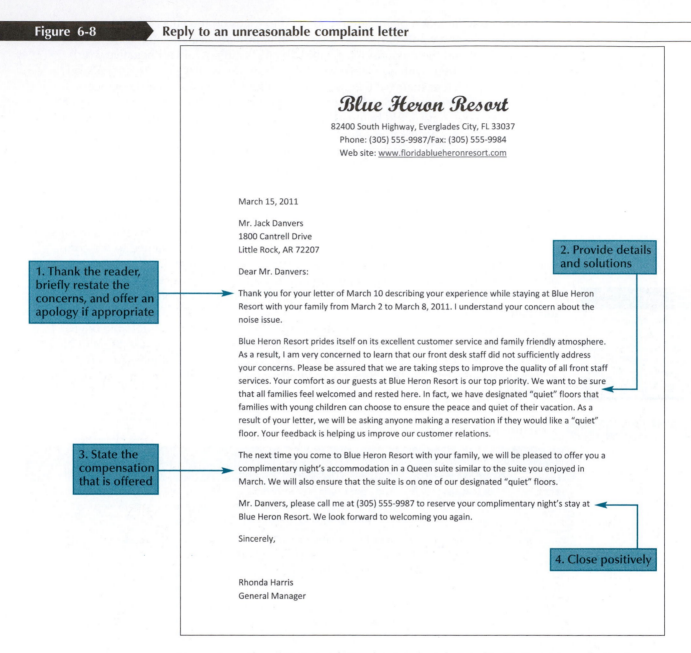

You can use the acceptance letter structure you learned in Project 4 to reply to a complaint letter that includes a request for compensation that you are able to grant. Figure 6-9 shows a positive reply to a reasonable complaint letter.

Figure 6-9	Positive reply to a reasonable complaint letter

Mr. Jack Danvers
1800 Cantrell Drive
Little Rock, AR 72207

Dear Mr. Danvers:

Thank you for your letter of March 10 describing your experience while staying at Blue Heron Resort with your family from March 2 to March 8, 2011. I am pleased to send you the refund you requested. The check is enclosed. I am also enclosing a $50 certificate, which you can use for room service, in one of our fine restaurants, or at our gift shop during your next visit.

Blue Heron Resort prides itself on its excellent customer service and family friendly atmosphere. As a result, I am very concerned to learn that our front desk staff did not sufficiently address your concerns. Please be assured that we are taking steps to improve the quality of all front staff services. Your comfort as our guests at Blue Heron Resort is our top priority. We want to be sure that all families feel welcomed and rested here.

Mr. Danvers, please call me at (305) 555-9987 when you are ready to reserve your next vacation at Blue Heron Resort. We look forward to welcoming you again.

Most people would prefer not to write, receive, or reply to complaint letters. However, when a complaint letter must be made or replied to, a focus on the facts and the use of a reasonable tone will help ensure a positive outcome.

Technology Skills – Creating Envelopes and Labels

After you have written a letter, you need to send it to the reader. In additional to having professional-looking letterhead, you can also create envelopes with typed addresses and return addresses. In Word, you can add an envelope to a letter and then print both at once. You can also print multiple addresses on sheets of labels, which are available at office supply stores. The Technology Skills steps cover these skills:

- Add an envelope to a letter
- Create a sheet of labels
- Modify a sheet of labels

To add an envelope to a business letter:

1. Open the file **Tech_06.docx** located in the Project.06 folder included with your Data Files, and then to avoid altering the original file, save the document as **Complaint Reply with Envelope** in the same folder.

2. Select the letterhead text from Bridges Bistro through the Web site address, press [**Ctrl**]+[**C**] to copy the letterhead onto the Clipboard, and then click away from the address to deselect it.

3. Click the **Mailings** tab, and then click **Envelopes** in the Create group. The Envelopes and Labels dialog box opens with the Envelopes tab active. Notice that the delivery address is already entered in the Delivery address area.

4. Click **Options**, click **Font** under Delivery address, select the **Calibri** font and **11 pt**, click **OK**, and then click **OK** again. The delivery address appears in the Calibri font.

5. Click in the blank box below Return address, and then press [**Ctrl**]+[**V**] to paste the company letterhead.

Tip

If the return address (in this example, Bridges Bistro) appears in the Delivery address area, click Cancel, and then in the document, click away from the selected text and repeat step 3.

6. Change the font for the return address to **Calibri** and **11 pt**. The Envelopes and Labels dialog box appears as shown in Figure 6-10.

Figure 6-10 ⟩ Envelopes and Labels dialog box

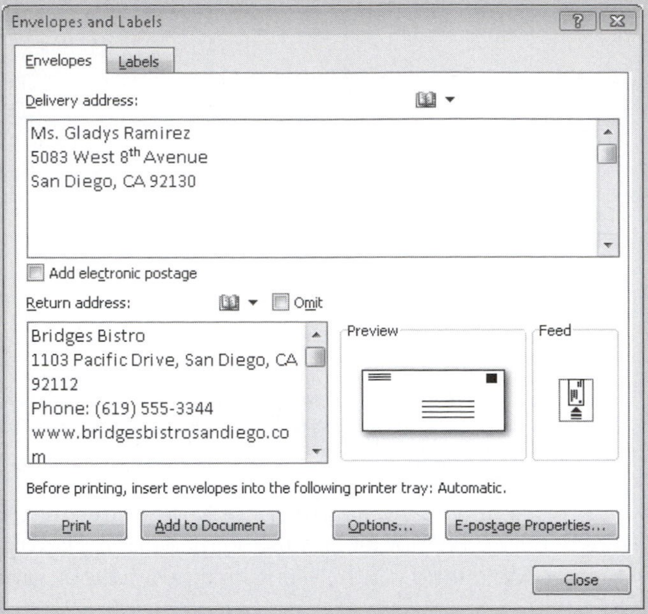

7. Click **Add to Document**, and then click **No** in response to the message. The envelope is added to the document.

8. Select **Bridges Bistro**, and then change the font to **Broadway** and the font size to **16 pt**.

9. Scroll down to view the letter, type your name where indicated in the complimentary closing, and then print a copy. If you have an envelope, you can insert it in your printer; otherwise, you can print both the envelope text and the letter on plain paper. If you are working with a network printer, you might need to check the printer settings before you print an envelope, even if you print it on plain paper. Check with your instructor or technical support person, if necessary.

10. Save the document and keep it open.

You can create sheets of labels for a wide variety of label types, including small address labels, shipping labels, business cards, nametags, and so on. You purchase the labels at an office supply store, and then format and print the labels in Word. Next, you create a sheet of labels.

To create a sheet of labels:

1. Scroll to the top of the document to view the envelope, click anywhere in the envelope area, click the **Mailings** tab, and then click **Labels** in the Create group.

2. Click the **Use return address** check box, and then click **Options**. In the Label Options dialog box, you can select the label style you require, depending on what kind of labels you purchase.

3. Verify that **Microsoft** appears in the Label vendors box, or click the list arrow and select Microsoft if another company name appears, click the second instance of **30 Per Page**, verify that the Height of the selected label type is 1" and the Width is 2.63" as shown in the Label information area, and then click **OK**.

Tip

If you are printing with real labels rather than on plain paper, you will find a code on the label package. You can use the code to select the label format you want.

4. Click **New Document** and then click **No** in response to the message. A sheet of labels appears.

On the sheet of labels you created, the return address is not formatted the way you want it to be. For example, the font sizes are not what you want and the street address, city, state, and ZIP code are all on one line. When you create a sheet of labels, you often need to experiment to find the best way of fitting the text onto the label. Next, you modify the labels so they are formatted attractively.

To modify a sheet of labels:

1. Close the document without saving it, click **Labels** in the Create group, click the **Use return address** check box, select **Bridges Bistro**, right-click the selected text, click **Font**, change the font size to **14 pt**, and then click **OK**.
2. Select all the address text (from 1103 to the end of the Web address), right-click the selected text, change the font size to **9 pt**, click **OK**, click **New Document**, and then click **No** again in response to the message. The sheet of labels looks better, but the street address should be evenly distributed across two lines.
3. Close the document without saving it, open the Envelopes and Labels dialog box again, click the **Use return address** check box again, click after **Drive**, delete the **comma** and the space that follows it, and then press the **Enter** key.
4. Select **Bridges Bistro**, right-click the selected text, click **Font**, verify the font size is **16 pt**, and then click **OK**.
5. Select all the address text (from 1103 to the end of the Web address), right-click the selected text, change the font size to **9 pt**, click **OK**, click **New Document**, click **No** in response to the message again, and then compare the label sheet to Figure 6-11.

Figure 6-11 Correctly formatted label sheet

Bridges Bistro 1103 Pacific Drive San Diego, CA 92112 Phone: (619) 555-3344 www.bridgesbistrosandiego.com	**Bridges Bistro** 1103 Pacific Drive San Diego, CA 92112 Phone: (619) 555-3344 www.bridgesbistrosandiego.com	**Bridges Bistro** 1103 Pacific Drive San Diego, CA 92112 Phone: (619) 555-3344 www.bridgesbistrosandiego.com
Bridges Bistro 1103 Pacific Drive San Diego, CA 92112 Phone: (619) 555-3344 www.bridgesbistrosandiego.com	**Bridges Bistro** 1103 Pacific Drive San Diego, CA 92112 Phone: (619) 555-3344 www.bridgesbistrosandiego.com	**Bridges Bistro** 1103 Pacific Drive San Diego, CA 92112 Phone: (619) 555-3344 www.bridgesbistrosandiego.com
Bridges Bistro 1103 Pacific Drive San Diego, CA 92112 Phone: (619) 555-3344 www.bridgesbistrosandiego.com	**Bridges Bistro** 1103 Pacific Drive San Diego, CA 92112 Phone: (619) 555-3344 www.bridgesbistrosandiego.com	**Bridges Bistro** 1103 Pacific Drive San Diego, CA 92112 Phone: (619) 555-3344 www.bridgesbistrosandiego.com
Bridges Bistro 1103 Pacific Drive San Diego, CA 92112 Phone: (619) 555-3344 www.bridgesbistrosandiego.com	**Bridges Bistro** 1103 Pacific Drive San Diego, CA 92112 Phone: (619) 555-3344 www.bridgesbistrosandiego.com	**Bridges Bistro** 1103 Pacific Drive San Diego, CA 92112 Phone: (619) 555-3344 www.bridgesbistrosandiego.com

6. Scroll to the bottom of the label sheet, replace the company name in the last label with your name, save the label sheet as **Label Sheet**, print a copy of the label sheet on plain paper, and then close the document.
7. Close the Complaint Reply with Envelope document.

Practice | Reply to Complaint Letter

You have just started working as the office manager for Greenock Communications, a new company that provides communications training seminars to clients in the Phoenix area. The overwhelming majority of participants in the seminars offered by Greenock Communications are extremely pleased with the quality of the teaching and the materials. However, occasionally, a participant is not satisfied with a seminar and sends a complaint letter or e-mail.

Follow the steps below to reply to the complaint letter shown in Figure 6-12 and then add an envelope and print a sheet of labels for the company.

Figure 6-12 **Complaint letter requiring a reply**

Sir/Madam:

I took your one-day Communication Skills seminar on March 3, 2011 at the Royal Phoenix Hotel and I wish to register my dissatisfaction with the experience.

The temperature in the room was either too hot or too cold, making learning a real chore. The seminar leader did try to remedy the situation, but to no avail. Several times I made my dissatisfaction known to her. In fact, at the end of the day, I asked for a refund, but to no avail. Apparently the deal was that I had attended the entire day and so presumably received some benefit.

Well, I'm not sure I did! Most of the time I was either sweating or shivering—a situation I find unacceptable. However, I must say that the leader did manage to impart some useful tips about communicating in the workplace.

Finally, the lunch provided was not vegetarian. I feel you should offer this option. In short, I would appreciate a full refund on the seminar.

1. Read the complaint letter shown in Figure 6-12 and note that the seminar participant requests a full refund for a seminar because the room temperature was not to his liking and because he did not receive a vegetarian meal at lunch. Note also that the participant stayed the entire day and felt that the seminar leader had imparted some useful information.
2. Open the file **Practice_06.docx** located in the Project.06 folder included with your Data Files and then, to avoid altering the original file, save the document as **Greenock Communications Reply to Complaint Letter**.
3. Note the directions in each paragraph and then replace the placeholder text with the required text. You cannot give the client a full refund; however, you can offer him a 10% discount off the next seminar he takes.
4. Enter your name where indicated in the complimentary closing.
5. Create an envelope for the letter, and then format the return and delivery addresses with the Calibri font and 11 pt.
6. On the envelope, change the font for the company name Greenock Communications to Impact and 14 pt.
7. Print a copy of the letter and envelope, and then save the document.
8. Create a sheet of labels using the return address; select Microsoft as the label vendor if it is not already selected, and then select the second listing for 30 Per Page in the Label Options dialog box.

9. Scroll to the bottom of the page, replace the company name in the last label with your name, save the label sheet as **Greenock Communications Label Sheet**, print a copy, and then close the document.

10. Close the letter document.

Revise	**Complaint Letter**

You work for Anderson Transport, a company that manages a fleet of luxury coach busses in Indianapolis and that specializes in providing coach busses for tours, weddings, corporate dinners, and other special events. A coworker has just had a negative experience with a printer and has written an angry complaint letter. Your coworker knows that the complaint letter is too harsh and asks you to rewrite it using a positive tone and including a request for specific compensation.

Follow the steps below to write a complaint letter that is likely to get positive results, and then add an envelope and print a sheet of labels for the company Anderson Transport.

1. Open the file **Revise_06.docx** located in the Project.06 folder included with your Data Files and then, to avoid altering the original file, save the document as **Anderson Transport Complaint Letter** in the same folder.

2. Read the letter and note its negative tone.

3. Write a new first paragraph that consists of two sentences. The first sentence should state clearly that you are informing the company about a concern you have with the lack of service you received for a recent rush order you placed with Printing Pals. The second sentence should state that Anderson Transport has been a customer of Printing Pals for several years and that you have been pleased with the service you received in the past.

4. Edit the current second paragraph to summarize your concerns. Use a neutral tone.

5. Write a third paragraph that states exactly what compensation you expect. In this instance, you feel that a free print run for 500 brochures might be reasonable. Also inquire how you should transmit the digital files in the future.

6. Complete the letter with a positive closing. If you wish, you can ask the reader to call you to discuss your proposal for compensation. Also mention that you hope Anderson Transport can continue to do business with Printing Pals.

7. Type your name where indicated in the complimentary closing, create an envelope for the letter, and then format the return and delivery addresses with the Calibri font and 11 pt.

8. On the envelope, change the font for the company Anderson Transport name to Tahoma and 16 pt, and the color to Olive Green, Accent 3, Darker 50%.

9. Print a copy of the letter and envelope, and then save the document.

10. With your insertion point on the envelope, create a sheet of labels for the company Anderson Transport (select Microsoft as the label vendor if it is not already selected, then select the second listing for 30 Per Page in the Label Options dialog box). To fit all the information on the label, you will need to modify the font size of the text. To modify a portion of a label in the Address box, select the text you want to change, right-click, click Font, and then select the required options. For example, you could change the font size of the company name Anderson Transport to 12 pt and the font size of the address information to 9 pt.

11. Replace the company name in the last label with your name, save the label sheet as **Anderson Transport Label Sheet**, print a copy, close the document, and then close the letter document.

Create		**Refusal Letter**

You can use the refusal letter structure to help you write refusal letters in a wide range of situations—from business to personal. Think of a situation in which you need to say *no* to someone who has considerable emotional or financial investment in a positive outcome. For example, you may need to say no to a community service group that has asked you to assist with an important fund-raising drive for which your skills are in great demand.

Follow the steps below to write your refusal letter so that it uses the five-paragraph structure, and then add an envelope and print a sheet of labels containing your name and address.

1. Complete the table below with the information you need to help you write the refusal letter. Note that you will need to make up information. Use fictitious but realistic details.

Information for a Refusal Letter
What is the name and address of the person who will receive your letter?
What is the request that you need to refuse?
Is there something you can thank the reader for? If yes, what?
What is the context for the refusal?
What is the positive alternative?

2. Create a new document in Word, and then save it as **Refusal Letter**.
3. Create an attractive letterhead using your own name and address information.
4. Include the current date below the letterhead and then enter the information for the inside address two lines below the date. Note that you can change the line spacing to 1.0 and remove After spacing so that the inside address information is single-spaced.
5. Include a salutation.
6. Start paragraph 1 by thanking the reader. For example, the opening to a letter related to a request for assistance at a fund-raising event could be: *Thank you for asking me to run the Holiday Book Fair fund-raiser for Literacy Now.* Follow this sentence with a sentence that extends goodwill.
7. In paragraph 2, provide the context for the refusal. Note that paragraph 2 is the most important (and the most difficult) paragraph to write in a refusal letter. Your goal is to lead the reader slowly toward the realization that you will be refusing the request. You want the reader to say no to him or herself before you do and to recognize that your refusal is both fair and reasonable.
8. Write a third paragraph that says no politely and respectfully.
9. Write a fourth paragraph that provides the reader with a positive alternative. For example, you could offer to take on another role at a future event or recommend someone who can take your place.

10. Close positively with a request for the reader to contact you if he or she has further questions, and include your name in the complimentary closing.
11. Create an envelope for the letter, and then format the return and delivery addresses with the Calibri font and 11 pt. Format your name differently from the rest of the address information.
12. Save the document, and then print a copy of the envelope and letter.
13. Create a sheet of labels for your name and address (select Microsoft as the label vendor if it is not already selected, and then select the second listing for 30 Per Page in the Label Options dialog box). Format your name with a different font and a larger font size. Note that you may need to generate a few sheets of labels before you are satisfied with the placement of your name and address information on each label. Experiment with different font sizes and line breaks.
14. Save the label sheet as **Refusal Letter Label Sheet**, print a copy, and then close the document. Do not save any of the label sheets that you do not intend to keep.
15. Close the letter document.

| Apply | **Case Study 1** |

Capstone College One of your duties as the program assistant for the Digital Arts Department at Capstone College in San Francisco is to inform students who have applied to one of the department's programs that they have not been accepted. Until recently, a very abrupt and unnecessarily dismissive refusal letter was sent to unsuccessful applicants. Fortunately, the new department head recognizes that these letters do not build goodwill for the department. He asks you to revise the current refusal letter so that it uses the five-paragraph refusal letter structure. To complete this case study, you rewrite the refusal letter.

1. Open the file **Case1_06.docx** located in the Project.06 folder included with your Data Files, and then save the document as **Digital Arts Refusal Letter** in the same folder.
2. Read the letter and note its dismissive and unpleasant tone.
3. Write a new first paragraph that consists of two sentences. The first sentence should thank the reader for applying to a program in the Digital Arts Department at Capstone College on a particular date, and the second sentence should extend goodwill. Note that you can use placeholders to indicate where variable information will be inserted. For example, [PROGRAM NAME] could be a placeholder since it will vary from letter to letter. Most refusal letters can be written as from letters so long as care is taken to include some personalized information.
4. Write a new second paragraph that provides the context for the refusal. Here is some information you might want to adapt:
   - The Digital Arts Department at Capstone College receives approximately 300 applications every year for 30 places in each of its three programs.
   - Applications come from all over the country, even from Canada and Mexico.
   - Most of the successful applicants have already had professional exhibitions; many have work experience in the digital animation field.
   Make sure that the second paragraph leads the reader slowly toward the no but that the reader can understand that the refusal is fair and reasonable.
5. Write a third paragraph that says no politely and respectfully.
6. Write a fourth paragraph that provides the reader with a positive alternative. You can refer the reader to the Web site of other colleges or programs that offer preparatory courses that the applicant could take before applying again for another term.
7. Complete the letter with a positive closing.

8. Type your name where indicated in the complimentary closing, save the document, and then print the letter.

9. Create a sheet of labels for Capstone College (select Microsoft as the label vendor if it is not already selected, and then select the second listing for 30 Per Page in the Label Options dialog box). Format the college name with a different font, size, and color. Note that you may need to generate a few sheets of labels before you are satisfied with the placement of the college name and address information on each label. Experiment with different font sizes and line breaks.

10. Replace the college name in the last label with your name, save the label sheet as **Digital Arts Labels**, print a copy, and then close the document. Do not save any of the label sheets that you do not intend to keep.

11. Close the letter document.

<table>
<tr><td>Apply</td><td>| Case Study 2</td></tr>
</table>

Otter Bay Kayaking Adventures   As one of Juneau's premier adventure tour companies, Otter Bay Kayaking Adventures has an excellent reputation for its superb customer service and the quality of the gourmet boxed lunches that every guest on a kayaking or whitewater rafting tour receives. The local company that supplies the boxed lunches was purchased recently by a large company based in Seattle. Unfortunately, the new company is supplying a much lower quality product. As a result, Otter Bay Kayaking Adventures has been receiving complaints from its guests about the stale sandwiches, bruised fruit, and tasteless cookies included in the boxed lunches. As the company's office manager, you have called the supplier and complained. The person you spoke with recommended that you write a letter to the company's head office in Seattle. To complete this case study, you write a complaint letter to Lunches On The Go, the company in Seattle that contracts with companies all over the United States to supply boxed lunches.

1. Open the file **Case2_06.docx** located in the Project.06 folder included with your Data Files, and then save the document as **Kayaking Supplier Complaint Letter** in the same folder.

2. Note the directions in each paragraph and then replace the placeholder text with the required text. Remember to use a respectful tone and avoid negative words.

3. Type your name where indicated in the complimentary closing, create an envelope for the letter, and then format the return and delivery addresses with the Arial font and 11 pt. Format the company name differently from the rest of the address information.

4. Save the document, and then print a copy of the envelope and letter.

5. Create a sheet of labels for Otter Bay Kayaking Adventures (select Microsoft as the label vendor if it is not already selected, then select the second listing for 30 Per Page in the Label Options dialog box). Format the company name with the Harrington font and 12 pt. Note that you may need to generate a few sheets of labels before you are satisfied with the placement of the company name and address information on each label. Experiment with different font sizes and line breaks.

6. Replace the company name in the last label with your name, save the label sheet as **Kayaking Labels**, print a copy, and then close the document. Do not save any of the label sheets that you do not intend to keep.

7. Close the letter document.

Apply | Case Study 3

An appeal letter is similar to a refusal or complaint letter because it also uses the persuasive letter structure. You write an appeal letter in response to a refusal. For example, you might write an appeal letter in response to a denial from an insurance company to honor an insurance claim. You can use the five-paragraph persuasive letter structure to write the appeal letter so that it states your case clearly and then requests fair compensation. The tone of an appeal letter should be positive and respectful. To complete this case study, you write an appeal letter for a situation of your choice.

1. Create a new document in Word, and then save it as **Appeal Letter**.
2. Create an attractive letterhead using your own name and address information. If you completed the Create exercise in this project, you can copy the letterhead from that letter to the current letter or even open the letter and adapt it. You save time by adapting documents rather than creating them from scratch.
3. Include the current date below the letterhead and then enter the information for the inside address two lines below the date. Note that you can change the line spacing to 1.0 and remove After spacing so that the inside address information is single-spaced.
4. Include a salutation.
5. Start paragraph 1 by thanking the reader for the opportunity to present your appeal. Include the subject of the appeal along with the relevant dates, if appropriate, or a case reference number if you have been given one.
6. In paragraphs 2 and 3, summarize the details of the appeal in neutral language. State timelines and describe the situation. Use bulleted lists or tables, where appropriate, to present the information clearly and succinctly.
7. In paragraph 4, clearly state the compensation required, and then in paragraph 5, close positively.
8. Include your name in the complimentary closing.
9. Create an envelope for the letter, format the return and delivery addresses with the Calibri font and 11 pt, format your name differently, and then print a copy of the envelope and letter.
10. Create a sheet of labels for your name and address (select select Microsoft as the label vendor if it is not already selected, then select the second listing for 30 Per Page in the Label Options dialog box). Format your name with a different font and a larger font size. Note that you may need to generate a few sheets of labels before you are satisfied with the placement of your name and address information on each label. Experiment with different font sizes and line breaks.
11. Save the label sheet as **Appeal Letter Labels**, print a copy, and then close the document. Do not save any of the label sheets that you do not intend to keep.
12. Save and close the letter document.

Press Releases

Introduction

Many newspapers, radio stations, and television stations depend on local businesses and organizations to supply them with content for news stories, community profiles, and features. You use a press release to communicate information to the media. A **press release** is often referred to as a **media release** and can be defined as a written announcement that informs publications and other news media about an important event, product launch, or other newsworthy story. A news media organization that receives a press release is free to use the content in a news story.

In this project, you identify the audience and purpose of a press release, organize content and develop an appropriate style for a press release, and use the reviewing features in Word to revise a press release.

Starting Data Files

Project.07

Tech_07.docx
Practice_07.docx
Revise_07.docx
Case2_07.docx
Research_07.docx

Press Release Essentials

A well-written press release that an editor approves and then publishes in a newspaper or broadcasts on the radio or television can garner excellent publicity for a company or organization. However, if the sole purpose of a press release is to generate publicity, an editor will likely not publish it. A press release cannot be a thinly veiled advertisement for a company's products or services. Instead, a press release must inform the public about a newsworthy event and contain information that will be of interest to a broad general audience.

Identifying the Press Release Audience

The **primary audience** for a press release is the editor of the news media that receives the press release. Many editors receive hundreds of press releases every week. The press releases they choose to publish must have a clear news focus, provide sufficient details, require very little editing, and use a recognized press release format.

The **secondary audience** for a press release is each person who will actually read, watch, or listen to the content, whether in the newspaper, or on radio, television, or the Internet. The editor who first receives the press release must ensure that the content will interest the market served by the media. For example, a press release that gives details about an upcoming rodeo might be accepted by the local country music radio station as being of interest to its listeners, but a national classical music station would likely refuse it as having too narrow a focus for its listeners.

Selecting Suitable Subjects for Press Releases

Many subjects are suitable for a press release so long as *news* is the central focus. A description of a company's products is not news. However, an interview with an inventor about a brand new product that will have a positive effect on people's lives is a suitable subject for a press release. Sometimes, an editor sees sufficient value in the content of a press release to send a reporter and possibly a photographer to interview a representative from the company or organization and then run a feature article.

From a company's point of view, a press release is an excellent marketing tool. First, press releases cost almost nothing to produce, apart from the time required to write them. If a news organization publishes a press release, the publicity is essentially free. A press release that results in a full page news story in a local newspaper can generate far more publicity for a company than even a full page advertisement. People read news stories, while they frequently ignore or skim over advertisements. The time invested in writing good press releases is time very well spent if they get published.

Figure 7-1 includes a list of common subjects for a press release, along with examples.

Figure 7-1	Suitable subjects for a press release

Subject	Example
Opening of a new facility or business	A new gourmet restaurant that serves only locally-grown food opens in the community. The press release is suitable for local newspapers and local radio stations because local people will be the target market for the restaurant. The press release may also be suitable for the local *What's On* Web site for a particular city or town.
Charity event	A charitable organization announces an upcoming charitable event, such as a Run for Cancer. A company that is sponsoring the event could also generate the press release. The press release is suitable for local publications, local radio or television stations, and community Web sites.
Sports or cultural event	A community art gallery sponsors an exhibition of paintings by a local artist. The press release is suitable for local publications and *What's On* sections of community Web sites. If the artist is known nationally and the exhibition is in a major gallery, then the press release could also be published in a national newspaper and featured in the arts section of national news Web sites.
Launch of a new product	A software designer launches a new software program that eliminates chances of identity theft. The press release may be suitable for national publications, depending on the size of the company. The launch of a new product by a major corporation usually gets national coverage. Information about the launch of a new product by a small local company may get a mention in a local community newspaper.
Hiring of new personnel	A charitable organization hires a new director. This subject would be newsworthy if the new person has a high profile in the community, for example, a local politician. The press release would be appropriate for a local newspaper unless the company is nationwide. For example, the hiring of a new CEO for a multinational corporation could be national news.
Educational event	A local college has started to provide summer cooking camps for children taught by a renowned local chef. The press release is suitable for a local community newspaper, community radio and television stations, and local news Web sites.
Other	Promotion of a high-profile person in the community to a responsible position, the participation of a company in a community project, awards either given or received by local companies or organizations, and celebrity appearances sponsored by a local company or organization.

Organizing Content for a Press Release

A press release communicates information about a newsworthy subject and therefore uses the news story structure. In the news story structure, you organize content from most important to least important as follows:

- Include a snappy title that attracts attention.
- Provide the most important information in the first two or three sentences.
- Include sufficient details: who, what, where, when, why, and how.
- Appeal to the interests and needs of the target audience.
- Feature quotations from at least two sources, when appropriate.
- Provide the information people need in order to respond or to find additional details, when appropriate.

Figure 7-2 summarizes each of these requirements.

Figure 7-2	Organizing press release content

Press Release Element	Purpose
Title	• Summarize the subject in a few well-chosen words that grab the editor's attention. Often the title will be the only thing the editor reads before moving on to the next press release. • Limit the length of the title of a press release to approximately five words or less. Sometimes you can include a subtitle that expands on the title.
Opening paragraph	• Stimulate interest in the subject. • Answer all, or at least most, of the 5W questions: who, what, where, when, and why.
Reader benefits	• Emphasize how readers benefit from reading the content of the press release; for example, how they could benefit from participating in an event or using a new product.
Additional details	• Expand on the information provided in paragraph 1. • Where possible, present additional details in the form of quotations from people involved in the event. • Present information in order of importance to the reader.

Quotations	• Include at least one quotation and preferably two quotations from two different people. Quotations from people outside the company or organization are particularly effective because they add credibility.
	• Check with the person quoted to verify the text of the quotation. Always use the person's exact words in a quotation.
	• Ensure the person quoted plays some significant role related to the newsworthy event. Examples include:
	  • Director of the gallery, the artist, or an art critic for the opening of an art exhibition
	  • President of the company, personnel director, or person promoted for a high-level promotion
	  • Inventor/adapter of a product, president of the company, or corporate customer for a product launch
	  • Director of the charity, participant in the event, or corporate sponsor for a charity event
	  • Principal of the school or college, a student and/or parent, or the instructor for an educational event

Response information	• Where relevant, include response information that informs readers how they can respond, such as to send in registration information, or how they can obtain further information, event tickets, etc.

Developing a Press Release Style and Format

A press release should conform to a conventional style and format that editors recognize. This style includes the following components, which are also summarized in Figure 7-3.

• Contact information included at the top of the press release
• City and date entered at the beginning of paragraph 1
• Third person used throughout (except in quotations)
• Quotations punctuated correctly
• Use of conventional formatting

Figure 7-3	Formatting a press release

Formatting Element	Description
Contact information	• Place the words *PRESS RELEASE, MEDIA RELEASE,* or *NEWS RELEASE* at the top of the document. • Include the name of the person to contact for further information or clarification and the name, address, telephone number, and e-mail address of the company or organization that produced the press release. You can also choose to include the company's letterhead and logo at the top of the press release. • Include the phrase FOR IMMEDIATE RELEASE: directly below and to the right of the contact information. This phrase means that the content in the press release should be published as soon as possible. If you do not want the content published until a certain date, use the phrase FOR RELEASE AFTER [DATE].
Location information	• Include the city where the press release originated and the current date at the beginning of the first paragraph followed by a dash: • Everglades City, February 15, 2011 –
Use of third person	• Use the third person instead of the second person (you) or first person (I). • For example, in a sales letter you might write: *If you love fine food, then you're in for a treat!* In a press release, you might write: *Lovers of fine food are in for a treat.*
Punctuate quotations correctly	• Use quotation marks for spoken words as follows: • *"Don't miss this opportunity,"* urges Rhonda Harris, the General Manager of Blue Heron Resort. *"Chef Pierre will be creating a selection of hot and cold appetizers that feature herbs from his native Provence. Guests can sample such gourmet treats as brie infused with lavender and truffles with lemon thyme."*

Press release format	• Double-space the body of a press release if possible so that the text is easy to read.
	• Limit the press release to one page whenever possible.
	  • If the press release is longer than a page, write *– more –* centered at the bottom of the first page to indicate that another page follows.
	  • Alternatively, change the line spacing to 1.5 so all the text fits on one page.
	• Indent the first line of each paragraph one tab stop if it helps make the document more readable.
	• Single-space the contact information at the top of the page.
	• Use a large, sans-serif font for the title.
	• Indicate the end of the press release by centering the word –END–. Other conventions include –End–, *–30–*, or -# # #-.

Key Point

The company or organization you work for may already use a style for its press releases. This style will likely include all the components listed previously; however, if it does not, you need to use the company's style until you are given permission to modify it.

Figure 7-4 shows a sample press release for a special event—a free reception to sample the cooking of Chef Pierre, the host of *Pierre's Provence,* a local television cooking show. The event also celebrates the opening of Chez Bleu, a new restaurant at Blue Heron Resort in southwest Florida. Note how paragraph 1 uses the *5W* format to communicate the most important information and how quotations are used to provide additional details.

Figure 7-4 **Sample press release**

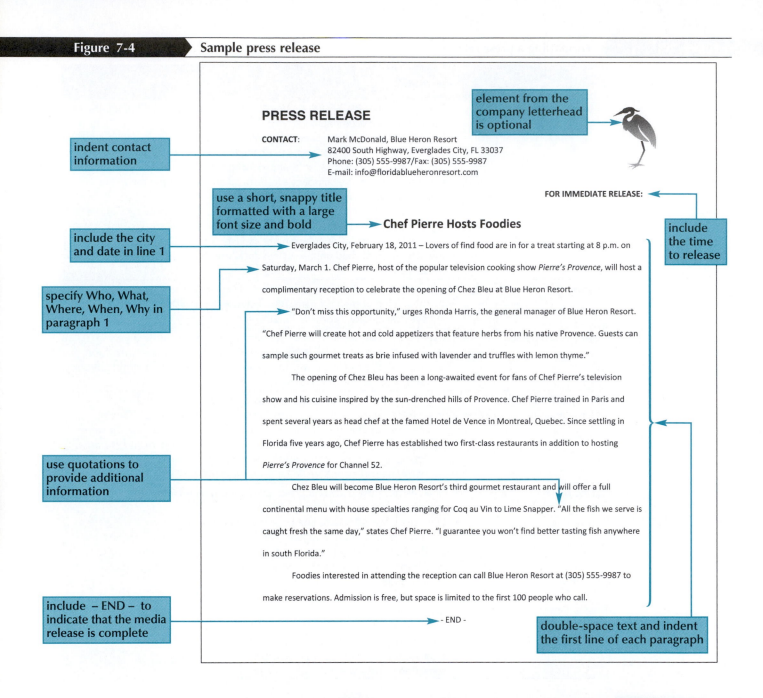

PRESS RELEASE

element from the company letterhead is optional

CONTACT: Mark McDonald, Blue Heron Resort
82400 South Highway, Everglades City, FL 33037
Phone: (305) 555-9987/Fax: (305) 555-9987
E-mail: info@floridablueheronresort.com

FOR IMMEDIATE RELEASE:

indent contact information

use a short, snappy title formatted with a large font size and bold

Chef Pierre Hosts Foodies

include the city and date in line 1

include the time to release

Everglades City, February 18, 2011 – Lovers of find food are in for a treat starting at 8 p.m. on

Saturday, March 1. Chef Pierre, host of the popular television cooking show *Pierre's Provence*, will host a

complimentary reception to celebrate the opening of Chez Bleu at Blue Heron Resort.

specify Who, What, Where, When, Why in paragraph 1

"Don't miss this opportunity," urges Rhonda Harris, the general manager of Blue Heron Resort.

"Chef Pierre will create hot and cold appetizers that feature herbs from his native Provence. Guests can

sample such gourmet treats as brie infused with lavender and truffles with lemon thyme."

The opening of Chez Bleu has been a long-awaited event for fans of Chef Pierre's television

show and his cuisine inspired by the sun-drenched hills of Provence. Chef Pierre trained in Paris and

spent several years as head chef at the famed Hotel de Vence in Montreal, Quebec. Since settling in

Florida five years ago, Chef Pierre has established two first-class restaurants in addition to hosting

Pierre's Provence for Channel 52.

use quotations to provide additional information

Chez Bleu will become Blue Heron Resort's third gourmet restaurant and will offer a full

continental menu with house specialties ranging for Coq au Vin to Lime Snapper. "All the fish we serve is

caught fresh the same day," states Chef Pierre. "I guarantee you won't find better tasting fish anywhere

in south Florida."

Foodies interested in attending the reception can call Blue Heron Resort at (305) 555-9987 to

make reservations. Admission is free, but space is limited to the first 100 people who call.

include – END – to indicate that the media release is complete

- END -

double-space text and indent the first line of each paragraph

Technology Skills – Using Reviewing Features

Once you have written and formatted one press release, you can easily adapt it for other press releases on related subjects. You use the Track Changes and Comments features on the Review tab in Microsoft Word to help you keep track of changes you make to a document. A **tracked change** is a change to the text that appears in a different format or in a balloon to the right of the text. You can also insert comments in the press release to ask a colleague questions and to clarify specific points. A **comment** is contained in a comment balloon that appears along the right side of your document. You use the Review features when you want to share writing duties with a colleague. Each person's changes are displayed in a different color so that you can see who made what changes.

The Technology Skills steps cover these skills:

- Turn on track changes
- Make changes to a document
- Insert comments
- Modify how changes appear in a document
- Review and accept changes
- Delete comments in a document

To turn on track changes and make changes to a document:

1. Start Word, open the file **Tech_07.docx** from the Project.07 folder included with your Data Files, and then to avoid altering the original file, save the document as **Tracking Changes** in the same folder.

2. Click the **Review** tab, and then click the **Track Changes** button in the Tracking group.

3. Select the name **Mark McDonald** at the top of the document, and then type **your name**.

4. Select the title **Ski for Your Heart**, and then type **Stay the Course**. The new text appears underlined and the deleted text appears as strikeout text.

5. Select **February 15** in the first line of the press release, type **April 20**, select **February 23**, type **May 3**, select **water-skiers**, and then type **runners**.

6. Select **water-ski**, type **half-**, press **Delete** to remove the extra space, select **off**, type **on**, select **Everglades Heart Fund** and type **10,000 Islands Community School**, and then scroll up so the title appears at the top of the screen. The changes to the title and paragraph 1 appear as shown in Figure 7-5.

Figure 7-5   **Changes to paragraph 1 of the adapted press release**

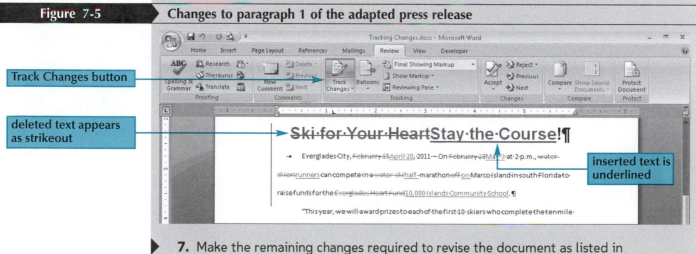

Track Changes button

deleted text appears as strikeout

inserted text is underlined

7. Make the remaining changes required to revise the document as listed in Figure 7-6.

Figure 7-6 **List of changes required**

Location	Original Text	Revised Text
Paragraph 2	skiers	runners
	ten (and the space following)	13- (close up the space following the dash if necessary)
	Mary-Low Knutson, chairperson	Janice Lee, principal
	Everglades Heart Fund	10,000 Islands Community School
	skier	runner
Paragraph 3	Liam McGregor	Marissa Schmidt
	gold	silver
	Water Skiing	Marathon
	Mr. McGregor	Ms. Schmidt
	give a demonstration of his incredible water-skiing skills.	hold a 30-minute running clinic for all participants.
Paragraph 5	water-ski	half- (close up the space following the dash if necessary)
	a CAT scanner for the Everglades Heart Fund	computers for the 10,000 Islands Community School

Comments are a useful way to communicate about specific details in a document, especially when you are collaborating with colleagues on the document. You might insert a comment to remind a colleague to check a fact or to explain to colleagues why you are suggesting a certain change. Each comment you insert appears in a comment balloon in the right margin. You use tools on the Reviewing tab in Word to navigate from one comment to another comment and to delete comments. Next, you insert a comment in a document.

To insert comments in a document:

1. Select the text **luxury weekend getaway** in the second paragraph.

2. Click the **New Comment** button in the Comments group, and then type **Should we also include a gourmet dinner for two?** The comment appears in a comment balloon as shown in Figure 7-7.

Figure 7-7 | **New comment**

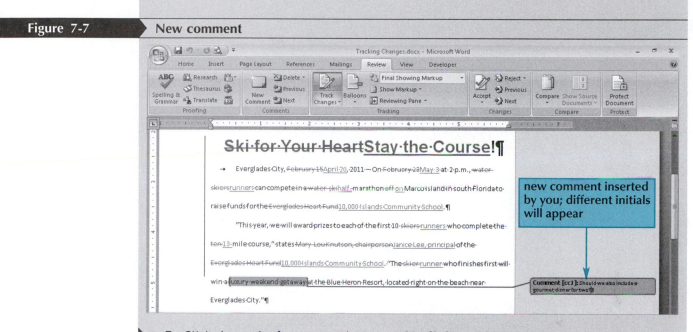

> **3.** Click the **main document**, then press [**Ctrl**]+[**Home**] to move to the top of the document.

By default, each reviewer is assigned a different color. A person looking at a document that includes tracked changes and comments can quickly determine which person made which edits and inserted which comments based on the color. In addition to color, markups such as insertions and deletions appear a certain way by default. You can modify how tracked changes and comments appear in a document to best meet your working style. Next, you modify how tracked changes and comments appear in a document.

To modify how changes and comments appear in a document:

1. Click the **Track Changes** list arrow in the Tracking group, and then click **Change Tracking Options**.

2. Click the **Insertions** list arrow, and then click **Double underline**. In the Track Changes Options dialog box, you can modify both the style and the color of every change you make to a document when the Track Changes button is active.

3. In the Balloons section at the bottom of the Track Changes Options dialog box, change the Preferred width of the balloon to **2"**.

4. Compare your screen to Figure 7-8 on the next page, then click **OK**. Double underlining appears under all the new text you inserted in the document and the comment is now 2" wide.

Figure 7-8 Track Changes Options dialog box

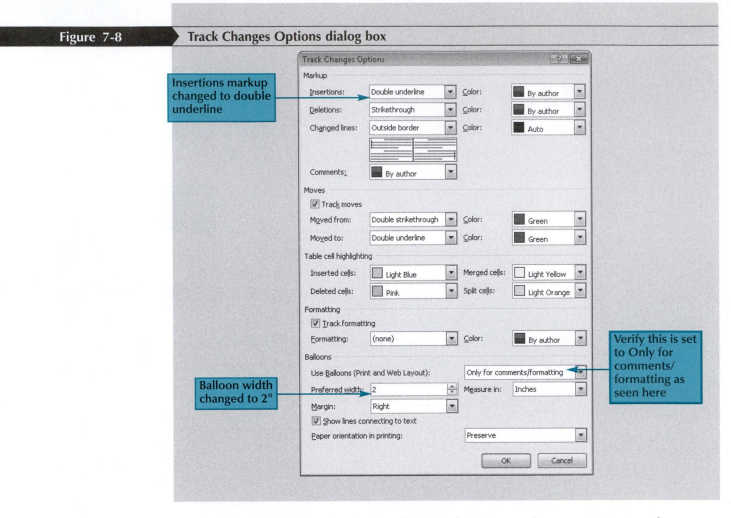

Insertions markup changed to double underline

Balloon width changed to 2"

Verify this is set to Only for comments/ formatting as seen here

In order to finalize a document with tracked changes and comments, you need to go through the document and accept or reject all tracked changes, and then delete all comments. Next, you review and accept changes, and delete all comments.

To review and accept changes in a document:

▶ 1. Click the **Next** button in the Changes group to move to the first change in the document, which is the deletion of Mark McDonald and the insertion of your name.

▶ 2. Click the **Accept** button to accept the deletion of *Mark McDonald*, and then click the **Accept** button again to accept the insertion of your name.

▶ 3. Click the **Next** button in the Comments group to highlight the comment, and then read the comment. After reading the comment, you delete the comment and make an addition to the text.

▶ 4. Click the **Delete** button in the Comments group, type **and a gourmet dinner for two**, and then press the **Spacebar**.

▶ 5. Press [**Ctrl**]+[**Home**] to move to the top of the document, click the **Accept** list arrow in the Changes group, and then click **Accept All Changes in Document**.

▶ 6. Click the **Track Changes list arrow** in the Tracking group, click **Change Tracking Options**, click the **Insertions** list arrow, click **Underline**, change the Preferred width of the balloon back to **3"**, and then click **OK**.

▶ 7. Click the **Track Changes button** to turn off track changes, print a copy of the final version of the revised press release, and then close the document.

Practice | Special Event Press Release

Local author Jared McGuire has just published a book called *Greenways* that provides people with tips on how to *go green* in their daily lives. To help promote the book, Jared will read excerpts at a book launch event to be held at a local community center. As part of his efforts to promote the event, Jared asks you to write a press release that he will send to three local newspapers and a community Web site.

Figure 7-9 includes answers to the 5W questions related to Jared's book launch. You will use this information in the press release.

Figure 7-9   **5W questions for book launch press release**

Question	Details
Who would be interested in the book launch?	People who want to find ways to save money and help improve the environment; members of local environmental groups.
Who is Jared McGuire?	Jared McGuire is the author of six books on a variety of topics related to the environment, including community initiatives, climate change, recycling, and energy options. He is also a frequent contributor to local and national publications and is often asked to speak about environmental issues. In addition, Jared teaches environmental science at Westview Community College. In 2009, Jared was awarded a gold medal by *Green Shift,* a national organization dedicated to helping people make positive changes in their lives.
What is the book?	*Greenways* is packed full of information to help people save money by *going green*. As Jared states, *Even small changes can make a big difference. In this book, you'll learn how to make saving energy a fun and easy activity that can involve the whole family.* *Greenways* is published by Global Press and will be available for sale at the book launch for $28.95.
Where is the book launch?	The book launch will be held in the lounge at the Westview Community Center at 555 Westview Road in your town. Refreshments will be provided.
When is the book launch?	Date: Two weeks from the current date Time: 7 p.m. to 9 p.m.
Why did Jared write the book?	Jared wants to share his *going green* tips with people and reassure them that even the smallest changes make a difference. Jared also plans to donate 20% of the sale price of each book to fund a new recycling program at Westview College.

Follow the steps below to write the press release for Jared.

1. Open the file **Practice_07.docx** from the Project.07 folder included with your Data Files, and then to avoid altering the original file, save the document as **Book Launch Press Release** in the same folder.
2. Where indicated, enter your name in the Contact line.
3. Write a snappy but informative title for the press release. Remember to limit the title if possible to five words or less. A good title should motivate an editor to read the press release.
4. Enter the name of your town or city and the current date in the space provided at the beginning of paragraph 1. Write the first paragraph of the press release. Remember to include brief answers to all the 5W questions, and write the paragraph to engage the reader's interest.

5. In paragraph 2, write a quotation from Melissa Renfrew, the science editor of the local newspaper (you determine the name of the newspaper). Melissa describes *Greenways* and stresses how people can learn what small changes they can make in their lives to save money and energy. You can adapt any of the information in Figure 7-9 for use in Melissa's quotation.

6. In paragraph 3, describe Jared's credentials. The purpose of this paragraph is to give Jared credibility so that people will be motivated to come to the book launch to listen to Jared read excerpts from *Greenways*. You can adapt the information provided in Figure 7-9 and make up additional information.

7. In paragraph 4, include a quotation from Jared that provides additional information about the book. Adapt information from Figure 7-9 and make up additional information.

8. In the final paragraph, include information about the cost of the book, the availability of refreshments at the book launch, and any additional information you have not already covered in the body of the press release.

9. Turn on Track Changes, add one comment to the document, insert a word or phrase, and then delete a word or phrase. You can choose to insert text to replace the text you delete.

10. Make sure the press release fits on one page. If the press release is longer than a page, either reduce the text or change the line spacing to 1.5. Print a copy of the press release, then save and close the file.

Revise | **New Restaurant Opening Press Release**

The owner of Blue Sky Bistro, a new restaurant in Seattle, has asked you to write a press release to announce the restaurant's grand opening. To help you get started, the owner sends you a press release he wrote for a restaurant he owns on Orcas Island in the San Juan Islands and asks you to adapt it for Blue Sky Bistro. In business, you can save time by revising an existing document rather than always creating a new document from scratch.

Follow the steps below to revise a press release.

1. Open the file **Revise_07.docx** from the Project.07 folder included with your Data Files, and then to avoid altering the original file, save the document as **Blue Sky Bistro Press Release** in the same folder.
2. Read the text of the press release, read all the comments, and note where changes are required. You may need to increase the zoom so that you can clearly read the text in the comment balloons.
3. Turn on track changes.
4. Revise the text of the press release as directed in the comments. You choose how and where you include the information supplied in the comments. Note that some of the required changes (for example, each instance of the restaurant name and the gender of the chef) are not highlighted by a comment. The owner presumes you will read the text closely to determine exactly what changes are needed to promote the opening of Blue Sky Bistro. You can make up additional information about the chef and the menu if needed, but limit the length of the press release to one page double-spaced.
5. Type **PRESS RELEASE** in bold at the top of the document and then after the last line in the press release, type and center the word **-End-** with dashes on either side. Note that you will need to undo the automatic bullet feature.
6. Double-space the press release and increase the font size of the title to 16-point.
7. Delete the comments.
8. Type your name where indicated in the contact line, save the document, then print a copy with all the tracked changes showing. Note that the press release will probably print over two pages because the tracked changes are showing.
9. Save the document again as **Blue Sky Bistro Press Release_Changes Accepted**.
10. Accept all the changes you made, adjust line spacing where necessary so the press release fits on one page, save the document, and then print a copy.

Create	**Charity Event Press Release**

You are working with a charitable organization that is putting on a special fund-raising event. You can choose the organization and the type of event. For example, a local hospital could sponsor a fun run to raise funds for a new piece of equipment, a non-profit community choir could put on a concert to raise funds to finance the choir's tour to Europe, or an affordable housing association could ask for volunteers to help build a house for a family in need.

Follow the steps below to create a press release.

1. Complete the table below with information about your charity event.

Information for a Press Release
What is the name of the charitable organization?
What is the event?
Why is the event being held?
Who benefits from the event? (e.g., for what purpose will the funds raised be used?)
Who will participate in the event?
When and where will the event be held?
Other questions

2. In Word, set up the press release using the format you learned in this project. Refer to Figure 7-4. Include your name in the contact information and single space the information.
3. Using the information you have developed about the charitable organization and the special event, write a one-page press release that includes a snappy title, at least four paragraphs, and appropriate quotations from two people. You can use the quotations to provide additional information about the event and the charitable organization, and to describe how the funds raised from the event will be used.
4. Format the press release attractively. Note that you can change the line spacing to 1.5 if all the text does not fit on one page. You can also remove extra space before and after paragraphs.
5. Save the press release as **Charity Press Release**, print a copy, and then close the document.
6. E-mail your press release to a colleague with instructions for them to turn on track changes, edit the press release, add comments where needed, save the press release as **Charity Press Release_Edited**, and then e-mail it back to you.
7. When you receive the edited press release, accept or reject changes, attend to the comments and then delete them, save a copy as **Charity Press Release_Revised**, print a copy of the revised press release, and then close the document.

Apply | Case Study 1

Capstone College   The Digital Arts Department at Capstone College in San Francisco, California, trains students in the very latest technology for jobs as animators, graphic artists, and video game developers. You work as a program assistant for the Digital Arts Department and have been asked to draft a press release to announce an exhibition of final projects by students graduating from the Digital Arts program. Figure 7-10 shows the information required for the press release. To complete this case study, you will write a press release using the information provided in Figure 7-10.

Figure 7-10 | **Information for Lakeview College press release**

Question	Description
Contact:	Capstone College, 640 Wharf Street San Francisco, CA 94133 (415) 555-9908; e-mail: info@capstonedigitalarts.com
What	Grand opening of the exhibition of final projects by students graduating from the Digital Arts program at Capstone College. Students have conceived, written, developed, and produced animations, software applications, and video games.
Who	Graduating seniors exhibiting their final projects.
Where	Capstone College Digital Arts Department in the Golden Gate Building, Room 2344.
When	The gala opening on May 18, 2011 from 6 p.m. to 9 p.m. is catered by students in Capstone College's Professional Chef program. The exhibition runs from May 18 to June 1.
Why	To showcase work by the entertainers of tomorrow. The projects these students have done provide a window into the future of animation, video games, and software development. Anyone who has ever played a video game or watched an animated movie or loaded a new software application will enjoy seeing the explosive creativity on display. All the students in this popular program get jobs within six months of graduation.
How	Tickets for the gala opening are available from any Digital Arts program student, from the Digital Arts Department office in the Golden Gate Building, and from the Student Union Building.
People to quote	• Mansur Singh, the faculty coordinator of the program • Donovan Voort, the president of Digital Divide, a large employer of students from the Capstone College Digital Arts program • Shari Eng, the top student in the program; her animated short film won *Best New Animation of the Year* from the California Film Fund • Wanda Bradley, faculty coordinator of the Professional Chef program

1. In Word, set up the press release using the format you learned in this project. Include your name in the contact information and single-space the information.

2. Using the information shown in Figure 7-10, write a one-page press release that includes a snappy title, at least four paragraphs, and appropriate quotations. Note that you should include quotations from two different people; you do not need to include quotations from all four people listed in Figure 7-10.

3. Format the press release attractively. Note that you can change the line spacing to 1.5 if all the text does not fit on one page. You can also remove extra line space before and after paragraphs.

4. Save the press release as **Digital Arts Press Release**, print a copy, and then close the document.

Apply	**Case Study 2**

Otter Bay Kayaking Adventures Tourists from all over the world enjoy kayaking trips led by the friendly guides at Otter Bay Kayaking Adventures in Juneau, Alaska. As an assistant in the Marketing Department, you are responsible for developing sales materials, dealing with customers, and announcing special events to the local media. To complete this case study, you will write a press release on behalf of Otter Bay Kayaking Adventures.

1. Open the file **Case2_07.docx** located in the Project.07 folder included with your Data Files. This document contains the source material you need to write the required documents.
2. Read the information in the document carefully to learn about Otter Bay Kayaking Adventures and determine the current requirements.
3. Start a new document in Word, and then, referring to the Information file, write and format a press release that announces a charity sea kayak race sponsored by Otter Bay Kayaking Adventures to raise money and food items for the local food bank.
4. Include your name as the contact person, save the press release as **Kayaking Press Release**, print a copy, and then close the document.

Research	**Case Study 3**

The Internet contains a wealth of information that you can use to help you determine where to send completed press releases. To complete this case study, you will gather information about local publications and other media outlets in your home town.

1. Open the file **Research_07.docx** located in the Project.07 folder in your Data Files, and then save the document as **Researching Media Companies** in the same folder.
2. Open your Web browser, and then search for companies in your home town that would be interested in receiving press releases. You can look for local newspapers, radio stations, and television stations.
3. Find contact information for five companies and enter the information in the space provided in the Researching Media Companies document. In the Description area, summarize how to submit a press release to this company. You should be able to find this information somewhere on the company's Web site, often from a *Contact Us* link.
4. Type your name in the footer where indicated, save the document, print a copy, and then close the document.

Proposals

Objectives

- Identify proposal types
- Develop proposal content
- Structure a proposal
- Format a proposal
- Outline a document in Word
- Generate a table of contents in Word
- Create sections in a Word document
- Insert headers, footers, and page numbers in Word

Introduction

You write a **proposal** when you need to persuade the reader to take a specific course of action with respect to a situation that requires significant effort and cost. For example, you could write a proposal to obtain $20,000 from a local school board to build a new playground at an elementary school, or you could write a proposal to request a partnership with a company that distributes the products you manufacture.

In this project, you explore types of proposals, identify the content required for a proposal, examine ways in which you can structure and format a proposal, and then work in Word to outline a document, generate a table of contents, create sections, and insert headers, footers, and page numbers.

Starting Data Files

Project.08

Tech_08.docx
Practice_08.docx
Revise_08.docx
Case1_08.docx
Case2_08.docx
Research_08.docx

Proposal Essentials

In many professions, your ability to write compelling proposals will help you progress in your career. You can train yourself to recognize opportunities by keeping an open mind and by asking questions. For example, if a procedure that you have been following for months seems outdated and perhaps even counterproductive, you could try approaching your supervisor and asking if you could write a proposal that describes and recommends a more effective procedure. Figure 8-1 lists some common reasons for writing proposals and provides examples.

Figure 8-1 ▶ **Reasons for writing proposals**

Reason	Example
To present a new idea to another company or within your own company	Obtain permission to develop a new 10-month certificate program called *Executive Administration* at a local college or university
To request funding for a project you want to complete	Obtain funding from a local government to hold an arts fair in the community; the government may supply forms that the proposer must complete with the proposal information
To propose a partnership with another individual or company	Obtain agreement from a small business to provide ongoing Web support
To request a contract to complete a specific project or job	Obtain a contract to write the policy and procedure manual for a large franchise

Identifying Proposal Types

The circumstances surrounding your decision to write a proposal affect the probable success of your proposal. A proposal can be **solicited** or **unsolicited**, or written in response to a formal **Request for Proposal (RFP)**. Figure 8-2 describes each of these three proposal types.

Figure 8-2 ▶ **Proposal types**

Proposal Type	Description
Solicited Proposal	• Write a solicited proposal in response to a specific request. For example, your supervisor may ask you to submit your idea about reorganizing the entire filing system in your office in the form of a proposal.
Unsolicited Proposal	• Write an unsolicited proposal to individuals or companies that might be interested in what you have to offer. For example, write a proposal to describe the landscaping services or Web design and maintenance services you can offer to a company.
Request for Proposal (RFP)	• Write a proposal in response to a formal Request for Proposal (RFP) distributed by companies and government agencies. For example, the organizing committee of a city that has won the bid to host the Olympics would develop RFPs for a wide variety of projects—from the construction of a new stadium, ski run, and arena, to the creation of an Olympic mascot and the training of volunteers. Companies respond using the format specified with a proposal that specifically addresses the needs outlined in the RFP.

Proposals can be either formal or informal. You usually write a **formal proposal** in response to an RFP. You can also submit a formal proposal as a solicited or an unsolicited proposal. An **informal proposal** is often a brief document of two to four pages that you submit for either a solicited or an unsolicited proposal. You use similar skills to develop all types of proposals, as discussed next.

Developing the Proposal Content

Regardless of the type of proposal you write, the ultimate purpose of your proposal is to win the contract, obtain the funding, get the job, and so on. As a result, everything you write in the proposal should reflect that purpose. You want to present the information in a way that persuades the reader to accept your proposal. The key word is *persuade*.

To determine what content you should include in a proposal, you can ask a series of questions, such as the following:

- What are you proposing?
- Who has requested the proposal?
- What need does your proposal address?
- What does the reader want?
- What is your competition (if any) doing?
- What are the characteristics of the product or service you are offering?
- What qualifications do you have to meet the needs of the proposal?
- What is the timeline for the project?
- How much will the proposed project cost?

Depending on the project, you might determine additional questions, such as, *Who will be affected by the proposal?*, *What is the timeline?*, and *What are some possible objections?* Figure 8-3 shows sample answers to questions about a proposal written by a parent group that is requesting funding to build a new playground at a local elementary school.

| Figure 8-3 | Identifying content for a proposal |

Question	Answer
What are you proposing?	To build a new playground containing safety-tested playground equipment for the children at Oak Park Elementary School.
Who requested the proposal?	The Oak Park School Board requested the proposal from the Oak Park Parent Advisory Council (OPPAC). The Board has not issued a formal Request for Proposal (RFP) to which other organizations could respond.
What need does the proposal meet?	The current playground is in a state of disrepair. Most of the swings are broken, the slide is cracked, and the old-fashioned metal climbing structure is unsafe. Several injuries have occurred in recent years as the result of the substandard equipment.
What does the reader want?	The school board wants to build a new playground for a reasonable cost that will provide safe recreational opportunities for children attending the school.
What is the competition doing?	A new playground similar to the playground proposed for Oak Park Elementary School was recently built at Arbutus Court Elementary School. This playground will be a model for the playground proposed for Oak Park.
What are the characteristics of the product or service you are offering?	The new playground consists of two sets of 10 swings, a large adventure playground structure with capacity for 20 children, and four coil spring rides. A detailed description of the new playground, including models and photographs of the Arbutus Court playground, will be included.

Figure 8-3 ▶ **Identifying content for a proposal (*continued*)**

Question	Answer
What qualifications do you have?	Marcus Watson is a professional architect with a practice in Portland. Mr. Watson is also a member of OPPAC and has agreed to donate his time to design the new playground. In addition, OPPAC can call upon up to 50 volunteers to do the work. A professional contractor will be hired and the entire project will be supervised by a school board inspector.
How much will the project cost?	The total cost will be $68,750 for the materials and labor. The architect and OPPAC members will be donating their time to save costs.

Key Point

The purpose of a proposal is to provide the reader with the information required to make a positive decision.

By answering a series of questions related to your proposal topic, you can identify the areas that make your proposal unique and then highlight these areas in the final proposal. You need to prove to the reader that your proposal has merit and that you or your company or organization is sufficiently qualified to implement the proposal.

Structuring a Proposal

After you have answered questions to identify the content of your proposal, you can organize the proposal into the following sections:

- Introduction
- Description of Need
- Scope of the Project
- Methods and Procedures
- Detailed Work Plan and Schedule
- Qualifications of the Company or Individual
- Projected Costs
- Conclusion
- Other Components (such as Appendices)

The order and titles of these sections might vary, depending on the needs of the company that requests the proposal. In some situations, the company or organization receiving the proposal will provide you with a set format that you must use. However, regardless of the format and the order, most of the sections listed previously will be required for all proposals. Following is a description of each of these sections in the context of a proposal to build a playground for the children of Oak Park Elementary School.

Introduction

In the **Introduction** section of a proposal, you describe the purpose of the proposed project and indicate the major topics. Figure 8-4 shows the introduction for the proposal to build a playground at Oak Park Elementary School.

Figure 8-4 ▶ **Introduction to playground proposal**

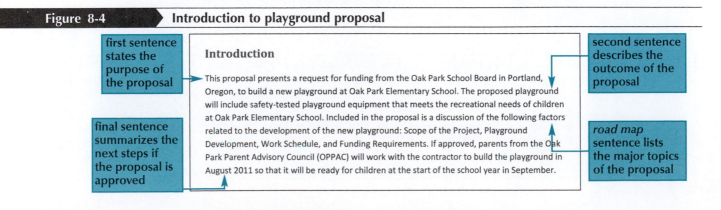

first sentence states the purpose of the proposal

second sentence describes the outcome of the proposal

final sentence summarizes the next steps if the proposal is approved

road map sentence lists the major topics of the proposal

Introduction

This proposal presents a request for funding from the Oak Park School Board in Portland, Oregon, to build a new playground at Oak Park Elementary School. The proposed playground will include safety-tested playground equipment that meets the recreational needs of children at Oak Park Elementary School. Included in the proposal is a discussion of the following factors related to the development of the new playground: Scope of the Project, Playground Development, Work Schedule, and Funding Requirements. If approved, parents from the Oak Park Parent Advisory Council (OPPAC) will work with the contractor to build the playground in August 2011 so that it will be ready for children at the start of the school year in September.

The first sentence of the introduction states the purpose of the proposal. You can start the proposal with the phrase *This proposal presents a request for...* and then complete the sentence with a precise summary of what you are proposing. The wording of the purpose statement is adapted from the answer to the first question shown in Figure 8-3: *What are you proposing?*

Following the one or two sentences required to state the purpose of the proposal, you should include a sentence that informs readers about the contents of the proposal. Readers appreciate this type of *road map* sentence. The final sentence in the sample introduction tells the reader what will happen if the proposal is accepted. The Introduction provides the reader with a context for reading the proposal.

Description of Need

As part of the introduction, you need to present a **Description of Need**, which includes any background information the reader requires to understand the need for the proposed project. For example, the playground proposal should include a description of how the current playground is both unsightly and unsafe. This section could also include pictures of the current playground, information from organizations that promote playground safety, and statistics related to how the playground is currently used.

Scope of the Project

In the **Scope of the Project** section of a proposal, you describe the limits of the project and supply details about dates and personnel. You can then include subsections that describe individual components of the project. Figure 8-5 shows the Scope of the Project section for the playground proposal.

| Figure 8-5 | Sample Scope of the Project section for the playground proposal |

Methods and Procedures

In the **Methods and Procedures** section, you tell the reader exactly what you plan to do to complete the project. This section could also be called *Products and Services, Project Components*, and so on.

You include information about personnel, equipment, materials, and any other relevant factors in the Methods and Procedures section, which usually forms the bulk of the proposal. For example, in a proposal to write a manual, the Methods and Procedures section may be called *Manual Contents* and would include a proposed table of contents for the manual, along with a sample chapter.

For the playground proposal, the heading *Playground Development* is used instead of *Methods and Procedures*. In this section, each of the bulleted items included in the Scope of the Project section is expanded. For example, the item *Final approval of the playground design created by Marcus Watson, a professional architect and a member of OPPAC*, is allocated a subsection titled *Design Approval* that includes pictures of the proposed playground design and equipment.

Detailed Work Plan and Schedule

This section, which might also simply be called *Work Schedule,* is required in a proposal for a project that needs to be completed within a certain time frame. You can use a table to present schedule information in an easy-to-read format.

Qualifications of Company or Individual

The reader of your proposal needs to know why the individuals making the proposal are qualified to complete the project. In this section, you describe the qualifications and background of the key players in the project, including any companies involved. In the playground proposal, a summary of the qualifications of the architect and the contractor would be included.

Projected Costs

From the reader's point of view, cost is one of the most important elements of a proposal. You can assist the reader in making an informed decision about your proposal by presenting cost information clearly and succinctly. You can include a spreadsheet to show the breakdown of expenses and then you can use a pie chart to illustrate cost information.

Conclusion

In the **Conclusion** section of a proposal, you summarize the rationale for the proposal and stress the benefits to the reader of accepting the proposal. You can also describe how the acceptance of the current proposal could lead to additional projects in the future.

Other Components

Many proposals include supporting information in an appendix or a series of appendices. An **appendix** is located at the end of a proposal and contains information that is too detailed to be included in the body of the proposal but is required for reference purposes. A proposal for a large project could include several appendices that contain financial statements, product specifications, references, and other technical information to which the reader might need to refer.

Not every proposal you write must include each one of the sections described previously. Sometimes, you might be able to provide enough information about the project in the Scope of the Project section, omit the Methods and Procedures section, and include the Schedule section. Figure 8-6 shows the table of contents containing the headings and subheadings for the playground proposal.

> **Key Point**
>
> A proposal must convince a reader to take a specific action, which is to approve the proposal. You need to organize the content coherently to lead the reader to a positive response.

Figure 8-6 ▶ **Table of Contents for the playground proposal**

Table of Contents

Formatting a Proposal

A proposal consists of multiple pages that you need to format clearly and attractively. For example, you do not want your reader to search through page after page of closely typed text to find information about projected costs. The reader should be able to find this type of information within seconds. As you have learned, some companies that request proposals provide a format that you need to follow. If such a format is not provided, you can format a proposal according to the guidelines described in Figure 8-7.

Figure 8-7 ▶ **Guidelines for formatting a proposal**

Component	Description
Title Page	• Include the title of the proposal, the name and title of the person or company who will receive the proposal, the name and title of the person who is submitting the proposal, and the current date. • Include a picture or a graphic such as a company logo, if appropriate. • Format the title page so that all the text is easy to read and attractively spaced; use a large font size for the proposal title.
Table of Contents	• List the principal headings and subheadings included in the proposal. • Use Word to generate a table of contents that you can update automatically. • Format the table of contents attractively, including using leader lines to help the readers associate a heading entry with a page number.
Header and Footer	• Create a header that includes the title of the proposal and the date and appears on the second and subsequent pages of the proposal text. • Create a footer for the table of contents page that includes the name of the individual or organization submitting the proposal at the left margin and the page number formatted as a lowercase Roman numeral at the right margin. • Modify the footer for the first and subsequent pages of the proposal text so that it includes the name of the submitting body at the left margin and the page number formatted in Arabic numerals beginning at 1 from the right margin.
Headings with Styles	• Use heading styles to format all the headings and subheadings in the proposal text consistently.
Tables and Graphics	• Format tables and other graphic elements, such as charts and illustrations, so that they are easy to read and understand.

As you have learned, the purpose of a proposal is to ask for approval, for either a project or a request of some significance. When you format the text in a proposal clearly and attractively, you help readers identify the information they need to make a positive decision. Figure 8-8 shows how pages 1 and 6 of the playground proposal text are formatted.

Figure 8-8   **Pages 1 and 6 of the sample proposal text**

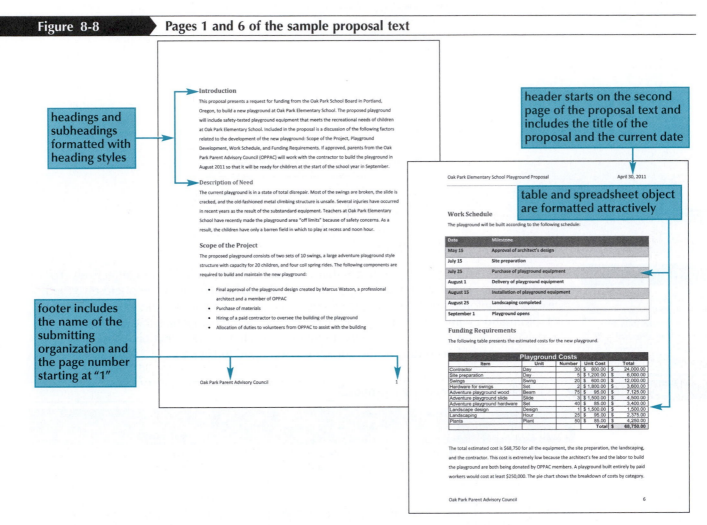

Technology Skills – Organizing Content in Word

You work in Outline view in Word to develop the structure of a document and then you generate a Table of Contents to list all the headings and subheadings. In addition, you can break the document into sections and add page numbers.

The **Outlining** feature in Word is designed to help you keep track of how all the topics and subtopics in your document fit together. In Outline view, you sort content into headings, subheadings, and body text, and then you can choose to view the main topics, or the topics with subtopics, or the entire text. The Technology Skills steps cover these skills:

- Use the Outlining feature to organize document content
- Edit a document structure in Outline view
- Add a table of contents to a document
- Break a document into sections
- Add headers, footers, and page numbers

Tip

You can modify the structure of your document by moving entire topics along with all their associated subtopics and text.

To use the Outlining feature to organize document content:

1. Open the file **Tech_08.docx** located in the Project.08 folder included with your Data Files and then, to avoid altering the original file, save the document as **Partnership Proposal** in the same folder. The document contains the text of a proposal between two companies to form a partnership.

2. Click the **Show/Hide ¶** button ¶ in the **Paragraph** group to show the paragraph marks, if necessary.

3. Click the **View** tab, and then click the **Outline** button in the Document Views group. In Outline view, you can assign levels to each heading and subheading. You assign Level 1 to the main headings, Level 2 to the subheadings under a main heading, Level 3 to the next level of subheadings, and so on. You can apply headings to nine levels; however, for most documents, three or at the most four levels are sufficient.

4. Press the **PgDn** key, click to the left of **Introduction** to position the insertion point, and then click the **Promote to Heading 1** button in the Outline Tools group. The heading is formatted as a Level 1 heading.

5. Click in the paragraph of text below Introduction, click the **Demote to Body Text** button in the Outline Tools group, click after the phrase **agreement will be negotiated.** at the end of the paragraph, press the **Enter** key, click the **Promote to Heading 1** button, type **Partnership Requirements**, and then press the **Enter** key.

6. Click the **Demote to Body Text** button, and then type **This section provides background information about PM Connections and Skill Mart and discusses how the partnership could benefit both companies.**

7. Click to the left of **Background Information**, click the **Promote to Heading 1** button once to move the heading to Level 1, and then click the **Demote** button once to move the heading to Level 2.

8. Click in the paragraph below the Background Information heading, and then click the **Demote to Body Text** button.

9. Apply outlining levels to the remaining headings and subheadings, as shown in Figure 8-9, and demote all the paragraphs of text to body text.

Figure 8-9 ▶ **Levels for headings and subheadings**

Heading Text	Level
PM Connections	3
Skill Mart	3
Benefits	2
PM Connections	3
Skill Mart	3
Financial Considerations	1
Projected Revenues	2
Financing Required	2
Proposed Seminars	1
PM Connections Seminars	2
Skill Mart Seminars	2
Conclusion	1

10. Scroll up to view the Benefits subheading, and then save the document.

The real benefit of working in Outline view becomes evident when you need to edit the structure of your document. You decide to move the Financial Considerations heading and all the text and subheadings associated with it from its current location to just above the Conclusion heading.

To edit a document structure in Outline view:

1. Click the **Show Level** list arrow in the Outline Tools group, and then click **Level 3**. Only the three levels of headings are displayed.

2. Move your mouse pointer over the **plus sign** ⊕ to the right of Financial Considerations and then click to select Financial Considerations and the two subheadings associated with it. The text associated with all three headings is also selected.

3. Click and drag the mouse down until a line appears above the Conclusion heading, and then release the mouse button. The selected text appears above the Conclusion heading, as shown in Figure 8-10. You can also click the Move Up button ⬆ and Move Down button ⬇ to move selected headings in Outline view.

Figure 8-10   **Moving text in Outline view**

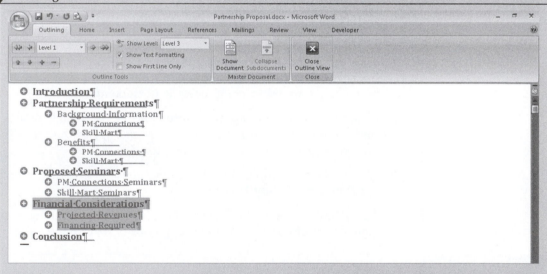

4. Double-click the **plus sign** ⊕ next to the Financial Considerations heading to expand only the subheadings and text associated with that heading.

5. Click the **Collapse** button ⊟ in the Outline Tools group two times to collapse the heading so only Financial Considerations appears. The other two headings and the text associated with them still exist; however, you hide them so that you can more easily analyze the structure of the document and move sections around.

6. Click the **Show Level** list arrow, click **Level 1** to show only the five main headings in the document, click the **Show Level** list arrow again, and then click **Level 2**.

7. Click the **Show Level** list arrow, and then click **All Levels** to show all the headings, subheadings, and accompanying text again.

8. Save the document.

A **table of contents** is an essential part of any long document because it provides your readers with a road map of your content. Readers can see at a glance the major headings and subheadings included in the document and can quickly determine the page number of a specific section.

You can use the Table of Contents feature in Word only if you format the headings and subheadings in a document with styles. When you work in Outline view to apply levels to headings and subheadings, the appropriate heading styles are applied automatically. For example, the Heading 1 style is applied to Level 1 text, the Heading 2 style is applied to Level 2 text, and so on.

To add a table of contents to a document:

► 1. Click the **Close Outline View** button in the Close group to return to Print Layout view, and then scroll to the Introduction. As you can see, the headings and subheadings are attractively formatted with the default heading styles.

► 2. Click to the left of Introduction, press [**Ctrl**][**Enter**], press the **up** arrow ↑ once, type **Table of Contents**, and then press the **Enter** key three times.

► 3. Select the text **Table of Contents**, format the text with **Bold**, **20-point**, and **Center** alignment, and then click to the left of the **paragraph mark** above the page break. Now your insertion point is in position to generate the table of contents.

► 4. Click the **References** tab, click **Table of Contents** in the Table of Contents group, click **Insert Table of Contents**, click the **Formats** list arrow, and then click **Formal**, as shown in Figure 8-11.

| Figure 8-11 | Selecting a format in the Table of Contents dialog box |

► 5. Click **OK**, and then save the document. The table of contents appears.

As you can see, the Introduction starts on page 3 in the table of contents you have generated. You need to divide the proposal into three sections so that you can use different page numbering options for each section as follows:

- Section 1 contains the title page and should not include a page number.
- Section 2 contains the table of contents page and should include a page number formatted as *i*.
- Section 3 contains the text of the proposal and should include a page number formatted in the *1, 2, 3* style and starting on page 1.

To divide a document into sections:

1. Press [**Ctrl**][**Home**] to move to the top of the document, press [**Ctrl**][**F**] to open the Find and Replace dialog box, click **More**, click **Special**, click **Manual Page Break**, and then click **Find Next**. You save time by using the Find command to search for the manual page break so you can replace it with a section break.
2. Move the dialog box so you can see the page break, click the selected text in the document (the page break), press the **Delete** key to remove the page break, click the **Page Layout** tab, click **Breaks** in the Page Setup group, and then click **Next Page** in the Section Breaks area to create a Next Page section break.
3. Click **Find Next** in the Find and Replace dialog box, close the Find and Replace dialog box, and then replace the page break between pages 2 and 3 with a Next Page section break. The document is now divided into three sections.
4. If necessary, press the **Delete** key to remove the extra paragraph mark above Introduction on page 3, and then save the document.

You add headers, footers, and page numbers to the proposal, remove selected text from the proposal, and then update the table of contents.

To add headers, footers, and page numbers:

Tip

You must deselect the Link to Previous button before you enter text into a header or footer to ensure the text does not appear in the previous section.

1. Scroll to and click anywhere on the table of contents page, click the **Insert** tab, click **Footer**, click the **Blank** option, press the **Delete** key two times to remove the text placeholder, and then click the **Link to Previous** button in the Navigation group. You deselect Link to Previous because you do not want the page number you enter in the footer to also appear in section 1 of the document. By default, the Link to Previous button is selected.
2. Type **your name**, press the **Tab** key twice, click the **Page Number** button in the Header & Footer group, point to **Current Position**, and then click **Plain Number**.
3. Click the **Page Number** button in the Header & Footer group again, click **Format Page Numbers**, click the **Number format** list arrow in the Page Number Format dialog box, and then select **i,ii,iii** as shown in Figure 8-12.

Figure 8-12 Page Number Format dialog box

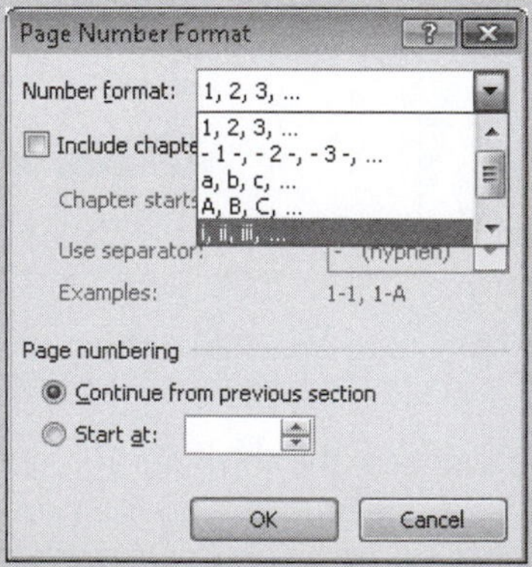

4. Click the **Start at** option button, click **OK**, and then click the **Next Section** button in the Navigation group to move to the footer for Section 3 of the proposal document. At present, a 2 appears in the footer and the Link to Previous button is again selected. You do not want the number in the footer to be linked to the text in the footer in section 2 because you want the number to be *1* instead of *2*.

5. Click the **Link to Previous** button to deselect it, click the **Page Number** button in the Header & Footer group, click **Format Page Numbers**, click the **Start at** option button, and then click **OK**. Your name appears at the left margin and a *1* now appears in the footer for page 1 of the proposal text.

6. Click **Go to Header** in the Navigation group, click the **Link to Previous** button to deselect it, type **Partnership Agreement Proposal**, select the text, center and bold the text, and then click **Close Header and Footer** in the Close group on the Header & Footer Design Tools tab.

7. Right-click the **table of contents**, click **Update Field**, click the **Update entire table** option button, and then click **OK**. Now the page number *1* appears next to Introduction. If you remove any text from the document, you can update the table of contents again and the new page numbers will be generated.

8. Type your name where indicated on the title page, save the document, print a copy, and then close the document.

One of your duties as the program assistant in the Business Department at Langton Community College in Tulsa, Oklahoma, is to help the director develop and format proposals made to the College administration to fund the purchase of equipment and software. The director has written the draft of a proposal and asks you to add additional material and modify the structure of the proposal, and then format it attractively for presentation to the College's Dean of Operations.

Follow the steps below to add content to a proposal and then format it.

1. Open the file **Practice_08.docx** located in the Project.08 folder included with your Data Files and then, to avoid altering the original file, save the document as **Software Upgrade Proposal** in the same folder.

2. Scroll to page 2, and then read the proposal to gain an understanding of the proposal purpose and scope.

3. Switch to Outline view, add *Description of Need* as a Level 2 heading under the Introduction paragraph, and then use the information shown below to write two or three sentences to describe why students in the Business Department require new software:
   a. Most colleges have already upgraded to the latest version of Windows.
   b. Students in the Business Department at Langton Community College need to learn the latest software in order to be competitive in the workplace.

4. Make *Work Schedule* in the Upgrading Activities section a Level 2 heading.

5. Collapse all the headings to Level 2, and then move the *Student Workers* heading below the *Work Schedule* heading.

6. Show all levels of the outline, switch to Print Layout view, and then insert a page break between the title page and the first page of the proposal text.

7. Type *Table of Contents* at the top of the new second page, center the text, and then enhance it with 16 pt and Bold.

8. Two lines below the title, generate a table of contents using the Distinctive format.

9. Use [Ctrl] + click to navigate to Benefits, switch to Outline view, delete Benefits and its subtext, return to Print Layout view, and then update the table of contents.

10. Replace the two manual page breaks in the document with Next Page section breaks.

11. Format headers, footers, and page numbers for the document as follows:
    a. Section 1: no header, footer, or page number
    b. Section 2: footer with your name at the left margin and the page number formatted as *i* at the right margin
    c. Section 3: header with *Software Upgrade Proposal* centered and bolded, and footer with your name at the left margin and the page number formatted in the *1, 2, 3* style at the right margin and starting on page 1.

12. Scroll through the document and where needed keep related text and headings together, update the table of contents, type your name where indicated in the title page, save the document, print a copy, and then close it. Note: To keep a head with its related subtext, select the head and at least one line of body text that follows, click the launcher in the Paragraph group on the Home tab, click the Line and Page Breaks tab, then click the Keep with next and the Keep lines together check boxes.

| Revise | **Proposal Revision** |

You can save time by modifying existing proposals to meet the requirements of new projects. You work for a company called Dynamic Physiotherapy Clinic, a large private clinic located in Brooklyn that specializes in providing a wide range of physiotherapy services to its clients. The clinic is doing well and looking for opportunities to expand. Several months ago, you wrote a proposal to form a partnership with the Brooklyn Fitness Center. This proposal was accepted and the resulting partnership has been very successful. Now you have been asked to write another proposal to form a partnership between Dynamic Physiotherapy Clinic and the Seaview Health Center, a small clinic that offers a range of restorative health services including massage therapy, acupuncture, and reflexology. You open the proposal you wrote for the partnership with the Brooklyn Fitness Center and revise it for a partnership with the Seaview Health Center.

Follow the steps below to review the content of the proposal and then format it for printing.

1. Open the file **Revise_08.docx** located in the Project.08 folder included with your Data Files and then, to avoid altering the original file, save the document as **Seaview Health Center Partnership Proposal** in the same folder.
2. Read the proposal and note where you will need to replace information about the Brooklyn Fitness Center with information about the Seaview Health Center. Note also that much of the information can remain the same.
3. Use Find and Replace to find every instance of *Brooklyn Fitness Center* and replace it with *Seaview Health Center.*
4. On the title page, change the name of the president of Seaview Health Center to George Ng.
5. Switch to Outline view, collapse the headings to level 2, and then move Seaview Health Center Facilities in the Products and Services section so it is below Dynamic Physiotherapy Clinic Services.
6. Show all levels and then refer to Figure 8-13 to make changes to the proposal content. Work in Outline view so you can concentrate solely on the content rather than the formatting.

> **Tip**
>
> Brooklyn Fitness Center in the Table of Contents is replaced by Seaview Health Center only after you use the Update Field command.

Figure 8-13 ▷ **Changes to proposal content**

Location	New Content Related to Seaview Health Center
Introduction	• Local facility that provides a range of restorative health services including massage therapy and acupuncture services • Terms of the partnership: October 11, 2011 to February 15, 2014
Background Information	• One of the Dynamic Physiotherapy Clinic therapists specializes in stress management treatments • Her services offered to clients of Seaview Health Center at a reduced rate • Location of Seaview Health Center: one block away • Maintains five treatment rooms • Excellent reputation for massage therapy and acupuncture treatments • Ranked the top restorative health facility in the area by local consumer groups
Benefits	• Set up a referral system between Dynamic Physiotherapy Clinic and Seaview Health Center; shared referrals will extend the market for both facilities • Clients of the Seaview Health Center can use the services of Dynamic Physiotherapy Clinic therapists at a reduced rate • 20% discount proposed

Figure 8-13	Changes to proposal content (*continued*)

Location	New Content Related to Seaview Health Center
Services	• Stress management treatments provided by Dynamic Physiotherapy Clinic to clients of Seaview Health Center • Restorative health services include massage therapy, acupuncture, and reflexology provided by Seaview Health Center to clients of Dynamic Physiotherapy Clinic
Financial Considerations	• Revise to reflect Seaview Health Center services; there are no product revenues • Increase is 25% for Seaview and 20% for Dynamic Physiotherapy Clinic
Conclusion	• Revise to reflect Seaview Health Center services

7. Return to Print Layout view, scroll to the column chart in the Projected Revenues section, right-click the chart, and then click Edit Data.

8. Change the data for the chart as follows: January: 30; February: 32; March: 38; and April: 45.

9. Close the Excel spreadsheet.

10. Divide the document into three sections and modify headers, footers, and page numbering as follows:

    a. Section 1: no header, footer, or page number

    b. Section 2: footer with your name at the left margin and the page number formatted as *i* at the right margin

    c. Section 3: header with *Partnership Agreement Proposal* centered and bolded, and footer with your name at the left margin and the page number formatted in the *1, 2, 3* style at the right margin and starting on page 1

11. Type your name where indicated on the title page, update the table of contents, save the document, and then print a copy.

Create | Proposal Sample

You work for a company called PM Connections that specializes in assisting companies and individuals in the Dallas area who need to write long documents such as proposals, reports, and newsletters. The company also conducts seminars on topics such as communication skills, effective leadership, and document development. Peter Marlin, the president of PM Connections, has decided to create a new seminar called *Effective Proposal Writing* and needs to write a sample proposal for the seminar participants. He asks you to determine a suitable subject for his sample proposal and then to answer questions to help him focus on the required content.

Follow the steps below to develop content for a proposal, and then to write and format the proposal.

1. Select a proposal subject that involves a significant change in a course, a program, or a company procedure. For example, you could request that a business program at a local college include more courses in business communications, you could propose setting up a flextime program at your company, you could request the purchase of new computer equipment, or you could propose a new marketing strategy for a particular product.

2. Complete the table below with the information you need to help you write the proposal. Note that you will need to make up information. Use fictitious but realistic details. Not all the questions will be relevant to your proposal. Answer questions that help you determine information for your proposal and identify additional questions and answers where needed. Your goal is to develop the *big picture* of your proposal—its purpose, characteristics, sections, etc.

Information for a Proposal
What are you proposing? *Hint*: Think in terms of making a change.
Who has requested the proposal?
What need does your proposal address?
What does the reader want?
What is the competition doing?
What are the characteristics of the project outcome (e.g., products and services, methods and procedures, etc.)?
What qualifications do you and/or other principal stakeholders have?
How much will the project cost?

3. Start a new document in Word, and then save it as **My Sample Proposal.docx**.
4. Switch to Outline view, type Introduction as a Level 1 heading, and then in the body text write an introduction to your proposal. Remember that your first sentence should start *This proposal presents a request...* and include a summary of what you are proposing. You might require two or even three sentences to summarize the proposal. Adapt the answers you provided to identify content for the proposal.
5. After the summary of the proposal, include a sentence in the introduction that identifies the four or five main sections of your proposal. Finally, include a sentence that describes the outcome of the proposal. Refer to the proposals you have worked on in this project for wording ideas.
6. Enter the main sections and subsections as Level 1 and Level 2 headings in Outline view.
7. Add appropriate content under each of the headings. When you work in Outline view, you can easily change your mind about how to organize the content. For example, you can decide to switch the order of certain sections. Include enough content so that the text of your completed proposal fills at least two pages.

8. In Print Layout view, add a title page as the first page. Include the name of the proposal, the name and title or organization of the person to whom you are submitting the proposal, your name as the person submitting the proposal and the organization or company you represent, and the current date. Refer to the title pages in the proposals you have worked on in this project for layout and formatting ideas.

9. On the second page of the document, add *Table of Contents* as the title, center it and format it with a large font size, and then generate a table of contents.

10. Divide the document into three sections and modify headers, footers, and page numbering as follows:
    a. Section 1: no header, footer, or page number
    b. Section 2: footer with your name at the left margin and the page number formatted as *i* at the right margin
    c. Section 3: header with the name of your proposal centered and bolded, and footer with your name at the left margin and the page number formatted in the *1, 2, 3* style at the right margin and starting on page 1

11. Update the table of contents, save the document, and then print a copy.

Apply | **Case Study 1**

Capstone College As the program assistant for the Digital Arts Department at Capstone College in San Francisco, you often help the department head to edit and format the proposals he writes to request new programs, additional funding, and so on, from Sara Yaretz, the vice president of Capstone College and the person responsible for allocating funds. The department head asks you to help him write a proposal requesting funding to take the students on a one-week trip to the animation studios at Disney World in Orlando, Florida. To complete this case study, you write the proposal.

1. Open the file **Case1_08.docx** located in the Project.08 folder included with your Data Files, and then save the document as **Digital Arts Proposal Questions** in the same folder.

2. Write answers to the questions to help you develop content ideas for the proposal. You are free to make any assumptions you want and can make up information about the students and the program. Thirty students will be going to Orlando for one week so your proposal should include information about costs. Check the Internet for flight information and hotel costs so that the cost information you provide is realistic.

3. Type your name where indicated in the footer, save the document, and then print a copy.

4. Open a new blank document, save it as **Digital Arts Proposal.docx**, switch to Outline view, and then write an outline for the proposal. Make the outline as detailed as you can so that you can write the proposal quickly.

5. In Print Layout view, write text for about 50% of the proposal. Make sure you include all the required topics and subtopics; however, you can omit text for some of the topics if you want. Make sure your proposal includes, at a minimum, an introduction, a description of the benefits of the trip to students and the college, a proposed schedule for the trip, and the cost information.

6. Add a title page and a table of contents to the proposal and format the page numbering correctly. Remember that you need to add a section break between the table of contents page and the first page of the proposal. The page numbers should be formatted in the *i* style for the table of contents page and the *1* style for the body of the proposal.

7. Include a header that starts on page 1 of the proposal text and contains the text *Orlando Trip Proposal* centered and in bold.

8. On the title page of the proposal, include the proposal title, the name of the vice president (Sara Yaretz, Vice President of Capstone College), your name followed by Digital Arts Department, and February 2, 2011 as the date. Format the text attractively.

9. Save the proposal, print a copy, and then close the document.

Apply	**Case Study 2**

Otter Bay Kayaking Adventures   Kay Johnson, the owner of Otter Bay Kayaking Adventures and your boss, has just been asked to create a proposal to partner with Cycle Juneau, another adventure tour company that offers mountain biking tours. She has listed the topics of the proposal in no particular order in a Word document, and then asks you to create a coherent outline for the proposal. To complete this case study, you create the outline.

1. Open the file **Case2_08.docx** located in the Project.08 folder included with your Data Files, and then save the document as **Otter Bay Partnership Proposal Outline** in the same folder.

2. Study the list of topics and subtopics included in the document, and then switch to Outline view.

3. In Outline view, organize the list of topics into a coherent outline that consists of three levels. Not every main heading will include subheadings. You can decide which items are main topics and which are subtopics, and the most logical order to present the topics.

4. Under the *Introduction* heading, write an introduction that states the purpose of the proposal (to partner with Cycle Juneau to offer one day adventure packages that combine kayaking and mountain biking) and describes the principal sections of the proposal in the order in which they will appear. Conclude the introduction with a sentence that describes the expected outcome—that the full day tour format should attract a high volume of participants who want to experience two outdoor adventures in one day.

5. Switch to Print Layout view, and then add page breaks in appropriate locations so the outline fills two pages.

6. Add a new page 1 with a section break between it and the first page of the proposal text. Type *Table of Contents* at the top of the new page, and then generate a table of contents using a format of your choice.

7. Add a header with the text *Kayaking and Cycling Tour Proposal,* center the text and start it on the first page of the proposal text.

8. Add a footer that includes your name at the left margin and the page number at the right margin to start on the table of contents page. In this document, page 1 will be the table of contents page and page 2 will be the first page of the document text.

9. Save the document and then print a copy.

Companies and individuals can use the Internet to find Requests for Proposals (RFPs) that they can respond to with proposals to complete specific projects or supply goods or services in a wide range of industries. For example, a company that conducts training seminars can search government Web sites to find RFPs for training services.

To complete this case study, you will gather information about two Web sites that provide companies and individuals with the opportunity to view and submit RFPs.

1. Open the file **Research_08.docx** located in the Project.08 folder in your Data Files, and then save the document as **Researching RFP Opportunities.docx** in the same folder.

2. Open your Web browser, and then search for Web sites that list RFP opportunities. You can use search terms such as *Request for Proposal Opportunities*, *Government RFP*, *state and federal RFP opportunities*, and so on. Your goal is to find Web sites that maintain listings of RFP opportunities. Note that some Web sites charge companies to access listings; however, you can determine information required to complete this case study without paying.

3. Find two Web sites that maintain listings of RFP opportunities.
   a. Enter information about each of the Web sites in the space provided in the Researching RFP Opportunities document. Note: To copy a Web address, click the Address box, be sure the URL is selected, press [Ctrl]+[C], switch to the Word document, click in the blank cell to the right of Web Site Address, and then press [Ctrl]+[V].

4. Type your name where indicated in the footer, save the document, print a copy, and then close the document.

Objectives

- Identify report types
- Develop the report structure
- Develop the report content
- Add reference materials
- Add support materials
- Add a cover page in Word
- Insert a footnote in Word
- Insert a chart in Word
- Add captions to figures in Word
- Generate a table of figures in Word
- Customize a table of contents in Word

Reports

Introduction

You write a **report** when you need to provide detailed information on a specific topic to people who will use the information to either support an existing decision or help them make a new decision.

Like proposals, reports consist of multiple pages and can be challenging to write. Few people can sit down and dash off a 10-page business report without extensive preparation. You need to identify a purpose, develop an outline, and gather the content. When you take the time to prepare thoroughly, the writing process itself usually goes quite smoothly.

In this project, you review the types of reports, investigate how to organize content for a report, identify the components of a report, and then work in Word to add a cover page to a report, insert a footnote, insert a chart, add captions to illustrations, generate a table of figures, and finally customize a table of contents.

Starting Data Files

Project.09

Tech_09.docx
Practice_09.docx
Revise_09.docx
Case1_09.docx
Case2_09.docx
Research_09.docx

Report Essentials

The word *report* is used to describe a wide range of documents—from a two-page memo that details the progress of a specific project to a 100-page annual report that describes the activities of a corporation to shareholders. In between, you find reports for specific purposes, such as incident reports, financial reports, and appraisal reports. Many of these types of reports are actually forms that include specified areas to complete.

Consider the proposal to build a new playground that you analyzed in Project 8. After the proposal is accepted, you might need to write a report that describes the building of the playground, makes observations related to how the playground is used, and provides recommendations regarding its ongoing maintenance. Unlike a proposal, a report does not ask for something; instead, it describes a situation and often recommends a specific course of action.

Identifying Report Types

You can categorize most reports, regardless of length and purpose, into three types: descriptive, comparative, and analytical. The type of report you choose to write determines how you will present the information to the reader. Each of the three types of reports is described next.

Descriptive Reports

A **descriptive report** provides the reader with the information needed to understand a specific situation. For example, you could write a descriptive report to summarize progress on a specific project and to describe the activities of a department or company during a set time frame. Often you write a descriptive report several months or even years after a new initiative has been put in place. Such a report describes how the new initiative has been implemented and includes recommendations for further development.

Figure 9-1 shows the outline of a report that describes the progress made by participants who attended a two-day business communication skills seminar.

Figure 9-1	Outline of a descriptive report

- ➕ **Introduction**
  - ⚫ This report describes the Business Communication Skills seminar presented by Business Connections on March 3 and 4 in Dallas in terms of three factors: Seminar Purpose, Seminar Content, and Seminar Evaluation.
- ➕ **Seminar Purpose**
  - ➖ **Learning Outcomes**
  - ➖ **Participant Needs**
- ➕ **Seminar Content**
  - ➕ **Day One**
    - ➖ **Sentence Writing**
    - ➖ **Punctuation**
  - ➕ **Day Two**
    - ➖ **Tone**
    - ➖ **Letter Writing**
- ➕ **Seminar Evaluation**
  - ➖ **Participant Feedback**
  - ➖ **Follow-up**

Notice that the paragraph under the Introduction heading begins with a sentence that summarizes the content of the report. This first sentence is the core sentence. You will learn how to use the core sentence format to help you identify the main topics of a report in the upcoming section, *Developing the Report Structure*.

Comparative Reports

You write a **comparative report** when you want to compare two or more factors that a reader needs to evaluate. For example, you would write a comparative report to describe the features of two brands available for the same product, such as a new computer system or a new photocopier. The comparative report presents the reader with a balanced view of both brands and then often concludes with a recommendation regarding which of the two brands to purchase. You can also write a comparative report to describe the pros and cons of two or more new product lines that a company contemplates developing or to analyze the relative merits and disadvantages of two locations for a new franchise.

Figure 9-2 shows the outline of a report that compares two small adventure travel companies in terms of potential profitability.

Figure 9-2 ▶ **Outline of a comparative report**

Key Point

The verb used in the core sentence is *compares* because the sentence summarizes how the comparative report presents information about two distinct companies.

⊕ **Introduction**
  ● This report compares the potential profitability of Great Northern Adventures and Wilderness Quest Tours in terms of three areas: Tours Offered, Market Share, and Potential Growth.
⊕ **Great Northern Adventures**
  ⊖ **Tours Offered**
  ⊖ **Market Share**
  ⊖ **Potential Growth**
⊕ **Wilderness Quest Tours**
  ⊖ **Tours Offered**
  ⊖ **Market Share**
  ⊖ **Potential Growth**
⊖ **Conclusions and Recommendations**
⊖

Analytical Reports

You write an **analytical report** when you want to provide your reader with an interpretation of factual information. For example, you could write an analytical report to analyze how a company uses the Internet to market its products. This analysis might include both a description of current Internet use, as well as a comparison of Internet use to other market strategies. An analytical report often includes both descriptive and comparative components. Another analytical report might explore why a product line is or is not profitable.

Figure 9-3 shows the outline of a report that analyzes the current way in which Simpson Communications is using the Internet to market its services. The three topics of the analytical report—Customer Access, Online Advertising Options, and Web Marketing Strategies—provide the reader with an easy-to-understand structure.

Figure 9-3 **Outline of an analytical report**

⊕ **Introduction**
 ● This report analyzes the marketing functions of the company Web site for Simpson Communications in terms of three areas: Customer Access, Online Advertising Options, and Web Marketing Strategies.
⊕ **Customer Access**
  ⊖ **Click-Throughs**
  ⊖ **Keyword Search**
  ⊖ **Direct Access**
⊕ **Online Advertising Options**
  ⊖ **Banner Ads**
  ⊖ **Affiliate Programs**
  ⊖ **E-Mail Marketing**
  ⊖ **Advertising Resources**
⊕ **Web Marketing Strategies**
  ⊕ **Market Research Options**
    ⊖ **Demographics**
    ⊖ **Psychographics**
  ⊖ **Customer Survey Results**
⊕ **Conclusions and Recommendations**
 ●

The type of report you choose to write depends on what you want your reader to do with the information you present.

- Write a descriptive report when you want the reader to take note of the information and perhaps use it to support the next step in a process.
- Write a comparative report when you want your reader to compare two or more products, services, or scenarios in order to make an informed decision based on certain criteria.
- Write an analytical report when you want to provide the reader with not only a description of a current situation but also your interpretation of the situation.

Developing the Report Structure

The more time you spend developing the structure for a report, the less time you will need to spend actually writing the report. You can use a three-step process to develop the report structure:

- Step 1: Identify the main topics
- Step 2: Write a core sentence
- Step 3: Develop an outline

Each of the three steps in the preparation process is discussed next.

Step 1: Identify the Main Topics

The main topics form the backbone of your report and give the reader a sense of the report's overall structure. One mistake people often make is to select a topic that is too large. For example, you could decide to write a report that describes the current state of your company and makes recommendations for improvements. This topic is far too comprehensive. The current state of your company could include any number of topics related to personnel, to marketing, to products, to customer service, to location, to physical plant, and the list could go on. You need to identify just two or three main areas that you will focus on in your report.

You can use the **brainstorming** technique to identify quickly the principal topics of your report. To start a brainstorming session, write the main topic of your report in the center of a blank sheet of paper and then circle the topic. Then, let your mind wander at will from topic to topic. Each time you think of a topic, no matter how seemingly irrelevant, write it down somewhere on the paper. Within minutes, you usually start to identify connections between the various topics. The procedure is a fluid and creative one that helps you identify connections that you might not see when you think sequentially and logically. After you have filled the page with topics, you can take different colored pens to circle all the subtopics related to each of the two or three main topics you identify. Figure 9-4 shows how the brainstorming technique is used to identify three main topics for a report about the current state of a company called Wilderness Quest Tours.

| Figure 9-4 | **Sample brainstorming session** |

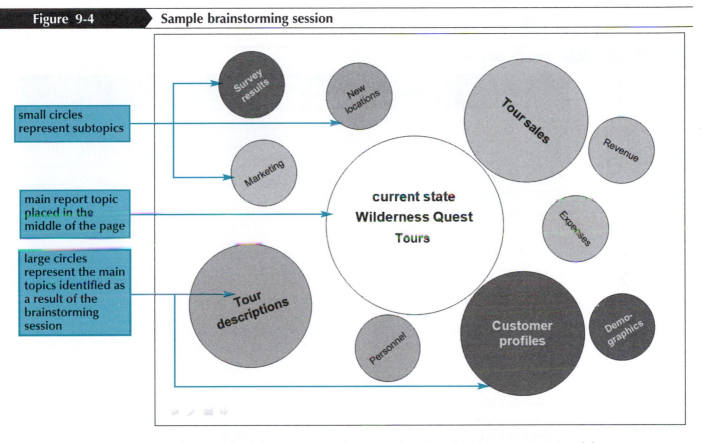

As a result of the random noting of topics related to the current state of the company, three principal topics were identified: Tour sales, Tour descriptions, and Customer profiles. Each of these principal topics was assigned a different color. Next, related subtopics were identified. These subtopics were enclosed in smaller circles, and then they were colored the same color as their corresponding main topic. Using different size circles and different colors can help you quickly associate subtopics with their main topics, even when they are not placed near each other. For example, you can see at a glance that the subtopics Survey results and Demographics correspond to the main topic, Customer profiles.

Step 2: Write a Core Sentence

Key Point

A core sentence reassures the reader that the report is structured coherently and probably worth the time required to read it.

After you have identified the main topics for your report, you develop your **core sentence**[1]. The core sentence presents the topics of your report, along with the two or three principal subtopics. It consists of the following parts:

- Subject: This report...
- Verb: describes, compares, or analyzes
- Object: Main topic of your report summarized in as few words as possible
- Linking phrase: in terms of or with regard to
- Number of main topics: Usually two, three, or four, followed by a colon
- Main topics listed in the order in which they will appear in the completed report

Figure 9-5 shows how a core sentence is deconstructed into its component parts.

Figure 9-5 | **Sample core sentence**

Component	Words from sample core sentence
Subject	This report
Verb	describes
Object	the state of Wilderness Quest Tours in 2011
Linking phrase	in terms of
Number of topics	three principal areas
Main topics	tour descriptions, customer profiles, and tour sales

When put together, the core sentence reads as follows:

This report describes the state of Wilderness Quest Tours in 2011 in terms of three principal areas: tour descriptions, customer profiles, and tour sales.

Readers appreciate reading a core sentence at or near the beginning of a report because it identifies exactly what the reader can expect to find in the report.

Step 3: Develop an Outline

Key Point

Your goal when writing your outline is to develop the report structure so thoroughly that the actual writing of the report requires relatively little time.

After you have determined the main topics of your report and written the core sentence, you need to expand the topics into an outline. You can return to your brainstorming sheet to find additional subtopics to include in the outline. An effective outline includes several layers of subtopics. As you learned in Project 8, you can work in Outline view in Word to develop the sequence of topics and subtopics required for a report outline.

Figure 9-6 shows the main topic and the subtopics in the sample outline of the Wilderness Quest Tours descriptive report.

[1]The core sentence concept was devised by Dr. Thomas W. McKeown in North Vancouver, BC, and is included in *Written Power Online*, an online business writing course accessible from www.writtenpower.com

| Figure 9-6 | Sample outline in Outline view |

You can significantly speed up the time you need to spend actually writing the report if you try to assign a heading for almost every paragraph in the report. For example, in the Category Descriptions section of the expanded outline shown in Figure 9-6, each of the sea kayaking subtopics *Queen Charlotte Islands*, *Vancouver Island*, and *Alaska Panhandle* will be accompanied in the finished report by a paragraph that describes the tours to each of these locations.

After you have developed an outline, you can conduct research, gather facts, and assemble supporting materials. Finally, you can write your report. You look next at how to develop content for the report.

Developing the Report Content

The time you spend preparing a comprehensive outline pays great dividends when you start developing content for the report. Your outline keeps you on track and focused. You gather only the content required to expand on the topics and subtopics included in the outline.

You gather content for a business report from sources such as the following:

- Interviews with customers, other employees, administrators, and so on
- Other company reports and documents, such as annual reports, financial reports, and memos
- Marketing materials such as brochures and newsletters
- Articles in publications and on Web sites

Figure 9-7 shows how tour information has been added in Outline view.

| Figure 9-7 | Adding content in Outline view |

Key Point

When you work in Outline view, you can quickly add content to the appropriate topics and subtopics in the outline.

○ **Introduction**
○ **Tour Descriptions**
　　○ **Category Descriptions**
　　　　● Wilderness Quest Tours has consistently sold all of its sea kayaking and mountain biking tours, with the backpacking, wilderness canoeing, and wildlife photography tours selling at approximately 75 percent capacity.
　　　　○ **Sea Kayaking**
　　　　　　● Sea kayaking tours are extremely popular. Visitors from all over the world have reported via surveys and e-mail feedback that they are enchanted by the peace and tranquility of the coastal waters. The occasional whale sighting adds a welcome level of excitement.
　　　　　　○ *Queen Charlotte Islands*
　　　　　　　　● Wilderness Quest Tours hosts two tours each summer to the Queen Charlotte Islands in British Columbia. Each tour lasts for one week and includes wilderness camping and whale watching. Both of these tours have sold out in each of the three years they have been offered. Total gross revenue exceeds $500,000.

Report Introduction

The **introduction** to a report includes the core sentence, a description of the reason for writing the report, and any background information that the reader might require to understand the content of the report. Figure 9-8 shows a short introduction to the descriptive report about Wilderness Quest Tours.

| Figure 9-8 | Report introduction |

Introduction

This report describes the state of Wilderness Quest Tours in 2011 in terms of three topics: Tour Descriptions, Customer Profiles, and Tour Sales. In particular, the report examines the impact of each of these three areas on the company's profitability in 2012. In addition to descriptions of the tours currently offered by Wilderness Quest Tours, this report explores the impact on current profits of the new wildlife photography tours offered for the first time in 2011, and discusses the anticipated impact of the enhanced mountain biking tours to be offered in 2012.

Report Writing Process

You can choose to write a report sequentially from start to finish or you can add content as you collect it. When you work in Outline view, you can add content in whichever order you please. If you get stuck on one section of your report, scroll through your outline to a section that you can write more easily. By the time you finish adding content to the new section, you might have come up with content for the section you set aside.

Write the report content quite quickly and without worrying about errors, writing style, and formatting. The hardest part of any writing assignment is getting the words down on paper or up on the computer screen. After you have written at least some text, you will find that additional content becomes increasingly easier to write. After you have written most of the content, you can then go back and make editing changes. Just before your final draft, you can correct spelling and grammar, rephrase sentences to use plenty of action verbs and the active voice, check for consistency of terms, and modify the document formatting.

Key Point

One of the greatest enemies of productivity is the preoccupation with getting everything perfect on the first draft.

Report Executive Summary

Key Point

The executive summary appears after the table of contents and table of figures.

Some reports include an **executive summary** that provides readers with a brief overview of the report contents and summarizes the recommendations. Many recipients of the report, particularly executives, read no further than the executive summary. If they need additional information, they turn to relevant sections in the report.

The executive summary consists of four parts as follows:

- Purpose of the report; can include the core sentence or a version of it
- Reason for writing the report
- Methods of investigation used to obtain the information contained in the report
- Conclusions and recommendations

For most reports, the executive summary consists of just one or two pages and is usually double spaced. Although you include the executive summary as the first page of text in a report, you write the executive summary after you have completed the report.

Figure 9-9 shows the executive summary for a report that analyzes the business communication seminars conducted for Silver Star Insurance.

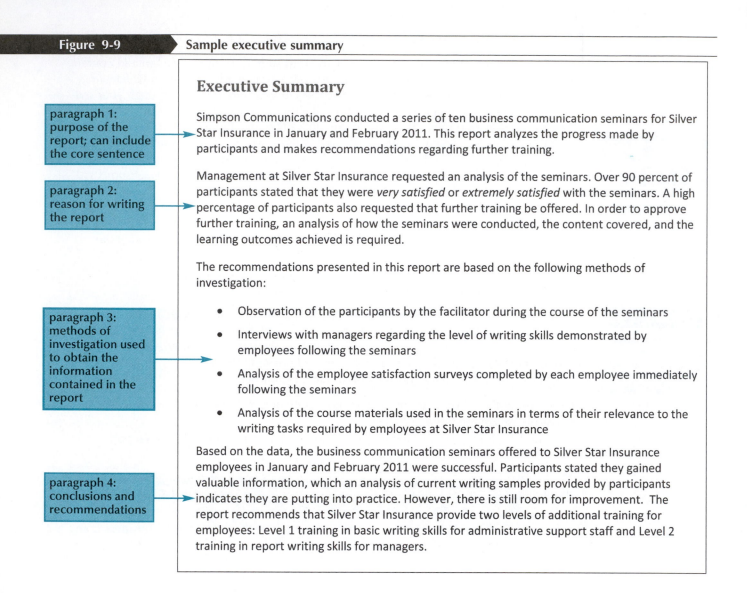

Figure 9-9 — Sample executive summary

Executive Summary

paragraph 1: purpose of the report; can include the core sentence

Simpson Communications conducted a series of ten business communication seminars for Silver Star Insurance in January and February 2011. This report analyzes the progress made by participants and makes recommendations regarding further training.

paragraph 2: reason for writing the report

Management at Silver Star Insurance requested an analysis of the seminars. Over 90 percent of participants stated that they were *very satisfied* or *extremely satisfied* with the seminars. A high percentage of participants also requested that further training be offered. In order to approve further training, an analysis of how the seminars were conducted, the content covered, and the learning outcomes achieved is required.

The recommendations presented in this report are based on the following methods of investigation:

paragraph 3: methods of investigation used to obtain the information contained in the report

- Observation of the participants by the facilitator during the course of the seminars
- Interviews with managers regarding the level of writing skills demonstrated by employees following the seminars
- Analysis of the employee satisfaction surveys completed by each employee immediately following the seminars
- Analysis of the course materials used in the seminars in terms of their relevance to the writing tasks required by employees at Silver Star Insurance

paragraph 4: conclusions and recommendations

Based on the data, the business communication seminars offered to Silver Star Insurance employees in January and February 2011 were successful. Participants stated they gained valuable information, which an analysis of current writing samples provided by participants indicates they are putting into practice. However, there is still room for improvement. The report recommends that Silver Star Insurance provide two levels of additional training for employees: Level 1 training in basic writing skills for administrative support staff and Level 2 training in report writing skills for managers.

Adding Reference Materials

Many reports include materials and information originally included in other sources such as books, Web sites, and articles. You must give credit to these sources using footnotes or citations. Reports also often include illustrations, such as charts and figures, as well as appendices. Figure 9-10 describes the reference materials commonly included in reports.

Figure 9-10 — Reference materials in reports

Component	Description
Footnotes	• Use **footnotes** to give credit to outside sources or to provide additional information about a specific point made in the report. A footnote appears at the bottom of the page on which the footnote reference appears. • Use **endnotes** when you want the information to appear at the end of the report.
Citations	• Insert a **citation** to give credit to a source. A citation usually includes the author and page number of the source.

Figure 9-10 **Reference materials in reports (*continued*)**

Component	Description
Illustrations	• Insert **charts** to show numerical information graphically. • Insert **figures** such as drawings, photographs, and diagrams to supplement the report text. • Add a **caption** to each illustration so you can generate a table of figures to follow the table of contents.
Appendices	• Include supporting information in **appendices**, such as the results of customer surveys, detailed financial information, and additional charts and tables required to clarify information.

Adding Support Materials

Most reports include a variety of additional materials, such as a cover page, a table of contents, and a letter of transmittal. Figure 9-11 describes each of these report components.

Figure 9-11 **Support materials for reports**

Component	Description
Cover page	• Include the title of the report, the name of both the report writer and the company or individual who requested the report, and the current date. • Do not include a page number on the report cover page. • Use one of Word's cover page formats when appropriate.

Letter of transmittal	• Write a letter of transmittal to accompany a report.
	• Include the following content in a letter of transmittal:
	  • Thank the reader for the opportunity to write the report.
	  • State the title of the report and the date it was requested.
	  • Briefly summarize the subject of the report.
	  • Briefly describe why the report was written.
	  • Close with an offer to discuss the report contents further.

Table of contents	• Include a table of contents in a report so that readers can see at a glance how you have organized the content.
Table of figures	• Include a table of figures following the table of contents in a report that contains numerous illustrations.

Technology Skills - Enhancing Multiple-Page Documents

In Word, you can enhance a multiple-page document by adding a cover page, inserting footnotes, inserting a chart, adding captions to figures such as charts and diagrams, generating a table of figures, and finally modifying a table of contents to include more than three heading levels. The Technology Skills steps cover these skills:

• Add a cover page
• Insert a footnote
• Insert a chart
• Add captions to figures
• Generate a table of figures
• Customize a table of contents

You can create a cover page in Word that includes placeholders for variable information. Word includes a variety of interesting formats for cover pages that add a professional look to your report.

To add a cover page to a report:

1. Open the file **Tech_09.docx** located in the Project.09 folder included with your Data Files, and then to avoid altering the original file, save the document as **Serenity Cosmetics Report** in the same folder. The document contains the text of a report.

2. Click the **Show/Hide ¶** button ¶ to turn on the display of paragraph marks, click the **Insert** tab, click **Cover Page** in the Pages group, and then click the **Cubicles** style. A new page appears containing content controls which you can add text to or delete.

3. Click the **content control** for Company, type **Serenity Cosmetics**, and then type **Progress Report** in the content control for document title.

4. Click the **document subtitle** content control, and then click the **Subtitle** tag as shown in Figure 9-12.

Figure 9-12   Subtitle content control tag selected

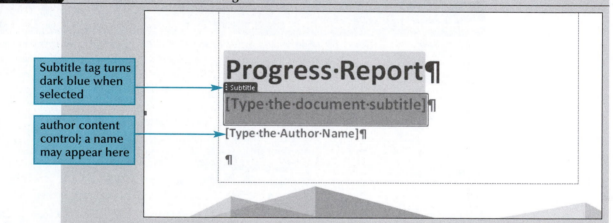

Subtitle tag turns dark blue when selected

author content control; a name may appear here

---

5. Press the **Delete** key. The entire content control is removed.

6. Type your name in the content control for author name.

7. Scroll to and then delete the content control for Year, type **January 11, 2012** in the text box that remains, and then change the font size for the date to **14 pt**.

8. Deselect the text, click outside the text box, and then save the document.

You use the **footnote** command to give credit to references made in the body of a report. You can also insert a footnote to provide additional information about a specific point made in the report. When you insert a footnote, the text of the footnote is entered at the bottom of the page on which the footnote reference number appears. You can also choose to add **endnotes**, which appear all together at the end of a document. Next, you insert a footnote in the report.

To add a footnote:

Tip

You can use the Find command to move quickly to the location where you need a footnote.

1. Press [**Ctrl**]+[**F**] to open the Find and Replace dialog box, type **holiday season**, click **Find Next**, and then click **Cancel** to close the Find and Replace dialog box.

2. Press the **right** arrow key once to move after the word *season*, click the **References** tab, then click **Insert Footnote** in the Footnotes group.

3. Type **The holiday season is defined as November 15 to January 5.**, and then click anywhere above the footnote divider line.

4. Save the document. Other footnotes in the document are renumbered automatically each time you add a new footnote.

Long documents such as reports often include figures containing charts, diagrams, and other illustrations. You can copy a chart from an Excel workbook or you can create a chart in a Word document. Next, you insert a pie chart on the last page of the report.

To insert a pie chart in a document:

1. Press [**Ctrl**]+[**End**] to move to the end of the document, then scroll up and click below the Sales paragraph.

2. Click the **Insert** tab, click the **Chart** button in the Illustrations group, click **Pie**, and then click **OK**. A worksheet opens in a Microsoft Excel window to the right of the Word document.

3. Click cell **A2** (contains 1st Qtr) in the Excel worksheet, type **Lavender**, press the **Tab** key, type **11560**, press the **Enter** key, and then enter the remaining data for the pie chart as shown in Figure 9-13, widening columns when necessary.

Figure 9-13 ⟩ **Pie chart data**

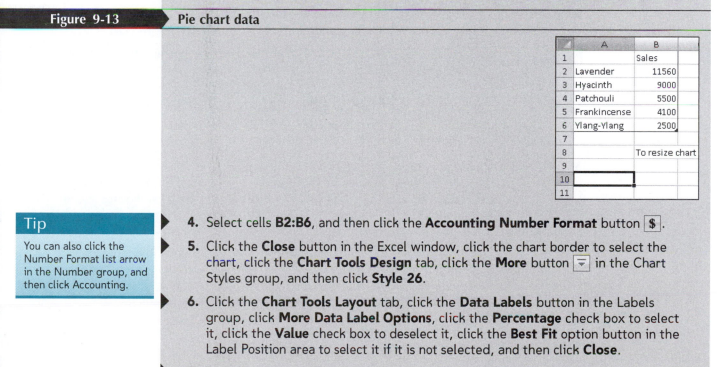

	A	B
1		Sales
2	Lavender	11560
3	Hyacinth	9000
4	Patchouli	5500
5	Frankincense	4100
6	Ylang-Ylang	2500
7		
8		To resize chart
9		
10		
11		

Tip

You can also click the Number Format list arrow in the Number group, and then click Accounting.

4. Select cells **B2:B6**, and then click the **Accounting Number Format** button $.

5. Click the **Close** button in the Excel window, click the chart border to select the chart, click the **Chart Tools Design** tab, click the **More** button ⩫ in the Chart Styles group, and then click **Style 26**.

6. Click the **Chart Tools Layout** tab, click the **Data Labels** button in the Labels group, click **More Data Label Options**, click the **Percentage** check box to select it, click the **Value** check box to deselect it, click the **Best Fit** option button in the Label Position area to select it if it is not selected, and then click **Close**.

7. Save the document.

You add a caption to each figure in a document when you want to be able to generate a table of figures. By default, a **caption** contains the text *Figure* followed by the caption number. Next, you add a caption to the two charts, as well as the photograph, in the report.

To add figure captions:

▶ **1.** With the chart still selected, click the **References** tab, and then click **Insert Caption** in the Captions group. The insertion point appears after Figure 1 in the Caption dialog box.

▶ **2.** Type a **colon (:)**, press the **Spacebar**, type **Aromatherapy Sales**, and then click **OK**.

▶ **3.** Scroll up to view the photograph in the New Marketing Image section, click the photograph, and then add a caption with the text: **Serenity's New Look** following Figure 1. Note that Figure 1 is entered because the photograph precedes the pie chart in the document.

▶ **4.** Scroll up to view the column chart, click the chart, and then add a caption with the text **Bath Products Sales** after Figure 1.

▶ **5.** Save the document.

A report that contains figures such as charts, diagrams, and pictures often includes a table of figures following the table of contents. You can only generate a table of figures if you have already added a caption to each of the figures in a document. Next, you generate a table of figures below the table of contents.

To generate a table of figures:

▶ **1.** Scroll to the page containing the table of contents, and then click to the left of the section break below the table of contents.

▶ **2.** Press the **Enter** key four times to move the section break down, and then click at the second paragraph mark below the table of contents.

▶ **3.** Type **Table of Figures**, select the **Table of Contents** heading at the top of the page, click the **Home** tab, click the **Format Painter** button in the Clipboard group, and then drag the pointer across **Table of Figures** to apply the same formatting.

▶ **4.** Click at the second paragraph mark below Table of Figures, click the **References** tab, click **Insert Table of Figures** in the Captions group, click the **Formats** list arrow, select **Formal**, and then click **OK**. The captions for the three figures in the document are listed.

You can customize a table of contents in a variety of ways. By default, a table of contents shows only three levels of headings. You can choose to show more levels and you can modify the appearance of the entries in the table of contents. Next, you show four levels in the table of contents and then modify the alignment of the headings.

To customize a table of contents:

▶ 1. Click anywhere in the table of contents above the table of figures, click **Table of Contents** in the Table of Contents group, click **Insert Table of Contents**, select the contents of the Show levels text box, and then type **4**.

▶ 2. Click **OK**, and then click **OK** again. The updated table of contents appears too widely spaced. Fortunately, you can adjust the formatting of levels in a table of contents by adjusting the style assigned to each level.

▶ 3. Click **Table of Contents** in the Table of Contents group, click **Insert Table of Contents**, click **Modify** in the Table of Contents dialog box, click **TOC 2** in the list of styles, click **Modify**, click the **Decrease Paragraph Spacing** button once, and then click **OK**.

▶ 4. Click **TOC 3**, click **Modify**, click the **Decrease Paragraph Spacing** button two times, click **OK**, click **TOC 4**, click **Modify**, click the **Decrease Paragraph Spacing** button two times, and then click **OK**.

▶ 5. Click **OK** until you see a message box with Yes, and then click **Yes** to return to the document.

▶ 6. Scroll through the document and adjust page breaks where necessary, type your name in the footer, save the document, print a copy, and then close the document.

Practice | Comparative Report Organization

You have been contracted to write a comparative report for Ever After Catering, a catering company that is considering a partnership with one of two wedding planning companies. You have received a description of the subject of the report and some notes for the executive summary. Your client asks you to send him a core sentence, outline, and executive summary of the report that he can approve before authorizing you to write the complete report. As you learned in this Project, you write the executive summary after you have completed the report. However, for this exercise you will write the executive summary using the information given so that you can practice how to organize the information into its four components.

Follow the steps below to write a core sentence, outline, and executive summary for a comparative report.

1. Open the file **Practice_09.docx** located in the Project.09 folder included with your Data Files and then, to avoid altering the original file, save the document as **Ever After Catering Report Organization** in the same folder.
2. Read the following description of the report subject:

   Ever After Catering specializes in taking care of all catering needs for weddings. The company is very successful and is now considering a partnership with one of two wedding planners. The first wedding planner is Giorgio Wedding Planner and the second wedding planner is Perfect on The Day. The report should compare the two companies in three areas: their current clientele, their products and services, and their financial situation.

3. In the space provided in the Ever After Catering Report Organization document, write an appropriate core sentence based on the above description. Remember to use the six-part format for a core sentence:
   a. Subject (This report)
   b. Verb (compares)
   c. Object: Main topic of your report summarized in as few words as possible
   d. Linking phrase: in terms of or with regard to
   e. Number of main topics: Usually two, three, or four, followed by a colon
   f. Main topics listed in the order in which they will appear in the completed report
4. Save the document and keep it open.
5. Start a new document in Word, save it as **Ever After Catering Report Outline**, and then switch to Outline view.
6. In Outline view, create an outline based on the three topics presented in the core sentence. Use the Promote and Demote buttons in Outline view to assign levels to each topic and subtopic. Make sure you assign Level 1 to the Introduction, the Conclusions and Recommendations, and the three main topics. You should then assign Level 2 to the subtopics, Level 3 to the sub-subtopics, and so on. You can choose to include up to four levels of subtopics, but you do not need to include four levels for each main topic.
7. In Outline view, adjust the page view so that all the outline levels appear in one screen.
8. Press the **Prnt Scrn** button to take a screen shot of the outline. The Prnt Scrn button is often located to the right of or above the function keys and could be called PrtScn or PrtSc.
9. Save and close the document, switch to the Ever After Catering Report Organization document, click below the paragraph on Outlining, and then press [**Ctrl**]+[**V**] to paste a copy of the screen shot.

10. Scroll to the Executive Summary heading, and then read the notes about the report for Ever After Catering.

11. In the space provided on page 3 of the document, write the Executive Summary based on the notes on page 2. Remember to organize the content presented in the notes into four sections as follows:

    - Purpose of the report
    - Reason for writing the report
    - Methods of investigation (use a bulleted list, if you wish)
    - Conclusions and recommendations

12. Use action verbs and the active voice wherever possible. Double-space the text of the executive summary.

13. Type your name where indicated in the footer, save the document, and then print a copy.

Tip

If the executive summary runs over one or two lines to page 2, adjust the line spacing as needed or open the Print Preview tab, then click the Shrink One Page button in the Preview group so the executive summary fits on one page.

Revise | Analytical Report

You work for an online company called GlobalHomeExchanges.com that arranges house exchanges between people worldwide. People interested in exchanging their homes with people in other parts of the world register with GlobalHomeExchanges.com and are matched with suitable homeowners. Your colleague, Sandra Long, has written an analytical report that analyzes the customer services activities of the company in terms of three areas: Customer Access, Contract Services, and Follow-Up Activities.

Sandra asks you to revise the report based on new information she has received and then to format it appropriately for printing. You will need to write a core sentence for the introduction, add a footnote, insert a chart, add captions to all the illustrations in the report, create a cover page, generate a table of figures, and finally customize the table of contents. Follow the steps below to revise and format the analytical report.

1. Open the file **Revise_09.docx** located in the Project.09 folder included with your Data Files and then, to avoid altering the original file, save the document as **Global Home Exchanges Web Site Report** in the same folder.

2. Switch to Outline view, scroll to the introduction, read the introduction and note the lack of a coherent core sentence. The introduction provides background information relevant to the report, but does not provide the reader with an overview of the report content.

3. Start a new paragraph below the first paragraph, and then write a core sentence. Note that the three major topics are Customer Access, Contract Services, and Follow-Up Activities, and that the purpose of the report is to analyze customer service activities. Use the correct core sentence format.

4. Switch to Print Layout view, use the Find feature to find the text **other home exchange Web sites**, and then insert a footnote with the text **The average fee for an annual membership in a home exchange Web site is $75**.

5. Find the text **Web site in 2002**, press the Enter key to start a new paragraph, center the paragraph mark, and then insert a column chart using the data shown in Figure 9-14.

Figure 9-14 Column chart data

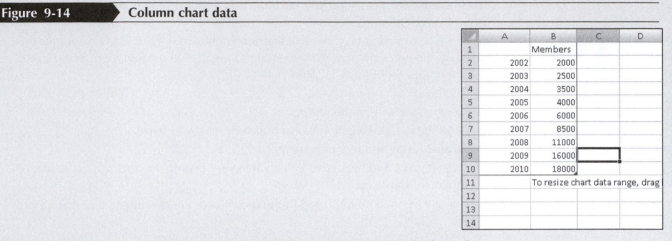

	A	B	C	D
1		Members		
2	2002	2000		
3	2003	2500		
4	2004	3500		
5	2005	4000		
6	2006	6000		
7	2007	8500		
8	2008	11000		
9	2009	16000		
10	2010	18000		
11		To resize chart data range, drag		
12				
13				
14				

6. Apply chart style 30 to the chart and delete the legend.

7. Add a caption to the chart with the text **Growth in Membership** following the figure number.

8. Go to the top of the document, and then scroll through the report and add captions with appropriate text to each of the other two figures in the report. Center the captions below the figures.

9. Return to the top of the document and create a cover page using the format of your choice form the Cover Page gallery. Include only the title of the report **Customer Service Analysis Report**, the name of the company **Global Home Exchanges**, your name as the author, and **March 24, 2011** as the date. Remove all other content controls.

10. Scroll to the table of contents, and then generate a table of figures below the table of contents. Use the Distinctive format. Enter **Table of Figures** above the table and format it so that it appears the same as the Table of Contents heading.

11. Customize the table of contents so that text formatted with the TOC 1 style is 12 pt.

12. Scroll through the report, add page breaks where needed to keep related materials together, type your name where indicated in the footer, save the document, and then print a copy.

Create | Report: Descriptive, Comparative, or Analytical

When you follow the guidelines presented in this project for developing the content of a report, you will find that the actual writing of the report goes quite smoothly. The key requirement is planning. Spend the time to brainstorm topics and subtopics, write the core sentence, and then develop the outline. You should never start writing a report until you have developed a sufficiently detailed outline.

Follow the steps below to write and format a report on a subject provided.

1. Choose a subject from the following list:
   - Recreation options in your home town
   - Ergonomic issues in the office
   - Interesting business to analyze (for example, a cycling tour company, a gourmet catering company, etc.)
   - Employment opportunities or comparison of two job offers in an industry of your choice

- Analysis of a program of studies at a local college or university
- Analysis of working from home

2. On a blank piece of paper, brainstorm topics and subtopics related to the topic you have chosen. Remember to write down any words that come to your mind. Your goal is to collect enough topics and subtopics so that you can identify three principal topics and related subtopics. You don't need to include all the topics you generated in the brainstorming session.

3. Write a core sentence that states the subject of the report along with the three principal topics. For example, a report with the subject *Working from home* could start with the core sentence: *This report analyzes the benefits and drawbacks of working from home in terms of three areas: Scheduling Logistics, Financial Issues, and Career Advancement.*

4. Make sure that the verb you select for the core sentence reflects the type of report you are writing. Your choices are *describes*, *compares*, and *analyzes*.

5. Open one of the reports you have completed in this project, for example, the Serenity Cosmetics Report or the Global Home Exchanges Web Site Report. You can save time by starting with an existing report so that you can edit footers and update a table of contents and table of figures, rather than creating all of them from scratch. If you did not already complete a report, start with a blank Word document.

6. Save the report as **My Report**, switch to Outline view, and then remove the text related to the original report.

7. In Outline view, create an outline based on the three topics in the core sentence. Use the Promote and Demote buttons in Outline view to assign levels to each topic and subtopic. Make sure you assign Level 1 to the Introduction, the Conclusion and Recommendations (if appropriate for your report), and the two or three main topics. You should then assign Level 2 to the subtopics, Level 3 to the sub-subtopics, and so on. You can include up to four levels of subtopics, if you wish.

8. Add content to each of the headings and subheadings in the outline. Your goal is to write a report of approximately three pages. Make up information where appropriate; use fictitious but realistic details.

9. Include at least one footnote in your report.

10. Include a chart and at least one other illustration such as a photograph or drawing, and then add captions to the figures in your report.

11. At the top of the document, replace the current cover page with another cover page. When you insert a new cover page, the old cover page is automatically replaced, but the information entered in the content controls is retained. Edit the content controls so they contain text appropriate for your report. Include at least the title of the report, your name, and the current date.

12. On the Table of Contents page, open the Table of Contents dialog box, change the format to a format of your choice, and then click OK. Open the Table of Contents dialog box again, and then modify some of the TOC levels. You can choose to modify the spacing or the appearance of the text.

13. Update the table of figures to list the figures included in your report.

14. Verify that the footer for the table of contents page contains the page number *ii*, and then verify that the footer on the first page of the report contains your name at the left margin and the page number (starting at 1) at the right margin.

15. Print a copy of the document, and then save and close it.

| Apply | | Case Study 1 |

Capstone College   One of your duties as the program assistant for the Digital Arts Department at Capstone College in San Francisco is to edit and format the reports produced by the department head on various aspects of the programs. The department head recently developed a new program called Game Art and Design that will be offered to students in the fall of 2011. He has written most of the text for a descriptive report that documents the progress made as of December 2010 toward getting the program approved and marketed. He asks you to write an appropriate core sentence, organize the headings and subheadings in Outline view, and then format the report. To complete this case study, you edit and format the report.

1. Open the file **Case1_09.docx** located in the Project.09 folder included with your Data Files, and then save the document as **Game Art and Design Descriptive Report** in the same folder.

2. Switch to Outline view, scroll to the first page of the report text (below the table of contents), and then as the last sentence in the Introduction, write a core sentence for the descriptive report that states the subject of the report and the three principal topics. The subject is this report, the verb is describes, the object is the development of the Game Art and Design program in the Digital Arts Department, and the three principal topics are Program Requirements, Program Contents, and Marketing and Recruitment.

3. Show three levels in the Outline, and then study the outline of the report. Evaluate the order in which the topics are presented and then change the order so that it reflects the order of topics presented in the core sentence.

4. In Print Layout view, use the Find feature to find the text **fill very quickly**, and then insert a footnote with the text **The five other colleges nationwide that offer a similar program regularly maintain waiting lists**.

5. Scroll to the Background Information: Program Focus section and then insert a pie chart using the data shown in the table in the report. Use the title **Number of Industry Jobs Available**. Apply the chart style of your choice and show the labels as values outside the pie.

6. Add a centered caption to the chart with the text **Number of Industry Jobs Available in January 2011** following the figure number.

7. Scroll through the report and add captions with appropriate text to each of the other two other figures in the report.

8. Return to the top of the document and create a cover page using the format of your choice from the Cover Page gallery. Include only the title of the report **Game Art and Design Program Development Report**, the name of the company **Digital Arts Program**, **Capstone College**, your name as the author, and the date **January 10, 2011**. Remove all other content controls.

9. Scroll to the table of contents, and then generate a table of figures below the table of contents. Enter Table of Figures above the table and format it so that it appears the same as the Table of Contents heading.

10. Customize the table of contents by reducing the spacing between all three TOC levels.

11. Type your name where indicated in the footer, save the document, and then print a copy.

Tip

If the Modify button is not active, click the Formats list arrow, and then click From template.

Apply | Case Study 2

Otter Bay Kayaking Adventures Tourists from all over the world enjoy kayaking trips led by the friendly guides at Otter Bay Kayaking Adventures in Juneau, Alaska. You run the office for Kay and are responsible for developing any documents that she may require. Two local companies, Ronda Foods and Jazz HeliTours, are for sale; and because Kay has been doing very well in recent years, she has decided that the time has come to expand. She wants to purchase one of the two companies. She asks you to outline a report that compares the two companies based on the criteria that Kay gives you. To complete this case study, you write an outline for the report, some of the text for the report, an introduction that includes the core sentence, and a one-page executive summary.

1. Open the file **Case2_09.docx** located in the Project.09 folder included with your Data Files, and then save the document as **Information for Otter Bay Kayaking Adventures Report** in the same folder. This document contains source material you need to outline the report.

2. Read the information in the document to learn about Otter Bay Kayaking Adventures and the two companies that Kay is considering acquiring.

3. Brainstorm topics for the comparative report and then write a core sentence. The core sentence should include two or three main topics and reference both companies: Ronda Foods and Jazz HeliTours.

4. In Word, work in Outline view to create an outline for the report. The outline should include an introduction, two or three main topics, two to four appropriate subtopics for each main topic, and a section called Conclusion and Recommendations.

5. Save the report as **Comparative Report for Otter Bay Kayaking Adventures**.

6. Write some of the content for the report so that the body of the report covers at least two pages. For example, you could include short descriptions of the two companies. Invent details as required. You should include all the headings and subheadings from your outline, but you don't need to include content for all of them.

7. Create a Cover page for the report. The report is being submitted to Paul Rose, the president of Juneau Bank. Mr. Rose will be helping to finance the acquisition of the company that Kay chooses. Include the text **Submitted to Paul Rose, President, Juneau Bank** in the subtitle content control. Include your name as the writer of the report and **April 7, 2011** as the date.

8. Create an executive summary that describes the purpose of the report, the reason for writing, the methods of investigation used to obtain information for the report (for example, interviews with the company owners and customers, analysis of financial statements, and so on), and your recommendation. You can choose which of the two companies you think Otter Bay Kayaking Adventures should purchase.

9. Generate a table of contents following the cover page that includes the executive summary and the headings and subheadings of the report. Modify the table of contents, if necessary, so that it presents the topics attractively.

10. On the Table of Contents and Executive Summary pages, include a footer with the page number centered and in lowercase Roman numerals. The Table of Contents page will be page i and the Executive Summary page will be page ii.

11. Starting on the first page of the report text, insert your name at the left margin and the page number starting at *1* at the right margin.

12. Customize the table of contents by modifying the spacing or font size of the various TOC levels.

13. Save the report, print a copy, and then close the document.

Tip

If the Modify button is not active, click the Formats list arrow, and then click From template.

In this project, you have learned about the three principal report types: descriptive, comparative, and analytical. Each of these report types requires a different focus. For example, the content in a comparative report focuses on describing the differences between two or more entities. To complete this case study, you describe an appropriate situation for each of the three report types.

1. Open the file **Research_09.docx** located in the Project.09 folder in your Data Files, and then save the document as **Content for Report Types** in the same folder. This document contains a table with space for you to describe a situation suitable for each of the three report types.

2. For each of the report types listed in the table, describe an appropriate situation that would require the specified report type. For example, if the report type is a descriptive report, describe a situation in which a descriptive report could be used to communicate information. Search the Web for examples of each type of report, or draw upon your own experiences at work and at school for ideas.

3. Type your name where indicated in the footer, save the document, print a copy, and then close the document.

Objectives

- Identify types of newsletters
- Develop newsletter stories
- Format a newsletter
- Modify a picture in Word
- Create and modify columns in Word
- Insert and format drop caps in Word
- Create and format a SmartArt diagram in Word
- Save a Word document as a PDF file

Newsletters

Introduction

The newsletter has grown in popularity over the years as more companies discover how they can use newsletters to help develop positive relationships with both customers and employees. A **newsletter** communicates news, announcements, and other stories of interest to a target market. You distribute a newsletter in print or electronic form over a set period of time, such as monthly, bimonthly, quarterly, or annually.

In this project, you identify the various types of newsletters, view examples of the kinds of stories and other content usually contained in a newsletter, and explore the newsletter formats. You also work in Word to modify a picture so that it appears lightly shaded behind text, format text in columns, add drop caps, create a SmartArt diagram, and save a Word document as a Portable Document Format (PDF) file.

Starting Data Files

Project.10

Tech_10.docx
Coast.jpg
Practice_10.docx
Revise1_10.docx
Revise2_10.docx
Case1_10.docx
Case2_10.docx

Newsletter Essentials

A newsletter provides information that recipients want to read because it relates to their interests or to their work. Some newsletters are distributed free of charge, whereas others require a paid subscription. In some professions, newsletters contain specialty information targeted at a specific audience. For example, a newsletter targeted at managers might contain articles written by management experts, such as highly respected company presidents and professional industry analysts.

Identifying Types of Newsletters

You can use the newsletter format to communicate information to coworkers, to other businesses, to members of an organization, and to donors or consumers. You can distribute each type of newsletter either electronically or on paper, depending on the location of the audience. For example, you might distribute a company newsletter via e-mail when you want to reach customers spread out over a wide geographic area. Most newsletters fall into one of three categories:

- **Company newsletter**
- **Consumer newsletter**
- **Organization newsletter**

Figure 10-1 describes each of these three newsletter types.

Figure 10-1 ▶ **Types of newsletters**

Newsletter Type	Description
Company newsletter	• Distribute to employees within a company. • Use to provide employees with a sense of purpose, to strengthen their commitment to the company, and to build employee morale by keeping everyone informed about current developments in the company and/or the industry. • Include profiles of successful employees, provide information about benefits and other practical information of interest to employees, describe new products or services, and celebrate company successes.
Consumer newsletter	• Distribute to customers who have agreed to receive it. Most consumer newsletters are distributed electronically via e-mail as an attachment or as inline text, or via the Web as a link that either opens or downloads the newsletter. • Obtain an e-mail address from customers who want to receive a newsletter that is distributed via e-mail. When a customer supplies an e-mail address to a company, the customer is giving the company permission to send a newsletter. • Use to keep customers informed about new products and services. • Include product-related information in articles that consumers find interesting and useful. For example, a company that sells camping equipment might distribute a newsletter that includes articles about great camping in Arizona or gourmet campfire chow.
Organization newsletter	• Distribute to members of nonprofit and other organizations such as charities, special interest groups, and clubs. • Use to keep members informed about activities, special events, and people. • Include articles related to members' interests. For example, a newsletter to members of a community arts organization could include a description of an upcoming art exhibition, a story about the winner of a fiction-writing contest, and information about volunteer opportunities at a special event.

Developing Newsletter Stories

The stories included in a newsletter are similar in many ways to the stories included in a typical newspaper, particularly a local community newspaper. A newspaper includes news items about current events; profiles of people and organizations; advice and how-to items; reviews of books, movies, restaurants, and so on; classified advertisements; and entertainment items, such as comics and crossword puzzles.

You should keep two things in mind as you select stories for a newsletter. First, you need to balance the needs and preferences of your audience for certain information with their desire for entertainment. Second, you need to remember the interests of the company or organization that sponsors the newsletter. Because most newsletters have some level of marketing focus, you need to be aware of how you can keep the company or organization at the forefront without seeming too commercial or self-serving.

A good newsletter contains interesting stories, so your first task when developing a newsletter is to determine what type of stories would appeal to your target audience. Figure 10-2 includes story topics appropriate for each of three newsletters—a company newsletter for Valley View Hospital, a consumer newsletter for a sporting goods store named Sports Heaven, and an organization newsletter for the members of the Passage Island Arts Council.

Figure 10-2 ▷ **Sample story topics**

Newsletter Type	Description	Story Ideas
Company newsletter	Valley View Hospital employs over 1000 people, including medical staff, administrative staff, and housekeeping staff. The hospital distributes a monthly newsletter to all staff to keep them informed about new hospital policies, special events, and general interest, health-related articles.	• Profile of Dr. Drake Moray who has just joined the hospital as the chief medical officer • News item describing the recent presence of a film crew in the hospital to shoot an episode of the new medical drama *Emergency!* • Article on how to choose comfortable and safe shoes for working on the hospital wards
Consumer newsletter	Over 30 Sports Heaven stores throughout the United States and Canada sell sports equipment for every possible sport—from skiing to hockey to yoga. Every three months, Sports Heaven sends an electronic newsletter to customers who have chosen to receive it.	• Profile of a pro football player who has endorsed Sports Heaven stores as his choice for all his personal training needs • Article describing three great ski resorts in the Pacific Northwest • Consumer report that compares four kinds of exercise bikes in terms of price, capacity, and features
Organization newsletter	Passage Island Arts Council, a small arts organization based on Passage Island off the coast of Maine, organizes exhibitions for the many artists and artisans who live on the island. The newsletter is distributed four times a year.	• Article on how wall hangings by a local weaver have attracted national attention • News item on the upcoming election of the organization's executive board • Profile of a new arts program in the local school that is run by island artists in consultation with teachers

After you have identified ideas for newsletter stories, you can start to develop appropriate content. The following sections provide information about how to create the various types of stories, such as articles, profiles, news items, and announcements, found in newsletters.

Articles

Key Point

The topics for articles suitable for a newsletter are as broad as the many hundreds of newsletter audiences.

Articles are the heart and soul of a newsletter. People enjoy reading articles on subjects that interest them and that they cannot find in other locations. Because newsletters are targeted at relatively specialized audiences, the articles can also be quite specialized.

The articles included in newsletters are not significantly different from articles included in publications such as magazines and newspapers or Web sites. You need to engage the reader's attention, present the information clearly, and focus on an angle that might provide an added level of entertainment. For example, instead of writing an article on *The History of the Stock Market* for an investment company's consumer newsletter, you could write an article titled *Where to Find an Extra $200 a Month*.

Readers want practical information related to their specific interests, rather than generic stories that they can find in any general interest magazine. As a result, articles featured in newsletters often include a *How-To* component. For example, a newsletter published by an airline might include an article on *How to Overcome Jet Lag* or an article on *Navigating the Hubs: Tips for Flying Through Dallas, Atlanta, Denver, and Chicago*.

Profiles

People love to read about people, which is why **profiles** of key personalities continue to be popular, particularly in company and organization newsletters. Following are tips related to writing a profile:

- Include quotations from the person being profiled. You can even choose to present the profile in the form of an interview.
- Include a picture if possible. Depending on the level of formality required, you can choose a professional photograph or a more casual photograph that shows the person doing something, such as a hobby, sport, or outside work.
- Briefly describe the person's background, but avoid merely summarizing a resume. A paragraph of biographical information is usually sufficient.
- Focus on what the person has done with respect to the company or organization.
- Describe what the person plans to do, particularly as related to the company or organization.

Figure 10-3 shows a profile of Patsy O'Brian, Pro-Line's Employee of the Month, that could be included in Pro-Line's company newsletter.

Figure 10-3 ▷ Sample profile

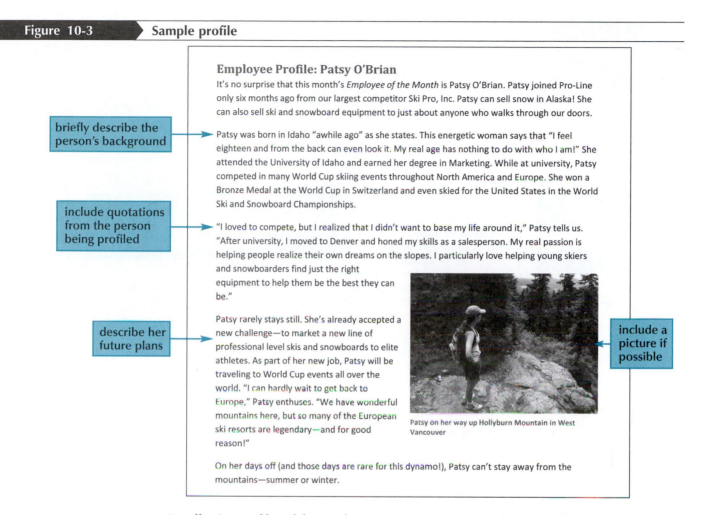

Employee Profile: Patsy O'Brian

It's no surprise that this month's *Employee of the Month* is Patsy O'Brian. Patsy joined Pro-Line only six months ago from our largest competitor Ski Pro, Inc. Patsy can sell snow in Alaska! She can also sell ski and snowboard equipment to just about anyone who walks through our doors.

Patsy was born in Idaho "awhile ago" as she states. This energetic woman says that "I feel eighteen and from the back can even look it. My real age has nothing to do with who I am!" She attended the University of Idaho and earned her degree in Marketing. While at university, Patsy competed in many World Cup skiing events throughout North America and Europe. She won a Bronze Medal at the World Cup in Switzerland and even skied for the United States in the World Ski and Snowboard Championships.

"I loved to compete, but I realized that I didn't want to base my life around it," Patsy tells us. "After university, I moved to Denver and honed my skills as a salesperson. My real passion is helping people realize their own dreams on the slopes. I particularly love helping young skiers and snowboarders find just the right equipment to help them be the best they can be."

Patsy rarely stays still. She's already accepted a new challenge—to market a new line of professional level skis and snowboards to elite athletes. As part of her new job, Patsy will be traveling to World Cup events all over the world. "I can hardly wait to get back to Europe," Patsy enthuses. "We have wonderful mountains here, but so many of the European ski resorts are legendary—and for good reason!"

On her days off (and those days are rare for this dynamo!), Patsy can't stay away from the mountains—summer or winter.

Patsy on her way up Hollyburn Mountain in West Vancouver

Labels:
briefly describe the person's background

include quotations from the person being profiled

describe her future plans

include a picture if possible

An effective profile celebrates the person's unique personality. Anecdotes, quotations, and personal observations engage readers, whereas stiff recitals of facts and figures make many readers turn to the next story.

News Items

News items include stories that relate to the daily operation of the company or organization. Following are some of the topics that can be expanded into news items for a newsletter:

- Promotions
- Awards
- Current and projected sales
- New product developments
- New policies
- Company activities such as relocation, purchase of a new franchise, expansion of a department, and so on

In a news item story, state the most important information first, and then include all the required details in order of importance. You can use the 5W technique, that is Who, What, Why, Where, When, and How questions, to help you develop information for a news story. Figure 10-4 shows a sample news story that announces the relocation of a company's offices.

Figure 10-4 | **Sample news story**

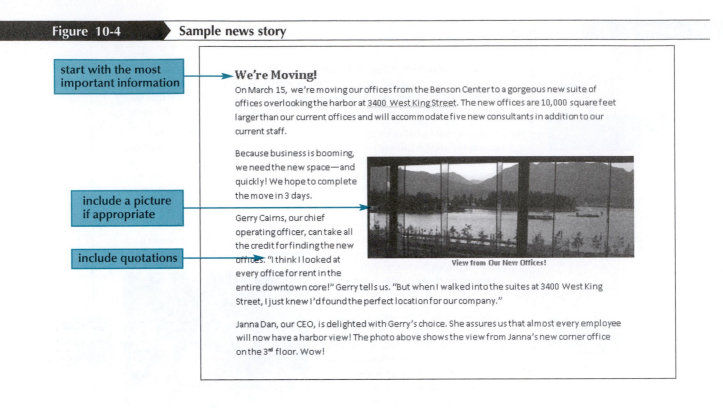

start with the most
important information

include a picture
if appropriate

include quotations

We're Moving!

On March 15, we're moving our offices from the Benson Center to a gorgeous new suite of offices overlooking the harbor at 3400 West King Street. The new offices are 10,000 square feet larger than our current offices and will accommodate five new consultants in addition to our current staff.

Because business is booming, we need the new space—and quickly! We hope to complete the move in 3 days.

Gerry Cairns, our chief operating officer, can take all the credit for finding the new offices. "I think I looked at every office for rent in the entire downtown core!" Gerry tells us. "But when I walked into the suites at 3400 West King Street, I just knew I'd found the perfect location for our company."

Janna Dan, our CEO, is delighted with Gerry's choice. She assures us that almost every employee will now have a harbor view! The photo above shows the view from Janna's new corner office on the 3rd floor. Wow!

View from Our New Offices!

Announcements

Most newsletters include a section for **announcements** about upcoming events, important dates, deadlines, and so on. When writing announcements, make sure you include all the required information. Use the 5W technique to make sure you do not miss anything. Newsletters often feature announcements in a boxed area on the front or back page. Sometimes the announcements are accompanied by the direction to refer to a specific page for more information. Announcements are usually easy to write. You just need to make sure you have the facts right. Figure 10-5 shows a sample list of announcements for an organization newsletter.

Figure 10-5 **Sample announcements for an organization newsletter**

> ### What's Up at MAC!
> Here are the latest announcements from Maplewood Arts Cooperative:
>
> **Exhibition on September 6**
> *The Abstract Eye: Paintings by Hartley Chan.* The opening will be held from 7 p.m. to 9 p.m. on September 6. Volunteers are needed to help staff the bar and provide food. For more information about Hartley Chan and his work, see his profile on page 1.
>
> **Annual General Meeting: September 20**
> All members of the Maplewood Arts Cooperative are welcome to attend the annual general meeting. This year, we'll also welcome Wendy Lalonde from the Art Gallery of Greater Chicago. Ms. Lalonde will be speaking to us about the role of community arts groups in the development of culture in this country.
>
> **It's a Girl!**
> Our Project Coordinator, Dorothy Feinstein, and her partner Keith Crane are delighted to announce the birth of their first child. At 8 pounds, 13 ounces, Josephine Crane has entered the world in fine health and with a hearty set of lungs. Congratulations Dorothy and Keith!

For most newsletters, you can use a relatively casual tone because you are speaking directly to subscribers. This casual tone is particularly appropriate for company and organization newsletters when you are communicating with a cohesive group.

Fillers

Fillers include items such as the *Inspiration of the Day* feature, puzzles, word games, and cartoons. Many printed newsletters include fillers, which are used literally to fill extra space. A key point is to choose fillers that relate to the subject of the newsletter. For example, a *Cool Words* filler for a newsletter for new computer users could include definitions for terms such as *podcast*, *terabyte*, and *SQL*.

You can find hundreds of great fillers suitable for newsletters. Think from the point of view of the readers to determine what topics will interest them. You can also get ideas by going online and exploring the Web sites of the thousands of companies that distribute newsletters. Many of these Web sites include archives of the newsletters they have distributed over the years.

Formatting a Newsletter

You format a newsletter according to how you plan to distribute it. You can choose to create a **paper newsletter** or an **electronic newsletter**. You can also choose to create a **combination newsletter**. Each of these distribution methods is described in Figure 10-6.

Figure 10-6 **Newsletter formats**

Format	Description
Paper	• Create a paper newsletter with a word-processing program, such as Word, or a desktop publishing program, such as Microsoft Publisher or Adobe PageMaker. • Paper newsletters are usually formatted in columns.
Electronic	• Create an electronic newsletter with a Web page design program, such as Macromedia Dreamweaver. • Newsletters created with Web page design programs are formatted as Web pages, which usually include navigational aids so that users can simply click a link to visit other parts of the Web site.

Figure 10-6 ▶ Newsletter formats *(continued)*

Format	Description
Combination	• Create a paper newsletter in Word or another desktop publishing program and then convert it into a Portable Document Format (PDF) file that you post on a Web site or send in an e-mail. When the PDF file format is used, the formatting used in the paper newsletter is retained when the file is distributed electronically. Users can read the newsletter on the Web page or print it.

Newsletters can be formatted in hundreds of different ways, depending on the creativity and skill of the newsletter designer. Most newsletters, particularly paper and combination newsletters, share several components, including the use of a **masthead**, columns (paper) or frames (electronic), and graphics. Figure 10-7 describes each of these characteristics.

Figure 10-7 ▶ Newsletter components

Component	Description
Newsletter masthead	• Include identifying information about the newsletter and the company or organization that created it, such as the name of the company, the title of the newsletter, the newsletter date, and sometimes the edition of the newsletter. • Maintain the same masthead for each newsletter with changes only to the date and edition.
Columns (paper version)	• Format paper newsletters in columns because most paper newsletters imitate the style of a newspaper and because column text can be scanned quickly for items of interest.
Tables or frames (electronic version)	• Format Web-based newsletters to resemble a typical Web page with lists of topics and links, for example, using tables or frames to create the newsletter masthead, navigation bars, and other features.
Graphics	• Include a variety of graphic objects, including photographs, drawings, charts, diagrams, and even cartoons to enhance content in a newsletter. • Use a word-processing program, such as Word, or use a desktop publishing program, such as Microsoft Publisher or Adobe PageMaker, to format a newsletter.

Figure 10-8 shows a one-page organization newsletter that can be distributed in print form or saved as a Portable Document Format (PDF) file and distributed electronically, such as via e-mail or via the Web. While most readers of the sample newsletter are members of the Maplewood Arts Cooperative, anyone visiting the Maplewood Arts Cooperative Web site can access and read the newsletter. Either way, readers are those who are interested in the arts. As a result, most of the newsletter content is arts-related. The main story describes an upcoming art exhibition at the art gallery run by the organization and another story showcases the winner of a fiction-writing contest for members of the cooperative.

Figure 10-8   Sample newsletter for an organization

Maplewood Arts Cooperative

Fall 2011 Newsletter

New Exhibition

Kicking off the Fall exhibition season on September 6 is *The Abstract Eye: Paintings by Hartley Chan*. Hartley is a new member of Maplewood Arts Cooperative, but certainly not new to the art world. Over the past ten years, Hartley has exhibited his stunning abstract paintings all over North America and Europe. Shown below is the image that will be used on the invitation to Hartley's exhibition. Entitled *Traces*, this work is a good example of Hartley's uncanny ability to capture the essence of light and color.

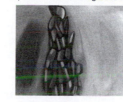

Online Gallery

We're online at www.maplewoodgallery.com. All of our artists are represented, along with images of their work. In a few more months, you'll even be able to purchase art online! We're working with a Web site developer right now to enable our site for e-commerce.

If you miss one of our openings, you can log on to our Web site and watch a video of the opening! We've installed a Web cam in the gallery so if the wind is blowing hard outside or your car has a flat tire, relax! Fire up your computer and come to a virtual opening.

Membership Drive

We are always ready to welcome new members! If you are interested in the arts and enjoy meeting artists, helping to run exhibitions, and lending a hand at openings, then please give us a call. We need your skills and your enthusiasm. And for our current members, how about asking a friend to join? For every member you sign up, you will receive $5.00 off your own annual membership fee. Since we're still keeping our annual membership fee at just $30.00, you just need to sign up six friends to enjoy a whole year of Maplewood Arts Cooperative for free!

Story Time

Maplewood Arts Cooperative counts many writers among its membership. In our last issue, we asked our writers to send us a thrilling beginning for a novel. Well we got what we asked for! The Story Committee stayed up half the night, on the edge of their seats, to read the submissions. The choice was tough, but finally the committee chose the novel beginning written by Ronnie Davidson. Here it is for your reading pleasure!

With breathtaking swiftness, the cold damp Pacific fog swallowed the Golden Gate Bridge. Only moments before, shafts of early morning sun had interlaced the bridge cables so that the bridge appeared to float in a sea of gold. The sudden plunge into obscurity was a good match for Betty's mood this last morning. Three months of searching from Beijing to Taiwan to Maui and finally here to San Francisco had yielded nothing. The fog that buried the entire city before her had more substance than the sum total of all the hours and days and weeks that stretched behind her.

"You've got to let it go."

Betty's shoulders flinched, but she didn't move from the window or turn around. She'd be the one to say when to let it go. He hadn't earned the right.

"I'll get the bags. The plane leaves in two hours and I heard on the radio that the traffic is murder."

The sound of his heels tapping across the wooden floor as he walked toward the bedroom irritated her almost beyond anything she'd yet felt.

When several minutes later she went looking for him after he failed to emerge with the bags, she was able to summon only token remorse. Of more immediate concern was the tiny jade dragon that had rolled out of his dead hand and come to rest almost at her feet.

The search was very suddenly over.

Technology Skills – Structuring Documents

In Word, you can modify a picture so that it appears lightly shaded behind text and you can structure a document so that the text flows into columns of the same or varying widths. In addition, you can enhance the first letter of a paragraph with a **drop cap**—a large initial capital letter that you can format with a different font. You can also add a **SmartArt diagram** to a document to show information graphically. Finally, you can save a Word document as a **Portable Document Format (PDF) file** that you can then distribute electronically. The person receiving a document saved as a PDF file needs to have the Adobe Reader software installed in order to read and print the document. The Technology Skills steps cover these skills:

- Modify pictures
- Create and modify columns in Word
- Insert and format drop caps in Word
- Create and format a SmartArt diagram in Word
- Save a Word document as a PDF file

You can insert a photograph in a document, modify its text wrapping so that it appears behind text or another object such as a WordArt object, and then adjust the brightness and contrast. You can also apply a preset picture style to a photograph.

To modify pictures:

1. Open the file **Tech_10.docx** located in the Project.10 folder included with your Data Files, and then to avoid altering the original file, save the document as **Coast Educational Foundation Newsletter** in the same folder. The document contains the text of a newsletter.

2. Click the **Show/Hide ¶** button ¶ in the Paragraph group to show the paragraph marks, if necessary.

3. Click to the left of **Coast Educational Foundation** near the top of the document, click the **Insert** tab, click **Picture** in the Illustrations group, navigate to the Project.10 folder, click **Coast.jpg**, and then click **Insert**. The picture appears in the document and the Picture Tools Format tab is active.

4. Click **Recolor** in the Adjust group, click the **Washout** option in the Color Modes section, click **Text Wrapping** in the Arrange group, and then click **Behind Text**.

5. Use your mouse to size and position the picture so that it appears as shown in Figure 10-9.

> **Tip**
>
> You work with the formatting marks visible when working with graphics to see the formatting changes you make more easily.

> **Tip**
>
> Use the ScreenTips to help you identify palette options.

Figure 10-9 — Masthead picture inserted, sized, and positioned

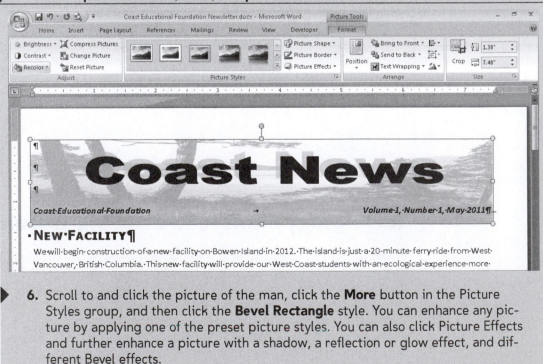

6. Scroll to and click the picture of the man, click the **More** button in the Picture Styles group, and then click the **Bevel Rectangle** style. You can enhance any picture by applying one of the preset picture styles. You can also click Picture Effects and further enhance a picture with a shadow, a reflection or glow effect, and different Bevel effects.

7. Save the document.

You can choose to format all or just a portion of text in a document in columns. You can also choose the number of columns, adjust the amount of white space displayed between columns, and include a vertical line between columns. When you format a portion of selected text in a document in columns, Word creates a section break between the text formatted in columns and the rest of the document.

To create and format selected text in columns:

1. Select the text from **New Facility** through **wood pulp!** at the end of the *A Whale of a Time* story, click the **Page Layout** tab, and then click **Columns** in the Page Setup group.

2. Click **More Columns** to open the Columns dialog box, select the **Left** column style, change the Spacing to **.3**, click the **Line between** check box to select it, and then click **OK**.

3. Click the **New Facility** heading, click the **Home** tab, click the **Line spacing** button in the Paragraph group, and then click **Remove Space Before Paragraph**. After you put text into columns, you sometimes need to adjust spacing.

4. Save the document.

Tip

You can also adjust column width by dragging the Move Column marker on the ruler or by typing new Width values in the Columns dialog box.

To make the text more attractive, you can format the first letter of each newsletter story with a drop cap. A **drop cap** is a large, dropped character that appears as the first character in a paragraph.

To insert and format a drop cap:

1. Click in the first paragraph of text under the New Facility heading (starts with the text "We will begin").

2. Click the **Insert** tab, click **Drop Cap** in the Text group, and then click **Drop Cap Options**. The Drop Cap dialog box opens.

3. Click **Dropped**, click the **Font** list arrow, scroll to and select **Brush Script MT**, and then click the **Lines to drop** down arrow once to reduce the lines to drop to **2**, as shown in Figure 10-10.

Figure 10-10 ▶ Drop Cap dialog box

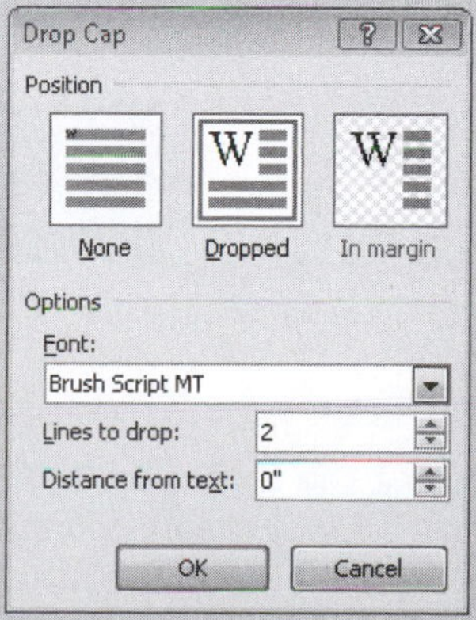

4. Click **OK**. The *W* is formatted as a drop cap in the Brush Script MT font. You decide you prefer a plain font.

5. Click **Drop Cap** in the Text group, click **Drop Cap Options**, change the font to **+Body** (top selection), and then click **OK**.

6. Add a drop cap with the default font to the first paragraph of the other three stories in the newsletter.

7. Adjust the size and position of the picture of the man so that the text in column 1, column 2, and the picture bottom align and *2010 Educational Programs* appears at the top of column 2, and then save the document.

You can create SmartArt graphics from seven categories in Word, including List, Process, Cycle, Hierarchy, Relationship, Matrix, and Pyramid. Within each category, you can select from a variety of layouts.

To create and format a SmartArt diagram:

1. Scroll to the end of the document, click after the text **at the helm** at the end of the last story, press the **Enter** key, and then click **SmartArt** in the Illustrations group.

2. Click **Hierarchy**, click the **Organization Chart** layout, and then click **OK**.

3. Type **Marion O'Brian**, press the **Enter** key, and then type **President**.

4. Click the **border** of the box below and to the left, press the **Delete** key to delete the box, type **Gerald Jansen** in the newly active box, press the **Enter** key, and then type **Vice President: Finance**.

5. Click the **Add Shape** list arrow in the Create Graphic group, click **Add Shape Below**, type **Donna Waring** on one line and **Accountant** on the next line, and then complete the organization chart so that it appears as shown in Figure 10-11. Note that you will need to delete one box and add another box.

Tip

To select the box, move the mouse near an edge of the box to show the ↖ and then click. You see sizing handles when a box is selected.

Figure 10-11 Text for the organization chart

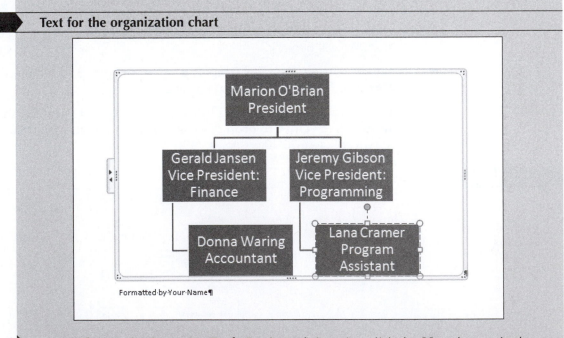

6. Verify that the **SmartArt Tools Design** tab is active, click the **More** button in the SmartArt Styles group, select the **Cartoon** style in the 3D section, click **Change Colors** in the SmartArt Styles group, and then select **Colorful Range – Accent Colors 3 to 4** in the Colorful section.

7. Click the **SmartArt Tools Format** tab, click the **Size** list arrow, and then change the Height to **2.5"** and the Width to **4"**.

Tip

You see sizing handles when a box is selected.

8. Click the **border** of the Gerald Jansen box, press and hold the **Shift** key, click the **border** of the Jeremy Gibson box so both boxes are selected, then drag the right middle handle of Jeremy's box to the right so that the titles associated with each vice president fit on one line, as shown in Figure 10-12.

Figure 10-12 ▶ **Resizing boxes in a SmartArt diagram**

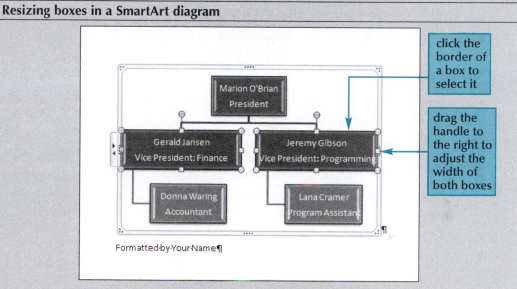

click the border of a box to select it

drag the handle to the right to adjust the width of both boxes

Tip

If you do not see Text Wrapping, click the Arrange button, then click Text Wrapping.

9. Click away from the selected boxes, click a blank area of the diagram to select it, click **Text Wrapping** in the Arrange group, click **Square**, switch to **One Page** view, use your mouse to position the SmartArt diagram to the right of the text so it appears as shown in Figure 10-13, and then save the document.

Figure 10-13 ▶ **Completed newsletter in One Page view**

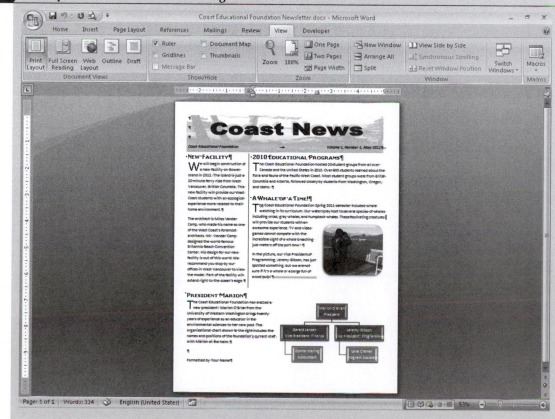

You convert a Word document into a Portable Document Format (PDF) file when you want to distribute the document to others who may not have Word installed on their computers. You need the Adobe Reader program to read a PDF file.

To convert a Word document into a Portable Document Format (PDF) file:

▶ **1.** Change to **Page Width** view, and then type your name where indicated at the bottom of the document.

▶ **2.** Click the **Office** button (⊞), point to **Save As**, and then click **PDF or XPS**.

▶ **3.** Press the **Enter** key to accept the current filename and publish the document as a PDF file.

▶ **4.** If the file does not automatically open in Adobe Reader, click the **Adobe Reader** button on the taskbar to show the document in Adobe Reader, and then exit the program.

▶ **5.** Print a copy of the newsletter from Word, save the document, and then close it.

Tip

If the PDF or XPS option is not available, download and install the Save as PDF or XPS add-in from Microsoft.

Practice | Consumer Newsletter

You work for Island Time Books, an independent bookstore located on Whidbey Island in Washington state. Every six months, the company creates a newsletter in both paper and electronic form for distribution to customers who have agreed to receive it. You have collected most of the information you plan to include in the newsletter. Now you need to organize the information into stories and then format the newsletter for publication as a PDF file that can be printed or attached to an e-mail.

Follow the steps below to organize and format the content of a consumer newsletter.

1. Open the file **Practice_10.docx** located in the Project.10 folder included with your Data Files and then, to avoid altering the original file, save the document as **Island Time Books Newsletter** in the same folder. This document includes two pictures along with notes that can be adapted as stories to be included in the one-page newsletter: three news items about upcoming events, one profile on Yolanda Larch, and filler information about Classic Travel books.

2. Read the document and note where you will need to rewrite the notes as prose appropriate for a newsletter. For the Spring Season Events story, do the following:
   a. Use the information in the bullet points to write a paragraph for both the *An Evening with Bart Grant* and *Book Launch of Greenways* events. Add additional information if you wish.
   b. Use the information in the bullet points for Yolanda Larch to write two paragraphs—one describing her background and another describing her upcoming appearance at Island Time Books.

3. Below the Yolanda Larch profile, create a SmartArt diagram using the Vertical Block List style in the List category that lists all four events and their dates as shown in Figure 10-14. To add a fourth row, click the May 3, 2011 text box, click Add Shape, click Add Shape After, and then click Add Bullet.

Figure 10-14   **SmartArt diagram listing all upcoming events**

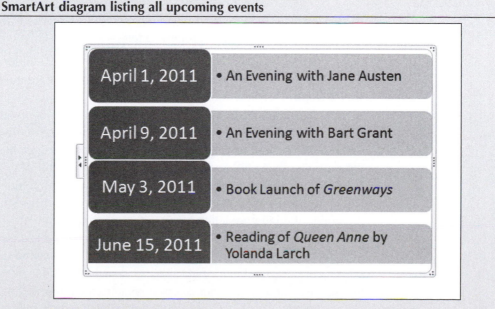

4. Apply the SmartArt style and color of your choice, and then verify the text wrapping for the object is set to In Line with Text. You will size and position the SmartArt diagram once you have completed formatting the newsletter.

5. In the Classic Travel Books section, apply the picture style of your choice to the picture of the Eiffel Tower and then change the text wrapping to Square. You will size and position the picture once you have completed formatting the newsletter.

6. Select the picture at the top of the document, apply the Washout color effect and Behind Text text wrapping, and then size and position the picture so that it appears behind the WordArt object containing the name of the newsletter (Island Time Books).

7. Add drop caps to the first letter of the paragraph below the Spring Season Events heading and the first paragraph below the heading for Yolanda Larch's profile. Set the lines to drop to 2.

8. Select all the text from Spring Season Events to the end of the document, then set columns using the Two format and .3″ spacing between columns.

9. In Two Pages view, adjust the sizes and positions of the graphic elements and text so that the entire newsletter fits attractively on one page. Note that you will need to remove the Before Paragraph Spacing from the headings as needed.

10. Type your name where indicated at the bottom of the document, save the document as a PDF file using the same name as the Word document, and then exit Adobe Reader.

11. From Word, save the document, and then print a copy.

> **Tip**
>
> Resize and move both images to page 1, place each image, and then continue to resize and move the images. Experiment with different picture styles. The process requires some time.

Revise | **Company Newsletter**

You work for The Travel Depot, a large chain of travel agents that specializes in providing clients with great deals on flights, package tours, and cruises. The company has grown considerably in recent years and employs a large staff of service agents. Every three months, the Human Resources department works with the Marketing department to produce a company newsletter for distribution to all staff. As an assistant in the Marketing department, you are responsible for updating the newsletter every three months with new stories and graphics.

Follow the steps below to revise the Summer newsletter for The Travel Depot so that it includes stories suitable for the Fall newsletter.

1. Open the file **Revise1_10.docx** located in the Project.10 folder included with your Data Files and then, to avoid altering the original file, save the document as **The Travel Depot Fall Newsletter** in the same folder.

2. Edit the masthead so the newsletter is suitable for fall—September to November. Change the fill and line colors of the WordArt object to an orange shade suitable for autumn. *Hint:* Double-click the WordArt object containing The Travel Depot, and then use the Shape Fill and Shape Outline buttons in the WordArt Styles group.

3. Open the file **Revise2_10.docx** located in the Project.10 folder included with your Data Files. This file contains the notes and some text for the stories you need to include in the fall newsletter, along with a photograph.

4. Keep the same heading styles for the headings. *Hint:* Type text for the new headings over the existing headings; to create the third heading, type the text above the SmartArt object, and then use the Format Painter to format the heading for the third story.

5. Revise the summer newsletter so that it contains the three stories for the fall newsletter. Delete the content under the headings, including the drop caps and the picture but not the SmartArt object, then use the notes provided in the Revise2_10.docx file as the basis for writing clear and interesting stories.

6. Modify the columns to use the Left column style with .3″ spacing and a line between columns. *Hint*: To modify columns, make sure your insertion point is positioned anywhere within an existing column, and then open the Columns dialog box.

7. Widen the left column as needed so that the heading Associate of the Season fits on one line.

8. Copy the pictures from the Revise2_10.docx document to appropriate places in the fall newsletter and then apply the picture styles of your choice and the Square text wrapping style. Note that you will need to adjust the size of each picture. Use your mouse to position each picture within its corresponding story.

9. Include a drop cap at the beginning of each of the three stories.

10. Modify the SmartArt diagram so that it reflects the information included in the Top Summer Tours story for the fall newsletter.

11. Apply the Inset SmartArt style to the SmartArt diagram, select a new color scheme, change the font size of the text in each box to 16 pt, and make sure that the number of tours appears on a separate line from each tour name. *Hint:* To change the font size of text in a SmartArt object, select the text in each object separately, and then change the font size.

12. Work in One Page view to ensure the text and graphics fit attractively on one page. Note that you will need to use your mouse to resize and position all the graphics.

13. Type your name where indicated at the bottom of the document, save the document as a PDF file using the same name as the Word document, and then exit Adobe Reader.

14. From Word, save the document, and then print a copy.

15. Close the Revise2_10.docx document without saving it.

> **Tip**
>
> Place the pointer over the ruler until you see Move Column. Then use the pointer to drag the Move Column marker to the right.

Create | Newsletter Sample

Develop the content for a newsletter for a company or organization of your choice and then format the content attractively. You need to select the newsletter type (Company, Consumer, or Organization), state the name of the company or organization, and then summarize the topic of each of the three stories. You can choose stories from any of the story types. For example, you could write an organization newsletter for a local charity that includes a news item, some announcements, and a profile.

Follow the steps below to write and format a newsletter.

1. On a blank piece of paper, identify a company or organization (it can be fictitious), and then brainstorm stories for the newsletter type you have chosen. You can adapt stories and articles you have written for other purposes or you can write new stories.

2. Complete the table below with the information you need to help you write the newsletter. Select a range of story types such as a profile, an article, and an announcement. For example, a consumer newsletter for a camera store could include an article titled "Traveling with Your Digital Camera," a profile of a local photographer who is having an exhibition at an art gallery, and an announcement about an upcoming seminar on landscape photography. Note that you will need to make up information. Use fictitious but realistic details.

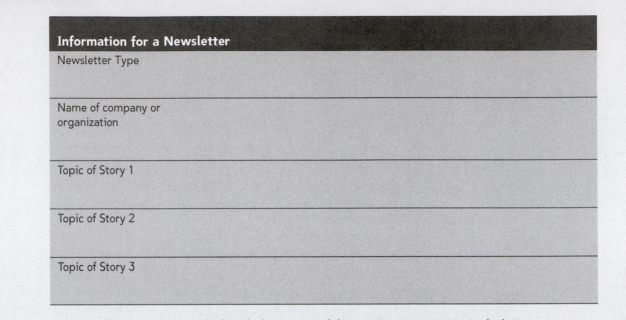

Information for a Newsletter

Newsletter Type	
Name of company or organization	
Topic of Story 1	
Topic of Story 2	
Topic of Story 3	

3. When you are satisfied with the topics of the stories you want to include in your newsletter, open a new document and write the text for each of the three stories.

4. Set all four margins at .5″, and then save the newsletter as **My Newsletter**.

5. Include a masthead for your newsletter. You can choose to include a WordArt object and a picture if you wish. Make sure you include a date for the newsletter (for example, *Fall 2011* or *April to June 2011*).

6. Format the heading for each story the same way and include a drop cap as the first letter for each of the three stories.

7. Add illustrations to your newsletter; at a minimum, include one picture formatted with the picture style of your choice. You can also include a SmartArt diagram if appropriate for the content.

8. Format some or all of the text in columns.

9. Limit the final length of the newsletter to one page.

10. Type your name at the bottom of the newsletter, save the document, and then print a copy.

Apply　　|　**Case Study 1**

Capstone College　Each year, over a hundred students graduate from the Digital Arts Department at Capstone College in San Francisco. Many of these students enjoy maintaining contact with the department by receiving the bi-annual newsletter distributed in June and December. You have collected stories for the July to December 2011 newsletter and saved them in a file. Now you need to organize these stories into a one-page newsletter for distribution in both paper and electronic form. To complete this case study, you create the newsletter.

1. Open the file **Case1_10.docx** located in the Project.10 folder included with your Data Files, and then save the document as **2011 Digital Arts Newsletter_July to December** in the same folder.

2. Read the stories and then create a heading for each story. You choose the wording. Format the heading for each story the same way. You can choose to increase the font size, change the font, select a new font color, and adjust the before and after spacing as needed.

3. Change the margins on all four sides to .5", and then create a masthead for the newsletter using the text *Digital Arts News* as a WordArt object and including the text *July to December 2011*. Select the settings you prefer for the WordArt object.

4. Select the text from the first story to the end of the document, and then apply two even columns. Decrease the spacing between the columns to .3".

5. Include a drop cap as the first letter for each of the three stories.

6. Format the picture with the picture style of your choice and select the Square text wrapping style.

7. Create a SmartArt diagram using the information in the table. You can modify the diagram any way you wish by removing selected objects, changing the font size of text, and applying new color schemes.

8. Work in One Page view to organize the stories and the illustrations so that all the text fills the two columns and fits on one page. You may need to change the order of the stories. Limit the final length of the newsletter to one page.

9. Type your name where indicated at the bottom of the newsletter, save the document, save the document again as a PDF file, close Adobe Reader, and then print a copy of the newsletter from Word.

| Apply | **Case Study 2** |

Otter Bay Kayaking Adventures   The primary target market for Otter Bay Kayaking Adventures is the group of tour coordinators who work on the cruise ships that visit Juneau each summer. Kay Johnson, the owner of Otter Bay Kayaking Adventures, has decided to develop a newsletter that she can send quarterly to the various cruise ship companies, as well as to independent tour coordinators. The purpose of the newsletter is to provide information about the company's tours, along with news about the tourist industry in Juneau that may interest the target market. Kay asks you to create a one-page newsletter containing three stories. To complete this case study, you write the newsletter using the source information provided.

1. Open the file **Case2_10.docx** located in the Project.10 folder included with your Data Files, and then save the document as **Otter Bay Kayaking Adventures Newsletter** in the same folder. This document contains source information and suggestions that you can use to write three stories.

2. Use the information provided to write the text for each of the three stories. You can add new text and make up additional details, but the completed newsletter should be no longer than one page, including illustrations.

3. Create an interesting heading for each story, format each heading the same way, and include a drop cap as the first letter for each of the three stories.

4. Create a masthead that includes a WordArt object with the text *Otter Bay Kayaking Adventures* and the subtitle *Newsletter: Spring 2011*.

5. Place the picture of the orange kayak included in the data file behind the WordArt object, modify the size, and change the coloring to Washout.

6. Add an appropriate picture to one of the stories; you can search Clip Art for a suitable picture or use one of your own photographs. For example, you could include a picture of a bicycle in the story about creating a partnership with Cycle Juneau or a picture of a whale or bear in the story about photography. Format the picture with the picture style of your choice and select the text wrapping style of your choice (usually Square or Inline with Text).

7. Create a SmartArt diagram using the Hierarchy layout to show the hierarchy of staff at Otter Bay Kayaking Adventures. You can modify the organization chart any way you wish by removing selected objects, changing the font size of text, and applying new color schemes.

8. Format all or some of the text in columns. You can choose to show some text in two columns and some text in one column (for example, the story containing the organization chart may look better formatted in one column). Work in One Page view to organize the stories and the illustrations until you are pleased with the overall effect. Note that you may need to change the order of the stories. Limit the final length of the newsletter to one page.

9. Type your name where indicated at the bottom of the document, save the document as a PDF file using the same name as the Word document, and then exit Adobe Reader.

10. From Word, save the document, and then print a copy.

| Research | | **Case Study 3** |

As you have learned in other projects, you can download templates for a variety of business documents from the Microsoft Office Templates Web site. Several good templates are available for newsletters. You can learn a great deal about the type of content included in these documents by studying the examples on the Microsoft Office Templates Web site. To complete this case study, you download a newsletter from the Microsoft Office Templates Web site and adapt it for a company of your choice.

1. Start Word, click the Office button, and then click New.

2. Scroll through the list under Microsoft Office Online, click Newsletters, and then explore the newsletter templates available.

3. When you find a newsletter template that appeals to you, follow the directions provided to download the template to your computer.

4. Save the template as a .docx file called **Sample Newsletter Template**. Note that the template may be a .doc file. You need to select Save As and the .docx file type, and then click OK to accept any messages. You need to save the document as a .docx file so that you can include a SmartArt diagram in the completed newsletter.

5. Read the text included in the template and then adapt it for a company or organization of your choice. You can delete text that you don't want to include. The completed newsletter should be no longer than two pages. Note that the template may contain text in text boxes. You can select and then delete a text box just as you would any graphic object.

6. Include a SmartArt diagram using the category and layout of your choice.

7. Include at least one photograph formatted with the picture style of your choice.

8. Include your name on the modified newsletter, save the document, print a copy, and then close the document.

Brochures

Introduction

Brochures come in all shapes and sizes and at various levels of production. A multipage brochure for a new car model costs many thousands of dollars to design and produce. A black-and-white trifold brochure that describes the benefits of drinking pure water can be created in a few hours and printed for pennies a copy. All brochures, regardless of topic, have one thing in common. A **brochure** contains text that describes a product or a service, or that describes a topic of interest for a target market.

In this project, you examine the principal uses for brochures, develop brochure content, and explore brochure formats. You then work in Word to create and edit styles, use style sets, and apply themes to provide documents with a unified look.

Starting Data Files

Project.11

Tech1_11.docx
Tech2_11.docx
Practice_11.docx
Revise1_11.docx
Revise2_11.docx
Case1_11.docx
Case2_11.docx
Research_11.docx

Brochure Essentials

People read brochures because they want to know more about a company's products or services or they want information about a specific topic. All brochures, regardless of type, need to contain enough content to make reading them worthwhile.

You organize content in a brochure into sections that correspond to the brochure format. For example, if the brochure you are creating includes six separate panels, you develop content to flow from panel to panel. If your brochure is organized into pages, you develop content for each page.

Exploring Brochure Formats

The typical brochure produced by a small company on a limited budget is the trifold brochure which is created by printing on both sides of an $8\frac{1}{2} \times 11$-inch piece of paper. Figure 11-1 shows how the six panels of a trifold brochure are positioned.

Figure 11-1   **Panel positions for a trifold brochure**

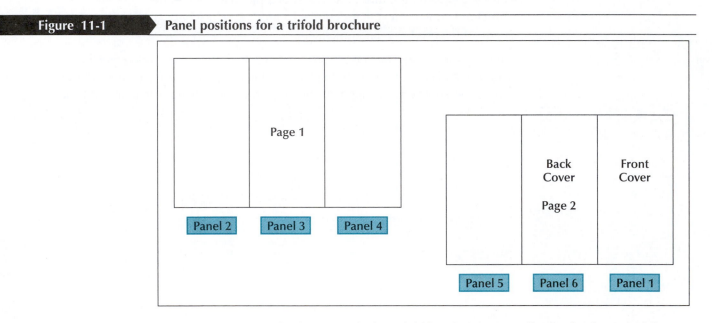

As you can see, the front panel of a trifold brochure is actually the third panel of the second page. When the brochure is folded, this panel becomes the cover panel. The back panel of a brochure is panel 6 and usually includes the contact information of the company or organization that wrote the brochure.

Panels 2, 3, and 4 are the three inside panels. These three panels face you when you open the brochure and so you usually include the most content on these three panels. Panel 5 is folded inward toward panels 2 and 3. When you open a trifold brochure, you see panel 5 briefly and then you usually open it out so that you can view panels 2, 3, and 4 in their entirety. On panel 5, you often include product specifications or how-to information that supplements the main content included in panels 2, 3, and 4.

Companies with large budgets can choose to create multipage brochures similar to a magazine that customers keep and refer to often. The brochures created by car companies and cruise ship lines are good examples of these types of brochures. If you are involved in writing text for a long brochure, you need to include a table of contents following the cover page so that readers can quickly find the products and services that interest them.

Most brochures are created to promote a company's products or services, or to provide readers with information about specific topics. The content required for both brochure types is described next.

Using Brochures to Promote Products and Services

A company creates a brochure to describe the benefits to customers of purchasing its products or services. Salespeople use brochures to generate leads, to introduce someone to the company prior to making a sales call, and to provide customers with additional information following a sales call. Many requests for information made by customers are answered with a letter or e-mail that includes a brochure, either in paper form or attached to an e-mail, generally as a PDF file.

A brochure that promotes a company's products or services is a persuasive document. As you learned in the discussion on sales letters in Project 5, a persuasive document must focus on how the reader will *benefit* from making a purchase. A brochure that merely describes features is not likely to attract potential customers. You can adapt the benefits identified in other sales literature, such as sales letters, for inclusion in a brochure.

You can use the **which means that** technique to reframe features as reader benefits. Suppose you need to write a brochure to promote a catering service. Figure 11-2 describes three of the features of the catering service along with potential benefits. The *which means that* phrase is used to show how a feature can be reframed as a benefit.

Figure 11-2   **Identifying reader benefits for a brochure on catering services**

Feature		Reader Benefit
An award-winning, European-trained chef	*which means that*	Your guests at the catered event will enjoy gourmet food and be impressed by your excellent taste.
An international menu that includes specialties from around the Pacific Rim	*which means that*	You please guests from different cultures and you cater to guests who are interested in food from cultures other than their own.
A traditional menu that includes "meat and potatoes" specialties	*which means that*	You ensure that your guests with more traditional food preferences also have great food available to them.

Once you have identified reader benefits, you organize the content for the brochure. You simplify the development of the brochure content by first dividing it into sections. Figure 11-3 summarizes how you can organize the content for a six-panel product brochure.

Figure 11-3   **Organizing content for a six-panel products brochure**

Location	Description of Content Required
Panel 1	• The name of the product or service and some motivational text designed to encourage readers to open the brochure. Panel 1 should attract attention and imply a benefit. • A graphic or picture that represents the product or service is often added.
Panel 2	• An overview of the product or service that stresses the benefits to the customer of purchasing that product or service. • Some of the text or a photograph included in a company's sales letter might be appropriate in this overview section of a brochure.
Panels 3 and 4	• A description of various components or features of the product. A lively writing style is used to paint a picture for readers. • Graphics or photographs, if available. The number and quality of the graphics you can use in a brochure depend on the level of design expertise and budget available. For example, the use of color photographs increases printing costs.

Figure 11-3	▶	**Organizing content for a six-panel products brochure (*continued*)**

Location	Description of Content Required
Panel 5	• A summary of product specifications or other details not described in the central part of the brochure. • A good location for an order form that customers can tear off and send in.
Panel 6	• Contact information about the company: include the company's address, phone number, fax number, and Web site address.

Figure 11-4 shows panels 2, 3, and 4 of a brochure designed to promote the catering services offered by Wild Greens, a whole foods café and retail store located in Auckland, New Zealand.

Figure 11-4	▶	**Content for panels 2, 3, and 4 of a products brochure**

CATERING EVENTS

The *Wild Green Chef* loves special events! He will transform the very freshest Wild Greens ingredients into fabulous feasts.

What's the one thing that people always comment on—for better or for worse—at any special event? That's right—the food! Great food makes a great event, and not-so-great food can well, you know...

You can depend on the *Wild Green Chef* to make your weddings, anniversaries, birthdays, dinner parties, and corporate events into events that your guests will remember for all the right reasons.

Weddings

You've imagined the perfect wedding for years and now finally, you're planning your own wedding. Congratulations! Now, what do you want your guests to eat at the reception? The typical wedding dinner buffet of over-cooked chicken and limp salads is not how you want your guests to remember *your* special day! Instead, give them something new. Give them an all-natural, all-organic, all-

gourmet wedding supper catered by Wild Greens. You can choose from two popular menus as follows:

Wild Greens Traditional

Mum and Dad and Auntie Doris from England still want roast lamb and mashed potatoes, so why not give them the Wild Greens version? Our traditional wedding feast is traditional in name only. You won't find our recipe for Kiwi-Lime-Cilantro Lamb anywhere in Granny's kitchen! Accompaniments include the *Wild Green Chef*'s signature mashed potatoes, wild asparagus, and ginger carrots. Even the most conservative taste buds will be wowed—and the success of your wedding buffet secured.

Wild Greens Exotic

Take your guests to the exotic climes of the Orient with a wedding supper loaded with the flavors of the Far East. Our *Wild Green Chef* creates a skillful blend of Japanese, Chinese, Vietnamese, and Indonesian dishes that will have your guests talking about your wedding until your Silver Anniversary!

Imagine fresh shrimp braised in mild chillies with a sweet sauce followed by crispy pork medallions in an orange-sesame sauce.

Special Events

Let the *Wild Green Chef* make your next dinner party an event your guests will rave about for years. Here are just some of the

ways in which Wild Greens can treat your guests at your next special event.

Dinner Parties

The *Wild Green Chef* will come to your home and whip up a gourmet meal for 2, for 4, for 24—you name the time and the place and the *Wild Green Chef* will arrive with all the food and a friendly, efficient wait staff. You just enjoy your guests and the fabulous food.

Birthday Parties

No one likes a birthday more than the *Wild Green Chef*! His specialty birthday cakes are legendary. Give the *Wild Green Chef* any theme—from Lord of the Rings to South Sea Luau and then just step back and enjoy!

Corporate Parties

Has your boss asked you to put together a reception for visiting dignitaries? Don't panic! The *Wild Green Chef* can put together a menu that features all New Zealand specialties so tasty that the dignitaries might decide not to go home.

As you can see, an overview of the catering services is provided on panel 2 and then the two principal event types that Wild Greens caters are described in some detail. Panels 2, 3, and 4 provide readers with a considerable amount of detailed information about the catering services offered by Wild Greens. The company hopes customers will keep this brochure and refer to it when they need catering services. Figure 11-5 shows panels 5, 6, and 1 of the brochure.

| Figure 11-5 | Content for panels 5, 6, and 1 of a services brochure |

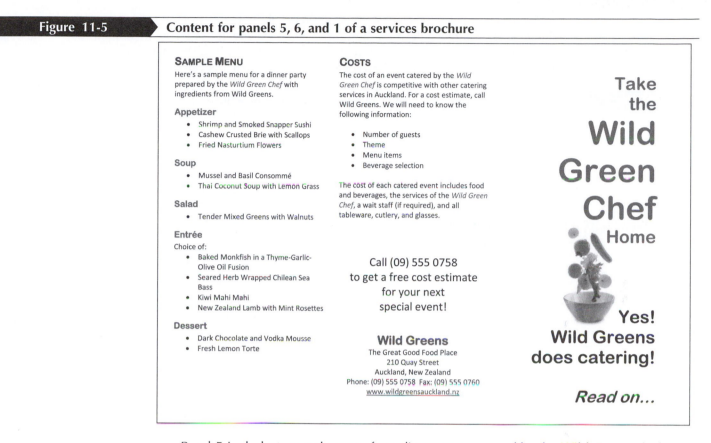

Panel 5 includes a sample menu for a dinner party catered by the Wild Green Chef and panel 6 includes the contact information. When the brochure is folded, panel 5 appears when the brochure is first opened and panel 6 is the back panel.

The content included on panel 1 is the most important content in the brochure because it must inspire people to pick up the brochure and open it. In panel 1 of the Wild Greens brochure, the statement *Take the Wild Green Chef Home* is intended to attract the attention of potential customers and then the phrase *Yes! Wild Greens does catering!* tells customers that the subject of the brochure is the catering services offered by Wild Greens.

You can transform some of the information you have developed about benefits into the text for the front panel. For example, if you have identified *great taste* as a benefit, you could write *Tickle Your Taste Buds* or *Taste the Wild Side*.

Using Brochures to Distribute Information

An informational brochure communicates information about specific topics, such as the benefits of drinking milk or how to childproof your home. Companies and organizations often include this kind of information in a brochure because the brochure format allows for the inclusion of a fair amount of information in a relatively compact space. In addition, people are accustomed to picking up a brochure to find out about a wide range of subjects, particularly health and safety-related subjects. Most waiting rooms in physicians' offices and hospitals include dozens of brochures on medical conditions ranging from athlete's foot to the Zoster virus.

Your first task when developing content for a brochure that distributes information about a specific topic of interest to a target audience is to create an outline that breaks your subject into main topics and subtopics. You can then divide the text across the brochure panels in much the same way as you do in a products and services brochure. The bulk of the information will appear in panels 2, 3, and 4.

Figure 11-6 shows the content included on panels 2, 3, and 4 of a brochure that describes the benefits of drinking filtered water. Wild Greens created this brochure to promote its brand of purified water. Each person who purchases the water at Wild Greens will receive the brochure, which will also be distributed to other stores that carry the water.

| **Figure 11-6** | **Content for panels 2, 3, and 4 of an informational brochure** |

Our Water

When you buy your filtered water from *Wild Greens*, you can be sure you're getting water that is not only crystal clear and safe, but great tasting! Drink a glass of tap water and then drink a glass of purified water, and you tell us which one tastes better.

You can't detect any chlorine or metal taste in a glass of purified water. In fact, the water contains less than three parts per million of minerals, and most of these minerals are reduced well below detectable limits.

Health Benefits

Here are the health benefits of drinking purified water:

- Increase your mental performance:
  o Our brains are 72% water!
- Increase your physical performance:
  o Our muscles are 75% water and our bones are 22% water
- Keep your skin healthy and glowing:
  o Our blood is 80% water
- Reduce headaches
- Digest your food properly
- Improve your energy
- Remove toxins from your body
- Live life with renewed health and vigor

Purification Process

The water purification process begins when the water is drawn from the municipal water system into the purifier. Six steps are required to purify the water as follows:

Step One: Particulate Filtration
A five-micron filter removes iron, dust, organic debris, mold, pollen, sand, silt, and other sediment. The filtration system removes particles 10 times smaller than the visible range of the human eye.

Step Two: Activated Carbon Absorption: Stage 1
A high-grade, five-micron, activated carbon block filter eliminates chlorine and a wide range of volatile halogens, pesticides, herbicides, and industrial solvents.

Step Three: Activated Carbon Absorption: Stage 2
A second, high-grade, commercial-quality, activated-carbon filter provides further protection.

Step Four: Reverse Osmosis Membrane Filtration
A powerful pump forces the water through a semipermeable membrane and separates out the dissolved minerals and unwelcome pathogens. The pores of this membrane are far smaller than bacteria and viruses so these microorganisms simply cannot get through. Reverse osmosis can eliminate "cysts" such as giardia and cryptosporidium, which chlorine cannot control.

Step Five: Solid Block Carbon Filtration
A five-micron, solid block carbon filter removes any traces of impurities.

Step Six: Ultraviolet Protection
The water is pumped through an ultraviolet (U.V.) lamp, which sterilizes the water before it reaches the bottle. The water you drink is as pure as science can make it.

Notice how headings and subheadings are used to neatly organize and present the content. Notice, too, how panels 3 and 4 have been combined into one column. The writing style is clear and informal. Although much of the subject is technical, the description aims to provide readers who are not experts in water purification techniques with a general idea about the process so that they understand why purified water might be better for them than tap water.

On panel 5, you can include additional details, appropriate specifications, or even a how-to section. On panel 6, which is the back panel of the brochure, you include contact information, just as you do in a brochure that promotes products and services. On panel 1, of course, you include text and possibly a graphic that describes the subject of the brochure and is interesting enough to invite readers to explore further. Figure 11-7 shows the content included on panels 5, 6, and 1 of the water purification brochure.

Figure 11-7 ▶ **Content for panels 5, 6, and 1 of an informational brochure**

Bottle Care

Reusable water bottles should give you years of service so long as you take care of them and keep them clean. A dirty bottle can contain millions of sprouting bacteria. You need to wash your bottles regularly and sanitize them periodically.

Bottle Washing
- Dissolve one tablespoon of baking soda in two liters of water.
- Shake well.
- Rinse well.
- Allow to air dry.
- Seal the bottle with its plastic cap.

Bottle Sanitizing
- Mix ½ teaspoon of chlorine bleach in a gallon of water.
- Seal the bottle with its plastic cap.
- Shake well.
- Place the bottle on the counter for three minutes.
- Rinse the bottle thoroughly with several changes of water.

Bottle Storage
- Store bottles away from sunlight and other heat sources.
- Store bottles with their lids on.
- Do not drop your bottles when full to avoid developing leaks.

Frequently Asked Questions

Is drinking purified water really better for my health?
Numerous studies have shown that drinking purified water has significant health benefits. See Health Benefits in this brochure for more information.

I heard that UV is dangerous and yet the water is pumped through UV filtration. Is that OK?
The process has been thoroughly tested. The type of UV lamp used to sterilize the water has been certified as safe by the Global Water Certification Agency.

What about metal bottles? Can I get purified water in them?
Yes! You can purchase your purified water in bulk and then fill and re-fill your metal water bottle.

Wild Greens

The Great Good Food Place
210 Quay Street
Auckland, New Zealand
Phone: (09) 555 0758 Fax: (09) 555 0760

www.wildgreensauckland.nz

Wild

Greens

Purified

Water

What You Need To Know

You can think of the content for an informational brochure as similar to the content included in a short, descriptive report. The difference is that an informational brochure must communicate the information very succinctly and usually less formally. Only the most important details are included.

When you take the time to develop appropriate content for a brochure, the design process usually goes quite smoothly. You can use many of the features in Word to help you lay out the content of a brochure in an attractive and compelling way.

Technology Skills – Working with Styles

Companies and organizations with healthy marketing budgets generally engage professional designers to lay out the text for a brochure and then prepare the brochure for printing. However, if you work for a smaller company or nonprofit organization, or you are just starting your career as an entrepreneur, you can use Word to create a perfectly acceptable trifold brochure.

You can use styles in Word to automate some of the brochure formatting tasks. A **style** consists of various formats, such as font, font size, and alignment, that are named and saved together as one set. For example, the default Heading 1 style in Word formats text with the Cambria font, 14 pt, bold, blue, and left alignment with Before spacing of 24 pt and After spacing of 0.

The Technology Skills steps cover these skills:

- Modify styles in Word
- Create new styles in Word
- Create a Quick Style Set in Word

Word includes several default styles that you can modify. These styles are available in the Styles group on the Home tab. When you modify a style, all text formatted with that style is also modified. Using styles to format text that you want formatted in the same way saves you a great deal of time. In the following steps, you learn two ways to modify a style.

To modify styles in Word:

1. Open the file **Tech1_11.docx** located in the Project.11 folder included with your Data Files, and then to avoid altering the original file, save the document as **Travel Brochure_Europe**. The document contains the text of a brochure that advertises a trip to France and Italy.

2. Click the **Show/Hide ¶** button ¶ in the **Paragraph** group to show the paragraph marks, if necessary. You will be working with styles to format the brochure and you can more easily see what formatting changes are being made if you work with the formatting marks visible.

3. Select **Tour Description**, and then note that Heading 1 is highlighted in the Styles group.

4. With Tour Description selected, open the Font dialog box, select the **Tahoma** font, change the color to **Green, Accent 1, Darker 50%**, click **Small caps** in the Effects area, and then click **OK**.

5. Right-click the selected text, point to **Styles**, and then click **Update Heading 1 to Match Selection** as shown in Figure 11-8. The Heading 1 style applied to Tour Highlights changes to match the formatting changes you made to the Tour Descriptions heading. You can also modify a style by right-clicking it in the Styles gallery.

Figure 11-8   **Updating a style**

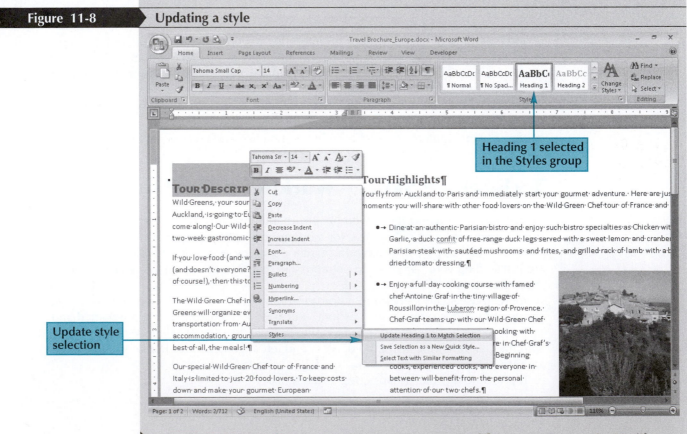

6. Right-click **Heading 1** in the Styles group, click **Modify**, click **Format** in the Modify Style dialog box, click **Paragraph**, change the **Before** spacing to **0 pt**, click **OK**, and then click **OK**. All text formatted with the Heading 1 style is updated automatically.

7. Scroll to the next page, select **Tour Itinerary** at the top of panel 5, and then click **Heading 1** in the Styles group. The Heading 1 style with the new formatting is applied to Tour Itinerary.

8. Scroll to the top of the document, and then save the document.

You can create custom styles for a paragraph style or a character style. A **paragraph style** is a combination of character and paragraph formats that you name and store as a set. The Heading 1 style you modified in the previous set of steps is a paragraph style. A **character style** includes character format settings, such as font, font color, and bold, that you name and store as a set. You apply a character style to selected text within a paragraph. Any text in the paragraph that is not formatted with the character style is formatted with the currently applied paragraph style.

To create a new character style in Word:

1. Select **Wild Green Chef** in paragraph 1 on page 1 of the brochure, change the color to **Green, Accent 1, Darker 25%**, and then apply **Bold** and **Italics**.

2. Right-click the selected text, point to **Styles**, and then click **Save Selection as a New Quick Style**.

3. Type **Wild Greens**, and then click **Modify**. You need to specify that the new style is a Character style that will be applied only to text within a paragraph without changing the formatting of surrounding text.

4. Click the **Style type** list arrow, click **Character**, and then click **OK**. You use the Replace function to find all instances of Wild Green Chef and replace it with the text formatted with the new Wild Greens character style.

5. Deselect the text, click **Replace** in the Editing group, type **Wild Green Chef**, click in the Replace with text box, and then type **Wild Green Chef**.

6. Click **More** to expand the dialog box, click **Format**, click **Style**, and then scroll to and click **Wild Greens** as shown in Figure 11-9.

Figure 11-9 ▸ Wild Greens Character style selected

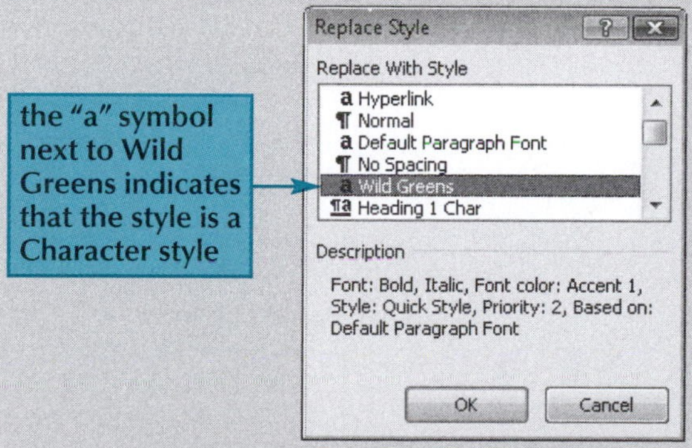

the "a" symbol next to Wild Greens indicates that the style is a Character style

7. Click **OK**, click **Replace All**, click **OK**, and then click **Close**.

8. Scroll to panel 1 on page 2 of the brochure (the far right panel containing the WordArt object), select Wild Green Chef, and then increase the font size to **20 pt**. Notice that even though a style has been applied to text, you can continue to format the text. The formatting changes you make to selected text will not affect a style, unless you save it as a style change.

9. Save the document.

After formatting a document with a selection of styles that includes both new and existing Quick Styles, you can save all the styles as a new Quick Style Set. You can then apply the Quick Style Set to other documents that you want formatted with the same styles. First, you check out one of the default Quick Style Sets and then you create a new Quick Style Set.

To create a Quick Style Set in Word:

▶ 1. Press [**Ctrl**][**Home**] to move back to the top of the document, click **Change Styles** in the Styles group, point to **Style Set**, and then click **Modern**. Text formatted with the default Heading 1 style is changed. The font size of the Normal style applied by default to all text not formatted with another style is also changed from 11 pt to 10 pt. You decide to return to your original formatting.

▶ 2. Click the **Undo** button [↩].

▶ 3. Click **Change Styles**, point to **Style Set**, and then click **Save as Quick Style Set**.

▶ 4. Type **Wild Greens Brochure**, and then click **Save**.

▶ 5. Type your name where indicated at the bottom of panel 6 (middle panel on page 2), and then view the brochure in Two Pages view. The completed brochure appears as shown in Figure 11-10.

Figure 11-10 ▶ **Completed brochure**

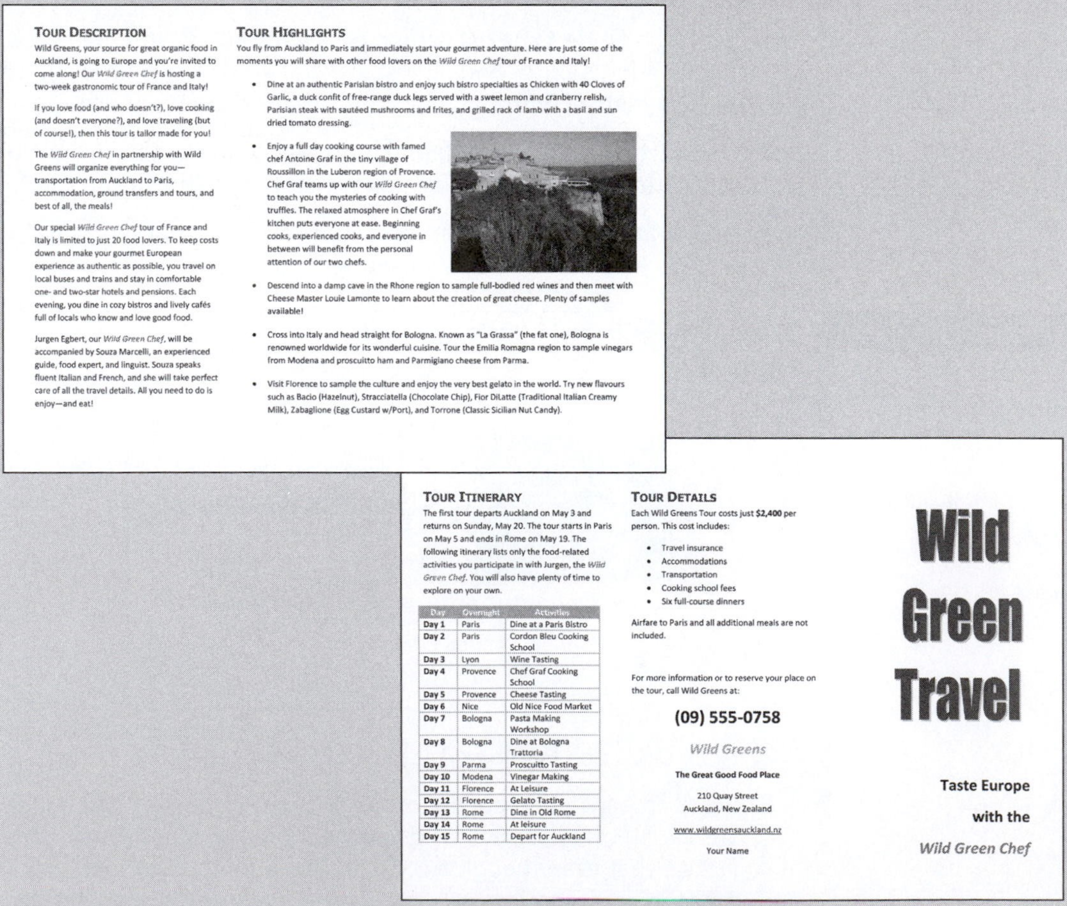

▶ 6. Print a copy of the brochure, and then save and close the document.

You create Quick Style Sets when you want to format several documents in the same way. By creating a Quick Style Set that includes all the modified and new styles required for a document, you save a great deal of formatting time.

To apply a new Quick Style Set:

1. Open the file **Tech2_11.docx** located in the Project.11 folder included with your Data Files, and then to avoid altering the original file, save the document as **Travel Brochure_England and Ireland**.

2. Click the **Change Styles** button, point to **Style Set**, and then click **Wild Greens Brochure**. The new style set is applied to the document. However, the color of the headings does not match the color of the headings in the Europe brochure because the color scheme applied to the Europe file was different. Color schemes are not included in style sets. You need to change the color scheme.

3. Click the **Changes Styles** button, point to **Colors**, and then click **Metro**. The headings are now the correct color. The heading color changes to the Green, Accent 1, Darker 50% used in the Europe brochure.

4. Use the Replace function to find all instances of **Wild Green Chef** in the document and replace it with Wild Green Chef formatted with the Wild Greens style.

5. On panel 1, change the font size of Wild Green Chef back to **20 pt**.

6. Double-click the WordArt object containing **Wild Green Travel**, click the **Shape Fill** button in the WordArt Styles group, and then select **Green, Accent 1, Darker 50%**.

7. Type your name where indicated at the bottom of panel 6 (middle panel on page 2), print a copy of the brochure, and then save and close the document.

Tip

If formatting appears under the Find what text box, click in the Find what text box, then click the No Formatting button at the bottom of the Find and Replace dialog box.

You work for Lakeland Cameras, a chain of camera stores in Wisconsin, Illinois, and Ohio. Your boss has decided to provide each person who purchases a digital camera with a six-panel printed brochure that describes how to take great pictures. Most of the content for the brochure has been written. Now you need to cut it down and organize it so that it can be formatted into a six-panel trifold brochure.

Follow the steps below to organize and format the content of an informational brochure.

1. Open the file **Practice_11.docx** located in the Project.11 folder included with your Data Files and then, to avoid altering the original file, save the document as **Digital Camera Information Brochure** in the same folder. This document contains the text you will adapt for the brochure and several pictures.

2. Read the document and note where you can use headings to divide the information into three or four major topics.

3. Divide the text into two or three main topics with appropriate headings. Also include subheadings where needed. Try to include at least two or three subheadings in the brochure. The subheadings do not all need to be under one heading.

4. Modify the text to make it clear and easy to read. Use bulleted points where appropriate and cut text that you don't feel is necessary. You decide how best to present the information. For example, you can change the order of topics and subtopics to fit the space better.

5. Change the margins to .5″ on all four sides of the page, and then change the page orientation to landscape. *Hint:* Click the Page Layout tab, click the Orientation button in the Page Setup group, and then click Landscape.

6. Create three columns with .2″ spacing between each column and then organize the content over six panels and two pages. Refer to the diagram of a six-panel, trifold brochure shown in Figure 11-1 to review how to distribute the information.

7. Select a new color scheme for the brochure.

8. Apply the Heading 1 style to the main headings and then change the font color, font style, and font size of the text. You can also choose to add a font effect, such as bold or small caps, and modify the Before and After spacing.

9. Create a new paragraph style called **Digital Brochure Subheading**, and then apply it to the subheadings.

10. Include each camera store's contact information on panel 6, create a new paragraph style called **Stores**, and then apply it to the four store locations but not to their addresses.

11. On panel 1 of the brochure, include the name of the camera store and a snappy title that reflects the contents of the brochure. Include a clip art picture or photograph of a camera if you wish.

12. Arrange the text and selected pictures over the six panels of the brochure. You will need to cut some of the text and some of the pictures, but use at least one picture in addition to whatever graphic you use on panel 1. Note that you need to change the text wrapping of the pictures to Square so that you can use your mouse to position them. You will also need to reduce the size of each picture you use.

13. Work in Two Pages view to organize the text and pictures attractively.

14. Create a new Quick Style Set called **Digital Camera Brochure**.

15. Type your name at the bottom of panel 6 (the middle panel of page 2), print a copy of the brochure on two pages, and then save and close the document.

Revise | **Services Brochure**

You work for Global Working Holidays, an organization that assists young people between the ages of 18 and 30 to supplement their travel expenses by working at casual jobs in foreign countries. The organization makes travel arrangements, hosts information meetings, assists with visa applications, and maintains offices in 20 countries worldwide. The organization publishes a glossy, 40-page magazine-style brochure each year that contains information about all the countries it works with. However, your supervisor would also like to publish a less expensive trifold brochure for each country. She has created brochures for Australia and Ireland that she would like you to format.

Follow the steps below to create styles for the Australia brochure and then use them in the Ireland brochure.

1. Open the file **Revise1_11.docx** located in the Project.11 folder included with your Data Files and then, to avoid altering the original file, save the document as **Global Working Holidays Brochure Australia** in the same folder.
2. Select the Trek color scheme for the brochure, modify the Heading 1 style so it is formatted with Juice ITC, a font size of 18, a font color of Brown, Accent 2, Darker 50%, and Before spacing set to 0, then update Heading 1 to match the selection.
3. Create a new paragraph style called **Global Subheadings** that uses the Calibri font style (the default), 14 pt, Bold, Orange, Accent 1, Darker 50%, and After spacing set to 0, and then apply it to each of the three subheadings in the brochure.
4. Format the text **Global Working Holidays** in paragraph 1 on page 1 of the brochure with Brown, Accent 2, Darker 50%, Bold, and Italic, and then create a new character style called **Global Company**. Make sure you select Character style.
5. Use the Replace function to find all instances of Global Working Holidays and replace it with the same text formatted with the Global Company character style.
6. Create a new Quick Style Set called **Global Brochure**.
7. Insert two photographs from the Clip Art gallery. Search for **Australia**.
8. View the document in Two Pages view, and then position the photographs and adjust the text flow in the brochure. Note that you may need to adjust column breaks so that the text and pictures fill the two pages of the brochure attractively.
9. Type your name where indicated at the bottom of panel 6, print a copy of the brochure, and then save and close the document.
10. Open the file **Revise2_11.docx** located in the Project.11 folder included with your Data Files, and then to avoid altering the original file, save the document as **Global Working Holidays Brochure Ireland**.
11. Select the Global Brochures Quick Style Set, and then apply the Global Subheadings style to the subheadings in the Our Services section.
12. Change the color scheme to Flow, use the Replace function to find all instances of Global Working Holidays, and then replace it with text formatted with the Global Company character style.
13. Insert two photographs from the Clip Art gallery. Search for **Ireland**.
14. View the document in Two Pages view, and then position the photographs and adjust the text flow in the brochure. Note that you may need to adjust column breaks so that the text and pictures fill the two pages of the brochure attractively.
15. Type your name where indicated at the bottom of panel 6, print a copy of the brochure, and then save and close the document.

Tip

If formatting is listed under either the Find what or the Replace with text box, click in the text box, and then click the No Formatting button.

Create | Products or Services Brochure

Create a two-page, six-panel brochure that advertises the products or services sold by a fictitious company of your choice. For example, you could create a brochure to advertise the programs offered by a public television station or to present the products sold by Quick Buzz, a company that sells high-energy snack foods. If you are involved in sports, your brochure could describe the sports training programs offered by a company called Fitness Forever, or if you are interested in art, your brochure could list the products sold by an art supply store called Painting Plus.

Follow the steps below to write and format a brochure.

1. Determine the name of your company and the products or services that it sells. Think of your own interests and then create a company that reflects these interests.

2. Select two or three products or services that your brochure will highlight. For example, a brochure for a landscaping company called Greenscapes could present information about bedding plant sales, landscaping design, and garden maintenance services.

3. Complete the table below with the information you need to help you write the brochure. Note that you will need to make up information. Use fictitious but realistic details.

Information for a Brochure
Company Name
Principal Products/Services
Text for Panel 1
Topics for Inside Panels (2, 3, and 4)
Topic for Panel 5
Contact Information for Panel 6

4. Allocate one of the three inside panels (1, 2, and 3) for each of the products or services you have selected. For example, if you wish to create a brochure for the Painting Plus art supply store, you could devote one panel to each of the three main types of products sold: Painting Supplies, Papers and Canvases, and Drawing Supplies. Alternatively, you could include two sections in panels 1, 2, and 3 of a brochure that advertises the sports training programs offered by Fitness Forever. Panel 1 could describe the sports facilities, and the weekly program schedule could be spread over panels 2 and 3.

5. When you are satisfied with the content you want to include in your brochure, open a new document and write the text.

6. Change the page orientation to landscape, set all four margins at .5", and then save the document as **My Brochure**.

7. Format the text in columns. You can choose to use three columns on each of the two pages, or two uneven columns on page 1 (use the Left format) and three even columns on page 2.

8. Select a new color scheme for the brochure, use the Heading 1 style to format the headings of each of the main topics, and then modify the heading style. You can also choose to create a new style to apply to subheadings, if your brochure includes subheadings.

9. Create a new character style and use it to format repeated text throughout the brochure, for example, the name of the company.

10. Add illustrations to your brochure in the form of pictures or clip art.

11. Create a new Quick Style Set called **My Brochure Styles**.

12. Type your name at the bottom of panel 6, save the document, and then print a copy.

Apply | **Case Study 1**

Capstone College   The Digital Arts Department at Capstone College in San Francisco has recently developed a new program called Game Art and Design that will be offered to students in the fall of 2012. As the program assistant in the department, you have been asked to create a simple brochure for distributing to students who may be interested in the program. To complete this case study, you create the brochure from information provided.

1. Open the file **Case1_11.docx** located in the Project.11 folder included with your Data Files, and then save the document as **Game Art and Design Program Brochure** in the same folder. This document contains information about the new game art and design program adapted from a descriptive report.

2. Read the information in the report and determine how you can adapt it for a six-panel, trifold brochure. You choose how to divide the information into topics and subtopics and how to display the information in six panels. Note that you will need to rewrite the information to make it more sales-oriented. Use *you* to speak directly to the readers and present the information in a way that will attract students and encourage them to apply for the program. You choose the order in which to present the information and the headings and subheadings to use.

3. Change the margins on all four sides to .5", change the page orientation to landscape, turn on columns with .2" between column spacing, and then organize the information into six panels.

4. Select a new color scheme, apply the Heading 1 style to the main topics, and then modify the style to include the formatting options of your choice.

5. Create a new style for subtopic headings (you determine the style name).

6. Create a new character style for specific text within the document (for example, Digital Arts Department or Game Art and Design.) Apply the character style to each instance of the text throughout the document.

7. Add appropriate illustrations; you can search Clip Art using keywords, such as **computers**, **computer game**, and **software**.

8. Work in Two Page view to organize the text and the illustrations so that all the text fills the three columns on the two pages. Make sure you include contact information on panel 6 and an appropriate title and subtitle on panel 1. You can also choose to include an illustration on panel 1 if you wish.

9. Type your name where indicated at the bottom of panel 6, save the document, and then print a copy.

Apply | **Case Study 2**

Otter Bay Kayaking Adventures   Tourists from all over the world enjoy kayaking trips led by the friendly guides at Otter Bay Kayaking Adventures in Juneau, Alaska. As an assistant in the Marketing Department, you help develop promotional materials, such as sales letters and brochures. To complete this case study, you write a brochure to advertise

Otter Bay Kayaking Adventures to visitors. The brochure will be distributed to tourist offices and sites around Juneau.

1. Open the file **Case2_11.docx** located in the Project.11 folder included with your Data Files, and then save the document as **Otter Bay Kayaking Adventures Brochure** in the same folder. This document contains source information and suggestions that you can use to create the brochure.

2. Start a new document, and then write content for the brochure. You can include additional information, such as a description of Juneau, how-to tips for kayaking, testimonials, and so on.

3. Format the brochure content over two pages with three columns on each page. Include any photographs and Clip Art pictures you want.

4. Select a new color scheme, modify the Heading 1 style, and create at least one new style.

5. Make sure you include contact information on panel 6 and an attractive headline and graphic on panel 1.

6. Type your name as the contact person on panel 6, print a copy of the brochure, and then close the document.

Research | **Case Study 3**

As you have learned, you can use the brochure format to present information on specific topics for a target audience. For example, you can create a brochure that explains how to engage in a specific activity, such as preparing for an earthquake or finding a job, or that provides information about a topic, such as charitable opportunities in your community or fire prevention tips. You can use the Internet as a source for information on just about any topic. To complete this case study, you collect information for a brochure on a subject of your choice, and then write the text for the brochure.

1. Determine a topic for your brochure. Think of your own interests and then think about how you can share information about them with others. For example, if you are interested in skiing, you could create a brochure containing information about the top five ski resorts in your area. If you are interested in computer games, you could create a brochure describing winning strategies for specific games.

2. Open **Research_11.docx** located in the Project.11 folder included with your Data Files, and then save the document as **Informational Brochure Content** in the same folder. This document contains a table you can complete with information about your brochure and a table to record Web references.

3. Research information about your chosen topic. Use the Internet if you wish, but make sure to rewrite any information you find on the Internet in your own words. As you research, keep track of the Web sites from which you adapt content. You need to include the Web site addresses of these sites in the project document.

4. Complete the table in the document with the topics, subtopics, and text you would include in your informational brochure. Write approximately 200 words for each of the three topics. Make the text lively and interesting to read. Note that your intention is not to fit the text into a trifold brochure. For this exercise, you want to focus only on creating interesting text.

5. Copy the Web site addresses of the Web sites you consulted into the source table provided.

6. Type your name in the footer where indicated, and then print a copy.

Project 12

Objectives

- Use Instant Messaging
- Define social media
- Explore Web site structure
- Create value-added Web content
- Create and format a blog in Word
- Insert hyperlinks and add ScreenTips in Word
- Edit hyperlinks in Word
- Learn how to publish a blog from Word

Web Communications

Introduction

The Internet has transformed how we communicate. Now communication means connectedness—24 hours a day, 7 days a week. One of your major challenges as a participant in the contemporary business world is to develop a balance between staying connected and staying sane. The ways in which you communicate on the Web are constantly expanding. In addition to e-mail, you can use Instant Messaging to converse online in real time, create and upload a blog to share articles and opinions, use social media tools to connect with coworkers, customers, and friends, and develop content for Web sites.

In this project, you explore how Instant Messaging is used in business, investigate the ever-expanding world of social media, and then learn how to develop content for Web sites. You also learn how to create and format a blog in Word, how to add and edit links (also called hyperlinks), and how to publish a blog from Word.

Starting Data Files

Project.12

Tech_12.docx
Practice_12.docx
Revise_12.docx
Case1_12.docx
Case2_12.docx
Research_12.docx

Web Communications Essentials

The immediacy of the Internet has significantly affected how people communicate. Instead of waiting for a paper message to be distributed, people can communicate virtually instantaneously. As a result, people sometimes put less thought into the text they send electronically simply because the medium is so fast—and apparently temporary. However, text uploaded to the Internet can stay on the Internet for a very long time—often for years.

When you communicate on the Internet, you need to keep in mind your reader's needs first and foremost. You want to avoid going so fast that your message is not clear or your reader misinterprets it. The information about tone you covered in Project 1 is particularly relevant when you communicate on the Internet.

Three Web communication areas are discussed next: Instant Messaging, social media, and Web sites.

Using Instant Messaging

Instant Messaging (IM) is a form of online communication that you can use to communicate in real time over the Internet. You can compare an IM conversation to a telephone conversation. However, instead of speaking into a telephone, you communicate by typing text. You type a question or a comment, press the Enter key, and moments later text typed by the person you are communicating with appears on your screen, to which you can again respond. IM is slower than talking on the phone because you must type your message and wait a moment while it is transmitted over the Internet. However, IM is slightly faster than e-mail because the person with whom you are communicating is online at the same time and so is able to respond immediately.

IM has been a popular form of personal communication, particularly with young people, for some time. Many people maintain accounts on Instant Messaging services such as MSN and AOL. When you set up an IM account, you can enter a list of buddies who also maintain an IM account and with whom you can communicate.

In business, more and more people are using IM to communicate. People who are accustomed to using IM in their personal lives are using the technology at work to chat about business matters with associates in the next cubicle or across the globe. For example, two people who are working on a project can use IM to check in with each other, ask questions, and monitor progress.

To use IM effectively and efficiently in business, you need to observe the guidelines discussed in Figure 12-1.

Key Point

Personnel in some companies use IM almost as frequently as e-mail and phone calls to conduct business.

| Figure 12-1 | Using Instant Messaging in business |

Guideline	Description
Identify appropriate uses	• Use IM to communicate with colleagues about routine business matters: confirm meetings, check to see if a colleague is available for an event, ask quick questions that require relatively quick answers, and monitor the status of a project. • Use IM to communicate with customers with whom your company has developed a longstanding relationship if the client is interested in using IM and if company policy allows you to do so.
Use an appropriate tone	• Use polite language and a businesslike approach. Anything you write in an IM should be suitable for an e-mail or a paper memo. • Avoid sarcastic comments and most attempts at humor that readers can easily misinterpret. • Avoid using IM to resolve conflicts. Typed text can easily be misinterpreted, sometimes with disastrous results. Use the telephone or conduct a face-to-face meeting to resolve conflict.

Figure 12-1 | **Using Instant Messaging in business** (*continued*)

Guideline	Description
Limit greetings and good-byes	• Get right to the point in an IM exchange, particularly when you are communicating with more than one other person. Here's an example of how time can be wasted in multiuser exchanges: Mary: Hi everyone. It's Mary. Sally: How's it going, Mary? John: Hi Mary. Steve: Hi! George: Hey, Mary! Dawn: Hi! • Identify yourself when you sign in (for example, *Hi, it's Martha*) when participating in an IM conversation with several people, and then remain quiet until everyone else has signed in. • Say good-bye and sign off when the conversation ends. You do not need to respond to each person's departure.
Ensure correctness	• Use correct grammar and punctuation when using IM for business. • Avoid IM Speak, a form of IM shorthand appropriate for private conversations, but not in business. For example, avoid using *u* for *you*, *r* for *are*, and *g2g* for *Got to Go*.
Maintain confidentiality and security	• Remember that IM is not a private form of communication. Anyone can paste an IM exchange into a Word document and then share it with others by printing or e-mailing the document. • Never write anything in an IM exchange that you would not want the whole world to read. • Never transmit confidential information such as a credit card number or your Social Security number.

In addition to the above guidelines, you should avoid the practice of blocking while engaging in an IM conversation. In the IM world, **blocking** is the practice of stopping an online conversation dead in its tracks—usually by providing responses that are too brief or not informative. Although blocking occurs more commonly in personal IM exchanges, it can also occur in business. Figure 12-2 compares two IM exchanges—one that ends because of blocking and one that is clear and businesslike.

Figure 12-2 | **Comparison of two IM exchanges**

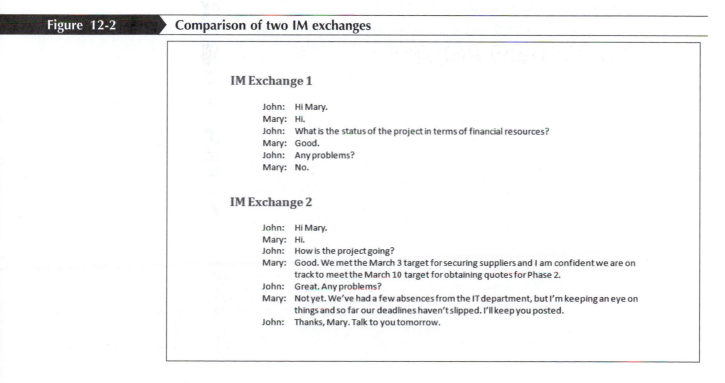

IM Exchange 1

John: Hi Mary.
Mary: Hi.
John: What is the status of the project in terms of financial resources?
Mary: Good.
John: Any problems?
Mary: No.

IM Exchange 2

John: Hi Mary.
Mary: Hi.
John: How is the project going?
Mary: Good. We met the March 3 target for securing suppliers and I am confident we are on track to meet the March 10 target for obtaining quotes for Phase 2.
John: Great. Any problems?
Mary: Not yet. We've had a few absences from the IT department, but I'm keeping an eye on things and so far our deadlines haven't slipped. I'll keep you posted.
John: Thanks, Mary. Talk to you tomorrow.

Key Point

Blocking conversations with noncommittal and uninformative responses frustrates colleagues and slows down productivity.

In IM Exchange 1, Mary is blocking communication. Her short replies do not provide John with sufficient information to reassure him about the current financial status of the project. In IM Exchange 2, Mary provides John with useful and complete information regarding the project. Even though IM entries need to be brief in order to keep the conversation rolling, they also need to be informative. When you use IM to conduct business, you always need to guard against wasting the time of others who are in the conversation.

Defining Social Media

Key Point

The purpose of social media tools is to build contacts and share information with hundreds, thousands, even millions of people worldwide.

Even though the text of an e-mail message or an IM exchange can be saved and distributed, many consider e-mail and instant messaging to be essentially private forms of online communication because they are often between two people or sometimes among small groups of people. In order to facilitate communication between individuals and the world, a whole new set of Internet communication tools has been designed. The term **social media** is the collective term that describes the set of tools used for sharing information online.

Anyone with a computer and Internet access can use social media tools to generate content, sometimes described as **user-generated content** or **consumer-generated media**. For example, you can post a comment on a travel Web site about your experience staying in a particular hotel or upload an article about recycling efforts in your workplace to an environmental Web site. Anyone can read what you have written and, in many cases, comment on it.

New social media tools are constantly being developed. Figure 12-3 describes some of the many categories of social media tools (listed in alphabetical order) and how they can be used in business. As you read the business applications, you will notice that many of these tools can be used for the same or similar purposes. You decide which social media tools to use based on the audience you want to reach, the technology tools available to you, and the financial resources allocated for social media.

Figure 12-3 ▶ **Social media tools**

Tool	General Application	Business Application
Blogs	• Provide information and express opinions through a series of postings displayed from newest to oldest • Allow readers to comment on postings	• Create a sense of community in an internal corporate blog by allowing employees to share information and ideas with one another • Maintain an external, publicly accessible corporate blog to build relationships with consumers by making announcements and providing information about the company
Internet forum	• Build a community based around the exchange of ideas and information between individual users • Share information within a directory-like framework in which users can interact and respond to each other's posts	• Provide information about upcoming company events, new policies, and ongoing projects, as well as facilitate the sharing of ideas between coworkers • Provide customers with a venue for discussing and sharing tips about a company's products and services
Media sharing	• Share pictures, video, and audio files through various methods including posting to a Web site or sending via e-mail	• Create and share videos about a company's products or services for marketing purposes in order to reach a wide audience online

Figure 12-3	Social media tools (*continued*)

Tool	General Application	Business Application
Microblogs	• Provide brief text updates which may either be viewed by anyone or by a specified group of individuals	• Keep employees up-to-date on company news and events • Supply customers with quick updates on new products, promotions, and news
Podcasts	• Broadcast audio or video content in a format similar to a radio show • Provide podcasts on a subscription basis, so that new content is downloaded automatically	• Provide regular updates on company products and share news about the company • Build public relations and customer loyalty by hosting interviews and discussions that respond to audience questions in real time
Social networking	• Share information and pictures within an online community • Strengthen existing relationships and build new relationships	• Connect with coworkers and fellow professionals within an online community • Share information, add events to a calendar, and post pictures • Broaden a customer base and receive feedback about products and services from consumers
Virtual reality	• Interact with other individuals in a real time and digitally-animated virtual world	• Hold virtual meetings with people across the world as a substitute for conference or video calls • Use as a marketing tool by creating virtual simulations of products with which users can view and interact
Vlogs	• Post video content in a blog format which allows other users to respond by leaving comments	• Build public relations and enhance a company's brand by relating information and news in an entertaining fashion
Wikis	• Create a collection of Web pages which may be added to and modified by any user	• Collaborate on projects and share information while reducing the need for conference calls and meetings

New social media tools are being developed almost daily. The key component of all social media tools is that they all encourage and facilitate communication. Figure 12-4 includes some guidelines for communicating effectively through social media.

Figure 12-4	Guidelines for communicating online

Guideline	Description
Identify appropriate uses	• Build a sense of community with colleagues by sharing information, discussing ideas, collaborating on projects, and planning events • Interact with customers in order to identify consumer needs, build public relations, and market new products
Communicate clearly and professionally	• Write in full sentences with proper grammar and punctuation to facilitate clear communication • Avoid the use of netspeak (for example, using *g2g* for *got to go*) when conducting business online
Use a clear format	• Use headings and spacing where possible to avoid long blocks of text, particularly in blogs • Use black text on a white background • Avoid fancy fonts, dark backgrounds, and unnecessary graphics
Maintain a respectful environment	• Respect the opinions of others; never engage in personal attacks • Read the rules/guidelines of a forum or community before posting

Exploring Web Site Structure

A **Web site** is a collection of pages that are linked together and share a common theme. Some companies maintain large, professionally designed Web sites where customers can go to engage in activities such as read more about the company, find answers to frequently asked questions, find contact information, and order products. Other companies maintain small Web sites that provide basic information in a few pages. These smaller Web sites are sometimes referred to as **Web brochures** or **brochureware** because they contain information normally found in a paper brochure. No matter what size the Web site is, the purpose is the same—to present the company to a worldwide audience.

To create a Web site, you need to identify the content required, determine a consistent design for each of the Web pages in the Web site, and select the technology tools you will use to create the Web site. This process can be extremely complex, depending on the size of the Web site. When working with Web site development, you must remember not to focus so much attention on the technological aspects of creating the Web site that you lose focus on the content of the site. The development of the Web site content is critical to its success.

A simple Web site for a small company describes the company and its products and services, and includes contact information. From this basic structure, you can develop Web sites that consist of just a handful of pages or thousands of pages. Figure 12-5 shows the basic structure of the Web site for Wild Greens, the New Zealand-based whole foods café and retail store you first encountered in Project 11 on Brochures.

| Figure 12-5 | Structure of Wild Greens Web site |

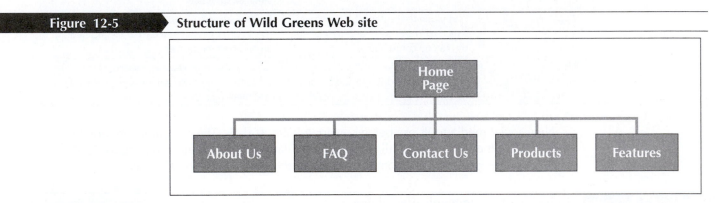

All Web sites include a home page, and most Web sites also include an About Us page, a FAQ page, and a Contact Us page. These pages provide readers with basic information about the company or organization. Following is a description of the content required for each of these pages.

Home Page

The **home page** is the first page that appears when you enter the Web address of a Web site into a Web browser. The home page welcomes people to the Web site, provides an overview of the Web site content, and includes a list of links to other pages in the site.

The appearance of a home page either encourages people to explore further or compels them to click away and go elsewhere. A great deal of thought is usually devoted to the physical appearance of a Web site, for example, the colors, the design elements, and the placement of the text and pictures on the screen. Certainly, people will usually click away quickly when they encounter a particularly visually unappealing or hard-to-read Web site. However, the principal reason why people either stay at a Web site or click away is because the first text they see tells them something they want to read.

You can use a variety of techniques to write compelling text to introduce a home page. Figure 12-6 describes some of these techniques.

Figure 12-6	Writing compelling home page headings

Technique	Example
Write a question	*Are you wild about today?* or *What are you cooking for dinner tonight?* can inspire readers to answer the question in their own mind and then read on to discover how the Web site answers the question.
Write a startling question	*Are you feeling green today?* This question is just strange enough to make someone pause, perhaps long enough to read about the new tour to Italy hosted by the Wild Green Chef and sponsored by Wild Greens.
Start the heading with *How to*	A heading such as *How to cook like a pro* or *How to eat healthy on a budget* appeals to people's need to improve. Often people go online because they want to know how to save money, how to find the perfect vacation destination, or how to get a job. A *How to* heading on a home page tells readers that they just might find something valuable if they explore some links.
Include an instruction	Headlines such as *Eat Your Way Across Europe* or *Save Money and Improve Your Health the Organic Way* tell people what to do. Because just about everyone enjoys eating and saving money, an instruction that includes those activities could well intrigue a reader into exploring the Web site further. The key to an effective instruction is that it communicates something that readers will perceive as a benefit—such as eating healthy or saving money.

After you have written a headline that includes a compelling appeal to your readers, you can expand on it, as well as add information that welcomes people to the Web site.

A successful Web site is similar to a successful newspaper or magazine. The text and pictures change daily, or at least monthly, while the look and feel stay the same. Figure 12-7 shows the text developed for the home page of the Wild Greens Web site in the few weeks prior to a cookbook-signing event at the Wild Greens store.

Key Point

Update a home page regularly so that when people return they always have something new to read.

Figure 12-7	Sample text for a home page

the question technique is used to attract reader attention

→ **What's Cooking at Wild Greens?**

An author cook off! That's right. At noon on May 20th, the authors of three earth-friendly cookbooks will demonstrate their favorite recipes at Wild Greens and then sign copies of their books.

If you buy any of the three cookbooks listed below on May 20th, you will receive 20% off all the groceries you buy at Wild Greens!

underlined text links to further information

- The Valiant Vegetable
- Fruits of Our Labors
- Polynesian Feast

The text shown in Figure 12-7 is adapted from a brochure that Wild Greens produced to advertise the three cookbooks. The original brochure included a description of each of the three books. On the home page of the Web site, the book titles become **links** that readers click to go to the descriptions. You use links to provide access to additional information on topics so you don't clutter a home page with too much text. Links give the visitor control over the content. A visitor can decide what information he or she wants to read by clicking or not clicking the links.

About Us Page

Key Point

Other common names for the Web page that describes company information are *Who We Are*, *About [Company Name]*, *Our Story*, and *About Our Company*.

Most Web sites include a page that describes the company or organization in more detail than is possible—or even desirable—on the home page. This company information page is often called **About Us**. Some companies include the company's history on the About Us page, whereas other companies describe the mission statement, corporate structure, and personnel. You often find the link to the About Us page at the bottom of the home page.

An About Us page should be relatively short and should be interesting to read. Most people do not want to read reams of materials about the company's corporate structure. However, this information could be included in the form of links that readers can explore if they want.

Figure 12-8 shows the text developed for the Wild Greens About Us page. The text on this page focuses on the story of Grace Holtz, the company founder and president, and is adapted from one of the company's flyers.

Figure 12-8 **Sample text for an About Us page**

underlined text links to further information

The Story of Wild Greens

One sunny Sunday back in 2001, Grace Holtz decided to take a drive into the country. She was fresh out of **university** and working as a computer programmer in Wellington. She was good at her job, but something was missing. She found it that sunny Sunday in the form of a **10-hectare hobby farm** with a For Sale sign. Grace bought the farm and within a year had converted most of her hectares into vegetable plots.

Grace grew everything organically and soon found herself with a surplus of great-tasting produce. She built a small roadside stand to sell her organically grown fruits and vegetables and within weeks she was attracting people from all over the greater Wellington area. But one customer in particular was to change Grace's direction forever.

Enter **Sean McNair**, an entrepreneur from Auckland. Mr. McNair stopped by Grace's roadside stand and bought a kilo of tomatoes and a kilo of apples. From the first bite of his apple, Sean was hooked. He found in Grace a dynamo waiting for an opportunity to take on the world. Together Grace and Sean formed a partnership and ***Wild Greens*** was born. The duo found premises on Prince's Wharf and set up shop. Three years later, they opened the Wild Greens Café next door.

Wild Greens has earned its five-star reputation by providing its customers with both a positive shopping experience and superior food products that taste good, look good, and are packed full of good nutrition.

FAQ Page

Key Point

On some Web sites, names such as *Help*, *Q&A*, *Common Questions*, and *Ask Us* designate where customers can go to obtain help.

People are accustomed to seeing a link to a FAQ page or similar Help page on a Web site and know that the link leads to a page that contains answers to common questions. The acronym FAQ stands for **Frequently Asked Questions**.

A FAQ page can be as simple as a Top 10 list of most frequently asked questions. You choose which questions to present based on the needs of your customers. When you compile a FAQ page, be sure to consult customer service representatives and other employees who have contact with customers and ask them what customers most often want to know. This information is then gathered into a question-and-answer format. Figure 12-9 shows some of the content that might be included on the FAQ page for Wild Greens.

Figure 12-9   **Sample content for a FAQ page**

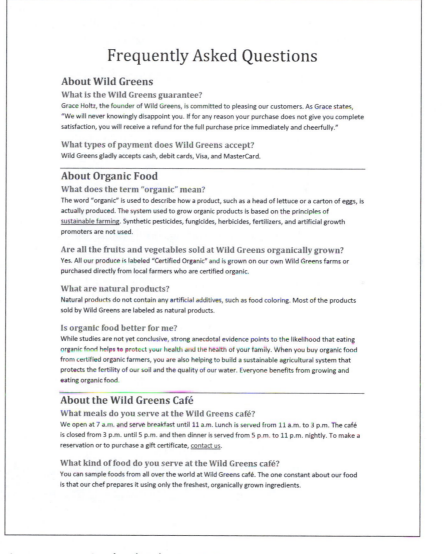

Following are some tips for developing FAQ pages:

- Provide a clear link to the FAQ or Help page from the Home page.
- Encourage customers to view the FAQ pages before sending an e-mail query or telephoning. Most common questions should be answered in the FAQ.
- Organize the questions into categories.
- Answer questions clearly and with a friendly tone.
- Present the questions and answers in a clear and easy-to-read format.
- Provide links within the answers to additional information and resources.
- Provide links from FAQ pages to other help options, such as e-mail, telephone, discussion forums, or live help.
- Update FAQ pages frequently.

Contact Us Page

A **Contact Us** page should include the company's address, phone numbers, and e-mail addresses arranged by department or person. In addition, you can include a form that people can complete to request additional information.

The content you develop for a home page and other information pages such as the About Us page, FAQ page, and Contact Us page should be updated frequently. One of the great advantages of maintaining a Web site is that you can change the content at any time and for very little cost. A brochure or other printed material can quickly go out of date, but a Web site can always remain current.

Creating Value-Added Web Content

The term **value-added content** is an extremely broad term that describes just about any content that a company includes on a Web site to attract readers and improve its relationship with customers. Some Web sites include articles related to the products they sell, whereas other Web sites include links to games, puzzles, questionnaires, video interviews and demonstrations, and customer forums.

The Web is all about content. It is interactive and not limited by schedules. People primarily surf the Web to find information, to be entertained, and to find and communicate with people who share similar interests. Purchasing a product is often a secondary activity that results from surfing, but is often not the surfer's initial reason for going to a Web site.

For example, someone who lives in Auckland, New Zealand, might browse the Internet looking for information about how to cook a Thai meal, follow a link to a recipe for a Thai meal, and land on the Wild Greens Web site. After arriving at the site, the person could spy a link to the cooking classes offered by the Wild Green Chef, follow the link, discover that a Thai cooking class is being offered in the near future, and then sign up. The person might also go to the Wild Greens store to purchase the ingredients to make the meal. The lesson here is that Wild Greens might attract more customers to its Web site if it includes value-added content, such as recipes, articles, and other information.

Figure 12-10 describes some of the extra content you could write for a company Web site and provides examples of how Wild Greens could use this content.

Figure 12-10 **Examples of value-added content**

Content Type	Wild Greens Examples
Articles	Articles on organic farming methods, organic food, and other related subjects written by local experts. The articles should be informative and interesting; thinly disguised advertisements will not hold surfers' attention.
Questionnaires	Questionnaires on food preferences, allergens, or other food-related topics. Many people like to complete a questionnaire if they receive some feedback. For example, after completing a questionnaire about food sensitivities, a list of foods to avoid, as well as a list of foods to substitute for nutritional value, could be provided.
Instructions	Recipes, tips for cooking with vegetables, instructions on how to grow your own vegetables, and so on. People surf the Web to find information and so a company that includes this information in the form of instructions provides readers with content they can value.
Personal stories, testimonials, and product reviews	Testimonials from satisfied customers, particularly in the form of stories on products purchased or classes taken at Wild Greens. People like reading what other customers have to say about a company's products or services. People also like to read product reviews provided by other customers and stories about how people have used a product or service. For example, a Web site such as TripAdvisor.com includes thousands of hotel reviews from people who have actually stayed at the hotels.

A company's Web site is considered a major marketing tool. As a result, many of the marketing materials prepared for the company are also included on the company's Web site. Content that you adapt or write for a Web site needs to be interesting enough to hold the attention of impatient readers. You want to avoid just copying chunks of text from the company's written materials onto its Web site without first editing the text to ensure brevity and clarity. In addition, use interesting headlines that attract reader attention and encourage them to read further. Remember, every Web site is just a click away from the competition!

Technology Skills – Working with Online Content

Microsoft Word includes tools related to developing online content. You can create and format a blog post in Word, and then upload it directly to a blogging Web site such as Blogger.com or Windows Live Spaces. You can also create a link from text in a Word document or a Word blog to other locations, such as a Web site or another document. The Technology Skills steps cover these skills:

- Create a blog in Word
- Format a blog in Word
- Insert hyperlinks and add ScreenTips in Word
- Edit hyperlinks in Word
- Learn how to publish a blog from Word

As you learned earlier in this Project, a **blog** or **weblog** is a Web page that you can use to share your writing with anyone who has access to the Internet. If you are posting to a blog as an employee of a company, you need to ensure that the contents of your posting are appropriate. Anything you post in a blog can be shared easily with the world. Just as with e-mail and Instant Messaging, your postings to a blog must be clear, concise, and easy to read. Avoid using emoticons, faulty grammar (such as incorrect punctuation or poor sentence structure), poor spelling, netspeak, and abbreviations.

Before you can upload your blog to the Internet, you need to create an account with a blog provider such as Blogger or Windows Live Spaces. Some company Web sites also include software for blogging that you can use to upload text you want to share internally with coworkers or externally with clients and others outside the company. Once you have a place you can upload your blogs to on the Internet, you can work in Word to create the text for the blog. An advantage of using Word to create your blog is that you have access to Word's formatting tools. You can also copy text from a Word document directly into the blog and then upload it to your blog provider.

To create a blog in Word:

1. In Word, click the **Office** button, click **New**, and then click **New blog post** in the Blank and recent category.

2. Click **Create**, and then if a registration notice appears, click **Register Later**. For this exercise, you will create and format a blog and then explore how you can acquire a blog account.

3. Click the placeholder text **[Enter Post Title Here]**, and then type **Improving E-Mail Efficiency**. You will be creating a post for a Business Communications blog that provides tips and techniques for how to write clearly and effectively in business.

4. Click below the line, click the **Save** button on the Quick Access toolbar, navigate to the folder where you save your solution files, and then save the blog as **E-Mail Communications Blog**.

5. Open the file **Tech_12.docx** located in the Project.12 folder included with your Data Files.

6. Press **[Ctrl][A]** to select all the text in the document, click the **Copy** button in the Clipboard group, and then close the document.

▶ **7.** Click the **Paste** button in the Clipboard group on the Blog Post tab.

▶ **8.** Press [**Ctrl**][**Home**] to move to the top of the blog, and then save it.

Once you have entered text into a blog or copied text from another source into the blog, you can use the tools provided to format the text. By default, each paragraph of text in a Word blog is formatted with After spacing of 10 pt. When you upload text to the blog provider, the text is converted into HTML, which results in spacing that can appear too wide.

Your blog posting will look more attractive if you modify the Normal style to remove the 10 pt After spacing. You can modify the Normal style just for the current document. Any changes you make to the Normal style are not applied to new documents. You can also apply Heading styles to headings.

To format a blog in Word:

▶ **1.** Right-click **Normal** in the Styles group, and then click **Modify**.

▶ **2.** Click **Format**, click **Paragraph**, select the content of the **After** text box (contains 10 pt), type **0**, click **OK**, and then click **OK**.

▶ **3.** Select **Overview** following paragraph 1, and then click the **Heading 2** style in the Styles group.

▶ **4.** With Overview still selected, click the right mouse button, click **Paragraph**, change the Before spacing of 10 pt to **0 pt**, and then click **OK**.

▶ **5.** Right-click the selected text, point to **Styles**, and then click **Update Heading 2 to Match Selection**. When the text is uploaded to the blog provider, some space will appear between the paragraphs because the default Paragraph style applied in HTML adds space above and below paragraphs.

▶ **6.** Save the blog.

Tip

If Heading 2 is not visible, click the More button in the Styles group to see the complete selection of Heading styles.

Tools are also available for inserting images and other graphics such as charts and SmartArt diagrams. However, these images will not be uploaded with the blog text unless you specify a location on the Web for the images. You will explore this issue further when you examine how to create a blog account and publish a blog.

As explained earlier, a link is text or a graphic that, when clicked, opens a file or a Web page, or moves to another location within a document. When you insert a hyperlink into a Word document, you can also enter text for a ScreenTip that will appear when the user moves the mouse over the hyperlink. The ScreenTip instructs the reader about the purpose of the hyperlink. You use the same method to insert a hyperlink in a Word blog as you do in a Word document.

To insert a hyperlink with a ScreenTip in a blog document:

▶ **1.** Scroll to the bottom of the document, and then select the text **Written Power Online**.

▶ **2.** Click the **Insert** tab, and then click the **Hyperlink** button in the Links group.

▶ **3.** Type the address **www.writtenpower.com** in the Address text box. Notice how the prefix http:// is entered automatically as soon as you type www to indicate that the link is going to a Web site.

▶ **4.** Click the **ScreenTip** button, and then type text for the ScreenTip as shown in Figure 12-11.

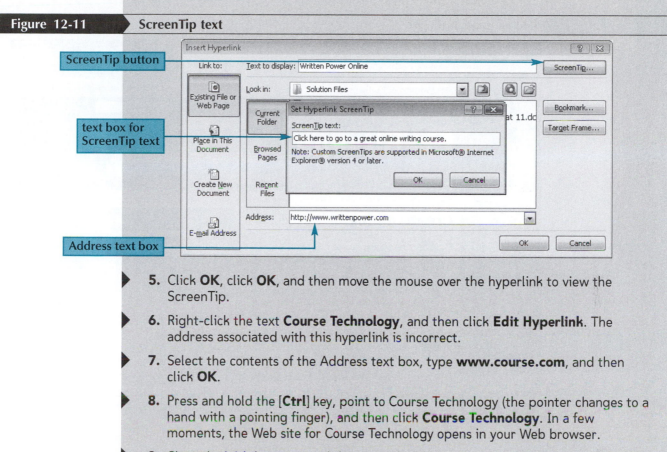

Figure 12-11 ScreenTip text

5. Click **OK**, click **OK**, and then move the mouse over the hyperlink to view the ScreenTip.

6. Right-click the text **Course Technology**, and then click **Edit Hyperlink**. The address associated with this hyperlink is incorrect.

7. Select the contents of the Address text box, type **www.course.com**, and then click **OK**.

8. Press and hold the [**Ctrl**] key, point to Course Technology (the pointer changes to a hand with a pointing finger), and then click **Course Technology**. In a few moments, the Web site for Course Technology opens in your Web browser.

9. Close the Web browser, and then save the blog.

You need to obtain an account with a blog provider before you can upload your blog to the Internet. Figure 12-12 shows the home page of Blogger, one of the blog providers that supports blogs published from Word. You create your own blog by clicking the Create a Blog button, and then following the steps provided. The Blogger service is free.

Figure 12-12 Home page of Blogger

The following steps describe how to create and manage a blog account on the Blogger.com Web site. Read the steps to understand the process but do not complete the steps unless you plan to start creating your own blog.

Tip

If you are registered with a blog provider, you publish the blog by clicking the Publish button in the Blog group on the Blog Post tab.

To publish a blog from Word:

1. Click the **Blog Post** tab, and then click **Manage Accounts**.

2. Click **New**, and then click the **Choose your blog provider** list arrow. The list of blog providers that support Microsoft Word opens, as shown in Figure 12-13. Note that additional or different blog providers may appear.

Figure 12-13   List of blog providers

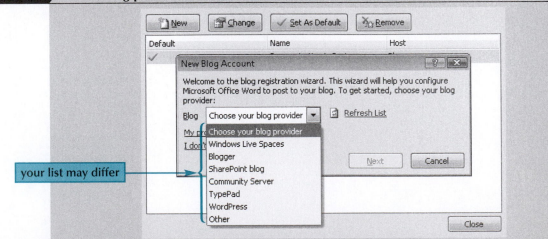

your list may differ

3. Click **Blogger**, and then click **Next**. In the New Blogger Account dialog box, you enter the user name and password you chose when you opened your account with the Blogger.com provider.

4. Leave the dialog box blank, click **Picture Options**, note the message in the Picture Options dialog box, and then click the **Picture provider** list arrow. You must specify a location for images if you intend to include them in your Word blog posts.

Tip

My own server refers to the server you use to host your pictures, which is different from the Blogger.com server.

5. Click **My own server**. In this dialog box, you enter the Web address (URL) of the location to which you upload images. You enter this information in the Upload URL text box. For example, you may have images stored on an image sharing Web site such as Flickr that you want to include in your blogs. In the Source URL box, you type the Web address that is used to display the pictures.

6. Click **Cancel**, click **Cancel**, and then click **Close**.

7. Print a copy of the document, and then save and close it. Figure 12-14 shows how the blog appears when published on Blogger.

Figure 12-14 | **Completed blog on Blogger**

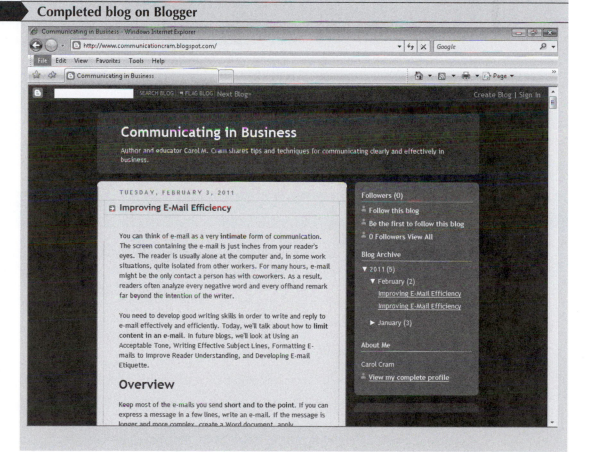

| Practice | **Web Site Content** |

As the executive assistant for Grace Holtz, the owner of Wild Greens, an organic food store and café, you are often asked to help develop content for the company's Web site. Grace likes to have new text on the Home page each month. She asks you to help her write text for the September home page that features information about an upcoming tour to Europe with the Wild Green Chef. Grace provides you with some of the text she used in the tour brochure and asks you to adapt it for the home page.

Follow the steps below to write content for the home page and identify text to be used as links.

1. Open the file **Practice_12.docx** located in the Project.12 folder included with your Data Files and then, to avoid altering the original file, save the document as **Web Site Content for September** in the same folder.
2. Study the source materials provided.
3. Complete the table on the second page of the document with a headline and two paragraphs of text about the tour.
4. Within each paragraph, include underlined text to indicate text that you will format as links on a real Web site. For example, you could underline the text *Wild Green Chef* to indicate that the text could link to a biography of Chef Jurgen Egbert.
5. Identify two examples of value-added content related specifically to the trip being advertised on the September Web site. You can adapt any of the content included in the source materials to describe the tour.
6. Type your name where indicated in the footer, save the document, and then print a copy.

| Revise | **Blog Article** |

As a marketing assistant at Global Working Holidays, an organization that helps young people go on working holidays in foreign countries, you have been asked to help maintain a blog that provides readers with travel tips. Your supervisor is new to blogging and has written a post on how to use the Internet to help make travel arrangements. She knows that her post needs revising before she publishes it online. She asks you to open the post and rewrite the content so that it is clear, interesting, easy-to-read, and free of spelling and grammar errors.

Follow the steps below to revise the blog post and create links.

1. Open the file **Revise_12.docx** located in the Project.12 folder included with your Data Files.
2. Start a new blog post in Word, copy the text from the Revise_12 document to the blog post, and then close the Revise_12 document.
3. Save the blog post as **Internet Travel Arrangements** to the Project.12 folder included with your Data Files.
4. Enter an appropriate title for the blog. You want a title that will attract attention and encourage people to open and read the blog.
5. Read the post carefully, and then organize it into three topics in addition to the introduction. Add a sentence to the introduction that names the three topics so readers know what to expect when they read the blog.
6. Write a heading formatted with the Heading 2 style for each topic.

7. Revise the text for each topic. You want to communicate the content clearly and succinctly. Rephrase any sentences you feel are awkward, add additional text to clarify the information, correct any spelling and grammar errors, and if necessary, rearrange the order in which the information within each topic is presented. The blog in its current format is not well written. Your goal is to develop a blog that contains useful information that is easy-to-read and understand.

8. In the appropriate areas, add text to describe at least three travel-related Web sites. For example, in the topic related to booking flights online, you could include a sentence that describes one or two popular sites for booking flights. *Hint:* To find appropriate Web sites, enter search keywords such as **travel journals**, **flights**, **airfare**, **hotels in [Location]**, and so on.

9. Make the name of each Web site you reference a hyperlink to the Web site. Create a ScreenTip for each hyperlink, and then test each hyperlink.

10. Modify the Normal style to remove all Before and After spacing and make the line spacing Single.

11. Modify the Heading 2 style to remove all Before and After spacing.

12. Type your name at the bottom of the blog, print a copy, and then save and close the blog.

Create | About Us and FAQ Pages

You can use the guidelines presented in this project to create an About Us page and a FAQ page. The About Us page should contain contact information about a fictitious company of your choice. The FAQ page should contain information about the products or services sold by the same fictitious company. For example, if you are interested in mountain biking, you can make up a company called *Velo-City* that sells bicycles and cycling accessories, provides bicycle repair workshops, and conducts cycling tours of your local area. If you love traveling, you can make up a company called *Travel Now!* that organizes custom tours to exotic locations around the world for small groups of adventurous travelers.

Follow the steps below to write content for an About Us page and a FAQ page.

1. Brainstorm ideas for a company that sells products or services that interest you.

2. Give your company a name and create contact information. Include an address, phone number, and Web site address. You can use "real" information or make it up.

3. Go online and look at Web sites that sell the type of products or services sold by your fictitious company. The goal of your search is to generate ideas for content.

4. Complete the table below with the information you need to help you write the brochure. Note that you will need to make up information. Use fictitious but realistic details.

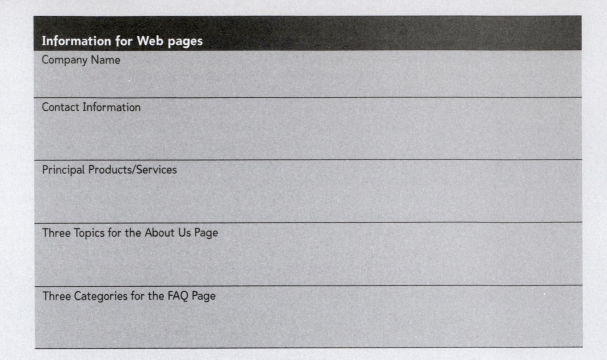

Information for Web pages

Company Name

Contact Information

Principal Products/Services

Three Topics for the About Us Page

Three Categories for the FAQ Page

5. Start a new document in Word, and then save it as **My About Us Page**.

6. Type the name of your company formatted with the Title style at the top of the page followed by the text **About Us** formatted with the Heading 1 style. Center both lines of text.

7. Write the content for a one-page About Us page that describes your company. Divide the text into three topics that include headings formatted with a heading style. Think about how you want the world to view your company—what aspects of your company do you want to highlight?

8. Include underlined text to indicate text that you will format as links on a real Web site. For example, you could underline the name of the company's founder to signify that a link would lead to his or her biography.

9. Type your name at the bottom of the document, print a copy, and then save and close it.

10. Start a new document in Word, and then save it as **My FAQ Page**.

11. Type the name of your company formatted with the Title style at the top of the page followed by the text **Frequently Asked Questions** formatted with the Heading 1 style. Center both lines of text.

12. Think about what a typical visitor to your Web site may wish to know, and then write questions and answers for up to 10 questions divided into three categories.

13. Use headings to designate the categories and include a horizontal line between each category. Format the category headings with the Heading 1 style and the questions with the Header 2 style.

14. Include at least two hyperlinks in the FAQ pages to other Web sites that provide appropriate information. For example, if your company sells cycling tours, you could include a link to a site that sells quality biking gear.

15. Include a ScreenTip with each hyperlink.

16. Insert a footer containing your name and the page number, print a copy of the FAQ page (or pages), and then save and close the document.

Tip

To create a hyperlink in Word, click the Insert tab, and then click the Hyperlink button in the Links group. You can then enter text for the hyperlink and create a ScreenTip in the same way as you do when inserting a hyperlink into a blog.

Research | Case Study 1

Capstone College   The Digital Arts Department at Capstone College in San Francisco offers programs in animation and software design, and is currently developing a new program called Game Art and Design. The department head would like to expand the department's Web site to include more opportunities for interaction with current and prospective students. He asks you to select three social media tools (for example, podcasts, media sharing, and wikis), and then to describe how the department could use these social media tools to expand communication and to build community. To complete this case study, you complete a table with information about three social media tools of your choice.

1. Open the file **Case1_12.docx** located in the Project.12 folder included with your Data Files, and then save the document as **Social Media Tools** in the same folder. This document contains a table you complete with information about three social media tools.
2. Enter the names of the three social media tools you have selected in the appropriate areas of the table. Refer to Figure 12-3 for a list of social media tools. You can also select new social media tools developed since the publication of this text.
3. Describe how the Digital Arts Department at Capstone College could use each tool to improve communication and build community with current, former, and prospective students. Use your imagination to think of new and interesting ways that the department could use the tools. Make each description approximately 50 to 100 words. Include more than one application for the tool if you can.
4. For each tool, include the name and Web site address of a Web site that either shows a sample version of the tool (for example, Wikipedia for wikis) or hosts the tool itself (for example, Facebook for social networking).
5. Make each Web site address a hyperlink that includes a ScreenTip, which provides a brief description of the site.
6. Type your name where indicated in the footer, save the document, and then print a copy.

Apply | Case Study 2

Otter Bay Kayaking Adventures   As an assistant in the Marketing Department for Otter Bay Kayaking Adventures, you help develop content for the company's Web page. You then send this content to a professional Web site developer who formats the text and uploads it to the Web site. To complete this case study, you write a FAQ page from information provided.

1. Open the file **Case2_12.docx** located in the Project.12 folder included with your Data Files, and then save the document as **Otter Bay Kayaking Adventures FAQ** in the same folder. This document contains the text for eight Frequently Asked Questions along with brief suggestions for answers.
2. Add two more questions.
3. Divide the questions into three categories and format the heading for each category with the Heading 1 style. You can change the order in which the questions appear so that they fit logically into the three categories you have determined.
4. Insert a horizontal line between each set of questions.
5. Format the questions with the Heading 2 style.

6. Supply complete answers to all ten questions. Partial answers that you can edit and expand are provided for some questions. Supply additional information. You can make any assumptions you need to about the company.

7. Type your name where indicated in the footer, print a copy of the document, and then close the document.

| Research | **Case Study 3**

The Internet contains numerous Web sites that provide you with information and advice about social media tools, as well as the future of social media tools, such as blogging and Twitter. You decide to investigate articles about the future of one or two social media tools in business so you can make up your own mind about the potential benefits or drawbacks of each. Is the social media tool something worth investing a company's time, energy, and fiscal resources in, or is it just another fad—here today and gone tomorrow? To complete this case study, you will search for and then summarize two recent articles—one related to the current use of a social media tool of your choice in business and one related to the future of that same social media tool in business.

1. Open the file **Research_12.docx** located in the Project.12 folder included with your Data Files, and then save the document as **Social Media in Business** in the same folder.

2. Identify a social media tool that you want to learn more about, both its current use in business and its future prospects. Refer to Figure 12-3 for some social media tools. You are not limited to the social tools discussed in this project.

3. Open your Web browser, and then go to the search engine of your choice (for example, *www.google.com* or *www.msn.com*).

4. Search for Web sites that contain articles about the use of the social media tool in business that you selected. Use keywords and keyword phrases associated with the social media tool of your choice, such as *blogging in business and the future of blogging in business*. Your goal is to find one recent article (e.g., written within the last year) related to the current use of the social media tool in business that you selected and one recent article related to the future use of that same social media tool in business. Avoid Web sites designed to sell you use of the social media tool you selected. You are looking for articles that provide information and opinions about the current and future use of the social media tool in business that you selected. You can also search news Web sites such as *www.internet.com* and *www.cnn.com* to find recent articles. Go to the sites and enter the appropriate search terms.

5. Select articles that are as recent as possible (preferably in the current year). Some articles may be in the form of blog postings. You are free to use a blog posting if you feel the content is useful.

6. Complete the table provided with information about each of the two articles you have chosen. If you cannot find information such as the author's name or the date the article was written, indicate Not Available in the appropriate table cell. Note that the Date Accessed is the date that you found and read the article.

7. If you copy text from a Web site (for example, the name of the article), format the text with the Normal style. All the text in the tables should use the Normal style, except the row headings.

8. Make the summary of each article between 100 and 150 words. Include the principal topics of the article and indicate the opinions expressed. Also, indicate your opinion about the usefulness and relevance of the article.

9. Type your name where indicated at the bottom of the document, save the document, print a copy, and then close the document.

Objectives

- Create cover letters
- Create networking, prospecting, and thank you letters
- Use the ASCENT guidelines to organize resume content
- Identify resume components
- Identify types of resumes
- Format a resume
- Modify line and paragraph spacing in Word
- Work with tabs in Word

Job Search Documents

Introduction

Of all the documents that you write during the course of your working life, the letters and resumes you prepare to obtain employment are some of the most important. In these documents, you present yourself to potential employers. How you express yourself and how you highlight your qualifications and experience can help employers see you as the answer to their recruitment dreams or cause them to pass over you in favor of another more favorable candidate.

In this project, you learn how to develop the letters used in the course of a job search and how to organize and format your resume for maximum impact. Finally, you explore how to modify line and paragraph spacing and how to set tabs in Word so you can format your resume attractively.

Starting Data Files

Project.13

Tech_13.docx
Practice_13.docx
Revise1_13.docx
Revise2_13.docx
Case1_13.docx

Job Search Documents Essentials

In the course of your job search efforts, you will almost certainly write cover letters and thank you letters. In addition, you may write prospecting and networking letters. You will also need to develop a resume that you modify throughout your career as you take on new responsibilities and develop new skills.

Creating Cover Letters

Whenever possible, you should accompany your resume with a **cover letter** that highlights the skills and qualifications that you feel best match the requirements of the particular position for which you are applying. In a cover letter, you can also demonstrate your written communication skills. A well-written cover letter can win you an interview even if your qualifications do not exactly match the position.

The key to writing an excellent cover letter is to put yourself in the potential employer's shoes. If you were the employer, what would you like to read about a prospective applicant? How would you like that information presented? The purpose of your cover letter is to show how the employer benefits by hiring you and not how you would benefit by getting the job.

Cover Letter Content

Most people write many cover letters in the course of their careers. Each of these letters should reference a specific job and prove to the employer that you are the best person for that job. To streamline your job search efforts, however, you can develop a template for a cover letter and then customize each letter for the requirements of each individual job.

All cover letters include the following content:

- Reference to the specific job
- Short description of how your qualifications match the required qualifications
- Description of any other skills you feel will benefit the employer
- How you can be contacted

The challenge is how to match your qualifications and experience with the requirements of the position. As a result, you need to examine carefully the information available about the position. Consider the advertisement for the project coordinator position shown in Figure 13-1.

Figure 13-1 | **Job posting for a project coordinator**

Project Coordinator

Description

You will be responsible for supporting three global project teams. Your duties include planning and coordinating team activities, organizing project meetings, and providing administrative support to the project managers. In addition, you assist the project managers to develop and maintain project plans and other project-related documentation, and you attend and document project meetings.

Requirements

You like to work independently but can also work well as part of a team. You pay attention to details and can complete work quickly and accurately. As a highly organized individual, you can prioritize activities to ensure the smooth running of business policies and procedures. Other qualifications include the following:

- Outstanding organizational and planning skills
- Excellent people skills and problem-solving abilities
- Expert skills in Microsoft Word, Excel, PowerPoint, and Outlook
- Proficiency in Microsoft Access, Microsoft Project, and Dreamweaver or another Web-authoring application
- Ability to create and deliver presentations on a wide range of subjects
- Very strong oral and written communication skills
- College degree or some college-level education preferred

Application

Send your resume and cover letter to Jason Kostiuk, Personnel Manager, Markham Square Developments, 409 Maple Avenue, Tulsa, OK 74132.

Key Point

Deconstruct a job posting by matching the requirements of the position with your own qualifications and experience.

Suppose you decide to apply for this position. The first thing you need to do is determine why you are the best person for the job. What strengths do you have that would benefit the employer? How can you show the employer these strengths? Figure 13-2 shows how the qualifications and experience of a typical applicant could fit some of the requirements of the advertised position.

Figure 13-2 | **Matching job requirements to qualifications and experience**

Job Requirement	Qualifications/Experience
Outstanding organizational and planning skills	Event coordinator for Executive Administration Certificate program at college: successfully planned a week-long trip for 30 classmates; three years' experience as a counselor at a youth camp
Excellent people skills and problem-solving abilities	Cashier at Martwise for four years; awarded Employee of the Month five times for excellent customer service; developed a new system for processing receipts
Expert skills in Microsoft Word, Excel, PowerPoint, and Outlook	Training to the expert level in all Microsoft Office programs as part of the recently completed Executive Administration Certificate program
Proficiency in Microsoft Access, Microsoft Project, and Dreamweaver or another Web-authoring program	Training in all these programs received as part of the Executive Administration Certificate program
Ability to create and deliver presentations on a wide range of subjects	Received outstanding marks in both the Training Skills and Presentation Skills courses in the Executive Administration Certificate program
Very strong communication and written skills	Editor of the company newsletter for Martwise (three years)
College degree or some college-level education preferred	B.A. in English and Executive Administration Certificate

After you have matched your qualifications and experience with the job description, you can select the areas you want to focus on in the cover letter. The applicant for this position will focus on three areas: the courses taken in the recently completed Executive Administration Certificate program, the Employee of the Month awards, and the experience as an event coordinator. Because he does not have a great deal of relevant work experience, he will focus in a positive way on his recent qualifications.

Cover Letter Structure

The purpose of a cover letter is to persuade a prospective employer to grant you an interview. You can adapt the persuasive letter structure you learned in Projects 5 and 6 to develop a cover letter. Figure 13-3 describes how to use the persuasive letter structure to create a cover letter.

Figure 13-3 ▶ **Using the persuasive letter structure in a cover letter**

Purpose	Description
Engage the reader	• State what position you are applying for. • Use the direct or the personal approach. Direct Approach: *I am applying for the position of project coordinator with Markham Square Developments. The enclosed resume details my qualifications and experience.* Personal Approach: *Your advertisement for a project coordinator in the Tulsa News attracted me immediately. My qualifications and interests closely match the job requirements.*
Stimulate interest	• Show the employer you are the best person for the job by describing two or three areas you identify as your greatest strengths in terms of the advertised position. • Frame your qualifications in terms of how they will help the employer.
Provide details	• Include a paragraph that provides additional details you think might be relevant to the employer if appropriate. For example, you might want to inform the employer that you are able to travel or that you are planning to move to the location of the employer if you currently reside elsewhere.
Inspire action	• Politely request an interview and provide the employer with contact information. • Close positively.

Cover Letter Format

You format a cover letter or any letter of application in the same way you format a regular business letter. You select either the full block or the modified block format, and you include your name and address as the letterhead. You want to be sure to include the same information in the same order in the letterhead as you do at the top of your resume.

Sample Cover Letter

The completed cover letter discussed in this section is shown in Figure 13-4. Notice that the letter resembles a sales letter in length because the purpose of a cover letter is to persuade the employer to consider you for the position.

Figure 13-4   **Sample cover letter**

introduction is direct and personable

qualifications and experience described in terms of their relation to the advertised position and how the company benefits

additional examples of how experience will benefit the company

final paragraph provides contact information and closes positively

Nick Renfrew
201 West 10th Street, Tulsa, OK 74121
Phone: (918) 555-2359

Current Date

Jason Kostiuk
Personnel Manager
Markham Square Developments
409 Maple Avenue
Tulsa, OK 74132

Dear Mr. Kostiuk:

Your advertisement for a project coordinator in the Tulsa News attracted me immediately. My qualifications and interests closely match the job requirements.

The training I received as part of the Executive Administration Certificate program at Maple Community College has equipped me with expert-level knowledge in all the software programs required for the project coordinator position. In particular, I can use Microsoft Project to coordinate the activities of the project teams. As the event coordinator for the Executive Administration program, I was responsible for organizing several successful events, including a one-week ski trip to Colorado for 30 students.

I enjoy working in a fast-paced environment where I can use my planning and people skills. While working at Martwise, I won the Employee of the Month award five times for providing excellent customer service. I am confident that this service ethic will assist me to plan and coordinate team activities and to provide reliable administrative support to the project managers.

Mr. Kostiuk, I am very interested in the employment opportunity at Markham Square Developments, and I feel that I could apply my skills effectively to the position of project coordinator. Please call me at (918) 555-2359 if you would like to discuss my suitability for the position. Thank you for your attention to my application. I look forward to hearing from you.

Sincerely,

Nick Renfrew

Creating Networking, Prospecting, and Thank You Letters

In addition to cover letters, you need to support your job search efforts with a variety of other types of letters. You might write letters or e-mails to network with people in a position to help you secure employment, and you might write letters to inquire about job opportunities in a company or area that interests you. You should always write a letter thanking an employer following a job interview. Each of these types of job search letters is discussed next.

Networking Letters

You write a **networking letter** to make contact with people in an industry or profession that interests you. A networking letter does not accompany a resume or refer to a particular position. Instead, the networking letter informs the reader that you are interested in seeking employment, and it asks if you can make further contact. For example, you might request a meeting to ask questions about a particular industry or maybe even to spend some time in the reader's workplace.

You usually write a networking letter either to someone you already know or to someone who has been recommended by a mutual associate. For example, if you are planning to pursue a career in journalism, you might discover that the mother of an acquaintance is a broadcast journalist. You can ask for permission to contact the person and ask her questions about her career. People are often flattered when they are contacted because they welcome the opportunity to help young people who are just getting started. You should be careful, however, not to assume that this is the case.

A networking letter is very similar to the everyday request letter you learned how to write in Project 4. The structure of a networking letter is as follows:

* Paragraph 1 states the reason for the letter and gives the name of the mutual contact.
* Paragraph 2 provides additional details about your career goals.
* Paragraph 3 thanks the reader and states when you hope to make further contact.

Figure 13-5 shows a sample networking letter.

Figure 13-5 ▶ **Sample networking letter**

Nick Renfrew
201 West 10th Street, Tulsa, OK 74121
Phone: (918) 555-2359

Current Date

Karen Knutsen
World News, Inc.
801 First Street
Tulsa, OK 74111

Dear Ms. Knutsen:

state the name of the mutual contact and the reason for the letter

Cheryl Elton, the editor of *Tulsa Today* and a personal friend of my mother's, suggested that I contact you. She thought that you might be able to provide me with some information about job opportunities in the news media industry.

provide details about your qualifications

I have a Bachelor's degree in English Literature and I have just completed the Executive Administration Certificate program at Maple Community College. In this program, I received advanced-level training in several software programs, business communications, special event planning, and project management. My goal is to use this combination of my education and my business skills to obtain an entry-level position in any area of broadcast journalism. My ultimate goal is to become a journalist—either in television like yourself or in print.

state when you would like to call

I will call you next week to ask if you have time to answer a few questions about the field of broadcast journalism. I'd particularly like to hear your insights regarding what types of jobs I should be applying for based on my qualifications. Thank you for considering my request. I look forward to speaking with you soon.

Sincerely,

Nick Renfrew

Networking is a powerful job search tool. In fact, many career specialists say that up to 80 percent of jobs are obtained as the result of networking. With odds like that, you will definitely benefit if you spend time developing a networking letter that you can customize for various situations.

Prospecting Letters

You write a **prospecting letter** to inquire about employment opportunities that match your qualifications. Instead of responding to a particular job posting, you write to request a meeting to discuss present and future opportunities. Sometimes prospecting letters lead to employment. If a company receives a prospecting letter from a candidate who has valuable qualifications, the company might call the candidate when a suitable position becomes available.

Like a networking letter, a prospecting letter adapts the request letter structure as follows:

- Paragraph 1 describes why you are interested in the company and inquires about employment opportunities.
- Paragraph 2 describes your qualifications and experience.
- Paragraph 3 states that a resume is enclosed and asks for an opportunity to discuss employment options within the company.

Figure 13-6 shows a sample prospecting letter.

| **Figure 13-6** | **Sample prospecting letter** |

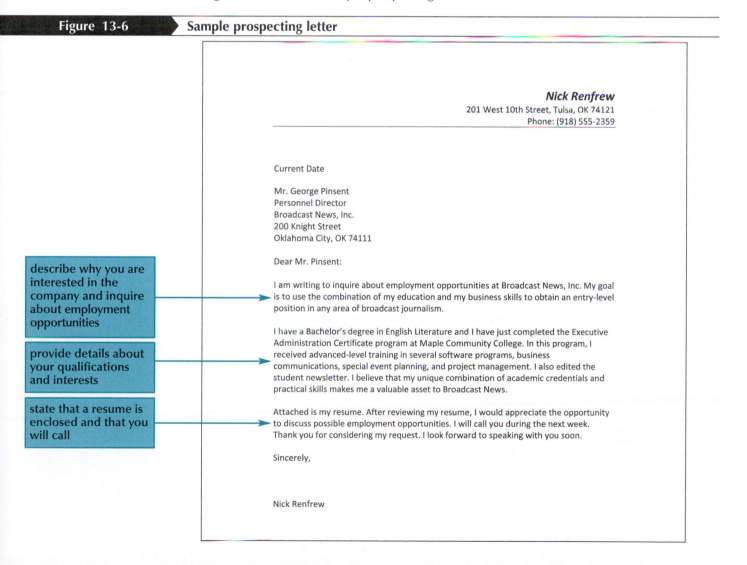

describe why you are interested in the company and inquire about employment opportunities

provide details about your qualifications and interests

state that a resume is enclosed and that you will call

Nick Renfrew
201 West 10th Street, Tulsa, OK 74121
Phone: (918) 555-2359

Current Date

Mr. George Pinsent
Personnel Director
Broadcast News, Inc.
200 Knight Street
Oklahoma City, OK 74111

Dear Mr. Pinsent:

I am writing to inquire about employment opportunities at Broadcast News, Inc. My goal is to use the combination of my education and my business skills to obtain an entry-level position in any area of broadcast journalism.

I have a Bachelor's degree in English Literature and I have just completed the Executive Administration Certificate program at Maple Community College. In this program, I received advanced-level training in several software programs, business communications, special event planning, and project management. I also edited the student newsletter. I believe that my unique combination of academic credentials and practical skills makes me a valuable asset to Broadcast News.

Attached is my resume. After reviewing my resume, I would appreciate the opportunity to discuss possible employment opportunities. I will call you during the next week. Thank you for considering my request. I look forward to speaking with you soon.

Sincerely,

Nick Renfrew

As part of your job search activities, you should spend some time researching the types of companies you would like to work for. When you find a company that you think would suit you, find out the name of the person responsible for hiring and then send a prospecting letter. Like the prospectors of old, you could strike gold.

Thank You Letters

Key Point

Most thank you letters are written on notepaper or included in attractive cards.

You write a **thank you letter** to the person who interviews you for a position. If you are interviewed by a panel, you address the letter to the principal interviewer and mention the members of the panel. Many job applicants do not take the time to send a thank you letter following an interview. However, those who do can have an edge over other applicants. Imagine you have interviewed three well-qualified candidates and are unsure which candidate to choose. The day following the interview, you receive a handwritten thank you note from just one of the candidates. All things being equal, you are very likely to award the position to the person who sent the thank you letter, presuming the letter is well written.

You can structure a thank you letter as follows:

Key Point

When you take the time to send a handwritten letter, you show potential employers that you are serious about wanting the position and willing to spend extra effort to secure it.

- Paragraph 1 thanks the interviewer for granting you the interview and states that you enjoyed the opportunity to meet.
- Paragraph 2 provides a very brief summary of how you see yourself making a positive contribution to the company. Avoid repeating what you have already said in the interview and included in your resume. Instead, mention something you learned about the company that attracts you further to the job or follow through on an issue that was discussed during the interview.
- Paragraph 3 provides your contact information and closes positively.

Figure 13-7 shows an example of a handwritten thank you letter.

Figure 13-7 ▶ **Sample thank you letter following an interview**

thank the interviewers →

stress why and how you are a good fit for the company →

provide contact information and offer to provide more information →

Dear Mr. Kostiuk,

Thank you for the opportunity to interview yesterday for the project coordinator position. I enjoyed learning more about Markham Square Developments and was happy to meet you, as well as Janet Harris and Robert Tilney.

I was particularly intrigued by your description of the team-based environment at Markham Square Developments. I have been fortunate to work on many teams both as a student and as an employee. I very much enjoy sharing a common focus with my coworkers.

Thank you again for the opportunity to meet you, Mr. Kostiuk, and to learn more about Markham Square Developments. I hope that after reviewing my resume and reflecting on my interview, you will find that my skills match your needs for the project coordinator position. If you have any further questions, please call me at (918) 555-2359.

Sincerely,

Nick Renfrew

You can also send an e-mail to thank an interviewer for interviewing you. However, sending a handwritten thank you letter is more effective.

Using the ASCENT Guidelines to Organize Resume Content

You can define a **resume** as a document that summarizes your work experience, education and qualifications, and other job-related information in a way that motivates an employer to interview you for a job. Many employers receive hundreds, even thousands, of resumes for a single job. Their first task is to reduce this number to a handful of resumes that they want to investigate further. You need to increase the chances of your resume making it into the *Investigate Further* pile.

You can apply the **ASCENT Guidelines** to help you construct a resume that gets the results you want. The acronym ASCENT stands for **A**ction-oriented, **S**trengths, **C**onsistent, **E**ngaging, **N**o errors, and **T**argeted. Each of these guidelines is described in Figure 13-8.

Figure 13-8	ASCENT resume guidelines

Key Point

Think of the resume as a persuasive document, much like a sales letter, but instead of selling a product, you are selling yourself.

Guideline	Description
Action-oriented	Use action verbs and specific nouns that show the employer what you can *do* for them.
Strengths	Match your qualifications to the qualifications required for the job and point out how your experience is relevant to the position for which you are applying.
Consistent	Format content consistently, that is, all headings use the same font and font size, bullets and punctuation are used consistently, and spacing between items is the same.
Engaging	Catch the reader's attention at the beginning of the resume so that they are inspired to read further.
No errors	Make sure that every word is spelled correctly and every punctuation mark is in the right place.
Targeted	Adapt your resume to highlight different strengths, depending on the job you are applying for.

Keep these ASCENT guidelines in mind as you organize content for your resume. You want to avoid creating a resume that is merely a dry recital of historical facts. Instead, your resume should present your qualifications and experience in a dynamic way that convinces an employer that you are the best person for the position.

Identifying Resume Components

Key Point

Like an advertisement, the purpose of a resume is to motivate someone to take a specific action.

You have very little time to impress a prospective employer with your resume. Many employers scan each resume for only a few seconds before deciding whether to discard the resume or to read it more closely. You need to catch their interest in the top half of the first page of your resume.

Your resume should include your contact information at the top, followed by text designed to get the attention of the employer. This text can be in the form of an objective, a summary of your qualifications, a description of your career highlights, or some combination. For example, you can include an objective and a list of career highlights, or you can include a short summary that includes an objective.

The content required for each of the resume components is described in the following sections in the order in which the components usually appear in a resume. Note that you do not need to include every component in your resume, nor do you need to use the same order as presented here. For example, if you are applying for a job that requires specific academic qualifications, you might want to feature your education before your work experience.

Contact Information

The first thing the employer sees at the top of your resume is your contact information. Keep it simple. Include your name, your street address, your phone number, your cell number, if applicable, and your e-mail address. You should not include your birth date, Social Security number, or any other personal information.

Objective

The objective will be the first substantive text the employer sees on your resume; so if you choose to include an objective, you need to make it specific and compelling. Remember that the *E* in the ASC**E**NT guidelines stands for *Engaging*. An effective objective engages the employer's attention by stating that you want the job being offered and that you have the qualities needed to succeed. Avoid including a generic objective such as *To obtain a challenging position in administration where I can apply my skills and abilities*. Such an objective tells a prospective employer almost nothing.

In your objective, specify the position you want, the type of organization you are interested in, and one or two of your personal strengths that show you are the person best suited for the job. Where possible, use some of the words from the job advertisement. For example, if the advertisement for an office manager mentions a busy office, you could mention *fast-paced environment* in the objective. Following are sample objectives for a resume.

Key Point

Write your objective from the point of view of the employer.

- An office manager in a fast-paced environment where I can apply my excellent computer skills to streamline office systems.
- A sales position in a publishing company where I can build upon my proven ability to generate new sales and provide outstanding customer service.
- A sales associate position in a busy retail environment requiring an enthusiastic commitment to customer service.
- A director of training in an organization that values a strong record of developing innovative and effective training experiences.

The *T* in the ASCEN**T** guidelines stands for *Targeted*. When you target your objective to the job you are applying for, you demonstrate your interest in what the employer has to offer. Many people use the *one-size-fits-all* resume; that is, they send the same resume in response to every job advertisement. From the employer's point of view, a resume naming a specific objective that meets the requirements of the job being offered is much more compelling than an obviously generic resume.

Key Point

Tweak your resume for each position you apply for and update your resume frequently as you progress through your career.

Summary of Qualifications

Because employers have little time to spend scanning each resume they receive, you want them to see your very strongest qualifications and experience at the beginning of the resume. You can choose to include a summary of qualifications (also called a *career summary*) following your objective, or you can include the objective within the summary of qualifications or career summary.

The *S* in the A**S**CENT guidelines stands for Strengths. In your summary of qualifications, you show the employer how your unique strengths can benefit an organization. Following is a sample summary of qualifications.

Highly motivated and enthusiastic communicator with proven ability to innovate and solve problems, to organize daily workload, to provide administrative support, and to meet deadlines. Expert-level knowledge of all Microsoft Office programs and a record of academic excellence.

This summary of qualifications clearly shows the employer how the candidate will benefit an organization because it describes how the candidate can organize the daily workload, provide administrative support to project team members, and meet deadlines. All of these activities are of value to the organization. Suitable topics for your summary of qualifications include your academic qualifications and a brief description of your experience.

Career Highlights

You can choose to provide a bulleted list of four or five career highlights, either instead of or in addition to a summary of qualifications. Each statement in your list of career highlights should be something specific and verifiable. Avoid vague descriptions such as *good organizational skills* or *excellent communication skills*. Instead, provide achievement-related examples such as *Developed and implemented a new filing system accessed by 40 staff at Tuftham Industries* or *Wrote and produced the company newsletter for 300 employees at Robinson Consultants for five years*.

Education

This section can be quite extensive, or very brief, depending on your career goals, time of life, and relevance to the position. You should list the degree, diploma, or certificate you attained, your specialty, the college you attended, and the date you graduated. If a job requires many of the skills you developed as part of your education, you need to make sure that your resume shows the related training. Figure 13-9 shows how a student who has just graduated from an Executive Administration Certificate program describes his education. This person is applying for positions such as project coordinator, executive assistant, and office manager, and so he wants to highlight his software and business skills.

Figure 13-9	**Sample description of education**

EDUCATION

Executive Administration Certificate   2011
Maple Community College, Tulsa, OK
- Dean's List
- Courses included:
  - Expert-level training in Microsoft Word, Excel, PowerPoint, and Access
  - Accounting Principles, Simply Accounting, Project Management, and Microsoft Project
  - Training and Presentation Skills, Event Management, Web Site Design, E-Commerce, Organizational Behavior, and Advanced Business Writing and Editing

Bachelor of Arts   2010
University of Oklahoma
- English Literature major and History minor
- Awarded scholarships annually for academic excellence
- Wrote, produced, and hosted a student recruitment video *University: The Life for You* now used as part of the high school recruitment program

Employment

An employer wants to see evidence that you have experience in areas related to the position. You want to show the employer what you have accomplished, not just what duties you performed. Compare the two employment descriptions shown in Figure 13-10.

Figure 13-10 | **Comparison of two employment descriptions**

Version 1: Duty oriented

Assistant Manager   2007 - 2011

The Natural Gardener, Tulsa, OK

Duties included: Assisting customers, working at the cash register, assisting with promotions, assisting with inventory

Version 2: Accomplishment oriented

Assistant Manager   2007 - 2011

The Natural Gardener, Tulsa, OK

- Assisted in preparing new store space for grand opening
- Promoted store locally by distributing fliers, sending follow-up thank you notes to valued customers, and consistently providing excellent customer service
- Developed and implemented a new inventory system

Both entries describe the same job. However, the second version is much more likely to attract an employer because instead of just describing the job duties, it provides specific examples of what the applicant accomplished in the job.

The *A* in the **A**SCENT guidelines stands for *Action-oriented*. Note how the descriptions in Figure 13-10 use action verbs. When you are developing content for the employment section of your resume, you want to find action verbs that express clearly your job-related accomplishments. Figure 13-11 lists some of the action verbs you can use. You use the past tense form (for example, Analyzed) to describe achievements at former jobs and the present tense form (for example, Calculate) for a current position.

Figure 13-11 | **Action verbs to describe job-related accomplishments**

Action Verb	Action Verb	Action Verb	Action Verb
Achieved	Adapted	Advised	Analyzed
Arranged	Assessed	Budgeted	Calculated
Collected	Communicated	Compiled	Controlled
Coordinated	Created	Demonstrated	Designed
Developed	Directed	Distributed	Evaluated
Generated	Handled	Implemented	Improved
Initiated	Inspected	Installed	Instructed
Investigated	Maintained	Managed	Motivated
Operated	Organized	Performed	Persuaded
Planned	Prepared	Presented	Processed
Produced	Promoted	Recommended	Reduced
Reviewed	Scheduled	Selected	Sold
Solved	Supervised	Supported	Taught
Trained	Updated	Verified	Wrote

Technical Skills

If you have relevant technical skills, list them toward the top of the resume. Include specific computer programs, programming languages, medical-related technology, and so on. You can also call this section simply *Skills* and include any foreign languages you speak, your keyboarding speed (if appropriate), and other job-related skills.

Affiliations, Licenses, Accreditations, and Certifications

You should include career-related affiliations such as *Vice-President: Tulsa Chamber of Commerce* and professional credentials such as *Investment Counselor Professional License*.

Publication List

A list of publications proves to an employer that you have been recognized for your communication skills. Include the title of the article or book, the name of the publisher, and the publication date. For example, you would list an article you wrote for a local magazine as follows:

The Challenges of Working at Home, *Home-Based Business Report*, Winter 2011.

If you have only one published article, you could include it in a list of awards and other achievements.

Awards and Other Achievements

Sometimes the only thing that separates you from another applicant with similar qualifications and experience are the entries in the awards and other achievements section. If both applicants are equal, the applicant who has listed *Awarded Mark Trent Memorial Scholarship* or *Five-time winner of the Employee of the Month Award at Burger Barn* could well have the edge.

Volunteer Experience

This section is important if you have valuable experience in a nonpaid position. For example, some students with excellent computer skills assist the lab managers at their schools. If so, ask the lab manager if you can list your work as a specific position. Listing volunteer experience is also valuable if you do not have very much work experience or if you are returning to the workforce after an extended absence.

Identifying Types of Resumes

You can classify resumes into two general categories: chronological and functional. Within these categories are many variations. You should study as many examples of resumes as you can to find a format and approach that present your qualifications and experience most effectively.

Chronological Resume

A **chronological resume** uses the traditional reverse-date chronological order to present your qualifications and experience. Within each section, you list each item in date order, starting from the most recent date and ending with the oldest date. The chronological resume is the most popular type, which means that employers are accustomed to seeing them and can easily compare several chronological resumes. Figure 13-12 shows an example of a chronological resume.

Figure 13-12 | **Sample chronological resume**

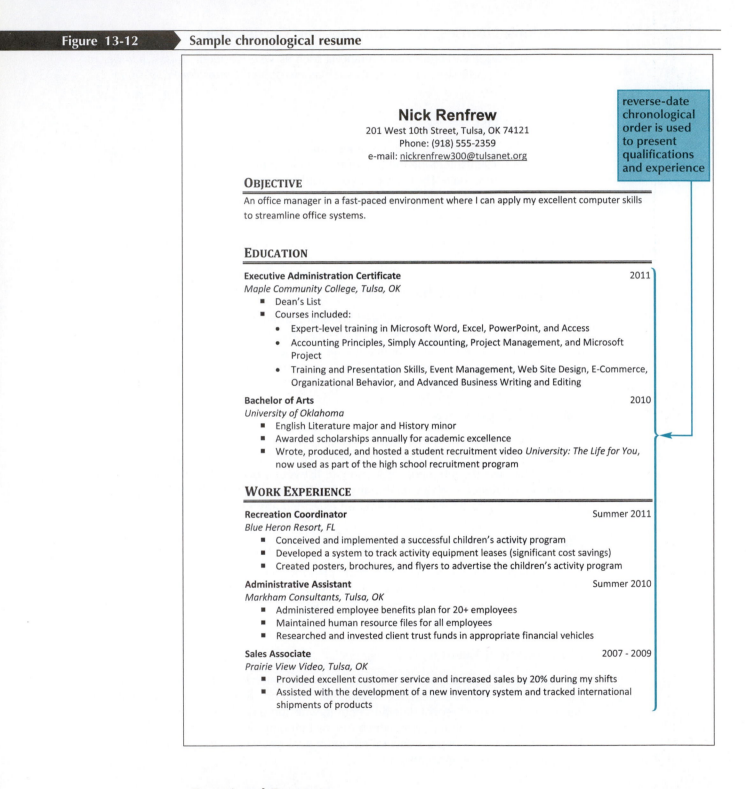

reverse-date chronological order is used to present qualifications and experience

Nick Renfrew
201 West 10th Street, Tulsa, OK 74121
Phone: (918) 555-2359
e-mail: nickrenfrew300@tulsanet.org

OBJECTIVE
An office manager in a fast-paced environment where I can apply my excellent computer skills to streamline office systems.

EDUCATION

Executive Administration Certificate   2011
Maple Community College, Tulsa, OK
- Dean's List
- Courses included:
  - Expert-level training in Microsoft Word, Excel, PowerPoint, and Access
  - Accounting Principles, Simply Accounting, Project Management, and Microsoft Project
  - Training and Presentation Skills, Event Management, Web Site Design, E-Commerce, Organizational Behavior, and Advanced Business Writing and Editing

Bachelor of Arts   2010
University of Oklahoma
- English Literature major and History minor
- Awarded scholarships annually for academic excellence
- Wrote, produced, and hosted a student recruitment video *University: The Life for You,* now used as part of the high school recruitment program

WORK EXPERIENCE

Recreation Coordinator   Summer 2011
Blue Heron Resort, FL
- Conceived and implemented a successful children's activity program
- Developed a system to track activity equipment leases (significant cost savings)
- Created posters, brochures, and flyers to advertise the children's activity program

Administrative Assistant   Summer 2010
Markham Consultants, Tulsa, OK
- Administered employee benefits plan for 20+ employees
- Maintained human resource files for all employees
- Researched and invested client trust funds in appropriate financial vehicles

Sales Associate   2007 - 2009
Prairie View Video, Tulsa, OK
- Provided excellent customer service and increased sales by 20% during my shifts
- Assisted with the development of a new inventory system and tracked international shipments of products

Functional Resume

The functional resume is less common and, therefore, might be a good choice simply because it could stand out from the crowd. In a **functional resume**, you organize your content in terms of categories of experience, skills, or functions. You might want to choose the functional format if you have been out of the workforce for a while and want to focus on what you have accomplished rather than how and when you accomplished it. Figure 13-13 shows an example of a functional resume.

Figure 13-13 **Sample functional resume**

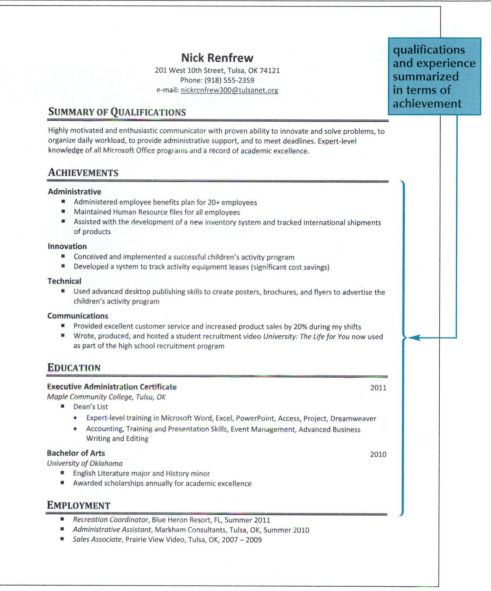

Nick Renfrew
201 West 10th Street, Tulsa, OK 74121
Phone: (918) 555-2359
e-mail: nickrenfrew300@tulsanet.org

SUMMARY OF QUALIFICATIONS

Highly motivated and enthusiastic communicator with proven ability to innovate and solve problems, to organize daily workload, to provide administrative support, and to meet deadlines. Expert-level knowledge of all Microsoft Office programs and a record of academic excellence.

ACHIEVEMENTS

Administrative
- Administered employee benefits plan for 20+ employees
- Maintained Human Resource files for all employees
- Assisted with the development of a new inventory system and tracked international shipments of products

Innovation
- Conceived and implemented a successful children's activity program
- Developed a system to track activity equipment leases (significant cost savings)

Technical
- Used advanced desktop publishing skills to create posters, brochures, and flyers to advertise the children's activity program

Communications
- Provided excellent customer service and increased product sales by 20% during my shifts
- Wrote, produced, and hosted a student recruitment video *University: The Life for You* now used as part of the high school recruitment program

EDUCATION

Executive Administration Certificate   2011
Maple Community College, Tulsa, OK
- Dean's List
  - Expert-level training in Microsoft Word, Excel, PowerPoint, Access, Project, Dreamweaver
  - Accounting, Training and Presentation Skills, Event Management, Advanced Business Writing and Editing

Bachelor of Arts   2010
University of Oklahoma
- English Literature major and History minor
- Awarded scholarships annually for academic excellence

EMPLOYMENT

- *Recreation Coordinator*, Blue Heron Resort, FL, Summer 2011
- *Administrative Assistant*, Markham Consultants, Tulsa, OK, Summer 2010
- *Sales Associate*, Prairie View Video, Tulsa, OK, 2007 – 2009

> qualifications and experience summarized in terms of achievement

You can also choose to combine elements from both categories. The key to a successful resume is its applicability to the job you are applying for. If a prospective employer can see that your combination of qualifications and experience matches the requirements of the posted job, you are on your way to getting the all-important interview.

Electronic Resume

You will likely conduct a great deal of your job searching on the Internet because so many companies now post job vacancies on their Web sites. To respond to a job advertisement posted on the Internet, you often must submit your resume electronically. You can also post your resume on dedicated employment Web sites such as the following: *www.monster.com* and *www.careers.com*.

An **electronic resume** is a resume formatted in plain text that contains keywords related to specific skills and abilities and can be searched by a computer. For example, if you are interested in working in accounting, you need to include words such as *accountant*, *budgeting*, *accounts receivable*, *cash flow*, and *costing* in your resume, generally in your summary of qualifications, career highlights, and descriptions of various positions you have held.

Figure 13-14 describes ways in which you can adapt your resume for distribution in electronic form. These guidelines are also relevant for print resumes that are scanned and entered into a database.

Figure 13-14 **Guidelines for creating electronic resumes**

Element	Description
Font style	Use only common fonts such as Calibri and Times New Roman. Do not use fancy or hard-to-read fonts.
Font size	Use common font sizes such as 12 pt. Avoid small or large font sizes (for example, under 10 pt or over 16 pt).
Text formatting	Use all capital letters very sparingly to emphasize important words and remove all bold, italic, and underlining. For some text such as book titles, you could use quotation marks to set them off.
Text alignment	Left-align all text, including heading text. Remove centering and right alignment.
Bulleted items	Use common keyboard symbols such as the dash (-) or asterisk (*) to designate bulleted items instead of the bullet symbols supplied by Word.
Tabs	Remove tabs; use colons followed by a space to show a relationship between items.
Headers and footers	Remove all headers and footers because an electronic resume is read as just one page, regardless of length.
File type	Save your resume as a plain text file (with the .txt file extension). In Word, click the Office button, point to Save As, click Other Formats, click the Save as type list arrow, and then select the .txt file type. When you save a file containing formatting as a plain text file, all the formatting is removed.

Each time you create a resume, get in the habit of creating two versions. Start by creating the formatted version that you will print and mail or send as an attachment to an e-mail. Then left-align all the text, remove tabs, clear formatting, enhance selected headings with all caps, and save the resume as a .txt file.

Formatting a Resume

You should limit your resume to one to two pages. Because a resume does not need to be an historical document, you should not include every detail about everything you have ever done. Instead, you want to select only the content that presents you as the best person for a particular job.

The *C* in the AS**C**ENT guidelines stands for *Consistent*. You can choose from many different resume formats; but after you choose a format, maintain consistency throughout. To understand the importance of using a clear, consistent, and attractive format, study the two resumes shown in Figure 13-15.

Figure 13-15 ▷ **Formatting comparison**

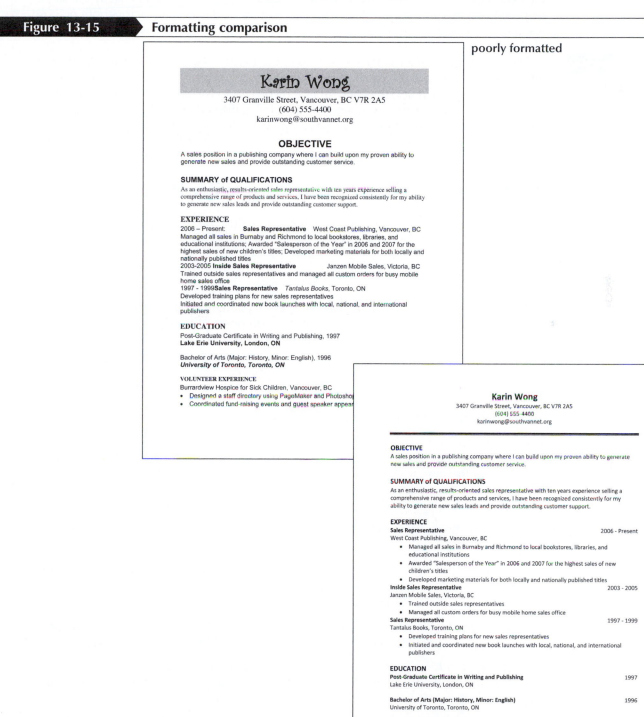

poorly formatted

attractively formatted

Both resumes contain identical information. However, the top version of the resume is sloppy and unprofessional because text is formatted with varying font styles and sizes, the spacing is uneven, and the use of bullets for list items is unpredictable. In the resume on the right, all text related to the same purpose is formatted in the same way. For example, all the headings use the same formatting, each bulleted list is formatted in exactly the same way, and bold is applied consistently to position names. If you came across both of these resumes while searching for a candidate to interview, which resume would you most likely give a second look?

The *N* in ASCENT stands for *No errors*. You need to read your resume carefully and many times over to make sure you catch every single error and inconsistency. Ask two or three other people to read your resume for errors and content. You should pay particular attention to punctuation. For example, if you include a period at the end of one bulleted point, you need to include a period at the end of every bulleted point, or vice versa.

Technology Skills – Working with Paragraphs

In Word, you work in the Paragraph dialog box to adjust the spacing between lines and paragraphs, and to set and modify tabs. The Technology Skills steps cover these skills:

• Modify line and paragraph spacing
• Set tabs

By default, Word adds 10 pt spacing after every paragraph formatted in the Normal style and sets the line spacing at 1.15. For many purposes, this default spacing works well. However, when you are creating a document such as a resume that often contains a great deal of information on only one or two pages, you need to adjust the spacing so that the information fits, but does not appear cramped.

To modify line and paragraph spacing:

1. Open the file **Tech_13.docx** located in the Project.13 folder included with your Data Files, and then to avoid altering the original file, save the document as **Kim Wilson Resume** in the same folder. The document contains the text for a chronological resume. Currently the text flows over two pages, but the resume should fit on one page.

2. Click the **Show/Hide ¶** button ¶ in the Paragraph group to show the paragraph marks, if necessary.

3. Scroll through the document to view the content and formatting, press [**Ctrl**][**Home**], press [**Ctrl**][**A**] to select all the text in the document, click the **Line spacing** button in the Paragraph group, and then click **1.0**.

4. Select the text from Kim Wilson through the e-mail address, click the **Line spacing** button in the Paragraph group, and then click **Line Spacing Options**.

5. Change the After spacing to **0**, click **OK**, and then scroll down to view the changes. The resume does not yet fit on one page. You can adjust the spacing attached to the Heading 1 style.

6. Select **Objective**, click the right mouse button, click **Paragraph**, change the Before spacing to **6 pt** and the After spacing to **3 pt**, click **OK**, right-click the selected text, point to **Styles**, and then click **Update Heading 1 to Match Selection.**

7. Select the two lines of text below Education: **North Shore College** and **Office Management Certificate**, click the **Line Spacing** button in the Paragraph group, and then click **Remove Space After Paragraph**.

8. Select **Allenham High School**, press and hold the **Ctrl** key, and then as shown in Figure 13-16, click the arrow pointer to the left of **Grade 12 Graduation**, **Branson's Bookkeeping**, **Office Assistant**, **Camp Shasta**, **Camp Counselor**, **Fabio's Pizza Palace**, and **Pizza cook** to select them. You save time by first selecting all the text you want to format.

Figure 13-16 | Selecting non-adjacent lines of text

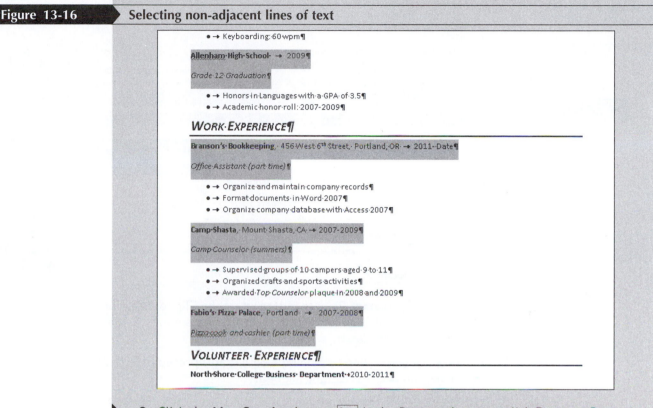

9. Click the **Line Spacing** button in the Paragraph group, click **Remove Space After Paragraph**, and then remove the space after **North Shore College Business Department** and **Big Brothers/Big Sisters** in the Volunteer Experience section.

10. Click in the *Student Activities Coordinator* line, click the **Line Spacing** button and then click **Add Space After Paragraph**.

11. Save the document. The resume now fits on one page.

By default, Word sets a tab every five spaces, which means that when you press the Tab key, the cursor moves to the right five spaces. To ensure that the dates in a resume line up attractively along the right side of the page, you set right tabs and then use the Format Painter button to apply the same tab setting to each line that includes a tab character.

To set a right tab:

1. Go to the top of the document, click in the line containing North Shore College under Education, and then note the tab character that appears following OR. When you set a new tab, the dates following OR will move to the right.

2. Click the launcher in the Paragraph group to open the Paragraph dialog box, and then click **Tabs**. The Tabs dialog box opens.

3. Type **6.5** as the Tab stop position, and then click the **Right** option button.

4. Click **Set**, and then click **OK**. The date moves to the right. You want the last digit in the date to line up with the end of the horizontal line.

5. Click the **View Ruler** button at the top of the vertical scroll bar, if necessary, to view the ruler.

6. Move the mouse over the Right tab marker on the ruler, and then drag it so the date right-aligns with the end of the rule (about **6.1**), as shown in Figure 13-17.

Tip

Drag the Right tab marker so it sits on the right edge of the Right margin marker to ensure the date and the rule right-align.

Figure 13-17 > Modifying a Right tab stop

Tab selector

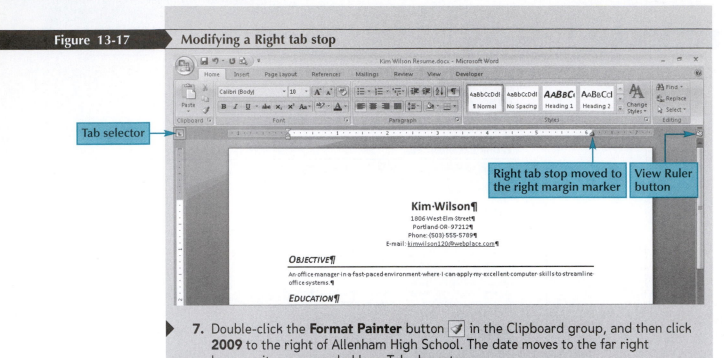

Right tab stop moved to the right margin marker

View Ruler button

Kim·Wilson¶
1806·West·Elm·Street¶
Portland·OR·97212¶
Phone:·(503)·555-5789¶
E-mail:·kimwilson120@webplace.com¶

OBJECTIVE¶

An·office·manager·in·a·fast-paced·environment·where·I·can·apply·my·excellent·computer·skills·to·streamline·office·systems.¶

EDUCATION¶

7. Double-click the **Format Painter** button in the Clipboard group, and then click **2009** to the right of Allenham High School. The date moves to the far right because it was preceded by a Tab character.

8. Click each remaining line containing a date that is preceded by a Tab character so that each of these dates is right-aligned.

9. Type your name in the footer where indicated, save the document, print a copy, and then close the document.

In addition to using the Tab dialog box to set margins, you can also use the Tab selector and the ruler. To use this method, click the Tab selector repeatedly until the tab type you want to select appears, then click the ruler at the location where you want to place the tab. When you need to set a tab position with an exact measurement, use the Tab dialog box; otherwise use the Tab selector. To remove a tab, simply drag the tab marker off the ruler. Figure 13-18 discusses the tabs available using the Tab selector.

Figure 13-18 > Tabs available using the Tab selector

Tab	Name	Description
⌞	Left tab	Sets the start position of text at the left so that all text as it is typed runs to the right
⊥	Center tab	Sets the start position of text at the middle so that all text as it is typed runs to the right and left
⌟	Right tab	Sets the start position of text at the right so that all text as it is typed runs to the left
⊥	Decimal tab	Aligns numbers around a decimal point so that the decimal point is always in the same position, regardless of the number of digits on either side of the decimal point
I	Bar tab	Inserts a vertical bar at the tab position

Practice | Job Posting Analysis and Cover Letter

Before you apply for a job, you need to spend some time analyzing how your qualifications and experience match the requirements set out in the job advertisement. You then use this information in the cover letter you write to accompany your resume. The purpose of the cover letter is to show the employer how you can benefit the company.

Follow the steps below to analyze a job advertisement of your choice and then write a cover letter.

1. Find an advertisement for a job that interests you. You can check career Web sites such as *www.monster.com* and *www.jobbankinfo.org* or you can check in your local newspaper.
2. Open the file **Practice_13.docx** located in the Project.13 folder included with your Data Files and then, to avoid altering the original file, save the document as **Job Posting Analysis** in the same folder.
3. In the space provided in the table, enter the position advertised and then list the requirements of the position in the left column. Make sure you match each requirement with your own qualifications and experience. Include examples, where possible, of how you have proven your abilities. For example, if the job requirement is problem-solving skills, then describe a situation where you confronted a job-related problem and solved it. Figure 13-19 provides a sample job analysis for a sales representative position.

Figure 13-19 ▸ Sample job analysis for a Sales Representative position

Job Requirement	Relevant Qualifications/Experience/Examples
Excellent communication and interpersonal skills especially in the area of customer service	Awarded *Salesperson of the Year* in 2009 and 2010 for the highest sales of new children's titles while working as a sales representative for West Coast Publishing
Experience in Microsoft Office applications including Word, Excel, and Outlook	Used Word to develop a wide range of marketing materials for both locally and nationally published titles and used Excel to manage all sales in Seattle and Tacoma to local bookstores, libraries, and educational institutions; also used Photoshop to modify illustrations for flyers and brochures
Strong organizational skills and the ability to prioritize and manage high volumes of work	Trained the sales representatives and managed all custom orders (sales representative at Marigold Books)
Ability to take initiative, prioritize, and manage time effectively	Developed training plans for new sales representatives and initiated and coordinated new book launches with local, national, and international publishers (sales representative at Marigold Books)
Some post-secondary education	Received Post-Graduate Certificate in Writing and Publishing from Seattle University and Bachelor of Arts (Major: History, Minor: English) from University of Western Washington

4. Type your name where indicated in the footer, save the document, and then print a copy and close the document.
5. Start a new document in Word, and then save the document as **My Cover Letter**.
6. Write the cover letter you would send to apply for the job you analyzed. Focus on showing the employer what you can do for the company.
7. Format the letter attractively on one page. Include a letterhead that contains your name and contact information.
8. Type your name in the closing, print a copy of the letter, and then save and close it.

Revise | Networking and Prospecting Letters

As you learned in this project, you write a networking letter to develop a relationship with people who work in industries that interest you and who might be able to provide some assistance with your job search efforts. You write a prospecting letter to a company that interests you but that doesn't have current job openings that match your qualifications. To help you develop a networking and a prospecting letter that you can use to help your job search efforts, you open two letters and adapt them for an individual, company, or industry of your choice.

Follow the steps below to adapt a networking letter and a prospecting letter.

1. Open the file **Revise1_13.docx** located in the Project.13 folder included with your Data Files and then, to avoid altering the original file, save the document as **My Networking Letter** in the same folder.
2. Think about the people you know and try to find an individual to whom you could write a networking letter. This person might be someone who works in an industry that interests you or who has contacts with an employer for whom you would like to work. Ask your friends and relatives for suggestions. If you are not able to find an individual to write a networking letter to, write a generic letter that you could adapt.
3. Read the networking letter provided and then adapt it for the individual to whom you wish to send the letter. Make sure you describe your own qualifications and experience.
4. Include your name and contact information in the letterhead and address the letter to the individual you have chosen to receive the networking letter. Leave the inside address blank if you do not yet have an individual.
5. Make sure the letter is formatted attractively and fits on one page, include your name in the closing, print a copy of the letter, and then save and close it.
6. Open the file **Revise2_13.docx** located in the Project.13 folder included with your Data Files and then, to avoid altering the original file, save the document as **My Prospecting Letter** in the same folder.
7. Think about a company that you would like to work for and then use the Internet to find the name of a suitable person to whom you can address a prospecting letter.
8. Read the prospecting letter provided and then adapt it for the company you wish to work for and to match your own qualifications and experience.
9. Include your name and contact information in the letterhead and address the letter to the individual you have chosen to receive the prospecting letter.
10. Make sure the letter is formatted attractively and fits on one page, include your name in the closing, print a copy of the letter, and then save and close it.

Create | Resume

Creating your own resume takes a great deal of time and effort. You need to gather the information you plan to include in the resume and then organize this information according to the ASCENT guidelines. You should create a generic resume that describes your qualifications and experience. You can then modify the resume to suit the specific requirements of each position you apply for. Follow the steps below to write and format a resume.

1. Find a job posting to which you wish to respond. You can use the same posting you analyzed in the Practice exercise if you wish.

2. Determine your objective. Think about how your skills will help the company that employs you. Refer to the sample objectives provided in this project and then enter your objective in the box below.

Resume Objective

3. In the table below, list the components related to your educational background, starting with your most recent school or college. Note the name of the institution, the certificate or degree you received, and a selection of the courses relevant to the type of work you are seeking.

Education			
Year(s)	Institution	Certificate/Degree	Courses

4. In the table below, list the details related to your work experience. Use parallel structure when listing your responsibilities; that is, make sure that each element uses the same grammatical structure. For example, you can start each point with a verb, such as *maintain, manage,* or *use,* and then follow it with the relevant object, for example, *maintain company records* and *use Microsoft Word 2007 to create promotional materials.*

Make sure you use the appropriate tense: present tense for your current position and past tense for former positions.

Employment		
Year(s)	Company or Institution	Responsibilities

5. In the table below, describe any volunteer experience and awards you have.

Volunteer Experience and Awards		
Year(s)	Volunteer Experience	
	Awards	

6. Start a blank document in Word, and then save it as **My Resume**.

7. Type your name and format it attractively, then enter and enhance the appropriate contact information. Don't forget to include your e-mail address and your Web site address, if you have them. Adjust the line and paragraph spacing as needed.

8. Refer to the sample resume included in this project and then create your resume. Adjust line and paragraph spacing as needed, and set right tabs for the dates.

9. Format the major headings in the resume (for example, *Objective*, *Work Experience*, and so on) with the Heading 1 style. Modify the Heading 1 style to use the paragraph spacing, font style, and effects you prefer. You can choose to include a border line below the heading if you wish.

10. Format information in the resume clearly and consistently. Avoid using unusual fonts and effects.

11. Fit the resume to one page, check spelling and grammar, print a copy, and then save and close the document.

Apply | Case Study 1

Capstone College   The Digital Arts Department at Capstone College in San Francisco includes a course designed to help students prepare their job search documents and get a job in their chosen field. As the departmental assistant, you sometimes help instructors prepare course materials. The instructor of the Job Search course asks you to format a sample resume that she will distribute to students. To complete this case study, you format the resume.

1. Open the file **Case1_13.docx** located in the Project.13 folder included with your Data Files, and then save the document as **Sample Digital Arts Resume** in the same folder.
2. Format the resume so that it fits attractively on one page. Use the Heading 1 style to format the headings, and then modify the style using the font, font effects, and spacing you prefer.
3. Modify the line and paragraph spacing where needed, and set a right tab for the dates.
4. Apply bullets where needed and modify the descriptions of job duties so that each duty begins with an action verb.
5. Replace *Paul Grant* at the top of the resume with your name.
6. Save the document, print a copy, and then close the document.

Apply | Case Study 2

Otter Bay Kayaking Adventures   The idea of working at a summer job with a tour company such as Otter Bay Kayaking Adventures appeals to you. You decide to write a prospecting letter to Otter Bay Kayaking Adventures or to a company of your choice to find out about summer job opportunities. To complete this case study, you write a prospecting letter.

1. Start a new document and save it as **Summer Job Prospecting Letter**.
2. Write a prospecting letter addressed to Otter Bay Kayaking Adventures or to another company of your choice to inquire about job opportunities. The contact and address information for Otter Bay Kayaking Adventures is as follows: Kay Johnson, 149 Seward Street, Juneau, Alaska 99804.
3. Alternatively, use the Internet to research real companies. You are looking for companies that may be interested in hiring you for a summer position. Think about your own interests and the type of summer job that you would like to do and for which you would be qualified.
4. Include your name and contact information in the letterhead.
5. Make sure the letter follows the three-paragraph format for a prospecting letter discussed in this project, is formatted attractively, and fits on one page. Include your name in the closing, print a copy of the letter, and then save and close it.

Research | **Case Study 3**

As you learned in this project, you can choose to create a chronological resume or a functional resume. In a functional resume, you organize your qualifications and experience in terms of categories, and then specify accomplishments under each category. For example, you could use *Communications* as a category under which you enter two bullets: *Wrote and produced the bi-annual newsletter for a local community-housing group* and *managed the telephone contact tree for parents at the community playschool*. Functional resumes are particularly useful for people who have been out of the work force for several years or who are making a career change and want to highlight their achievements rather than provide an historical overview of their work experience.

The Internet is an excellent resource for finding out more information about how to put together a functional resume, and for viewing sample functional resumes. To complete this case study, you find examples of functional resumes on the Internet and then you create your own functional resume.

1. Open your Web browser, and then go to the search engine of your choice (for example, *www.google.com* or *www.msn.com*).
2. Use keywords such as *functional resume samples* to find sample functional resumes that you can refer to as you create your own functional resume. Try to find sample resumes for people with similar qualifications and experience to your own. For example, if you have a background in marketing, look for *functional resumes marketing*.
3. Open a new document in Word, and then save it as **My Functional Resume**.
4. Using the sample resumes you find online and the sample shown in Figure 13-13, create your own functional resume. You will need to determine the categories to use for the Achievements section. Note that you can also call the section *Career Highlights*, *Skill and Abilities*, or some other title. Check out a variety of sample functional resumes for ideas.
5. Format the resume attractively to fit on one page. Adjust line and paragraph spacing as needed, and set right tabs for the dates. Format the major headings in the resume with the Heading 1 style. Modify the Heading 1 style to use the paragraph spacing, font style, and effects you prefer. You can choose to include a border line below the heading if you wish.
6. Check the spelling and grammar, print a copy, then save and close the document.

Presentation Planning

Introduction

You will very likely be called upon to deliver presentations on many occasions during the course of your career. Sometimes, this presentation involves the use of overhead transparencies or an on-screen slide show created with PowerPoint. All good presentations share one thing—they are planned. Planning involves five distinct steps as follows:

Step 1: Determine the *purpose* of the presentation

Step 2: Analyze the *audience* for your presentation

Step 3: Develop the *content* for the presentation

Step 4: Use *electronic* technology to prepare the presentation

Step 5: Practice *delivery* of the presentation

You can summarize these five steps by remembering the word **PACED**, which stands for **P**urpose, **A**udience, **C**ontent, **E**lectronic Preparation, and **D**elivery Practice.

In this project, you learn how to use the PACED method to plan a presentation, and you review how to create a presentation in PowerPoint that includes information contained in a Word document.

Starting Data Files

Project.14

Tech1_14.docx
Tech2_14.jpg
Practice_14.docx
Revise_14.pptx
Case1_14.docx
Case2_14.docx

Presentation Planning Essentials

When you use the PACED method to develop a presentation, you ensure that your presentation engages the audience with interesting content and progresses at a steady rate within a limited time frame. Few things are more distressing to an audience than a disorganized presentation that plods on too long. A discussion of presentation planning essentials focusing on the PACED steps, as shown in Figure 14-1, follows.

| Figure 14-1 | PACED presentation planning |

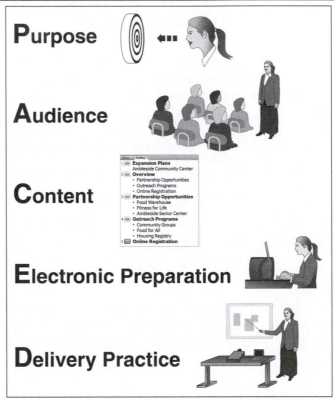

PACED Step 1: Determine the Purpose of the Presentation

First, you need to determine the **purpose** of your presentation. Often the purpose is tied to what you want your presentation to accomplish. For example, the purpose of a presentation could be to persuade a group of clients to buy your products, to describe the operations of your company to a group of investors, or to teach a class of students about a particular subject.

Once you know the purpose of your presentation, you determine what type of presentation will help you achieve its purpose. There are three types, or categories, of presentations: persuasive, descriptive, and instructional. Figure 14-2 describes each of these categories and provides examples.

Figure 14-2 **Presentation categories**

Presentation Category	Used To
Persuasive presentation	• Encourage an audience to think or to act in a certain way. 　• A sales presentation should persuade the audience to purchase the product or service (for example, a time-share condominium) described in the presentation. 　• A motivational presentation should convince the audience to accept and then act upon a strategy, such as using the power of positive thinking to lose weight.
Descriptive presentation	• Communicate information about a specific topic or strategy. 　• A staff orientation presentation should inform new employees about company policies and procedures. 　• A project update presentation should inform stakeholders of the progress of a project, such as the building of a new hospital facility.
Instructional presentation	• Teach skills and concepts to audience members who will then be expected to prove mastery of the content. 　• A technology skills presentation should inform the audience how to use a specific tool, such as Access, to build a data report that summarizes student achievement.

Some presentations have multiple purposes. For example, a descriptive presentation that outlines company operations to a group of new employees also has a persuasive component. The presenter wants to both convince new employees that they have made the right choice in joining the company and motivate them to work hard and make a positive contribution.

PACED Step 2: Analyze the Audience for Your Presentation

Key Point

You analyze audience expectations, determine outcomes, and identify audience characteristics so that you develop appropriate content.

You deliver a presentation in front of an **audience**, which is a group of people gathered together for the sole purpose of listening to you. Your responsibility as a presenter is to ensure that your audience's time is spent wisely. Even the most beautifully prepared and formatted presentation will fall flat if it is not tailored to the needs and expectations of the audience. As part of the presentation planning process, you need to determine answers to the following questions:

• Why have participants come to the presentation?
• What do participants hope to do or learn as the result of attending the presentation?
• What are the average background and characteristics of the participants?

Figure 14-3 explores the answers to these questions.

Figure 14-3 **Presentation audience requirements**

Requirement	Description
Identify audience expectations	• Think about your presentation from the point of view of your audience to ensure you do not omit important information. • A young person attending an information session at a local college would expect the presentation to include information about course fees, living on campus, and recreational facilities. • A professional attending a seminar at a conference would expect to obtain up-to-date information about topics listed in the seminar description or implied by the seminar title.
Determine outcomes	• Identify what you want the participants to do as the result of attending the presentation. • Employees at a staff orientation should learn how to obtain benefits, understand company policies, and feel motivated to make a strong contribution to the company. • Potential customers at a sales presentation should feel motivated to purchase the products or services described in the presentation.
Identify audience characteristics	• Identify any common characteristics related to background and expectations of audience members so you can develop appropriate content. • Modify a presentation on a new park for an audience of senior citizens and for an audience of teens. • Modify a presentation on children's nutrition for an audience of health-care professionals and for an audience of PTA members.

Key Point

At any point during the presentation, audience members should know approximately where they are in relation to the main topics.

PACED Step 3: Develop the Content for the Presentation

You organize the content of a presentation into a structure that your audience can easily identify and understand. One of the most effective ways to organize your presentation is to divide it into three distinct topic areas and then include up to three subtopics under each main topic. Figure 14-4 shows the outline of a presentation organized into three main topics with subtopics.

Figure 14-4 **Well-structured presentation outline**

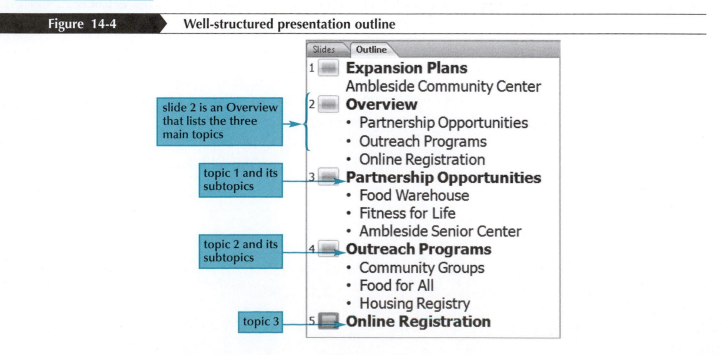

As you can see, the three main topics in this presentation are identified under the Overview heading at the beginning of the outline. Each of these three main topics includes subtopics. For example, the subtopics for the Partnership Opportunities topic are the three organizations that Ambleside Community Center plans to partner with: Food Warehouse, Fitness for Life, and Ambleside Senior Center.

Although the three-part structure works well for many presentations, you can also choose to adapt it, depending on the content you wish to present. For example, you may occasionally divide a presentation into two or even four main topics, and omit subtopics from some main topics. The key is to impose a simple structure on the content so that the audience can understand the content easily.

Once you have determined the topics and subtopics for your presentation, you need to develop appropriate content. Figure 14-5 shows an outline of a descriptive presentation. Notice how only a few bullet points are added to the subtopics. When you create content for a presentation, you do not need to write down every word you plan to say. Add just a few short points and then during the course of your presentation, expand on the points verbally.

Key Point

Limit the content to only the most important topics and subtopics.

Figure 14-5 ▶ **Partial outline of a descriptive presentation**

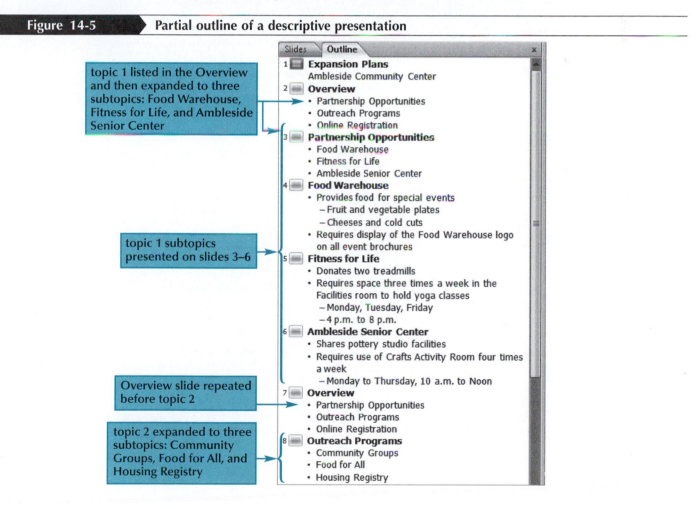

topic 1 listed in the Overview and then expanded to three subtopics: Food Warehouse, Fitness for Life, and Ambleside Senior Center

topic 1 subtopics presented on slides 3–6

Overview slide repeated before topic 2

topic 2 expanded to three subtopics: Community Groups, Food for All, and Housing Registry

PACED Step 4: Use Electronic Technology to Prepare the Presentation

Many presentations are accompanied by a series of slides, often created in PowerPoint for electronic delivery, which means that the slides are projected from the computer screen to a large screen that audience members can see easily. Each slide includes a title and either text in the form of three or four bulleted points or a graphic such as a chart, a table, some pictures, or a video clip. A typical 10-minute presentation usually consists of between 10 and 15 slides.

When you prepare the content of your presentation for delivery, you need to select the text content, format the content attractively, choose appropriate graphics, and include a summary slide. Figure 14-6 describes each of these tasks.

Figure 14-6 | **Preparing a presentation for delivery**

Requirement	Description
Selecting the text content	• Limit the number of bulleted items to three or at the most four • Include only phrases and key terms; avoid long sentences • Ensure all text is readable • Use the text on each slide as a starting point for additional comments and examples that you provide verbally • Insert the Overview slide and bold the upcoming topic each time the main topic changes in the presentation

Formatting content	• Use a consistent format for each slide in a presentation
	  • Use the same background color for every slide
	  • Enhance all the text at each level with the same font size and style
	• Use subtle colors and clear fonts to draw attention to the presentation content
	• Select light colors for the slide backgrounds and dark colors for slide text

Choosing graphics	• Use charts to display statistical and other numerical information in a visual way that audience members can understand easily • Make sure the chart is large and easy to read • Use illustrations sparingly and only to enhance specific information or to emphasize a specific point • Include a logo or other identifying graphic in one corner of every slide in a presentation when appropriate
Adding a summary slide	• Include a very short summary of the presentation or contact information on the last slide • Leave the last slide on-screen until people have left the presentation

Presentations consisting of poorly formatted slides distract your audience from the presentation content. Instead of focusing on your words and the purpose of the presentation, the audience focuses on trying to understand what they see displayed on the slides. Figure 14-7 compares three poorly formatted slides with three well-formatted slides.

Figure 14-7 | **Slide formatting comparison**

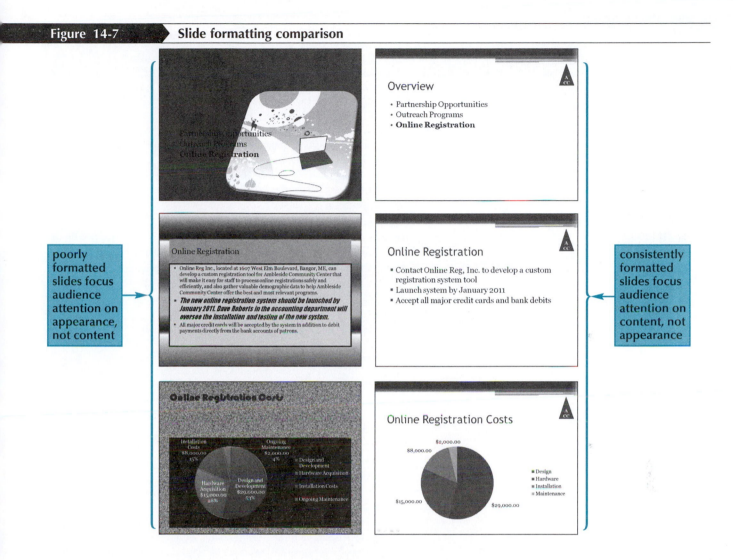

poorly formatted slides focus audience attention on appearance, not content

consistently formatted slides focus audience attention on content, not appearance

PACED Step 5: Practice Delivery of the Presentation

Your presentation should be tightly organized and then delivered in a relaxed manner that appears unstudied and spontaneous. The key word is *appears*. You should know exactly what you want to say and have rehearsed your delivery thoroughly. Your audience should see a presenter who delivers the content with confidence and flair, and seems to be talking *off the cuff*. Figure 14-8 describes three major factors related to the delivery of a presentation: communicating the content, coping with nerves, and managing the location.

Figure 14-8 | **Presentation delivery factors**

Factors to Consider	Description
Communicating the content	• Never read the text of your presentation. Almost as soon as a slide is projected, people in the audience have read the content. Reading the slide text bores your audience. • Expand on the content by providing additional and interesting comments and examples, by asking questions of the audience, and by responding to questions asked by audience members. • Display a slide, pause for only a second or two, and then start to talk about the content. The slides are not the presentation. The slides are only the presentation backup.
Coping with nerves	• Be very well prepared and know the content well. • Memorize your opening statements and then practice them several times before starting the presentation. The hardest part of any presentation is the beginning. Since most people in the audience are willing to give you about five minutes of their attention before they decide whether you are worth listening to, you have very little time to make a good impression. • Be prepared to answer questions as they arise. • Make eye contact with individual audience members periodically as you deliver your presentation. People want to feel like they are included in your presentation. • Engage an audience by asking questions and encouraging discussion if appropriate. • Appear relaxed and friendly. In any presentation, the presenter is by far the most important aspect. The focus of the audience should be on you and not on a screen showing PowerPoint slides. • Speak clearly and at a slightly slower pace than you would use for normal conversation.
Managing the location	• Deliver your presentation in a well-lit, temperature-controlled room where participants sit on comfortable chairs and can easily see and hear you. • Arrive at least one hour before the start of the presentation so that you can set up the equipment and verify that it works correctly. • Bring a copy of the presentation slides on overhead transparencies and on paper. If the projector does not work, you can use the overhead transparencies. If an overhead projector is not available, you can distribute paper copies of the presentation.

Technology Skills — Creating a Presentation in PowerPoint

Microsoft PowerPoint provides the tools you need to create both the electronic presentation and the handouts that accompany your presentation. First, you enter the content for each slide in Outline view. You can type the text directly into PowerPoint or you can import text from a Word document. Most slides will consist of a title and three or four bulleted points. Once you have entered text for each slide, you modify the appearance of the presentation by applying and then editing a theme. Finally, you prepare the presentation for delivery.

The Technology Skills steps cover these skills:

- Outline a presentation in PowerPoint
- Add content to a presentation from Word
- Apply and modify a theme
- Insert clip art
- Print presentation handouts

To outline a presentation in PowerPoint:

▶ **1.** Start PowerPoint, save the presentation as **Nutrition Workshop** in the Project.14 folder included with your Data Files, click the **Outline** tab, and then click next to the **slide icon** in the Outline pane, as shown in Figure 14-9.

Figure 14-9 ▶ **Positioning the insertion point in the Outline pane**

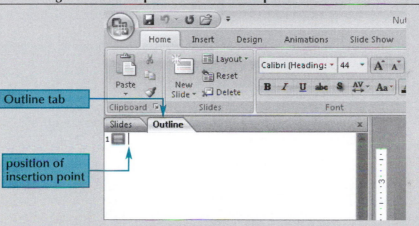

▶ **2.** Type **Nutrition Workshop**, press the **Enter** key to move to slide 2, and then press the **Tab** key to move back to the subtitle of slide 1.

▶ **3.** Type **Lakeview Wellness Clinic**, press the **Enter** key to move to the line below the subtitle, and then type your name.

▶ **4.** Press the **Enter** key after your name and then press [**Shift**]+[**Tab**]. This action starts a new slide. The insertion point moves to the left margin of the Outline pane next to the icon for slide 2 and to the Title placeholder on the slide. By default, the Title & Text slide format is applied to the second and all subsequent slides in a presentation.

▶ **5.** Type **Overview**, press the **Enter** key to move to slide 3, and then press the **Tab** key to move back to the text of slide 2.

▶ **6.** Type **Basic Principles**, press the **Enter** key to move down one line, type **Shopping and Cooking Tips**, press the **Enter** key to move down another line, and then type **Eating Out**.

▶ **7.** Press the **Enter** key to move down one line, press [**Shift**]+[**Tab**] to start a new slide, and then enter the slide title and bulleted items, as shown in Figure 14-10. This slide includes information related to Topic 1: Basic Principles. You press the Tab key to insert bullets and subbullets, and [Shift]+[Tab] to move back to the slide title or to move to a higher level in a bulleted list.

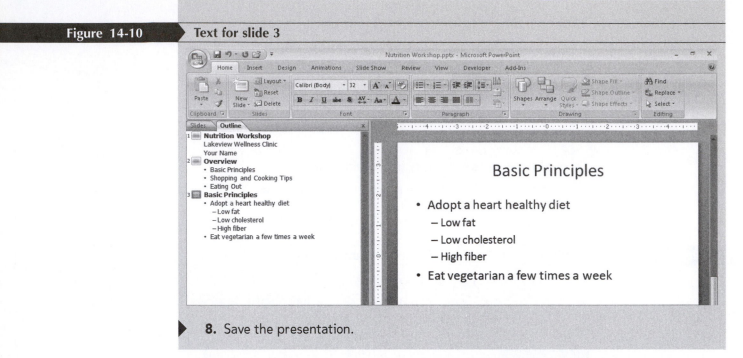

Figure 14-10 | Text for slide 3

8. Save the presentation.

You can continue to enter all the text required for the presentation in Outline view or you can add content from other sources, such as Microsoft Word. Next, you create more slides based on content in a Word outline.

To import content from a Word document into a PowerPoint presentation:

Tip

Before you import content from a Word document, make sure the appropriate heading styles are applied to text that will become slide titles and bulleted items in PowerPoint.

1. Click the **New Slide** list arrow in the Slides group, and then click **Slides from Outline**.

2. Navigate to the Project.14 folder included with your Data Files, click **Tech1_14.docx** in the list of files, and then click **Insert**. The text from the Word document appears in the PowerPoint presentation. All the text formatted with the Heading 1 style in Word appears as a slide title in PowerPoint, and all text formatted with the Heading 2 and Heading 3 styles in Word appears as bulleted items.

3. Click the **Next Slide** button (bottom of the vertical scroll bar to the right of the slide window) to move from slide to slide in the presentation and read the text.

4. Scroll to the top of the presentation, click the **Slides** tab in the left pane, and then save the presentation.

Key Point

An effective presentation format is a format that your audience barely notices.

You can modify the themes included with PowerPoint in hundreds of different ways. You should avoid using a theme without modifying it in some way because PowerPoint includes a limited number of themes and many audience members will have seen them in other presentations. The key point is to keep the format clean and simple. Next, you apply and modify a presentation theme.

To apply and modify a presentation theme:

1. Click the **Design** tab, click the **More** button ☰ in the Themes group to expand the selection of themes, and then point to the Origin theme as shown in Figure 14-11.

Figure 14-11 ▸ Selecting the Origin theme

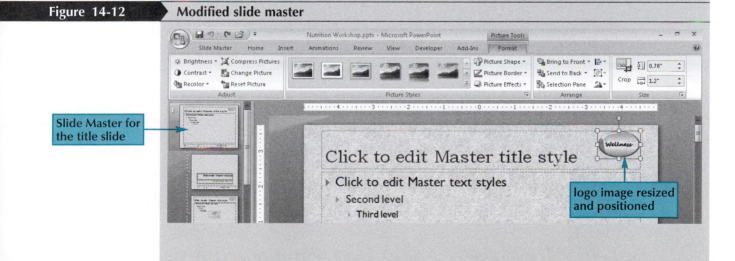

Origin theme selected

2. Click the **Origin** theme, click **Colors** in the Themes group, and then select the **Technic** color scheme.

3. Click **Background Styles** in the Background group, click **Format Background**, and then click the **Picture or texture fill** radio button.

4. Click the **Texture** list arrow, select the **Blue tissue paper** texture, click **Apply to All**, and then click **Close**.

5. Click the **View** tab, click **Slide Master** in the Presentation Views group, and then click the top slide master in the left task pane.

6. Click the text **Click to edit Master title style**, click the **Home** tab, click the **Font Size** list arrow in the Font group, select **36**, click the text **Click to edit Master text styles**, and then click the **Increase Font Size** button ⒜ in the Font group one time (to 28 pt).

7. Click the **Insert** tab, click **Picture** in the Illustrations group, navigate to the Project.14 folder included with your Data Files, click **Tech2_14.jpg** in the list of files, and then click **Insert**.

8. Click **Recolor** in the Adjust group, click **Set Transparent Color**, and then click a white area of the image you inserted. The image appears to float over the slide background.

9. Size and position the logo image so that it appears in the top right corner of the slide master as shown in Figure 14-12.

Figure 14-12 ▸ Modified slide master

Slide Master for the title slide

Click to edit Master title style

Click to edit Master text styles
Second level
Third level

logo image resized and positioned

10. Click the second slide master (the Title Slide Layout) to show the slide master for the title slide, click the **Hide Background Graphics** check box in the Background group to select it, click the **Close Master View** button in the Close group, scroll through the presentation to view each slide, and then save the presentation. The logo for Westview Wellness Clinic appears on every slide in the presentation, except the title slide.

To add interest to your presentation, you can add clip art. **Clip art** is a collection of images including pictures and drawings that you insert from the Clip Art task pane. Next, you insert a piece of clip art on slide 5 of your presentation.

To insert clip art in a presentation:

1. Scroll to slide 5 of the presentation, click the **Insert** tab, and then click the **Clip Art** button in the Illustrations group. The Clip Art task pane opens.

2. Enter **groceries** in the Search for text box, click **Go**, and then select a picture of your choice. You can choose to select a clip art picture or a photograph.

3. Size and position the picture so that it fills the lower right corner of the slide, close the Clip Art task pane, and then save the presentation.

Once your presentation is completed, you need to read through it again to look for content, format, spelling, and grammar errors. You can also print copies of your presentation to distribute as handouts. Next, you edit the presentation and then print the slides as a handout.

To edit and print a presentation:

1. Scroll to slide 2 of the presentation, and then apply bold to **Basic Principles**.

2. Scroll to slide 4 of the presentation. As you can see, the text is colored blue, which is different from the text on slides 2 and 3.

3. With slide 4 active, click the **Reset** button in the Slides group. All the text is formatted using the settings you selected in the Slide Master.

4. Apply Bold to **Shopping and Cooking Tips**. You bold the upcoming topic on the Overview slide after you reset the layout. If you apply bold first and then reset the layout, the bold is removed.

5. Reset the slide layout on all the remaining slides in the presentation, and apply bold to **Eating Out** on slide 8. Note that you will need to reset the layout on each slide individually.

6. Click the **Office** button, point to **Print**, click **Print**, click the **Print what** list arrow in the Print dialog box, and then click **Handouts**.

7. Click the **Slides per page** list arrow, click **9**, and then click **OK**. All nine slides in the presentation are printed on one page.

8. Save and close the presentation.

Practice	**Volunteer Orientation Presentation**

Joanna Lund, the director of the Ambleside Community Center in Bangor, Maine, needs to develop a presentation that she can deliver to volunteers interested in helping out at the Center. The volunteers need to understand something about the operations of the Center, how they should conduct themselves at the center, and what kinds of volunteer jobs are available.

Figure 14-13 includes the information that Joanna wants to present. Follow the steps below as you work in PowerPoint and in Word to organize this information into slide titles and bulleted items.

Figure 14-13   **Information for volunteer orientation presentation**

Topic	Information
Center operations	Ambleside Community Center was founded in 1972 to provide community-based recreational programs and services and specialty programs for seniors, adults, teens, and children. The courses and activities offered at the Center fall into the following categories: arts and crafts, dance, aquatics, fitness classes (30 per week!), and sports including soccer, hockey, basketball, racquetball, and badminton. The full-time staff at the center consists of Joanna Lund, the director; Donald Vance, the program coordinator; Judy Watson, the marketing assistant; Sara Perkins and Alex Carson on the front desk; and facilities manager Karen Chow.
Volunteer conduct	Volunteers are expected to arrive on time, be courteous and helpful to facility visitors and staff, verify instructions with supervisors, and provide sufficient notice of absences. A performance review is conducted on every volunteer once every six months to celebrate successes and identify areas for improvement.
Volunteer jobs	Volunteer jobs include assisting instructors with Aquatics, Fitness, Arts and Crafts, and Dance classes, assisting front desk staff with answering phones, directing visitors, and assisting with course registrations, and assisting facilities maintenance staff to set up for special events and assist with clean up duties. Before beginning work at the Center, all volunteers need to complete the Volunteer Application Form and submit it to Joanna Lund. It is important that the volunteer include all phone numbers, including both home and cell phone numbers.

1. Create a new blank presentation in PowerPoint, click the Outline tab, enter **Volunteer Orientation** as the presentation title on slide 1 followed by **Ambleside Community Center** and your name on two separate lines in the subtitle, and then save the file as **Volunteer Orientation** in the Project.14 folder.
2. On slide 2 in Outline view, enter **Overview** as the slide title, and then enter the three topics for the presentation: **Center Overview**, **Volunteer Conduct**, and **Volunteer Jobs**.
3. In Word, open the file **Practice_14.docx** located in the Project.14 folder included with your Data Files, and then to avoid altering the original file, save the document as **Volunteer Orientation Outline** in the same folder.
4. Switch to Outline view in Word.
5. Refer to the information provided in Figure 14-13 and then replace the placeholder text with appropriate slide titles and bulleted items. Remember that slide titles are Level 1 headings in Word and bulleted items are Level 2 and 3 headings in Word. You determine how to divide the information into slides and how to condense the information into bulleted points. Assign two to three slides to each of the three main topics.

6. You should aim to create a presentation consisting of about 12 slides, including the title slide, overview slides, and a summary slide containing contact information. You can refer to volunteers directly as *you* in the presentation. For example, instead of writing *Volunteers are expected to arrive on time.*, you could write *Please arrive on time.*

7. Save and close the Word file, and then in PowerPoint, import the Word outline into the active presentation. Be sure to copy slide 2, the Overview slide, so it appears before each main topic. Also, be sure to bold the bullet for the main topic being discussed in the next set of slides.

8. In PowerPoint, apply the presentation theme of your choice, select a new color scheme, and then change the background style to the textured or gradient fill style of your choice. Remember to select a subtle style that will not overwhelm the text.

9. In Slide Master view, modify the font style of the slide title (you choose the font style, size, and enhancements you prefer). You can choose to change the color of the font to better match the background style you selected.

10. Create a logo to appear on every slide in the presentation except the title slide. The logo can consist of a simple shape such as a circle or a triangle containing the initials of the community center (e.g., ACC). In PowerPoint, you use the same procedure as in Word to draw a shape and then fill it with text. Position the logo in the top or bottom right corner of the screen.

11. Review the presentation and reset the layout where needed on specific slides. Note that you may also need to reapply the slide layout to slides imported from Word. To do so, click the Layout button in the Slides group, and then click Title and Content.

12. Print the presentation as handouts containing six slides to the page, save the presentation, and then close the presentation and exit PowerPoint and Word.

Revise | **Instructional Presentation**

You are the office manager for Greenock Communications, a new company that provides communication training seminars to clients in the Phoenix area. One of your duties is to assist the owner of the company to create instructional presentations. A client has asked for training in how to create clear and effective presentations. You already have a PowerPoint presentation that contains the required information.

Follow the steps below to impose a clear structure on the content to make the presentation ready to use in the seminar and then format the presentation attractively for delivery as an online presentation.

1. Start PowerPoint, open the file **Revise_14.pptx** located in the Project.14 folder included with your Data Files, and then to avoid altering the original file, save the presentation as **Effective Presentations** in the same folder.

2. Type your name where indicated on slide 1 of the presentation.

3. Make sure the Outline tab is showing in the left pane, click the slide icon for slide 1, and then insert a new blank slide. *Hint:* Click the New Slide button in the Slides group.

4. On the new slide (slide 2), type **Overview** as the slide title and then enter three main topics for the presentation: **Presentation Requirements**, **Presentation Method**, and **Presentation Enhancements**.

5. Apply bold to the first of the three topics.

6. Scroll to slide 4 (Audience Involvement), and add **Ask questions** as a third main bullet point.

7. Scroll to slide 8, add three bullet points under the title Presentation Method: **Select the presentation subject**, **Write the outline**, and **Add enhancements**.

8. Each time the main topic changes, insert the slide you created for slide 2 and then bold the bullet text for the main topic being discussed in the next set of slides. To copy a slide, click the Slides tab, click the slide, press [Ctrl]+[C], move to the slide just before you want the new slide to appear, and then press [Ctrl]+[V].

9. Change the color scheme of the current presentation theme, and then modify the background style. You can choose to include a plain colored background if you wish. Remember to keep the background color light.

10. Modify the font styles and sizes in the Slide Master slightly.

11. Print a copy of the presentation as handouts of six slides to the page.

12. Save and close the presentation.

Create	Descriptive Presentation

You have been asked by a local community group to create a presentation of approximately 12 to 15 slides that shares information about one of your hobbies or interests. For example, if you are an avid mountain biker, you could create a presentation to inform people about great mountain biking routes in your area. If you are interested in photography, you could create a presentation that describes how to set up an online photo album.

Follow the steps below to create a presentation on an area of interest to you.

1. Complete the table below with information about your presentation.

Information for a PowerPoint Presentation
Presentation Topic
Presentation Purpose: complete the sentence *The purpose of my presentation is to...*
Why have participants come to the presentation?
What are the average background and characteristics of the participants?
What background knowledge about my presentation topic might the audience have?
What are the three main topics I plan to cover in my presentation?

2. Start Word, and then switch to Outline view.

3. Enter the three main topics for your presentation as three separate Level 1 headings.

4. Under each of the three main topics, add content in the form of bulleted items (Level 2 headings). Limit the number of slides for each main topic to no more than three.

5. Save the document as **Descriptive Presentation_Outline**, and then exit Word.

6. In PowerPoint, show the Outline tab, type the presentation title and your name as the subtitle on slide 1, and then on slide 2 type **Overview** as the slide title followed by the three main topics. Be sure to copy the Overview slide so it appears before each change in topic. Also, be sure to bold the topic on the Overview slide that will be discussed next in the presentation.

7. Save the presentation as **Descriptive Presentation**, import the Word document into your presentation starting on slide 3, and be sure a summary slide is the last slide. This slide could include your contact information or a brief summary of the presentation content.

8. Apply the design theme of your choice, and then change the color scheme.

9. In the Slide Master, modify the Master title and Master text styles, and then add a logo or small clip art picture to every slide in the presentation except the title slide.

10. Reset the layout on each slide as needed.

11. Add clip art pictures or photographs to selected slides in your presentation if you wish. To insert a picture, click the Insert Picture button in the Illustrations group on the Insert tab. You size and position a picture in PowerPoint in the same way you do in Word.

12. Print the presentation as handouts of six slides to the page, save and close the presentation, and then exit PowerPoint.

Apply | **Case Study 1**

Capstone College   The Digital Arts Department at Capstone College in San Francisco, California, trains students in the very latest technology for jobs as animators, graphic artists, and video game developers. In your position as the program assistant for the Digital Arts Department, you are responsible for creating presentations for delivery to students, other faculty, and members of the business community. The department coordinator asks you to create a presentation to welcome new students to the department. Most of the information required for the presentation is included in a Word file. To complete this case study, you create the student orientation presentation.

1. Start a new blank presentation in PowerPoint, show the Outline tab, and then type the title **Student Orientation** on the first slide in the presentation. Below the title, type **Capstone College Digital Arts Program** on one line and your name on the next line.

2. On the second slide, type **Overview**, and then type the three main topics: **College Information**, **Digital Arts Program Information**, and **Student Expectations**.

3. Save the presentation as **Digital Arts Student Orientation** in the Project.14 folder included with your Data Files.

4. Insert slides from the Word file **Case1_14.docx** located in the Project.14 folder included with your Data Files.

5. Apply a theme to the presentation and then modify the color scheme.

6. Open the Slide Master and modify the slide title text and the slide text. You can choose to change the font sizes, styles, and colors.

7. Show each slide in the presentation and reset the layout as needed so that all the text in the presentation is formatted consistently. As you are going through the slides, apply bold and a different color to the appropriate bulleted item on each of the overview slides. For example, you will need to enhance the *College Information* bullet on slide 2 of the presentation.

8. Add Clip Art pictures or photographs to at least three of the slides in the presentation.

9. Print a copy of the presentation as handouts of six slides to the page, and then save and close the presentation.

| Apply | **Case Study 2** |

Otter Bay Kayaking Adventures Tourists from all over the world enjoy kayaking trips led by the friendly guides at Otter Bay Kayaking Adventures in Juneau, Alaska. As the marketing assistant, you develop presentations to help market the kayaking tours. Kay Johnson, the owner of Otter Bay Kayaking Adventures, has sent you a Word document containing information for a presentation she needs you to create in PowerPoint. The purpose of the presentation is to describe Otter Bay Kayaking Adventures to people in the tourism industry who are attending a conference on recreational opportunities in Alaska. To complete this case study, you create the presentation to describe the tours.

1. Open the file **Case2_14.docx** located in the Project.14 folder included with your Data Files, and then print a copy. This document contains some of the information that you can adapt to create the presentation at the tourism conference.

2. Start PowerPoint, and then type the title **Kayaking Tours** on the first slide in the presentation. Below the title, type **Otter Bay Kayaking Adventures** on one line and your name on the next line.

3. On the second slide, type **Overview**, and then enter the three main topics: **Tours Available**, **What's Included**, and **Tour Prices**.

4. Save the presentation as **Kayaking Presentation** in the Project.14 folder included with your Data Files.

5. Enter content for each of the three topics. Refer to the Word document for information. You will need to organize the content into the three topics, and then use bulleted lists to communicate the required information. Limit the information on each slide to no more than two or three points in addition to the slide title. For this presentation, you do not need to repeat the Overview slide before each topic change because you are presenting a limited amount of information about each topic.

6. Create content for no more than nine slides, including the title slide.

7. Include contact information for Otter Bay Kayaking Adventures (included in the Word document) on the last slide of the presentation.

8. Add Clip Art pictures to at least two of the slides in the presentation.

9. Apply a design to the presentation and then modify the color scheme as needed. You can also modify the background style if you wish.

10. Open the Slide Master and modify the slide title text and the slide text to make the presentation attractive and easy to read. You can change the font sizes, styles, and colors.

11. Reset the slide layouts where needed, and then print a copy of the presentation as handouts of six slides to the page.

12. Save and close the presentation.

Microsoft PowerPoint includes numerous presentation designs that you can download to enhance your presentations. You access these designs from the New Presentation dialog box. To complete this case study, you explore the sample PowerPoint designs available for download, and then you download two designs to create two short presentations.

1. Start PowerPoint, click the Office button, and then click New.
2. Click Design slides in the list under Microsoft Office Online. A large selection of Design slides categories appears.
3. Spend some time exploring the many designs available.
4. When you find a design you like, click the picture of the design, and then note its name and category. If a License Agreement for Community Templates appears in the right pane, read the agreement, and accept or decline the agreement. If you decline the agreement, select a different design.
5. When you see a Download button in the right pane, click Download, and then click Continue. If you receive a message that you cannot download the template, check with your instructor or technical service support.
6. When the design appears in PowerPoint, type the name of the design on slide 1 followed by the category and your name.
7. Insert a new slide 2, type **Rationale** as the slide title on slide 2, and then at the first bullet, briefly describe why you chose the design.
8. Save the presentation as **Presentation Design 1** in the Project.14 folder included with your Data Files, and then print a copy of both slides in the presentation.
9. Repeat steps 4 to 7 to select and download a design from a different category, and then to create a second two-slide presentation.
10. Save the presentation as **Presentation Design 2** in the Project.14 folder included with your Data Files, and then print a copy of both slides in the presentation.

Objectives

- Identify guidelines for sales presentations
- Develop content for a sales presentation
- Use diagrams to present content
- Deliver a sales presentation
- Create diagrams in PowerPoint
- Create tables in PowerPoint
- Animate charts and diagrams in PowerPoint

Sales Presentations

Introduction

The purpose of a **sales presentation**, like the purpose of a sales letter or any sales-oriented publication, is to persuade people to purchase the product or service described in the sales presentation. A sales presentation differs from a sales-oriented document only in terms of its delivery method. Instead of reading a document, potential buyers listen to a speaker describe how a specific product or service will help them.

In this project, you explore guidelines for developing sales presentations, learn how to develop appropriate content for a sales presentation, and identify delivery methods. Finally, you learn how to use PowerPoint to enhance a sales presentation with tables and animated charts and diagrams.

Starting Data Files

Project.15

Tech_15.pptx
Practice1_15.docx
Practice2_15.pptx
Revise_15.pptx
Case1_15.docx
Case2_15.docx
Case3_15.pptx

Sales Presentations Essentials

A successful sales presentation shows an audience how a product or service will solve a specific problem and provide specific benefits. For example, imagine that the executives at a large corporation need their key employees to work together in teams. A tour company could present these executives with a sales presentation designed to show them the value of sending their employees on an adventure tour that will include teamwork activities and show employees they are valued.

Identifying Guidelines for a Sales Presentation

You need to consider the following guidelines when developing content for a sales presentation:

- Identify three key points.
- Customize the presentation to a specific audience.
- Emphasize benefits.

Following is an analysis of each of these guidelines.

Key Points

> **Key Point**
>
> The action you require from an audience for a sales presentation is to purchase your product or service.

People will not remember every word you say in a presentation, nor will they be able to recall the content of every slide. In the previous project on Presentation Planning, you learned that you should organize a presentation into three main topics. When you create a sales presentation that must persuade an audience to take a specific action, you identify the three key points that you want your audience to remember so they are able to take the required action.

Think about a presentation or class that you attended a few days ago. How many key points can you remember without consulting your notes? Most people can remember just a few points—usually those points that relate in some way to their own interests and concerns. Consider the sales presentation to executives about adventure tour options. The three key points that you might want the executives to remember above all else could be as follows:

- Shared adventures build teamwork.
- Participating in outdoor recreational activities reduces stress.
- Appreciated employees are productive employees.

> **Key Point**
>
> Identify three key points that relate to something that audience members regard as important.

When you identify the three key points you want to communicate in a presentation, you ensure that your presentation stays on track and remains focused. You evaluate the content you plan to include in the presentation in terms of its relationship to the three key points. For example, if you include photographs in your presentation, you want to select photographs that provide a visual backup to at least one of the key points. If one of these key points is *Shared adventures build teamwork*, you would want to include photographs that show people working together to accomplish a specific task, such as building a wilderness shelter or cooking dinner over a campfire. As you progress through your presentation, you emphasize the key points by stating verbally how they relate to the slide content. Then, just before the final slide in your presentation that contains the contact information, you can choose to include a slide that provides your audience with a clear summary of the key points.

> **Key Point**
>
> Audience members should perceive immediately that your goal is to show them how your product or service will solve their particular set of problems or concerns.

Customization

You design a sales presentation to appeal directly to the needs of a specific audience. Few businesspeople are willing to listen to a presentation that has obviously been given many times before to many other prospective clients. Corporate clients are particularly unwilling to pay attention to a generic presentation simply because many of them have listened to hundreds of sales presentations throughout their careers.

To customize a presentation for a specific audience, you first need to determine the priorities of the audience. For example, one group of executives might put a high priority on developing employee morale, whereas another group of executives at a different company might put a high priority on obtaining the best possible tour at the most reasonable price.

Figure 15-1 compares a generic description of a kayaking tour offered by Catalyst Adventure Tours to a customized description of the same tour for Mark One Industries, a company interested in purchasing an adventure tour package for 50 of its employees.

| Figure 15-1 | Comparison of a generic product description to a customized product description |

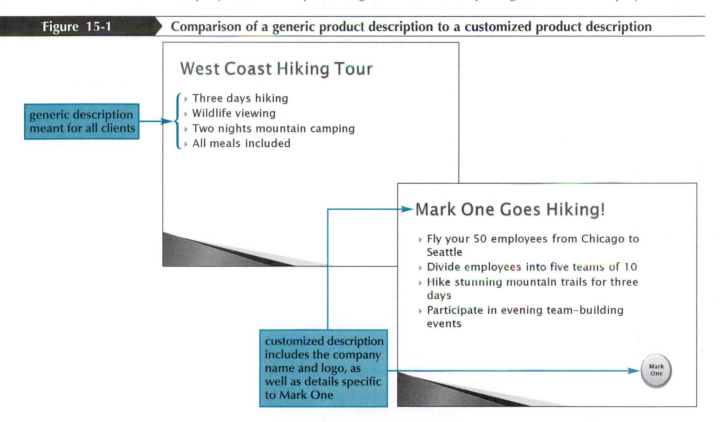

The customized description of the kayaking tour includes the name of the company and the company logo. In addition, the text describes the particular, customized trip that employees from Mark One Industries will experience.

Benefits

A sales presentation, like a sales letter, a promotional brochure, or any other kind of sales-oriented document, needs to emphasize how a particular product will benefit a particular audience. When you deliver a presentation, you can see and hear your audience, which is not possible when you send out a letter or a brochure. As a result, you can receive immediate feedback from the audience, which can help you determine what benefits appeal to the audience most.

For example, you might decide to focus on saving money as a benefit for executives who want to send employees on a reasonably priced adventure tour instead of to a luxury resort. During the presentation, the executives ask you how the tour will help build employee morale. Even if you are not able to change the content of the slides while you are in the middle of delivering a presentation, you can easily change the benefits you stress in the presentation from saving money to building morale.

One of the most appealing features of the presentation format is its flexibility. If you determine that an audience is not interested in a particular part of your presentation, you can skip to a new part. Of course, to do so, you need to have complete control over the content of your presentation. You need to be able to change the order of the topics you present at the last moment and expand existing topics with additional material that directly interests your audience.

Developing Content for a Sales Presentation

As you have learned, an effective sales presentation should include content relevant to the needs of the audience. This content is in the form of text presented in bulleted points and tables, and visual elements in the form of photographs, charts, and diagrams. Your first step in the content development process is to organize the content in a logical sequence. After you are satisfied with this sequence, you can add text and visuals.

Text Content

For most audiences, the content for a sales presentation consists of three principal areas as follows:

- Overview of participant needs
- Description of the product
- Cost information

Figure 15-2 shows an outline of the content that needs to be included in a short sales presentation on cycling tours in southern Utah offered by Catalyst Adventure Tours.

Figure 15-2 ▶ **Outline of content for a sales presentation**

| Slides | Outline |

1. **Slick Rock Cycling Tours**
2. **Overview**
   - Tour Basics
   - Tour Categories
   - Tour Costs
3. **Tour Participants**
   - Small groups
   - Tailored to ability level and interests
   - Bicycles and all accessories provided
   - All tours based in southern Utah
4. **Gourmet Meals**
   - Superb gourmet food in a wilderness setting
   - Sample dinner menu:
     - Deep-fried cactus-coated chicken
     - Wild rice with toasted pecans
     - Mesquite-roasted vegetables
     - Mocha-raspberry cheesecake
5. **Full-Day Tours**
   - Seven hours
   - Customized to all levels
   - Gourmet lunch and two snacks
   - Some technical instruction
6. **Two-Day Tours**
   - Overnight camping in a wilderness area
   - All equipment provided
   - All meals and snacks provided
   - Suitable for intermediate and advanced cyclists
7. **One-Week Tours**
   - Overnight camping in wilderness areas
   - All equipment and transport
   - Four sites in Utah
   - All meals and snacks
   - Suitable for intermediate and advanced cyclists
8. **Tour Costs**
9. **Breakdown of One-Week Costs**

In this presentation, information about the participants and the gourmet food they can expect on a typical tour is provided first so that audience members can *see* themselves enjoying a tour. Next, information about the three tour categories is provided: Full-Day, Two-Day, and One-Week. If audience members were intrigued by the tour information given in the first few slides, they can now determine their level of interest. In other words, are they intrigued enough to try a one-day tour or will they choose the one-week tour? Finally, the sales presentation provides information about tour prices and the breakdown of costs.

Visual Content

When you accompany a sales presentation with slides created in PowerPoint, you need to find ways to make your presentation content as visually stimulating as possible. Figure 15-3 shows the slides in the sales presentation outlined in Figure 15-2.

| Figure 15-3 | Content for a sales presentation |

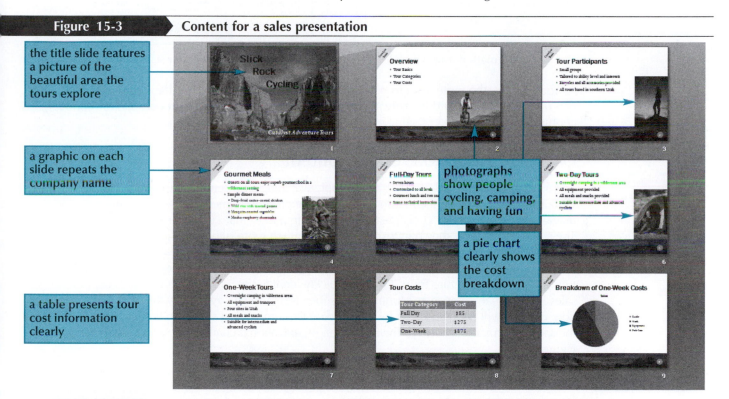

the title slide features a picture of the beautiful area the tours explore

a graphic on each slide repeats the company name

photographs show people cycling, camping, and having fun

a pie chart clearly shows the cost breakdown

a table presents tour cost information clearly

Notice how photographs and other graphic elements add interest to the presentation. Photographs are particularly appealing when used sparingly in a sales presentation. As advertisers are well aware, people like to see pictures of people enjoying the products or services they might consider purchasing for themselves.

You can also use colors, shading, and animations to draw attention to specific information in a presentation. In Figure 15-3, a colorful but simple table presents the cost information, and a pie chart is used to present the breakdown of costs by category (for example, Equipment, Meals, and so on). Your first priority when you include visual elements in a presentation is visibility. Audience members need to be able to grasp the significance of the visual element almost immediately.

You can understand the importance of using clear visual elements to communicate information when you look at a slide that does the opposite. The first slide in Figure 15-4 shows the schedule of tours offered by Catalyst Adventure Tours in April, May, and June. Suppose the audience for this presentation is interested only in tours to Europe. Can you quickly identify the European-based tours in the first slide shown in Figure 15-4? Eventually you would be able to determine the locations of the various European tours; however, you should not need to work so hard in order to do so. As shown in the second slide in Figure 15-4, the presenter can use shading to highlight the European tours while still showing the wide range of tours offered.

Figure 15-4 | **Comparison of unformatted and formatted tour schedule**

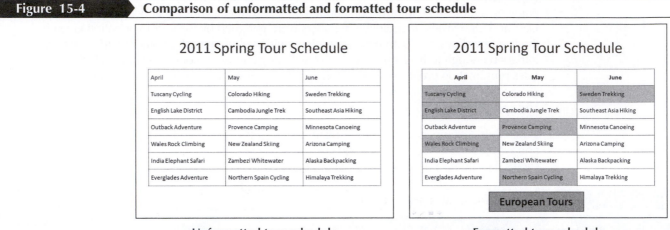

Unformatted tour schedule   Formatted tour schedule

You can use the table form to organize and present information so that your audience can read and understand it easily. You can also use diagrams to present complex or conceptual information.

Using Diagrams to Present Content

As you learned in the previous sections, people watching a presentation appreciate seeing visuals that contribute to their understanding of the presenter's message. You can create a **diagram** to communicate conceptual information in a form that audiences can understand. The same information shown in text form is often much more difficult to grasp, particularly by audience members who are sitting some distance away from the presentation slides. The first slide in Figure 15-5 shows a slide containing text that describes the organizational structure of Catalyst Adventure Tours. Can you quickly identify the name of the vice president of sales or how many managers Muriel Vance supervises? You can eventually find this information, but you will need to search for it. Compare the information shown in the first slide with the same information shown in the form of an organizational chart in the second slide in Figure 15-5.

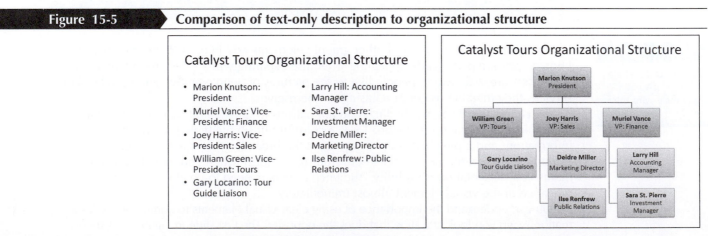

Poorly formatted text-only   Clearly formatted

Now you can see at a glance that Joey Harris is the vice president of sales and that Muriel Vance supervises two managers.

As you learned in Project 10 when you created organizational charts and lists, you use the SmartArt feature to create diagrams. This feature is also available in PowerPoint. SmartArt diagrams (also called SmartArt graphics) are particularly useful in presentations because you very often need your audience to view information in a clear and visually appealing way. SmartArt graphics are available in the seven categories described in Figure 15-6. Within each category are several subcategories, some of which overlap. For example, you will find a Vertical List diagram in both the List and Process categories.

Figure 15-6 **SmartArt diagram categories**

Category	Information Illustrated
List	A series of non-sequential or grouped blocks of information
Process	A progression or sequential steps in a task
Cycle diagram	A process that has a continuous cycle
Hierarchy	A hierarchy, often of positions within a company
Relationship	The relationship between several related elements to a core element
Matrix	Areas of overlap between two or more elements
Pyramid diagram	A hierarchical relationship between several elements that each has a different weight

To determine how to use a specific SmartArt diagram, view the description of the diagram that appears when you click the SmartArt button in the Insert tab and then select a diagram type. Figure 15-7 and Figure 15-8 provide examples of two diagrams from two different SmartArt diagram categories that you can use to display information in a presentation graphically.

Figure 15-7 **Text Cycle diagram from the Cycle category**

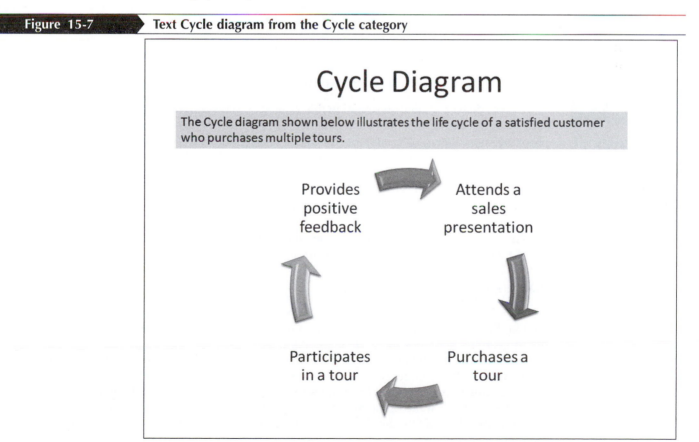

Figure 15-8 | Basic Radial diagram from the Relationship category

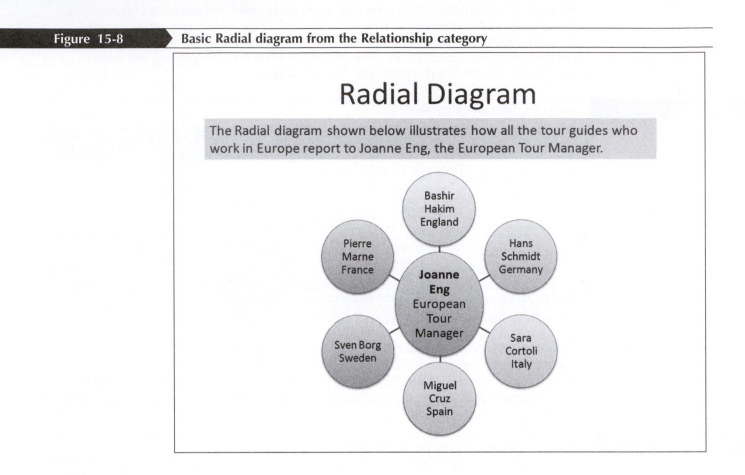

Delivering a Sales Presentation

When you deliver a sales presentation that consists of PowerPoint slide after PowerPoint slide, you risk boring your audience simply because most people in your audience have probably seen many PowerPoint presentations before. You can use PowerPoint slides to provide a visual and even an auditory backup for your words; however, you want to minimize the number of slides and maximize their impact. Each slide should pack a punch. As a result, you do not need to include text on every slide in the presentation. Sometimes just a picture gets the attention of audience members. The presenter then supplies the words.

When you deliver a sales presentation, you need to engage your audience, use a variety of media, and end the presentation strongly.

Audience Engagement

You should start a sales presentation by stating the most important thing that you want your audience to remember. A presentation is not a mystery novel. That is, its purpose is not to keep the audience in the dark about the most important points until the very end. Instead, you want to let the audience know right at the beginning why they should seriously consider the product or service you are describing.

You can use many different techniques to engage an audience at the beginning of a sales presentation. Some of the most effective techniques are those that directly involve audience members. For example, you could start a sales presentation about a whitewater rafting tour by asking the audience a question such as *What do you think would happen if all your sales managers piled into a raft and plunged down the Colorado River? Which managers would love it? Which would want out?*

Such a question could spark a lively discussion that sets the stage for the rest of the presentation. The purpose of this type of opening is to intrigue audience members so that they want to listen to the presentation.

Other methods you can use to engage audience members at the beginning of a presentation include asking them to play a short game, performing a demonstration of a product, or giving them an activity to complete. Figure 15-9 provides examples of several methods you can use to engage an audience at the beginning of the presentation and the purpose of these methods.

Figure 15-9 | Methods of engaging an audience

Method	Example	Purpose
Demonstrate the product	The presenter shows the audience a short video on how to negotiate whitewater rapids.	To stimulate excitement before introducing a sales presentation on a whitewater kayaking adventure tour
Complete an activity	Two audience members set up a tent within a certain time frame.	To emphasize the importance of teamwork before introducing a sales presentation on a hiking adventure tour
Play a game	Audience members complete a simple crossword puzzle with clues about the geographical location of the adventure tour.	To stimulate interest in the location before introducing a sales presentation on an adventure tour to a new and exotic location
Answer a question	Audience members answer a question such as *How many days does it take to hike the length of the Grand Canyon?*.	To engage interest by stimulating a discussion about the tour location; questions that do not have a right or wrong answer work best
Discuss an issue	Audience members are given a topic such as *teamwork* and are asked to brainstorm five characteristics of effective teamwork.	To focus attention on the importance of teamwork to the success of a company before introducing a sales presentation on a wilderness survival adventure tour

Any opening activity you use to engage an audience should have a purpose that relates to the topic of the sales presentation. Audience members do not want to waste time playing games or engaging in activities that appear to have no relevance to the presentation.

Multimedia Components

> **Key Point**
>
> People can get weary staring at a screen. Give them a break by engaging them in a variety of ways, including asking and answering questions.

A PowerPoint presentation should not be the only backup to your presentation. You can also write on flip charts, a chalkboard, or overhead transparencies, and you can distribute handouts or play videos and music. In fact, you can often revive a lackluster presentation just by turning off the PowerPoint presentation and switching to a different media such as a flip chart.

Remember that the most important part of any presentation, regardless of type, is the presenter. A beautifully formatted PowerPoint presentation can fall flat if the presenter does not engage the audience. When you are delivering a presentation, try to identify at least three ways in which you will present information in addition to PowerPoint slides.

Sales Presentation Ending

At the end of a sales presentation, the hope of the presenter is that audience members will want to purchase the product or service described in the presentation. From the audience members' point of view, the end of a sales presentation signals the time when they can think about what they have seen and heard. They do not necessarily want to make a decision.

Key Point

Requiring people to make a purchasing decision immediately following a presentation is a hard sales technique that can easily negate all the work that you put into preparing and delivering the presentation.

As a presenter, you need to give audience members the space to think about the presentation without feeling pressured. A good technique is to end the presentation with a slide that includes your contact information. This information is also duplicated on a handout that audience members can take away.

You can then leave the final slide up and complete your presentation with a short question-and-answer period. You should also invite people to speak with you following the presentation and tell them that they can call or e-mail you.

Technology Skills – Working with Visuals in PowerPoint

In PowerPoint, you include graphics such as tables, charts, and diagrams to provide a visual backup to your words. The key point about all such graphics is that they must be very easy to see and read. Complicated charts and tables containing a great deal of information can be included in handouts, but not on PowerPoint slides. The Technology Skills steps cover these skills:

- Create a diagram in PowerPoint
- Create a table in PowerPoint
- Animate a chart in PowerPoint
- Animate a diagram in PowerPoint

You create a diagram to simplify the communication of complex information. The key point is simplicity. Select a diagram type from the collection of SmartArt graphics that best displays the information you want audiences to understand. In these steps, you create a Radial diagram to show how a selection of activities all contribute to a central goal.

Tip

You can also open the text pane by clicking the control on the left side of the SmartArt graphic.

To create a Radial diagram:

1. Start PowerPoint, open the file **Tech_15.pptx** located in the Project.15 folder included with your Data Files, and then to avoid altering the original file, save the document as **Sales Presentation for Watson Enterprises** in the same folder.

2. Scroll through the presentation to determine how the content is organized, and then go to Slide 4: Building Morale.

3. Click the **Insert** tab, and then click the **SmartArt** button in the Illustrations group.

4. Click **Cycle** in the list of Categories, click **Basic Radial** (third row, second column), click **OK**, and then click the **Text Pane** button in the Create Graphic group on the SmartArt Tools Design tab to open the text pane, if necessary.

5. Click the **Add Shape** button in the Create Graphic group once to insert another shape so that the diagram contains five circles in addition to the middle circle.

6. Click the **middle circle**, type **Building Employee Morale**, click the **top circle**, type **Challenge**, and then enter text in the remaining circles, as shown in the text pane in Figure 15-10. You can enter text in a SmartArt graphic either in the text boxes in the SmartArt graphic or in the text pane.

Figure 15-10 ▶ **Text entered in a SmartArt graphic**

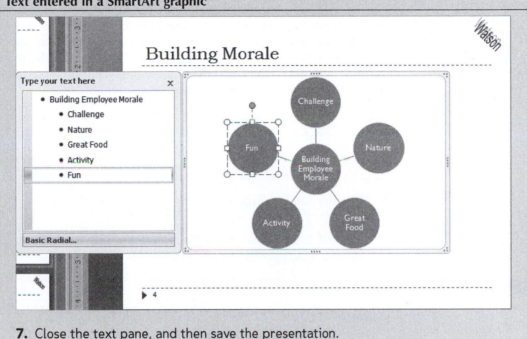

7. Close the text pane, and then save the presentation.

After you have created a diagram, you can change the layout, apply one of the preset formats, and then make additional adjustments to the various diagram elements so that the information is presented clearly and concisely.

To format a diagram:

1. Click the **SmartArt Tools Design** tab if necessary, click the **More** button ⧉ in the Layouts group, and then click **Diverging Radial** (use the ScreenTips to help you identify the layout).

2. Click the **More** button ⧉ in the SmartArt Styles group, and then select the **Inset** effect in the 3D area.

3. Click the circle containing the text **Building Employee Morale**, click the **SmartArt Tools Format** tab, and then click **Larger** in the Shapes group two times to increase the size of the middle circle only.

4. Select the text **Building Employee Morale**, click the **Home** tab, apply **Bold**, and then click the **Increase Font Size** button once.

5. Click the top circle (contains Challenge), press and hold the **[Ctrl]** key, and then click each of the outside circles so that all five circles are selected. You can modify one or all of the shapes in a SmartArt graphic.

6. Click the **Shape Fill** list arrow in the Drawing group, and then select **Dark Blue, Accent 3, Darker 25%**.

7. Click away from the selected circles to deselect them, and then save the presentation.

PowerPoint includes an Insert Table function that you can use to create a simple **table** that consists of rows and columns, exactly like tables you create in Word. A key requirement of a table that you include in a PowerPoint slide is that it should contain limited information in large, easy-to-read type. When you use tables to display information in a presentation, you need to make sure that all the text is readable. You should limit the number of columns to three and the number of rows to no more than eight, and format text in a table with at least the 18-pt font size.

To create and modify a table:

1. Go to Slide 9 in the presentation, click the **Insert** tab, click **Table** in the Tables group, and then click **Insert Table**.

2. Press the **Tab** key, type **3**, and then click **OK**. A table grid consisting of five columns and three rows appears on the slide.

3. Press the **Tab** key once, type **May**, press the **Tab** key, type **June**, and then enter the remaining text, as shown in Figure 15-11.

Figure 15-11 ▸ Table text entered

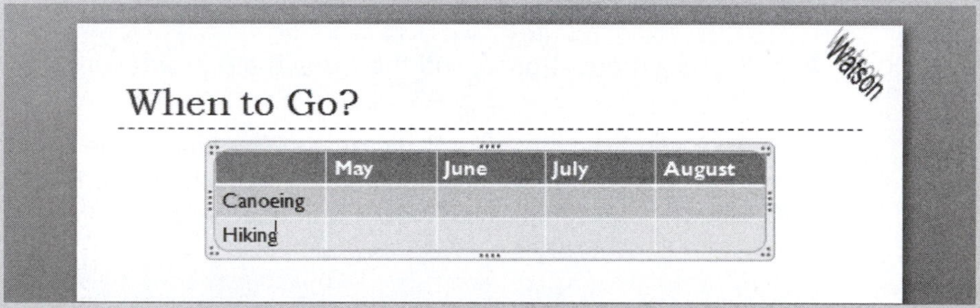

4. Click the border of the table so that the entire table is selected, click the **More** button ⬇ in the Table Styles group, and then select the **No Style**, **Table Grid** format (use the ScreenTips to find the format).

5. With the table still selected, click the **Table Tools Layout** tab, select the contents of the **Height** text box in the Table Size group, type **3.5**, and then press [**Enter**].

6. Click the **Center** button ≡ and the **Center Vertically** button ▤ in the Alignment group.

7. Click the blank cell below June in the Canoeing row, click the **Table Tools Design** tab, click the **Shading** list arrow ▨ ▾ in the Table Styles group, and then click **Dark Green, Accent 4, Lighter 40%**.

8. Fill the **Canoeing cells** for July and August, and the **Hiking cells** for May and June with **Dark Green, Accent 4, Lighter 40%**.

9. Position the table on the slide as shown in Figure 15-12, and then save the presentation.

Figure 15-12 **Selected cells filled with green**

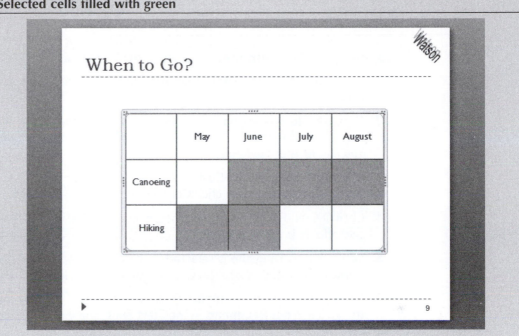

All charts you include in a PowerPoint presentation should be simple and easy to understand. To add excitement to an on-screen presentation, you can animate a chart so that its component parts appear on-screen sequentially.

To animate the elements of a chart:

1. Go to Slide 10 in the presentation, and then click the chart to select it.

2. Click the **Animations** tab, and then click the **No Animation** list arrow in the Animations group. The various ways in which you can animate a chart are listed.

3. Click **By Category** in the Fly In group. The animation is applied to the chart. You can further customize the animation.

4. Click **Custom Animation** in the Animations group to open the Custom Animation task pane.

5. Verify that **Chart 3: Background** is selected in the Custom Animation task pane, and then click the **Change** button at the top of the task pane.

6. Point to **Entrance**, click **More Effects**, scroll to **Exciting**, click **Spiral In**, and then click **OK**.

7. Click the **Speed** list arrow in the Custom Animation task pane, and then click **Medium**.

8. Click **Play**, and then save the presentation. The chart background appears followed sequentially by each column in the chart.

> **Tip**
>
> If you do not see the Change button, click the Add Effect button.

You use the same method to animate the components that make up a SmartArt graphic so that each component appears on-screen separately.

To animate the elements of a SmartArt graphic:

▶ **1.** Go to Slide 4 which contains the radial diagram, and then click the diagram to select it.

▶ **2.** Click the **No Animation** list arrow in the Animations group, and then click **From center one by one** in the Wipe group. The animation is applied to the diagram. You can further customize the animation.

▶ **3.** Click **Add Effect** in the Custom Animation task pane, point to **Emphasis**, click **More Effects**, and then click **Contrasting Color** in the Subtle category.

▶ **4.** Click **OK**, and then click **Play**. The effect is interesting but you decide that having two effects is too much.

▶ **5.** Verify that **7. Diagram** is selected in the Custom Animation task pane, click **Remove**, and then close the Custom Animation task pane.

▶ **6.** Enter your name where indicated on the title slide, click the **Slide Show** tab, and then click **From Beginning** in the Start Slide Show group.

▶ **7.** Use your Spacebar or click the mouse button to view each slide in the presentation and the animations.

▶ **8.** Click the **Office** button, point to **Print**, click **Print**, click the **Print what** list arrow, click **Handouts**, click the **Slides per page** list arrow, click **6** if necessary, and then click **OK**.

▶ **9.** Close the presentation, and then exit PowerPoint.

Marion Knutson, the owner of Catalyst Adventure Tours, needs to give a sales presentation to two very different companies that are both interested in the Canyon Hiking Adventure through Zion National Park in southern Utah. Marion asks you to read a short description of each of the two companies and then to develop the key points she should stress in each presentation.

Follow the steps below to develop key points for two presentations, and then create content for one of the presentations.

1. Open the file **Practice1_15.docx** located in the Project.15 folder included with your Data Files and then, to avoid altering the original file, save the document as **Customizing a Sales Presentation** in the same folder.

2. Read the description of each of the two companies that is interested in the Canyon Hiking Adventure.

3. Write your own entries in the appropriate areas of the table to identify three key points to stress for each presentation. Note that a key point is an idea or fact that you want to stress in the presentation. For example, a key point for Lambert Consultants could be *Managers deserve a reward for their outstanding effort.* Think from the point of view of the executives who are deciding whether to purchase the Canyon Hiking Adventure. What are the three main points you should make to convince them to purchase the tour?

4. Type your name where indicated in the document footer, save the document, and then print a copy.

5. Open the file **Practice2_15.pptx** located in the Project.15 folder included with your Data Files and then, to avoid altering the original file, save the presentation as **Lambert Consultants Sales Presentation**. The file contains content for a generic sales presentation about the Canyon Hiking Adventure. All the required information about the tour is included; however, the information is not customized to the requirements of a specific company.

6. Add *Lambert Consultants* as a footer that appears on every slide in the presentation except the first slide. *Hint*: Click the Insert tab, click the Header and Footer button in the Text group, click the Footer check box, enter the name of the company in the space provided, click the Don't show on title slide check box to deselect it if necessary, and then click Apply to All.

7. In the Notes area of Slide 2, paste the key points you included in the Customizing a Sales Presentation document for Lambert Consultants.

8. Refer to the key points you developed for Lambert Consultants, and then modify the presentation to reflect the company's concerns. For example, if you identified *rewarding managers* as a key point, include somewhere in the presentation a reference to how the tour provides participants with opportunities to celebrate their successes. You can modify text on existing slides and insert one or two new slides. Limit the final number of slides to no more than 12. You might also add a slide before the contact information that summarizes the key points relevant to the company in bullet form.

9. On one of the slides in the presentation, include a diagram created as a SmartArt graphic. You determine appropriate content for the diagram. You may decide to have the diagram reflect one or more of your key points.

10. Format the diagram attractively, and then apply the animation effect of your choice to the diagram so that each of the diagram components appears sequentially.

11. On the Tour Costs slide, include a simple table that includes per person cost information as follows: **Transportation: $50**, **Equipment: $100**, **Meals: $150**, **Activities: $50**, and the total cost.

12. Apply the table AutoFormat of your choice and increase the font size of the text so it is easy to read.

13. Insert appropriate pictures in the presentation to emphasize the key points. For example, if one of the key points is that an adventure tour in the outdoors appeals to the company's young, sports-oriented managers, include pictures that show people enjoying the outdoors.

14. Enter your name where indicated on the title slide, view the presentation in Slide Show view, print a copy of the presentation as handouts, six to the page, and then save and close the presentation.

Revise | Corporate Sales Presentation

You work for a public relations firm called Star Events that organizes special events for corporations. One of your duties is to provide short sales presentations to corporations interested in hiring the company to organize a special event. To save time, you often adapt existing presentations to meet the needs of an individual client. You have a presentation you've created for the Renfrew Corporation about a banquet for 500 people. Now you need to adapt the presentation for Galaxy Books, an educational publishing company that wants to provide attendees at a three-day conference with a special event on the evening of Day 2.

Follow the steps below to adapt a sales presentation.

1. Open the file **Revise_15.pptx** located in the Project.15 folder included with your Data Files and then, to avoid altering the original file, save the presentation as **Galaxy Books Special Event** in the same folder.

2. Change the footer text to **Galaxy Books**. *Hint*: Change the text in the Header and Footer dialog box, not on the slide.

3. Refer to the information in Figure 15-13, and then modify information in the presentation so that it relates to the special event for Galaxy Books.

Figure 15-13 ▸ **Information for Galaxy Books**

Slide	Content
Title	Change the name of the company to Galaxy Books. Change the title of the event to *Literary Legends Special Event*. Modify the font sizes to fit in the available space.
Overview	Add a picture of a stack of books (search Clip Art).
Event Theme	The special event will be a celebration of famous literary figures from Shakespeare to Hemingway. Specify some of the activities related to the event theme.
Requirements	The special event also includes a banquet for 200 people in the ballroom at the Westview Resort on May 3 starting at 7 p.m.
Catering	The chef is Ronald Deville from Paris.
Suggested Menu	Create a table containing a description of each of the four courses for the banquet. Format the table attractively.
Merchandise	Literary-themed merchandise of your choice.

Figure 15-13 ▶   **Information for Galaxy Books** (*continued*)

Slide	Content
Event Costs	Insert a SmartArt diagram to create a Pyramid chart showing total costs of $15,000 for the event divided into categories from largest to smallest. You determine the breakdown of costs for Catering, Entertainment, Merchandise, and Venue Rental. Format the pyramid chart attractively.

4. Read the following key points and then adapt the text and any of the graphics in the presentation so that these points are emphasized. You can also choose to add a shape containing text to a slide. You determine how best to customize the presentation for the client.

   • Key Point 1: Conference attendees have worked hard for two days in conference sessions and deserve a chance to relax and be entertained.

   • Key Point 2: Galaxy Books is an innovative company that places a very high value on meeting each customer's unique needs.

   • Key Point 3: Conference attendees appreciate the opportunity to network with other attendees.

5. Add appropriate pictures to one or more of the slides, and then animate the SmartArt diagram using the settings of your choice.

6. Enter your name where indicated on the title slide, print a copy of the presentation as handouts, six to the page, and then save and close the presentation.

Create | Sales Presentation

Create a sales presentation consisting of between eight and 12 slides that you could give on behalf of a company of your choice to a company of your choice. For example, you could create a sales presentation that describes the training seminars offered by a company called Great West Trainers for a large company called Janzen Enterprises that is requesting leadership training for its 200 middle managers.

Follow the steps below to create the sales presentation.

1. Determine the name of your company and the products or services that it sells. Think of your own interests and then create a company that reflects these interests.

2. Determine the name and characteristics of the company to which you will deliver the sales presentation. Think about how you can customize the presentation to meet the needs of the company.

3. Complete the table below with the information you need to help you create content for the sales presentation. Note that you will need to make up information. Use fictitious but realistic details. Sample topics for a company offering training seminars could be *Skills Assessment, Training Topics,* and *Training Delivery*.

Information to create a sales presentation
Presentation Title
Presentation Subtitle (For example: Customized for [Name of Company] By [Name of Company])

Information to create a sales presentation (continued)

Overview (Three key topics)

1.

2.

3.

Main Topic 1 (from Overview)

Subtopic 1

Subtopic 2

Subtopic 3

Main Topic 2 (from Overview)

Subtopic 1

Subtopic 2

Subtopic 3

Main Topic 3 (from Overview)

Subtopic 1

Subtopic 2

Subtopic 3

Prices

Contact Information (Name and address of the company delivering the presentation)

4. Create a new presentation in PowerPoint and save it as **My Sales Presentation**.
5. Enter the text you wish to include on each slide in your sales presentation. Include the contact information for your company on the last slide in the presentation. Limit the presentation length to eight to 12 slides.
6. Apply the presentation design of your choice to the presentation and then modify the color scheme. You can also choose to modify the background color for each slide.
7. Insert the slide number and the name of the company receiving the presentation on every slide in the presentation except the title slide. Work in Slide Master view to modify the positioning of the slide number and footer text if necessary.
8. In the Notes area of Slide 1 of your presentation, identify three key points that you want to emphasize in the presentation. These points should relate to areas that your target audience considers important. For example, in a presentation on training seminars, key points could be:
   a. Key Point 1: Training employees helps the company save money by contributing to higher employee retention.
   b. Key Point 2: Trained employees are more efficient, which also saves the company money.
   c. Key Point 3: Training programs can be customized to meet the individual needs of the company.

9. Incorporate the key points into your presentation—in text and/or in graphics. Your goal is to ensure that the content supports your key points.

10. On one of the slides in the presentation, include a diagram created as a SmartArt graphic. You determine appropriate content for the diagram. You may decide to have the diagram reflect one of your key points.

11. Format the diagram attractively, and then apply the animation effect of your choice to the diagram so that each of the diagram components appears sequentially.

12. On one of the slides in the presentation, include a simple table. Use shading to emphasize key information.

13. Include appropriate pictures in the presentation. You can use your own photographs or insert pictures from the Clip Art task pane.

14. In the Notes area on Slide 2 of your presentation, write a short description of how you could engage the audience at the beginning of the presentation. Think of an activity that you could have audience members participate in. Refer to the description of activities included in Figure 15-9 for ideas.

15. Enter your name on the title slide, print a copy of the presentation as handouts, six to the page, and then save and close the presentation.

Apply | Case Study 1

Capstone College   The new Game Art and Design program at the Digital Arts Department at Capstone College in San Francisco will be offered to students in the fall of 2012. In the spring, the department is holding regular information sessions to describe the program to students who may be interested in enrolling. As the program assistant in the department, you have been asked to create a PowerPoint presentation about the new program. To complete this case study, you create the presentation from information provided.

1. Open the file **Case1_15.docx** located in the Project.15 folder included with your Data Files, print a copy to refer to as you create the presentation, and then close the document. The document contains information about the new game art and design program.

2. Read the information in the document and determine how you can adapt it for a sales presentation consisting of between eight and 12 slides. You choose which information to include, how to divide the information into topics and subtopics, and how to display the information. You don't need to include all the information in the document. Think from the point of view of the students viewing the presentation. What information do they need to encourage them to apply for the Game Art and Design program?

3. Create a new presentation in PowerPoint and save it as **Digital Arts Game Art and Design Presentation**.

4. In the Notes area of Slide 1 of your presentation, identify three key points that you want to emphasize in the presentation. These points should relate to areas that prospective students consider important.

5. Enter the text you wish to include on each slide in your sales presentation. Include contact information for the Digital Arts Department on the last slide in the presentation. Limit the presentation length to 10 to 15 slides.

6. Incorporate the key points into your presentation—in text and/or in graphics. Your goal is to ensure that the content supports your key points.

7. Apply the presentation design of your choice to the presentation and then modify the color scheme.

8. On one of the slides in the presentation, include a diagram created as a SmartArt graphic. You determine appropriate content for the diagram. You may decide to have the diagram reflect one of your key points.

9. Format the diagram attractively, and then apply the animation effect of your choice to the diagram so that each of the diagram components appears sequentially.

10. On at least one of the slides in the presentation, include a simple table. Use shading to emphasize key information.

11. Add appropriate illustrations; you can search Clip Art using keywords, such as *computers*, *computer game*, and *software*.

12. Include a footer with the text *Game Art and Design* and a slide number on every slide except the title slide.

13. Enter your name on the title slide, print a copy of the presentation as handouts, six to the page, and then save and close the presentation.

Apply	**Case Study 2**

Otter Bay Kayaking Adventures   Tourists from all over the world enjoy kayaking trips led by the friendly guides at Otter Bay Kayaking Adventures in Juneau, Alaska. As one of the two assistants who work in the office, you often help develop sales presentations for the tours. Kay Johnson, the owner of the company, has asked you to create a sales presentation designed for a corporate client who is considering hiring Otter Bay Kayaking Adventures to provide a kayaking tour for 20 employees. The presentation will present information about two tour options: a two-day kayaking adventure and a five-day kayaking adventure. To complete this case study, you create the presentation from information provided.

1. Open the file **Case2_15.docx** located in the Project.15 folder included with your Data Files, and then print a copy. This document contains some of the information that you can adapt to create the sales presentation for Evergreen Consultants, a corporate client based in Seattle, Washington.

2. Start PowerPoint and then enter the title **Custom Kayaking Tours** on the first slide in the presentation. Following the title, enter **Evergreen Consultants** on one line and your name on the next line.

3. Save the presentation as **Sales Presentation for Evergreen Consultants**.

4. In the Notes area of Slide 1 of your presentation, identify three key points that you want to emphasize in the presentation. These points should relate to areas that executives at Evergreen Consultants who are considering purchasing a kayaking tour for their employees consider important.

5. On the second slide, type **Overview**, and then enter the three main topics: **Tours Available**, **What's Included**, and **Tour Prices**.

6. Enter content for each of these three topics. Refer to the Word document you printed for source materials. Incorporate the key points into your presentation—in text and/or in graphics. Your goal is to ensure that the content supports your key points.

7. Include at least one table in the presentation.

8. Limit the information on each slide so that all the text is readable, use list form, and avoid reproducing the sentences included in the Word document.

9. Create content for nine to 12 slides, including the title slide.

10. Apply a design to the presentation and then modify the color scheme so the presentation is attractive and easy to read.

11. Include the name of the company and a slide number on every slide in the presentation except the title slide.

12. Include a diagram on one slide of the presentation to communicate information visually that might be of interest to the client.

13. Apply a custom animation to the diagram.

14. In the Notes area on Slide 2 of your presentation, write a short description of how you could engage the audience at the beginning of the presentation. Refer to the description of activities included in Figure 15-9 for ideas.

15. Print a copy of the presentation as a handout of six slides to the page.

16. Save and close the presentation.

Apply	**Case Study 3**

You can choose to publish a PowerPoint presentation to the Internet so that it is accessible from a Web site. This option is useful when you want to provide access to the presentation content for someone who was not able to attend an in-person delivery of the presentation. For example, an artist who made a sales presentation at a luncheon for architects and commercial developers in the hopes of being asked to create installations for new office buildings in the area might decide to post his PowerPoint sales presentation to his Web site. He can then invite architects and commercial developers he meets who were not at the luncheon to view the presentation online. To complete this case study, you save a presentation for viewing on the Internet.

1. Open the file **Case3_15.pptx** located in the Project.15 folder included with your Data Files, and then, to avoid altering the original file, save the presentation as **Art Presentation**. The file contains a short presentation highlighting the work of a local artist.

2. Scroll through the presentation to view the contents.

3. On Slide 1 of the presentation, type your name below the subtitle.

4. Change the background color of all slides to black. *Hint*: Click the Design tab, click Background Styles in the Background group, and then click the black box. Note that the font color will change automatically to white.

5. Save the presentation.

6. Click the Office button, point to Save As, and then click Other Formats.

7. Click the Save as type list arrow, and then select Web Page (*.htm;*.html).

8. Click Publish to open the Publish as Web Page dialog box.

9. Click the Display speaker notes check box to deselect it, and then click the Open published Web page in browser check box to select it.

Tip

If a warning message appears, click the *here* link to continue.

10. Click Publish. The presentation appears in your default browser.

11. Click each slide title to view the presentation. Note that the presentation may not look the same as the presentation in PowerPoint. You close the presentation and open it directly in Internet Explorer.

12. Close the presentation, and then launch Internet Explorer.

13. Click File on the menu bar in Internet Explorer, click Open, and then navigate to the location where you saved the Art Presentation file. Note that you will see a folder called Art Presentation_files and a file called Art Presentation.htm.

14. Double-click Art Presentation.htm, and then click OK in the Open dialog box.

15. If a message regarding blocked content appears along the top of the browser window, click the message to allow the content, click Allow Blocked Content, and then click Yes in the message box that opens.

16. View the presentation in the browser, print a copy of Slide 1 containing your name, and then close the browser.

My Portfolio

Employers value excellent communication skills. Applicants who present a portfolio of current documents that they have created have an advantage over applicants who present only a resume. A **portfolio** is a collection of documents designed to showcase your talents. In the following exercise, you will bring together a selection of the documents you created while working through the projects in this book, or you can create the documents in this exercise from scratch. Your portfolio should demonstrate to current and future employers your business communications skills and your software skills, especially in the areas of word processing and presentation development.

Collecting Documents

Use the guidelines presented below to select the documents to include in your portfolio.

Document	Description
Cover Page	Use the Word Cover Page feature in the Pages group on the Insert tab to create a one-page cover page that precedes all the documents in the portfolio. Include the following information on the cover page: *Business Communications Portfolio* as the title; your name and contact information, including your e-mail address; and the current date. Use the cover page style of your choice, and delete any content controls you do not use.
Table of Contents	Create a table of contents that clearly identifies each of the items in your portfolio. The table of contents helps the reviewer see at a glance the documents included in your portfolio. You can use the words or phrases in the left column of this table as the entries in your table of contents.
Resume	Select one of the personal resumes you created in **Project 13: Job Search Documents**. You can choose the chronological or the functional version, depending on how you want to present your qualifications and experience.
Cover Letter as a Main Document	Adapt one of the cover letters you created in **Project 13: Job Search Documents** so that it matches a job of your choice and the resume you are including in your portfolio. Save the cover letter as a main document for a mail merge, allocate fields for a data source, and then add the fields to the cover letter main document.
Data Source	As you learned in **Project 4: Everyday Letters**, create a data source that includes five entries. Make up suitable contact information to include in the data source or use one of the data sources you created. Include a printout of the data source in your portfolio.
General Business Communications	Choose one of the documents you created in **Project 1: Business Communications**. Be sure the document illustrates an understanding of reader needs and clearly identifies the action expected from the reader.
E-mail	Choose one of the e-mails you created in **Project 2: E-Mail** and print a copy from Outlook or another e-mail provider. Be sure the e-mail clearly states its purpose and uses a positive tone.
Memo	Choose one of the three memo types you created in **Project 3: Memos**: Defining Procedures, Making Requests, or Summarizing Progress. Make sure the content of the memo fills one to two pages and includes appropriate formatting, such as tables and lists, to make the content clear and easy to read.
Everyday Letter	Choose one of the five types of everyday letters you created in **Project 4: Everyday Letters**: Request, Confirmation, Transmittal, Acceptance, or Personal. Use a consistent letter style and include a simple letterhead.

Portfolio Projects

Document	Description
Sales Letter	Choose one of the sales letters you created in **Project 5: Sales Letters**. Use a consistent letter style and include a letterhead containing a WordArt object or a piece of modified clip art.
Letter Presenting Negative News	Choose one of the letters presenting negative news that you created in **Project 6: Messages with Negative News**. Be sure the document illustrates how you can encourage the reader to accept the negative news as fair and reasonable.
Press Release	Choose one of the press releases you created in **Project 7: Press Releases**. Make sure the press release includes a snappy title that will attract the attention of an editor.
Proposal	Choose one of the proposals you created in **Project 8: Proposals**. Make sure your proposal clearly states your request and provides the reader with the information needed to make an informed decision.
Report	Choose one of the reports you created in **Project 9: Reports**. You can choose a descriptive, comparative, or analytical report. Make sure your report includes a core sentence, appropriate page numbering, illustrations, a table of contents, and a cover page. You can also choose to include an Executive Summary.
Newsletter	Choose one of the newsletters you created in **Project 10: Newsletters**. Use columns to present the information, and include a diagram or chart and drop caps.
Brochure	Choose one of the brochures you created in **Project 11: Brochures**. Format all headings with styles. Print the brochure on two sides of one sheet of paper. You can also choose to include a folded version of the brochure in your portfolio.
Web Content	Choose either one of the blog posts or one of the Web pages, such as a Home Page, FAQ page, or About Us page that you created in **Project 12: Web Communications**. Format the text simply; your focus is on presenting the content, not on reproducing the design of a Web site.
Presentation	Choose one of the presentations you created in either **Project 14: Presentation Planning** or **Project 15: Sales Presentations**. Print the presentation as handouts of six slides per page for inclusion in your portfolio.

Creating the Portfolio

1. Carefully review each of the documents you have selected, and make revisions as needed. The goal of these documents is to showcase your writing and formatting abilities. Make sure each document clearly demonstrates the skills you bring to the work force.
2. Create a folder named **My Portfolio** on your hard drive, a flash drive, or the Web. Copy the documents you have selected into the My Portfolio folder.
3. Print a copy of each of the documents in your portfolio.
4. Arrange the printed documents in an attractive folder or three-ring binder with the cover page as the first page, followed by the table of contents.

Glossary/Index